# RELIC QUEST

## A GUIDE TO RESPONSIBLE RELIC RECOVERY TECHNIQUES WITH METAL DETECTORS

# Other Books by Stephen L. Moore

*Battle Surface! Lawson P. "Red" Ramage and the USS Parche in the Pacific War.* Annapolis, MD: Naval Institute Press, 2011.

*Savage Frontier: Rangers, Riflemen, and Indian Wars in Texas. Volume IV: 1842–1845.* Denton: University of North Texas Press, 2010.

*European Metal Detecting Guide: Tips, Techniques and Treasures.* Garland, TX: RAM Books, 2009.

*Last Stand of the Texas Cherokees: Chief Bowles and the 1839 Cherokee War in Texas.* Garland, TX: RAM Books, 2009.

*Presumed Lost. The Incredible Ordeal of America's Submarine Veteran POWs of World War II.* Annapolis, MD: Naval Institute Press, 2009.

*War of the Wolf: Texas' Memorial Submarine, World War II's Famous USS Seawolf.* Dallas, TX: Atriad Press, 2008.

*Savage Frontier: Rangers, Riflemen, and Indian Wars in Texas. Volume III: 1840–1841.* Denton: University of North Texas Press, 2007.

*Savage Frontier: Rangers, Riflemen, and Indian Wars in Texas. Volume II: 1838–1839.* Denton: University of North Texas Press, 2006.

*Spadefish: On Patrol With a Top-Scoring World War II Submarine.* Dallas, TX: Atriad Press, 2006.

*Eighteen Minutes: The Battle of San Jacinto and the Texas Independence Campaign.* Plano: Republic of Texas Press, 2004.

*Savage Frontier: Rangers, Riflemen, and Indian Wars in Texas. Volume I: 1835–1837.* Denton: University of North Texas Press, 2002.

*Taming Texas. Captain William T. Sadler's Lone Star Service.* Austin, TX: State House Press, 2000.

With William J. Shinneman and Robert W. Gruebel. *The Buzzard Brigade: Torpedo Squadron Ten at War.* Missoula, MT: Pictorial Histories Publishing, 1996.

For more information, visit www.stephenlmoore.com

## A GUIDE TO RESPONSIBLE RELIC RECOVERY
## TECHNIQUES WITH METAL DETECTORS

Updated Second Edition

# STEPHEN L. MOORE

*Relic Quest: A Guide to Responsible Relic
Recovery Techniques with Metal Detectors*
Third Printing, June 2013

Library of Congress Cataloging-in-Publication Data

Moore, Stephen L.
  Relic quest : a guide to responsible relic recovery techniques with metal detectors / Stephen L. Moore.
      p. cm.
  Includes bibliographical references.
  ISBN 978-0-9818991-9-0 (alk. paper)
  1. Treasure troves. 2. Metal detectors. I. Title.
  G525.M589 2010
  622'.19--dc22
                    2010049497

Published by RAM Books
A Division of Garrett Metal Detectors

Charles Garrett and other professional treasure hunters also bring the hobby of metal detecting to life in treasure hunting and prospecting videos. To order a RAM book or a treasure hunting video, call 1-800-527-4011 or visit www. garrett.com for more information.

# CONTENTS

# Table of Contents

*(From the cover)* This group of bullets, buttons, buckles, and jewelry is a sample of what relic hunter Brian Pennington has recovered in the past decade.

# Author's Note

My deep interest in history began in childhood and I've always enjoyed visiting museums to study artifacts recovered from earlier periods. My career path led me into marketing, advertising and journalism, but my interest in the past has kept me busy researching the past in my spare time. This research has spawned books on topics that interest me such as World War II, the Texas Revolution and the Texas Rangers.

My cousins and I had played around with a metal detector when we were younger, but it wasn't until more recent years that I've found the time to really learn the true enjoyment that can be derived from this hobby. It is only fitting that my love for history has evolved into a passion for digging relics with metal detectors.

Fortunately, the contacts I had developed while researching the Texas Indian Wars and revolutionary period helped to open doors to good detecting sites. In 2008, Eagle Douglas of the American Indian Cultural Society agreed that I could bring a group of detectorists onto his group's land to search for artifacts from the largest ever battle between Texas Rangers and Native Americans. We agreed that whatever was found would be preserved for future generations to appreciate. Our artifact recoveries and the history of this 1839 Indian battle are chronicled in *Last Stand of the Texas Cherokees*, released by RAM Books.

Months later, I organized another search team which included Charles Garrett to work hand-in-hand with Texas Parks & Wildlife officials and archaeologists on the San Jacinto battleground. Two of my great-great-great grandfathers had helped wrestle Texas independence from Mexico in 1836 on these state-protected grounds. I have participated in several hunts on and around San Jacinto with archaeologists. Regardless of how much or how little we found on each search, the quest for history on such important soil was always as much of a thrill as each recovery.

There is so much history to be recovered with metal detectors that it is almost necessary to start a "wish list" of places to hunt in one's lifetime. More recently, I have been able to journey to Civil War sites to field test new Garrett detectors. Like so many Americans, my family was heavily involved in this bitter conflict that is often called the "War Between the States." Although I can claim some Cherokee blood in my ancestry, my ancestors primarily made their way to North America hundreds of years ago from England, Ireland and the Germanic settlements. European detecting trips I have made thus have special significance, also.

Relic hunting is a hobby that can be gratifying to history nuts of all ages. You need not travel the country or the world to find interesting artifacts. Start with your family's own property or within the community where you were raised. Some of the best detector finds you can experience—be it relics, coins or jewelry—are those items that have the most personal connection with you.

Recovered artifacts are pieces of history that can be preserved and appreciated. Centuries of heritage can come to life with any given swing of the searchcoil. The purpose of this book is to pass along tips and techniques that can help you to become more successful at relic recovery with a metal detector. Good finds do not always come easy. In most cases, you or one of your hunting companions will have conducted research and worked with landowners to secure their blessings to hunt certain properties. Your search and recovery time in the field is the payoff to the hours you put in before you leave the Internet, libraries, books, maps and telephone far behind. The exercise, fresh air and new friends you enjoy along the way are merely fringe benefits of this hobby.

The roads to recovering history sometimes end in digging out more than relics—but it's all part of the game of relic hunting!

I make no claims to being a metal detecting expert. Rather, I hope to continue to refine my relic recovery skills every time I venture into the fields, forests or streams. *Relic Quest* is instead the result of many people coming together to share their knowledge. I can offer some tips from my decades of researching and writing history, as well as what I've learned so far in the field. Other relic hunters, however, can provide much more knowledge that they have compiled from their own experiences. To each of them who have contributed to this collection, I am forever indebted.

Foremost on this list is Charles Garrett—a true pioneer of today's advanced metal detectors. He has spent decades in the field hunting and testing technology that he and his engineers have implemented into Garrett detectors. I must thank him for the many stories he has shared about his relic hunting experiences and for the advice he has provided along the way in compiling this book. We also spent several hours culling through one of Mr. Garrett's vaults, which was a special treat as he related stories of his finds.

Senior Vice President and Director of Engineering Bob Podhrasky and Director of Product Development Brent Weaver, the leading engineers for Garrett Metal Detectors, served as my technical advisors. Brent particularly offered much insight on the science of how and why metal detectors and searchcoils operate as they do. Brian McKenzie accompanied me on many detecting trips described in this text to document the finds with his cameras. Many of the close-up relic gallery photos and the superb technical illustrations are also the handiwork of Brian's photography, Illustrator and Photoshop skills. I am also grateful for the editorial skills of Hal Dawson and for artist John Lowe's efforts to improve some of this book's design elements.

Beyond these key technical contributors, dozens of successful relic hunters offered their searching secrets and photos of their favorite finds. Although many searchers are named only by their first name (per their request), they all deserve recognition for their contributions. Many others shared stories with me either in person or via email. Successes of such experienced detectorists offer the key to learning how to become a better relic hunter.

Key image contributors Butch Holcombe, Charlie Harris, Harry Ridgeway, Spencer Barker, Larry Cissna, Bobby McKinney and Tom Henrique each helped complete the relic recognition galleries by opening their personal photo archives. Harris, author of *Civil War Relics of the Western Campaigns,* has accumulated more than 11,500 Civil War relic photos. The other photos were either taken by Brian McKenzie, myself or one of the dozens of relic hunters who generously allowed me to use images of their favorite recoveries. The recovered relics seen in this book were found with various brands of metal detectors over many years.

Perhaps you will be able to find an exciting piece of your family's history. Maybe you will help reunite some lost item of deep personal importance with its owner. Perhaps you will be one of the fortunate to dig a rare Confederate belt plate or a Revolutionary War buckle.

At the end of a long day in the field, I often emerge looking like I've wrestled with the wilderness and lost. My ankles itch from bug bites, my arms are scratched and cut from briars, my clothes

Author Steve Moore shows a minié ball dug while using an *AT Pro* metal detector near a Civil War battlefield in the Lowcountry region of South Carolina.

are wringing wet with sweat, my boots are caked in mud, and my pants are smudged with the color of the local soil. In spite of whatever haggard appearance I may convey, I am all smiles on the inside if my little fly fishing "goodie box" has fresh relics packed into its cotton-filled compartments. This is always a sure sign that the day's quest has been fulfilled.

I am an advocate of responsible relic recovery. This means helping out where you can with archaeological recovery work. It also means documenting your significant finds and sharing that data and/or finds with local historical societies. Responsible relic recovery is also a code of ethics that you must maintain in the field. How you conduct yourself on someone else's property reflects not just upon you but the entire community of hobby detectorists as well. This means filling in the holes you dig, properly disposing of junk metal that you dig, hunting on others' land only with the proper permission, and respecting livestock by closing gates on farmland. There is nothing more disturbing to me than the carelessness of eager hunters I have seen during organized hunts and rallies—namely open holes in the field or discarded trash metal left on the surface that others must "find" all over again.

Relic hunting with metal detectors is a leisure sport for some and a very serious endeavor for others. For both factions, my hope is that this text will offer some additional insight into metal detector basics, research techniques, field reconnaissance and the identification of recovered artifacts. I hope to continue to learn as I go diggin' in new places and learn new techniques from other veterans. I wish you the best of success in the field. Happy hunting!

Stephen L. Moore

# CONTRIBUTORS

Many metal detectorists and landowners contributed to this book by sharing their techniques, their tips, their photos or by helping to research particular sites. Special thanks are also due to some of the landowners who allowed our search teams to hunt their property. *For those whose last name has not been used in this text, the initials of their home state is given in parenthesis below.*

Rick Anderson
Gene Bakner
Spencer Barker
Steve Beck
Michael Bennett
Franco Berlingieri
Joe Bogosian
David Booth
John Bortscher
Earl Boyd
Rich Brown
Maxim Burmistrov
Matt Bruce
Bob Bruce
Garrett Brumit
Helen Cade
Kenneth Cade
Gilles Cavaillé
Larry Cissna
Paul Claunch
Keith Cochran
Glenn Collins
Ian Conway
Beverly Cournoyer
Raymond Cruz
Rusty Curry
Joseph D. (NC)

Bart Davis
Retchey Davis
Ron Dean
Herman Denzler
Bobby DePalo
Dr. Gregg Dimmick
Joe Dinisio
Bradley Dixon
Steven Doering
Jason Ebeyer
Jerry Eckhart
Dave Edwards
Linda Edwards
Michael Edwards
James Ellis
Steve Evans
Tom Ference
Bill Fogelsanger
James Ford
David Foss
Scott Foss
Dan Frezza
John Frezza
Charles Garrett
William Godfrey
Scott Graham
Evan Granger

Jim and Lou Griffin
Joey Gunnels
Vance Gwinn
Gary Hall
Lucas Hall
Mark Hallai
Brian Hanisco
Charles Harris
Steve Hathcock
Joe Hennig
Tom Henrique
John Hitt
Anita Holcombe
Butch Holcombe
Curt Hollifield
John Howland
David Hugg
Rick Hutson
Mark Ickx
Derek Ingram
Nigel Ingram
Dalton Jordan
Robert Jordan
Stephen Jordan
Dustin Juhasz
Jimmi K. (GA)
Bill Kasellman

Davy Keith
Adrian Kelly
John Kendrick
Rose Kendrick
Kevin (TN)
Doug King
Mitch King
Leo Kooistra
Melvin Lane
Jim Leonard
Douglas Mangum
Sir Robert Marx
James Massey
Stan May
Tom McDowell
Warren McGrath
Bobby McKinney
Gerry McMullen
Travis McMullen
Brett McWilliams
Scott Mitchen
Ron Montgomery
Roger Moore
Steve Morgan
Richard Murphy
Lewis Murray
Reece Muru
Regis Najac
Gary Norman
Danny Norris

Beau Ouimette
Brian Pennington
Pavel Popov
Jason Price
Randy Pyle
Rick Range
Kelly Rea
Jason Reep
Tony Reeves
Danny Reijnders
Julie Reiter
Spencer Alan Reiter
Autry Reynolds
Ron Rutledge
Andy Sabisch
Brad Saunders
Jocelyn Savoie
Tim Saylor
Eric Schoppman
Bonnie Schubert
Robert Silverstein
Reggie Simmons
Larry Simpson
Mike Skinner
Terry Smith
Wilson Smith
Keith Southern
Lana Spence
Bob Spratley
Glen Stephens

Rob Stephens
Michael Strutt
Mark Sweburg
Keith Sylvester
Greg T. (SC)
David Thatcher
Scott Thomson
Dave Totzke
Ed Verboort
Linda W. (WY)
Roger W. (IN)
John Walsh
Nikki Walsh
Brent Weaver
Charlie Weaver
Pete Welch
Ted Wells
Megahn White
Keith Wills
Jerry Wilson
Joe Wilson
Paul Wilson
Sue Wilson
Al Winters
George Wyant
Dimitry Zatsepin
Tim Zissett
George Zuk

# FOREWORD

It gives me a great deal of personal pleasure to welcome this book to RAM Publishing's *Treasure Hunting Library* because it serves as a valuable addition. Plus, it's a guide book, filled with interesting stories and colorful picture. It is sure to help many relic hunters—beginners as well as "old pros"—in both North America and Europe.

Hunting with a metal detector has always been thrilling for me over the past 60 years. When I turn on the instrument and sweep its searchcoil over the ground, I'm always excited about what I'm going to find. Maybe it's just a modern-day coin I quickly spend. But, over the many years I've been enthralled by listening to detectors and responding to their signals, my results have often been far more eye-opening.

I've probably done more than my share of hunting remnants of times gone by and achieved a considerable amount of success. For example, you'll see in this book the 500-plus relics I dug from a long-ago British fort on a Caribbean island. Photographing them brought back wonderful memories and reminded me of the frontier sites all over the United States, the gold fields of the Northwest and the battlefields and castles in Europe where I've unearthed ancient objects. Many of the adventures were described in *Ghost Town Treasures* which I wrote some 15 years ago.

Yet the use of metal detectors for finding such artifacts has grown rapidly over these years, and the time has come for a new all-encompassing guidebook on seeking out, digging and restoring relics. Like all of our RAM books, *Relic Quest* is based on solid, in-the-field treasure hunting experience. You will read amazing stories, and get valuable relic-hunting tips.

This book is written by RAM Publishing's Steve Moore, a successful relic hunter himself who certainly shares my enthusiasm for metal detecting. He comes from the same part of East Texas where I grew up, and he and I have hunted side by side with my Garrett detectors more than once.

In putting together this book, Steve has sought out responsible relic hunters far and wide and reported their experiences. *Relic Quest* is, therefore, a grand compilation of what he and I have learned in the field plus all that he has gained from hunting with others and listening to their wisdom. His eagerness to share all of this will be welcomed, and I hope that some of you who have never really considered hunting for relics will join us in this fascinating pastime. You'll be amazed at what you can find.

I know you will enjoy this book even as much as I did when I first read it. Even now, each time I scan its pages I marvel at the information Steve has placed within its covers and the tremendous treasures displayed in the book's photography. Good hunting to you. I hope we will see you in the field.

*Charles Garrett*

Garland, Texas

Charles Garrett shows recovered Civil War plates from his collection.

# CHAPTER 1

# HUNTING HISTORY

Relic hunting is not a new fad. In fact, when the Civil War in America erupted 150 years ago, the musket smoke had scarcely cleared the air before the first souvenir hunters came out to examine the Manassas battlegrounds near present Washington, DC.

The quest to locate and preserve artifacts from significant eras of our history has not faded. Rather, it has gained momentum as technological advances continue to open new doors of discovery. Metal detectors have played a significant role in the unearthing of artifacts in the past 60 years that previously could have been found only by chance or accident.

Military surplus mine detectors found their way into consumer hands following World War II and men soon ventured into the field to search for their own souvenirs and wealth in the form of war relics, lost money, precious minerals and hidden caches. The earliest hunters had very little competition and could thus clean up on finds in spite of the limited technology of their early metal detectors. Two of the most common detector types in the early decades of searching were beat frequency oscillators (BFOs) and transmitter-receiver (TR) machines. While these instruments were quite effective in locating metallic objects in average soil, their design did not allow them to effectively discriminate out ferrous "junk" targets such as small nails or to deeply penetrate the mineralized ground that was prevalent in regions where the significant relics might be found.

As metal detector technology has advanced during the past 40 years, the hobby of searching for metallic items has increased in popularity with each advance that makes the instruments of discovery simpler to operate. Thousands take up metal detecting each year and find it be a truly enjoyable way to pass time. Many are thrilled to search for coins and jewelry on beaches, in parks, on their own land or on sites where people have congregated and lost items of value.

Those of us who engage in "relic hunting" are a different breed. Relic hunting is truly hunting, where what is hunted is that elusive site that has not been found by other searchers. It takes determination and persistence to sniff out such productive sites. But rest assured, they still exist. That said, the sites we seek to search are often not as readily available as they were decades earlier.

The sites that are easiest to find and easiest to work have been hit hard for many years now. Research is vital to find the elusive productive areas, such as virgin camp sites, and getting into such places is often a challenge in itself. In North America, early colonial sites, Revolutionary War and Civil War camps may be deep in the forest and shrouded by heavy overgrowth. Other areas that still hold vast deposits of relics are heavily overlaid with modern trash or in heavily mineralized ground—these being two prime challenges to the casual hunter.

These and other roadblocks can be circumvented with the use of the right detecting equipment and the willingness of the hunter to invest the sweat equity to sniff out those untouched sites. This book is intended to serve as a road map for those who are interested in finding good detecting sites. Initially, we will discuss the types of detectors, searchcoils and other technology that is currently available and the pros and cons of each.

Other chapters in this book will offer insight into methods of research, safety, preparedness for the field, relic identification, preservation methods, and sections dedicated to specific areas of relic hunting. The information has been gathered from personal experiences and from the decades of field experience possessed by dozens of other relic hunters who possess techniques and success stories that will, hopefully, provide some useful bits of information to most any searcher.

In addition to understanding the metal detector technology and spending the time to locate potentially productive areas, today's successful relic hunter must also be a person of good moral character. You must gain the trust of landowners for their permission to allow you onto their property. You must prove your respect to their land by leaving it in a better condition than you found it. This means filling in every hole you dig and hauling out every piece of junk metal and other trash that you encounter. It means closing gates and being respectful of livestock and crops in rural areas. It means respecting the law and never trespassing or hunting on park service land or in national park areas.

Because the hobby of relic hunting has become more and more controversial, it is important to understand both sides of the efforts to preserve history.

———

**The Great Relic Hunting Debate**

The term "treasure hunter" is not favored in today's history circle. The poor judgement of a few often cloud the future for the rest of us who possess the best of intentions. Suburban development and farmers' plows periodically churn up relics of history in areas that have long been forgotten. Most other pieces of world history are unearthed by individuals using metal detectors either as a form of hobby recreation or during true archeological excavations on historic sites.

There is, however, a long-standing debate between archaeologists and relic hunters over the rights of individuals to use metal detectors to seek historic items. Many state and federal entities would love nothing better than to shut down relic hunters from being able to hunt. Some items will remain in decent shape in the ground for thousands of years. Other artifacts deteriorate in the ground. Ferrous items eventually are reclaimed by the earth's acidic soils and simply dissolve over hundreds or thousands of years. Much of what is found by relic hunters would probably not otherwise come to light by chance discoveries made by farmers or modern construction.

Thousands of relics are found each year on private property that simply would not be searched by archaeological efforts. There are simply not enough of these specialists who want to dig every potential site. The responsible relic hunter will keep careful notes of important finds that can be relayed on to historians. They also preserve the precious items they recover. Responsible metal detectorists can also get involved with archaeological projects, offering their special skills to help preserve and add to their nation's heritage.

England is a country which has established an artifact-finding program for detectorists which is beneficial to all. Anyone who finds a piece of treasure (as defined by UK laws) is required to report the item or items to local-level authorities. In return, the found artifacts are studied, the information is logged and then one of two things happens. The government either eventually decides to pay the finder fair market value for the find or it is returned to the finder. This practice has dramatically increased the number of historic artifacts now on display in the UK. This model would well serve many other countries, where the existing laws which forbid the recovery of historic artifacts often compel the finders simply to keep the pieces in secrecy—thus negating the ability of the general public and historians to ever benefit from the valuable knowledge that these pieces might have offered.

Organized rallies held in the UK often have proper officials on hand who log in the various finds and often return to the finders those pieces not desired for display. The European relic hunting chapter provides more details on the various treasure laws of international countries.

*Where are the best places to relic hunt?* The answer to this question, at the risk of sounding like a smart-aleck, is **anywhere in the** *world people have lived in the past 10,000 years.* More specifically, worthwhile relic hunting opportunities exists anywhere that metallic objects have been used by these same inhabitants in the form of tools, weapons, money, jewelry and for household purposes.

Copper was used by early civilized man to form arrowheads, fish hooks, axe heads, and other tools more than 6,000 years ago. Metal detectorists have retrieved such ancient historic implements from sites in Europe, North America and other parts of the earth for many years.

Any worries that treasure fields would be picked clean of riches have been laid aside during the past 20 years as metal detectors have become more and more technologically advanced. Charles Garrett, a pioneering engineer of today's modern metal detector and an avid treasure hunter himself, estimates that more than 95 percent of the world's treasures remain to be discovered in the fields, streams, oceans, mountains, countrysides and settlements of Mother Earth. Add to this estimate the undeniable fact that millions of new coins and other metallic items are lost or discarded across the world each year, providing a vast treasure trove that continues to replenish itself daily.

Experienced relic hunters know that the same well-hunted field can still continue to produce finds year after year. Some such hunters simply return to their favorite hot spots after a farmer has plowed his land in preparation for the planting season. A fresh plowing produces a fresh hunting field.

Today's metal detectors continue to become more sophisticated with electronics that allow them to search deeper and to better discriminate out unwanted "junk metal" targets. Newer detectors have microprocessors or even digital signal processors that can be adapted to the ground mineralization and to the swing speed of the hunter. In many cases, the hunter once had to swing his or her older machine at a controlled, slower speed to make certain the equipment properly processed treasure signals.

Today, many amateur (advocational) archaeologists take to the field every day to help uncover significant pieces of man's past.

Regulations are increasingly adopted to draw the line between what is acceptable conduct for "treasure hunters" and what is not. Some countries have exceedingly stringent laws while others have literally forbidden the use of metal detectors by anyone not carrying credentials.

I have volunteered on several archeological projects and know many others who have done the same. Veteran relic hunters are often used on such projects to verify research, to scout out productive artifact areas on large pieces of property and to generally make the most efficient use of time and money on a project. Seasoned relic hunters are familiar with the techniques of separating the good targets from the bad in trashy areas. Many of those who have volunteered on archeological projects have a certain amount of pride in contributing to the preservation of history, particularly on battlefields or sites to which they feel a certain connection.

The challenge detectorists now face is how to comply with the local regulations while appealing for their right to hunt fairly within less constrictive boundaries. Those who follow the general metal detecting code of ethics will help demonstrate to the historians that metal detecting can be enjoyed without disrupting the quest to preserve history.

---

### Those *Whooo-Hooo!* Moments

The benefits, potential payoffs and enjoyment of relic hunting are similar in nature to what fishermen or large game hunters experience in the field. Each of these sports offers the participant a certain mental escape from the realities of life with the potential of a great fulfillment of obtaining certain goals.

The bass fisherman seeks that big lunker that will fight him until the last possible moment and will ultimately be landed. The "prize" fish may be appreciated and released, weighed and photographed or perhaps even mounted above the fireplace. Such moments of satisfaction are, however, truly few and far between for most fishermen. Many "small fry" are caught and thrown back or perhaps fried up for a satisfactory meal—while the "big one" still remains out there, just waiting to be caught or at least fought.

For deer hunters or other big game sportsmen, the challenge is similar in nature. Their determination, persistence and abilities often pay dividends in the form of downing or at least admiring lesser targets while the desired trophy buck always remains just over the horizon or in another thicket just out of sight.

Relic hunting is comparable in many of the same ways. This sport enables the participant to get out in nature, enjoy the fresh air and sunshine, relax from life's daily grind, benefit from physical exercise, and generally forget about life's other stresses for a short while. Many hunts prove to be unproductive but the avid relic hunter still enjoys the mental escape of trying his or her luck just as much as game hunters or fishermen enjoy their escapes.

The true thrill of fulfillment for a relic hunter comes with the occasional good find. For some, this thrill comes more often than others. Regardless, for those of us that stick with the hobby long enough, there will be a *wooo-hooo!* moment at some point. This is the moment where sweat equity and research finally pay off in the form of a highly-desired target coming to the surface.

For me, I will always remember the exhilaration of digging that first minié ball. I will also remember the certain deep inner satisfaction of pinpointing a battle site—after long hours of studying maps and documents and just feeling that this "has to be" the right spot. Whether openly expressed or suppressed deep within, I would venture to bet that most relic hunters have a prize target they hope to one day find—be it a gold coin cache, a Revolutionary War buckle, a Civil War sword plate, or even an ancestor's heirloom lost on family property.

There is no prescribed method for how relic hunters are to celebrate that coveted recovery when it finally happens. For some, it might be a howled *whooo-hooo!* that echoes through the forest. For others, it may be a hearty laugh of joy, a rebel yell, or even an exclamation which is unprintable in this text. Whether you shake like a deer hunter with buck fever, break out in a sweat of nervous energy, or just shout with joy, you deserve to enjoy the payoff moment to your long hours of searching when a dream is fulfilled.

Sure, there are plenty of those hunters who maintain a poker face and nonchalantly mutter, "Hey, I just dug a Confederate belt plate" as casually as though they had just discovered the daily newspaper in their driveway once again. But for those who wish to let it out, I say, "Go for it!"

There are more types of relics to be found than can be discussed in the limited space of this book. Photo galleries are presented in many of the chapters to help with basic identification of some of the more commonly found artifacts. Other found items are so unique that identifying them can become a whole new research project in itself. While chance discoveries are frequently made by beginners and even veterans, those who are consistently productive in their relic quests are usually diligent in researching the areas they are hunting and in understanding the techniques and tools necessary to be successful in a given environment.

With a little luck, patience and research, dedicated detectorists also afford themselves the opportunity to make a truly remarkable or historic discovery.

## A Relic Hunter's Dream Becomes a Reality

Jerry Eckhart began relic hunting in the 1950s when hobby metal detectors were not common. "I used only a short handled hoe, a shovel, probe and my eyeballs," he wrote. "At that time, relics were easily available in many of the outlying areas. Most folks considered them junk and let them lay."

As metal detectors improved in quality, Jerry developed a passion for hunting with them. His excitement grew as his recovery rates increased. "Relics are in every state in the Union," Jerry testifies. These may vary from Civil War relics, Revolutionary War relics, Indian relics, pioneer relics or turn-of-the-century items. Many of us dream of searching for such items in distant states "but you can still find excellent relics right where you live."

He has done just that in his countless hunts around the central Texas area that he calls home. In 2001, Jerry had a dream of opening what he planned to call the Texas Treasure Hunting Museum in his hometown of Cisco. His dream became a reality in May 2009 when he and local history professor Duane Hale opened the Lela Latch Lloyd Memorial Museum.

"Texas licensing snafus made it simpler to set the organization up as a nonprofit general interest museum," he explained. "As a result, the museum was named in honor of the lady who made it all possible."

The treasure museum is housed in an old three-story brick building that served as Cisco's city hall and police station from 1915 until about 1990. The local Southwestern Searchers metal detecting club and the Texas Council of Treasure Clubs stepped in to assist with restoration, funding and filling the 5,000-square-foot building with history.

*(Left)* Veteran Texas detectorist Jerry Eckhart at "work" in the field.

*(Above)* Jerry recovered this six-pound prairie howitzer cannonball from an unnamed frontier fort.

*(Above)* Artifacts found with metal detectors that Jerry has on display in the treasure hunters' section of the history museum he helped to create in Cisco.

*(Left)* This early period carved sandstone head was found near Putnam, Texas by a farmer as he plowed his fields. Imagine his surprise when he rolled this large stone over to find the carved face.

*(Below)* Relic hunters often find many non-metallic artifacts as they search the land. Jerry's museum has an impressive collection of Indian arrowheads.

One upstairs room is filled with many hundreds of rare treasure hunting books and magazines which researchers may browse through. The museum's upstairs area also features a vaudeville auditorium on whose stage such well-known stars as Elvis Presley, Minnie Pearl and Lawrence Welk once played.

The first floor rooms are filled with displays of all sorts of history, including one room with strictly treasure hunting displays. Dozens of antique detectors hanging on the wall were once produced by Garrett, Fisher, White's, Tesoro and D-Tex. The display cases contain Spanish and Indian artifacts, as well as many early Texas history relics and coins.

Visitors can see relics recovered from an old Spanish iron smelter from the 1600s in what is now Callahan County, Texas. Dr. Hale found one half of a large smelter rake and Jerry was later to recover the other half with his metal detector.

Another display is dedicated to artifacts from Fort Phantom Hill. Jerry served as the caretaker of this property from 1986–1990, clearing brush and restoring buildings. He was able to find and donate more than 300 relics to the land owners. He notes that many good finds can be made on private lands adjoining those that are nationally protected.

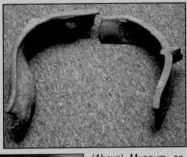

*(Above)* Museum co-founders Jerry Eckhart and Duane Hale found these two halves of a smelter rake from a 17th century Spanish smelter.

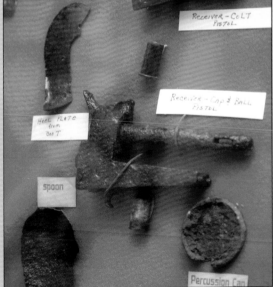

*(Left)* Other artifacts that can be seen in the Texas Treasure Hunter's Museum are these relics recovered by Jerry and his hunting buddies from an 1860s Texas Rangers outpost called Fort Salmon.

More of Jerry's handiwork with the metal detector can be seen in form of artifacts from Camp Salmon that he and his detecting buddies recovered years ago in northeast Callahan County, Texas. Named for Texas Ranger Captain John Salmon, this frontier post was manned by Rangers of the Frontier Regiment during the Civil War to protect settlers from Indian attacks and to handle deserters from the Confederate forces.

This relic hunter's museum—open on Saturdays—is worth a visit to visually sample the artifacts that can be found with metal detectors.

*(Above)* Historic helmets and body armor on display in the Cisco museum.

*(Right)* One of the remaining stone buildings at Fort Phantom Hill, a U.S. Army outpost used in the 1850s. Metal detecting is not permitted on this historical site.

*(Below)* These artifacts were recovered from private land near the fort in the late 1980s using metal detectors.

# CHAPTER 2

# DETECTOR TECHNOLOGY AND SEARCHCOIL TYPES

### Early Relic Hunting Metal Detectors

The earliest finds of Civil War and early Americana relics were picked up after farmers plowed a field and tilled up the artifacts. Most other artifacts of these periods entered the marketplace after they were discovered in trunks and attics, long tucked away by someone's ancestor. It was not until surplus military mine detectors began to reach the marketplace after World War II that early relic hunters made their way to the fields to search for battleground souvenirs.

Scientists and engineers actually began experimenting with electrical theory in the late 1800s to create a machine that could pinpoint metal in order to locate various ore-bearing rocks. Among the early scientists working on what were the forerunners of modern metal detectors was Scottish physicist Alexander Graham Bell, better known as the inventor of the telephone. Bell was working on an electrical induction balance device for locating metals in 1881, when U.S. President James Garfield was severely wounded in an assassination attempt. He was called upon to use his new device to locate a bullet lodged in the President's chest. Dr. Bell's attempts to locate the bullet, however, were unsuccessful before President Garfield died.

The popularity of hobby metal detecting surged following World War II when thousands of surplus military metal detectors were put on the market in America. Prior to 1945, the military had used detectors for minesweeping purposes. Lieutenant Josef Stanislaw Kosacki, a Polish officer attached to a unit stationed in Scotland, had refined earlier metal detector designs into a more practical unit. Although his creation was heavy, ran on vacuum tubes and needed separate battery packs, this mine detector was used to clear the minefields of retreating Germans during the Second Battle of El Alamein. The Allies also used military mine detectors to clear the beaches during the invasions of Normandy, Sicily and Italy. Following the war, former American soldiers who had been trained with these detectors purchased surplus units to hunt for coins as well as American Revolutionary War and Civil War artifacts. By the 1950s several companies were manufacturing somewhat more modern metal detectors for hobby enthusiasts.

The number of different types of metal detectors offered on the market today and the claims of their manufacturers can make the purchase decision a daunting task. It is good to understand the essential components of a metal detector and the advantages and disadvantages of the different technologies involved. Key among the components worthy of discussion here are: **detection technologies, searchcoils, target identification** and **signal processing**.

---

### Detection Technologies: Single versus Multiple Frequency

A metal detector transmits magnetic energy into the ground and senses distortion in the magnetic field caused by the presence of a metal object. The frequency content, temporal form and amplitude of this magnetic energy can affect detection capabilities and overall performance characteristics.

The two primary metal detection technologies used in today's detectors are **Single-Frequency** (also known as Continuous Wave or VLF) and **Multiple-Frequency** (examples include Pulse Induction and Dual Frequency). Since each technology has its own detection characteristics, understanding these will enable the purchaser to choose the right detector for his or her treasure hunting needs.

***Single Frequency Detection:*** Most commonly-used modern metal detectors are **VLF** (Very Low Frequency) models whose single frequency generally ranges between 3 kHz and 30 kHz. Such single-frequency detectors are the most sensitive in lightly mineralized soils where they are able to offer the most accurate and reliable target ID and discrimination.

Continuous Wave may be a more descriptive term for Single Frequency technology because it works as the name suggests. The magnetic field generated via Single Frequency technology resembles the continuous flow of waves onto a beach, which results from the continual transmission of energy from the coil. As a result, all of the detector's magnetic energy is focused at a single, powerful frequency *(see illustration on page 18)*. For the vast majority of hobbyists, their best detector will use Single Frequency (VLF) technol-

*(Right)* Examples of Multiple Frequency/Pulse Induction (PI) detectors are Garrett's *Sea Hunter Mark II* and *Infinium LS* models.

*(Below)* Examples of Single Frequency, VLF detectors are Garrett's *GTI 2500*, *AT Pro* and *ACE 350*.

ogy because it offers greater depth capabilities, better discrimination and enhanced target ID in those soil conditions where most treasure hunting occurs.

Single Frequency detectors also offer the greatest number of features—such as Target ID, Tone ID, Notch Discrimination and Imaging. Many of today's Single Frequency detectors offer both All-Metal and Discrimination modes. Such machines can be used for coin, cache and artifact hunting as well as prospecting on land and in streams. These detectors are more stable and less susceptible to electrical interference because of their focused bandwidth. Single Frequency machines are also very energy efficient, thus providing longer battery life. They are the most commonly purchased detectors because they are the most appropriate for detecting the broadest range of targets in most soils.

Prehistoric volcanic activity seeded much of our land with microscopic iron particles. In most areas, this content is so low that is has little effect on the transmission signals of a metal detector. In other areas, however, the iron content of the ground is high enough that the ground is considered to be "hot" or very mineralized. Older metal detectors utilized technology that reacted to such mineralized soils as though it contained pieces of metal.

The introduction of the VLF machines offered better soil depth penetration and ground elimination than their **TR** (Transmitter/Receiver) or **BFO** (Beat Frequency Oscillator) predecessors. Their low frequency circuitry allowed their transmission signals to more easily pass through soil minerals to seek out artifacts. Relic hunters were thus able to search more effectively in areas of hot soil than during previous decades. Gaining extra depth allowed them to dig items that the early model detectors simply could not reach. Some detectorists still employ detectors with TR technology for coin hunting, but their general lack of discrimination have made them less desirable.

The Single Frequency machine, however, can suffer performance loss in saltwater and over heavily mineralized soils. Large mineral deposits generate strong signals that can distort a target's

# SINGLE VERSUS MULTIPLE FREQUENCY DETECTORS

### ADVANTAGES OF SINGLE FREQUENCY (VLF) DETECTORS

- More sensitive in the most common environments
- Most accurate and reliable target ID and discrimination
- Very energy efficient (long battery life)
- Less susceptible to external noise and interference
- Most appropriate technology for detecting the broadest range of targets over the most common ground conditions
- Majority of hobby detectors use single frequency (VLF) technology

### DISADVANTAGES OF SINGLE FREQUENCY (VLF) DETECTORS

- Loss of detection depth and target ID accuracy in saltwater environments and over heavily mineralized soils

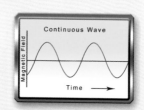

*(Above)* With a Continuous Wave detector, the magnetic field is continually alternating from positive to negative, thousands of times per second.

*(Below)* All of the magnetic energy from a Continuous Wave (VLF) detector is focused at one frequency, hence the term "Single Frequency."

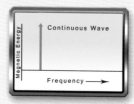

### ADVANTAGES OF MULTIPLE FREQUENCY (PI) DETECTORS

- Provide the best results over mineralized ground and in saltwater environments due to its ability to ignore minerals by virtue of their pulse characteristics

### DISADVANTAGES OF MULTIPLE FREQUENCY (PI) DETECTORS

- Target ID accuracy suffers, primarily in the region of iron identification
- Size and depth measurement and advanced discrimination modes suffer or are not available
- Inherently less sensitive than Single Frequency
- Typically less energy efficient, requiring many models to use larger batteries
- More susceptible to external noise and interference

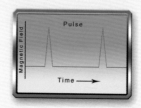

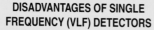

*(Above)* With a Pulse Induction (PI) detector, the magnetic field is produced by very brief, repetitive spikes or pulses.

*(Below)* The magnetic energy of a Pulse Induction detector is spread out among many different frequency harmonies, hence the term "Multiple Frequency."

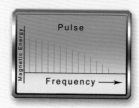

## FREQUENCY VERSUS POWER AND PERFORMANCE

A metal detector transmitting multiple frequencies does not guarantee it will locate more treasures. The Multiple Frequency illustration (B) depicts 18 frequencies (indicated by 18 arrows), which might make you believe you have 18 times the power and performance than that of a Single Frequency detector. In reality, what each arrow in illustration (B) represents is a frequency component with only a fraction of the power and performance found in a Single Frequency detector (illustration A).

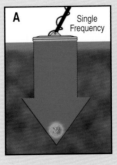

Simply stated, detectors represented by illustrations (A) and (B) contain the same amount of power and potential performance. The difference is that a Single Frequency detector focuses 100% of its power at a nominal frequency that finds the most treasure over the most common ground conditions. In contrast, a Multiple Frequency detector divides its power into 2, 18 or more frequencies for the purpose of overcoming heavily mineralized soils. So, when deciding which technology—Single or Multiple Frequency—is best for you, consider where you will do most of your metal detecting. If you will hunt in difficult conditions where mineralization is a problem, use a Multiple Frequency detector. However, if you plan on hunting in lightly mineralized fields, use a Single Frequency detector.

true signal, resulting in loss of depth and target ID accuracy. For example, a detector using Single Frequency technology may detect a target at ten inches in lightly mineralized soil but may detect the same target at only four to eight inches in heavily mineralized soil. Though the detector's magnetic field is still penetrating at least ten inches into the mineralized soil, its ability to recognize the presence of a target at 10 inches is limited by the vast amounts of minerals present in the soil. This loss of depth in highly mineralized ground in areas such as Virginia limits Single Frequency detectors from finding the deeper relics.

***Multiple Frequency (PI) Detection:*** Where Single Frequency technology suffers (i.e. in saltwater environments and highly mineralized soils) Multiple Frequency technology prevails. The best Multiple Frequency technology is found in many of today's specialty metal detectors.

Though technically interchangeable with Multiple Frequency, the term Pulse Induction (PI) may offer a clearer idea of how the spectrum of multiple frequencies is typically generated and utilized. To illustrate, the repetitive transmission of magnetic pulses is similar to the recurring transmission of sonar "pings" (each ping being analogous to an individual magnetic pulse). The spectrum, or frequency content, of the sonar ping contains numerous frequencies called harmonics. This describes how the brief ping can be mathematically represented by the combination of many different frequency components, known as the Fourier Transform *(see illustration on page 25)*.

In much the same way, the magnetic spectrum of the Pulse Induction wave contains multiple frequencies or harmonics. Stating that a detector operates with 18 frequencies, for example, only shows its pulse wave is made up of 18 significant harmonics. It does not mean a detector is 18 times better, nor the equivalent of 18 detectors operating at once *(see illustration on facing page)*.

Pulse Induction/Multiple Frequency is simply another way of driving the detector's magnetic energy into the ground. However, just as sonar may be superior to other sensing technologies in certain applications, there are some environments where Pulse Induction has an advantage over Single Frequency technology and vice-versa.

Multiple Frequency technology, which is most commonly implemented as Pulse Induction, was initially designed specifically for use in highly mineralized soils like those found on certain beaches or in the gold fields. Wreck divers and prospectors who hunt in areas of high ground mineralization generally use specialized PI detectors due to the extra stability they offer. However, target ID accuracy will typically be poor with these detectors, primarily in the region of iron identification. Many PI detectors, in fact, do not include a target ID at all. In addition, other important features found on Single Frequency detectors, such as True Size and Depth measurement, Tone ID and advanced discrimination modes either suffer or are not available on Multiple Frequency instruments. Such PI detectors are also less energy efficient, often requiring large and heavy battery packs.

---

### VLF Frequency: Higher or Lower?

The performance of a Single-Frequency (Continuous Wave or VLF) detector that operates at a set frequency varies on certain target types and on the prevailing type of soil conditions. Although some more expensive VLF models allow the user to switch from one frequency to another based upon hunting environments, the operating frequency is more often than not fixed. Some allow minor shifts of frequency to overcome signal interference but these basically operate within a very tight frequency range.

Frequency can be defined as the number of times that a signal or wave completes a full cycle per second and is measured in hertz (Hz). Frequency is also defined as the inverse of the wave's period (i.e. frequency = 1/period). For example, if a signal repeats itself 20 times each second, the signal's frequency is 20 Hz. Metal detector frequencies are commonly referenced in kilohertz (kHz). This is a unit of frequency equal to 1000 hertz (or 1000 cycles per second).

Manufacturer's engineers determine what is believed to be the best all-around operating frequency based on a particular detector model's primary searching purpose. American-made Single Frequency metal detectors which sell for less than $500 generally operate at a frequency from 6.5 kHz to 8.5 kHz, with only a few exceptions. American-made VLF detectors priced above $500 have operating frequencies ranging from 6.5 kHz up to 18 kHz.

European manufacturers tend to produce detectors (even their less expensive models) with higher frequencies. There are more areas of lightly mineralized to highly mineralized grounds that can be encountered across the continent. Some of the desired targets—such as thin, hammered Roman and Celtic coins—are best detected with higher frequencies.

There are general advantages and disadvantages offered by

low and high frequency detectors.

*Lower frequency*—generally tends to be more sensitive to more highly conductive metals such as silver or brass. Lower frequencies tend to detect larger targets deeper in the ground than higher frequencies. These machines also perform better in most water hunting environments.

*Higher frequency*—generally more sensitive to lower to mid-conductive metals such as gold, platinum and lead. These also improve the ability to find tiny targets that can missed by lower frequency detectors. European hunters benefit from higher frequencies in their increased ability to find very thin and small hammered coins. Higher frequencies are generally preferred by prospectors who are seeking small gold nuggets, although as the frequency continues to increase there is a reduction in detection depth. High frequency machines also see a decline in detection depth on highly conductive targets (such as silver) as the frequency increases.

————

**Searchcoil Essentials**

The second essential component of metal detecting is the searchcoil—also known as search head, loop, coil or head.

Choosing the right searchcoil from all the different *sizes, shapes, configurations* and *construction* types available is one of the most important aspects of becoming a successful treasure hunter. Searchcoils are generally plastic, molded resin or epoxy-filled housings that contain many thin copper wire windings that send and receive the signals. Most quality manufacturers make watertight searchcoils that can be totally immersed in water without affecting any of the wire loops inside.

The searchcoil attaches to the end of the detector's stem. A coil cable usually winds around the stem and plugs into the detector's control housing. Most searchcoils operate with two separate internal sets of coiled wires, a transmit coil (TX) and a receive coil (RX). Mono coils can be different since one coil acts as both the

## WHAT SIZE SEARCHCOIL SHOULD I USE?

Large searchcoils offer the ability to cover more ground and search deeper. There is, however, a relationship between searchcoil diameter and effective search depth. As a rule of thumb, use a standard size coin (such as a quarter) to gauge effective detection depth.

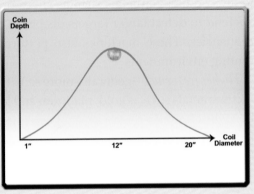

For example, a 4-inch coil will very effectively locate a quarter at a 4-inch depth. A 12-inch coil will effectively find the same quarter at about a 12-inch depth. As seen in the illustration above, however, the coin-sized target becomes more difficult for searchcoils to detect effectively as the coil diameter continues to increase. By the time you reach a 20-inch coil, the coin-sized object can only be detected at perhaps 2.5 inches depth. It is important to remember that the magnetic energy of the searchcoil is much more heavily concentrated in smaller diameter coils.

TX and the RX. When the metal detector is turned on, an electromagnetic field generated by the transmitter winding flows out into whatever medium is present—soil, rock, water, sand, wood, air or whatever else might be encountered. When a metallic object is within this generated magnetic field, it will create a distortion in the field. The RX coil will sense this distortion and send a signal to the control housing. A searchcoil's detection pattern is determined by the combination of the TX's generated field pattern and the RX's sensing field pattern.

Because searchcoil construction quality can vary, it is important to choose a reputable manufacturer. Consult fellow detectorists, read reviews and ask the advice of your dealer before opting for the cheapest coil on the market. Although some inexpensive metal detectors may come with a permanently mounted searchcoil, most quality detectors have a stem assembly that allows the user to switch searchcoils based on different hunting needs.

*Searchcoil Size:* As you gain experience in the field, you will learn that there is no such thing as "the best searchcoil" for all applications. The same coil that performs well in a plowed field may be challenged on a trash-filled beach. Searchcoils are thus available in a wide range of sizes.

Bigger searchcoils do not necessarily guarantee greater detection depth with all targets. Larger targets will certainly be detected at greater depths with larger searchcoils. Small-sized objects can be missed when hunting with a searchcoil that is too large. *(See the illustration on previous page.)*

A metal detector typically puts out a fixed amount of energy regardless of the size of the searchcoil. However, the volume or region into which that energy is transmitted is determined by the size of the coil. A larger coil transmits into a larger region, both deeper and wider while a small coil transmits into a smaller region. Therefore, the energy will be much more concentrated and intense beneath a smaller coil. Conversely, the bigger coil takes that same amount of energy and spreads it into a larger and deeper area, but with less concentration and intensity. As a result, the smaller coil with its concentrated energy field is able to detect small objects better than the larger coil with its dispersed field. It is true that bigger searchcoils will search deeper but the size-versus-energy concentration has an effect on what size target can be discovered as the size of the coil increases.

For effective hunting, you should use smaller coils to seek small, shallow targets. Use larger coils to detect larger, deeply buried objects. For general-purpose hunting, use 7-inch to 10-inch coils.

**Small Coils (4–6 inch diameter):** Because the magnetic field of a small searchcoil is concentrated within a small area, that coil size is the best choice for hunting where a lot of metal debris is encountered. This allows the user to maneuver through and around trash to locate good targets, especially when searching in tight places where large searchcoils cannot fit. However, because a small searchcoil provides less coverage and less depth per sweep, more scans will be required to cover a search area.

## SEARCHCOIL DETECTION DEPTH

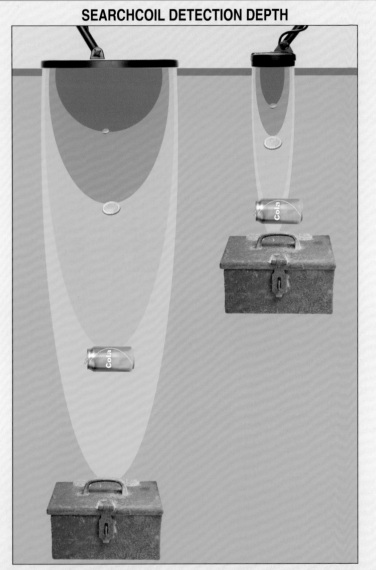

These illustrations compare the average detection capabilities of a larger diameter search-coil (12 to 14") versus a small searchcoil (4.5" diameter). Larger coils achieve greater detection depths.

Larger items can be detected at greater depths than smaller items. Each shaded region represents the detection limits for the particular sized item shown. The items shown are a tiny silver coin, a modern clad coin, a soda can and a large money box.

It only takes a tiny piece of metal to disturb the magnetic field below the searchcoil when using smaller searchcoils with more heavily-concentrated fields. As long as the object is within reach of the diameter of your coil, it will be more easily detected by these smaller coils.

This smaller size searchcoil is referred to as a *Super Sniper* by Garrett. Its intense electromagnetic field gives good detection of very small objects, and its narrow pattern permits excellent target isolation and precise pinpointing. Depth of detection is not as great as that of larger sizes. In high junk areas it is possible to find coins with a *Super Sniper* that would be masked by adjacent junk signals if a larger coil were used.

**Medium Coils (7–10 inch diameter):** This size searchcoil is furnished with most detectors because it is usually the best size for coin hunting and other general purpose uses. These searchcoils are lightweight, have good scanning width and are sensitive to a wide range of targets. Small objects can be detected, and good ground coverage can be obtained. Scanning width is approximately equal to the diameter of the searchcoil. Depth of detection is excellent for most targets with a searchcoil of this size.

**Large Coils (12-inch and larger diameter):** Searchcoils this large, while able to detect larger coins and artifacts at greater depths, are also classified as the best searchcoils for cache and artifact hunting. Precise pinpointing is obviously more difficult with the larger sizes, and their increased weight usually necessitates the use of an arm cuff or a hip-mounted control housing, especially when the detector is used for long periods of time. You will want to use this larger searchcoil when you expect to search deeply for caches or similar treasures.

When you are hunting coins, how do you know when to switch from your "standard" size to the larger searchcoil? The search conditions often help dictate when you should make a switch. For example, suppose you locate a target at the fringe of detection. You know from the weak audio signals that you are at the outer edges of your detector's capability with this searchcoil.

# SEARCHCOIL CONFIGURATIONS AND SHAPES

TX (Outside Coil)   RX (Inside Coil)

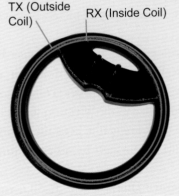

*Mono Searchcoil with Circular Shape*

TX (Outside Coil)   RX (Inside Coil)

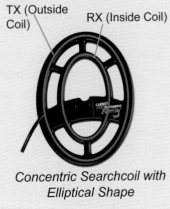

*Concentric Searchcoil with Elliptical Shape*

RX   TX

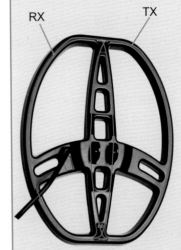

*Double-D Searchcoil with Elliptical Shape*

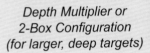

*Depth Multiplier or 2-Box Configuration (for larger, deep targets)*

TX   RX 1   RX 2

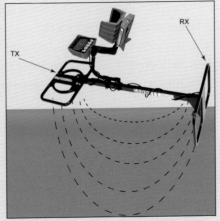

*Circular, Imaging Searchcoil*

TX   RX

By using a larger size, you will generally detect deeper but run the risk the losing smaller targets as the coil size increases. Larger coils also present the increased risk that you will pass over iron rubbish and coins at the same time because of the increased region into which they transmit energy. The iron garbage can "mask" the good target you were hoping to find; more on target masking will be discussed in Chapter 4. The "Searchcoil Detection Depth" illustration *(see page 24)* depicts the average detection depth capabilities of a large coil versus a much smaller coil.

*Searchcoil Shape:* The two most common shapes of searchcoils are *circular (round)* and *elliptical.* Searchcoil *shape is independent* from searchcoil configuration and should not be confused.

**Elliptical shaped searchcoils** are built for both Double-D and concentric search configurations. An elliptical searchcoil is more maneuverable than a circular searchcoil due to its elongated length. However, because a **circular searchcoil** has slightly more detection depth and sensitivity because of the maximum loop area being utilized, it is still the most commonly used shape. Circular coils provide the most uniform pinpointing because of their symmetry. A circular coil can also be either concentric or Double-D in configuration.

An elliptical-shaped coil's narrow width provides more maneuverability for working in tight areas. An elliptical 6 x 10" coil is 15" wide and 10" long from heel to toe versus a 10" circular coil, which offers greater search area with 10 inches in each direction. The equivalent diameter of a 6 x 10" coil is the average of the two dimensions, or equivalent to the performance of an 8" circular coil. Again, the elliptical coil potentially gives up a little bit of depth but offers better maneuverability in tight areas.

*Searchcoil Configurations:* There are a variety of searchcoil configurations available, each with various benefits for different hunting applications and ground conditions. The "configuration" of a searchcoil refers to the arrangement of the TX and RX coils within the searchcoil shell. There are basically five configurations: Concentric, Mono, Imaging, Double-D and 2-box. The searchcoil's

Searchcoils are available in many shapes and sizes for various hunting uses. Shown above, starting clockwise from top, are: an 8" mono coil, a 4.5" *Super Sniper* circular coil, a 6.5" x 9" elliptical-shaped concentric coil, a 9.5" circular imaging coil, a 10" x 14" elliptical Double-D coil and an 8.5" x 11" blunted, elliptical Double-D coil.

*configuration* is more important than the shape of the coil.

The **concentric configuration** consists of a TX coil and RX coil which are usually circular and arranged *(see adjacent page)*. The advantage of this configuration is that both the TX and RX coils can be wound as large as possible within a given searchcoil diameter. The size of these windings dictates the size of the detection field that will be generated by the searchcoil. In a conventional VLF detector the RX coil must be physically separated from the TX. They cannot be stacked directly on top of each other or the transmitter coil would completely overload the receiver coil and thus prevent detection. (For PI machines, the TX and RX coils do not have to be separated.)

In the concentric configuration, the TX coil is generally made larger than the RX coil to provide the necessary separation. The concentric coil configuration offers the largest possible detection field, greatest potential detection depth and greatest potential sensitivity because the coil loop area within the searchcoil's housing has been maximized. The bigger the coil windings are, the greater the detection depth.

In addition, concentric coils also provide the most symmetrical detection field, allowing ease in pinpointing and consistency in target identification. For these reasons, they are the most commonly used and such coils will provide the best overall performance in most environments. For all of its virtues the concentric coil does have its drawback. Because it transmits the greatest amount of energy into the ground, it is also the coil configuration that will receive the greatest amount of interference from ground minerals. This results in substantial loss of performance when used over heavily mineralized ground. Detectorists working such areas therefore often opt for Double-D searchcoil configurations.

A **mono-coil** is available only on Pulse Induction (PI) detectors and is a variation of the concentric configuration. In VLF detectors, the TX and RX coils cannot be located on top of each other because they are transmitting constantly. In a PI machine, the mono-coil can be manufactured with the TX and RX coils located together or as a single coil acting as both TX and RX. The detection and performance characteristics of the mono-coil are essentially the same as the concentric in that it provides the maximum possible sensitivity, but suffers some performance loss in mineralized ground. The mono-coils on PI machines offer better sensitivity and depth because of their maximum loop area. In the most extreme mineralization conditions, a Double-D searchcoil will offer performance advantages.

An **Imaging searchcoil** is an enhanced version of the concentric configuration that features an additional RX coil. This extra coil provides the detector with additional target information necessary for true target-depth perception and true target-sizing capabilities.

With this additional sizing information, the detector can more fully characterize a target and for the first time distinguish between trash and good targets of the same conductivity (e.g. a coin vs. a soda can). Garrett's *GTI (Graphic Target Imaging)* metal detectors have imaging searchcoils that use this advanced technology.

Imaging searchcoils use a second RX coil that acts like a person's second eye. The second receiver is smaller than the first receiver and helps judge depth and size of objects by offering a second perspective.

The **Double-D coil configuration** is designed to significantly reduce ground interference and, thereby, recover the performance lost by a concentric coil over mineralized soil. This configuration is called DD because both TX and RX coils are in the shape of a "D." The interior DD coils can be housed within a searchcoil that is elliptical, round or even square in shape.

The Double-D arrangement of TX and RX coils produces a canceling effect of ground signals. The positive detection field of the DD is located beneath the overlapping center section from front-to-back. The remaining portion of the coil actually produces negative (i.e. canceling) detection fields. It is this canceling field that allows the DD coil to cancel the effects of mineralized ground and maintain its performance over such ground *(see illustration on page 31)*. Double-D coils are useful when hunting highly mineralized grounds and also experience less saltwater interference.

A 10-inch DD searchcoil containing slightly overlapping six inch RX and TX coils does not offer the same 10-inch search area that a 10-inch concentric coil offers. Because of its small positive detection field, the DD is inherently less sensitive than a concentric searchcoil of the same size over non-mineralized ground. The Double-D will, however, outperform the concentric coil over mineralized ground. For this reason, it is highly recommended for hunting mineralized ground often found when prospecting and relic hunting.

In terms of pinpointing with different coil configurations, most beginners find a concentric searchcoil to be easy for learning. More

## DOUBLE-D VERSUS CONCENTRIC SEARCHCOILS

The DD searchcoil has a much different detection field than a concentric coil. The DD's positive detection field is highly concentrated in the center, with negative fields on either side which provide the cancellation of the ground signals.

The concentric searchcoil provides the largest possible detection field and greater detection depth in normal soil conditions but is more susceptible to ground minerals. The concentric coil also offers greater ease in pinpointing targets and in target ID.

As depicted, the detection depth with a DD coil becomes superior to that of a concentric coil as the level of ground mineralization increases.

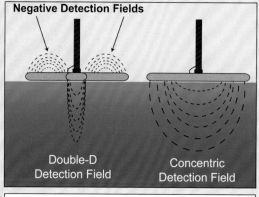

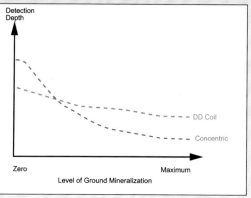

experienced users, however, will realize that with its more tightly defined "hot spot" where the RX and TX coils overlap, a DD coil actually offers more precise pinpointing.

Another type of searchcoil configuration is the **depth multiplier or 2-box configuration** for ultra-deep detecting. In this configuration, the TX and RX coils are physically separated by a significant distance (e.g. 1 meter). This provides a lightweight, manageable means of achieving the performance of a 1-meter-diameter searchcoil that can be physically managed. Because of its large size, and consequently large detection field, the 2-box is the best choice for detecting large, deeply buried objects such as caches. Also, because of its large detection field, it ignores objects smaller than about 7

Depth multipliers or 2-box searchcoil configurations mount to select metal detectors and operate in the All-Metal mode. This specialized setup allows the detector to search for larger, deeply buried targets well beyond the depths of conventional searchcoils while ignoring small trash items.

cm in diameter. This characteristic is advantageous when hunting in areas heavily littered with small trash objects. The depth multiplier configuration is recommended when searching for coin or weapons caches, large artifacts, safes or cannons.

Garrett offers an exclusive, enhanced version of this 2-box configuration known as the *Treasure Hound with Eagle-Eye* pinpointing. This version incorporates an additional pinpointing coil in the front for precise target location.

*Searchcoil construction:* There are three main types of searchcoil construction. An **air-filled** searchcoil is basically a plastic shell that houses the RX and TX coil windings. This is the lightest weight configuration but it is also the least durable without a solid internal structure for support. Air-filled searchcoils traditionally do not seal well and can suffer from leakage in wet environments which can quickly ruin a searchcoil.

The second type of coil construction is a plastic shell that is **foam-filled**. This can be pre-cut foam or expandable foam that fills the housing. This provides a relatively light-weight coil with some added structure for the internal coil windings. This coil still suffers from water leaks because it is not truly watertight.

The third type of searchcoil construction is an **epoxy-filled** searchcoil. It is the most durable version as a rock-hard epoxy protects the windings. The only drawback is that this makes the searchcoil heavier; therefore, most epoxy-filled coils have openings cut through the coil versus a solid housing. An advantage of these openings is visibility through the coil to see the ground as a target is pinpointed. The epoxy-filled coil is rugged and offers the best protection from water because the internal windings are fully sealed.

Make certain you understand the water-resistant capabilities of your searchcoil. *Splashproof* indicates that operation will not be affected if a small amount of water gets on the searchcoil, such as light rain or moisture from wet grass. *Weatherproof* (sometimes called waterproof) means that the searchcoil can be operated in heavy rain with no danger from the moisture. *Submersible* indicates that a searchcoil can be fully submerged as deep as the cable connector, without affecting the detector's operation.

Avoid "bargain" searchcoils. A good searchcoil is vital to the success of a metal detector. It should be light, but it must also be sturdy and capable of rugged treatment. A good searchcoil has a tough exterior that will not abrade or crack easily on rough ground. Searchcoils must withstand the greatest abuse of any detector component because they are constantly being slid across the ground, bumped into rocks and trees, submerged in water and generally mistreated in every way.

**Skid plates or coil covers** are available that protect the surface of a coil from being damaged or heavily scratched by rough ground, rocks, roots and other obstacles a searchcoil brushes against. Coil covers prevent the search head from eventually becoming so scuffed that cracks form which can cause leakage into the inner coil wires, rendering the coil useless. Such covers are thus a wise investment to prolong the life of valuable searchcoils.

———

A quality detector always includes a quality searchcoil but it is important to understand the various other coil options that are available for your search efforts. Hopefully, the above information will assist in your decision-making process in regards to the various searchcoil and metal detection technologies. The other two essentials components of a metal detector—target identification and signal processing—will be reviewed in equal depth in the next chapter.

Successful relic hunters know when to use various searchcoil types and they understand the signals their detector is providing. The success of Tony Reeves—as seen in one of his Civil War relic cases—proves the value of understanding target signals.

# CHAPTER 3

# TARGET IDENTIFICATION AND SIGNAL PROCESSING

In the previous chapter, we identified four essential elements of a metal detector to consider when making a purchase decision: **detection technologies, searchcoils, target identification** and **signal processing.** Having covered the first two essentials, this chapter will focus in-depth on the various types of Target ID features and on signal processing.

Your style and experience in relic hunting will help dictate which type of metal detector and which particular features are most important. Some seasoned hunters prefer to hunt only with a True All-Metal Mode detector to hear every subtle nuance of every target's characteristics. Many searchers also find it very important to have ample iron resolution to be able to discriminate out only certain targets. Still others may want to "notch out" certain segments—such as pop tops or foil—while detecting everything else.

To decide what features are important to you, it is worthy to consider the two main detector types (motion versus non-motion detectors), how targets are interpreted and identified on various machines, and other key metal detector features that can change your success in the field. Knowledge of these key areas will ultimately lead you to making a purchase decision that fulfills your hunting needs.

***

## All-Metal (Non-Motion) Detectors versus Discrimination/ Target ID (Motion) Detectors

The earliest metal detectors operated in an All-Metal mode without any discrimination. They simply identified all types of metal that their searchcoil passed over. Many detectorists today wish to ignore small iron and pull tabs, which requires a detector with discrimination settings that can be applied. It is important to note some of the key differences between the two primary detector types that are sold today.

In a true **All-Metal**, Non-Motion metal detector, the machine responds to all types of metals it encounters. One advantage of an All-Metal detector is that because it is not trying to analyze whether a target is worthy or not, the detector can provide the greatest possible depth and sensitivity—often achieving depths up to twice that of a discrimination detector. The other advantage of All-Metal detectors is that they operate without requiring the searchcoil to be in motion. This static, or very near static, operation mode is the reason that All-Metal machines are referred to as *Non-Motion* or Motionless detectors.

Such a detector allows you to approach a target, hover over a target or creep around a target with your searchcoil. You will hear every nuance and every subtle increase or decrease in target response as you approach it and leave it. When veteran detectorists hear every characteristic of their target, they can literally hear the shape or size of a target as the audio changes. This continuous audio response helps distinguish a target's features.

The principle drawback to this continuous audio response is that you also hear every subtle nuance of the environment. The biggest environmental factor, of course, is the ground itself, which contains all types of minerals. This can include ferrous minerals, conductive minerals and moisture, which all produce responses. Some rocks—known as "hot rocks"—contain concentrated minerals and can produce a significant audio response. You thus have to become adept at distinguishing the sounds of ground response from the sound of a good target's response.

The first thing to do with an All-Metal detector is ground balance it. Without ground balancing, the ground itself will produce such strong signals that you can not hope to find a target. Until you ground balance your machine, all you will hear is *ground noise* when you move your coil. Ground balancing is literally adjusting and tuning the electronics of your detector so that the ground response is essentially ignored. Whenever ground mineralization shifts, however, you must ground balance your detector again to this new environment. This can be challenging for new detectorists.

Circuitry or signals in an All-Metal detector can potentially drift, adding another challenge to the operator. Drift in the ambient background signal can be caused by drift in the electronics (although modern electronics are extremely stable); temperature drift as you might move from the hot sun into a cool, shady spot; and changes in the ground mineralization. You must remain aware of this ever-changing environment because of the sensitivity of an All-Metal detector.

A good quality All-Metal mode detector has features to help overcome the difficulties presented by ground balancing and drift. To keep these effects to a minimum, a quality All-Metal detector has features like Auto Threshold and Auto GroundTrack. With *Auto Threshold*, the detector automatically monitors the ambient signal; if it starts drifting because of temperature changes, etc., the Auto Threshold will work to suppress this. In *Auto GroundTrack*, the detector continually monitors the ground conditions and adjusts itself to these changes.

When discrimination detectors utilize pinpointing abilities, they are basically switching into an All-Metal mode to allow you to continually hear the target response as you move the searchcoil over the target. Examples of this are the *ACE 350* and *AT Pro* detectors by Garrett, which temporarily switch into All-Metal operation when you hold down the Pinpoint button.

When the *ACE 350* and *AT Pro* in their Pinpoint modes put the machine into an All-Metal mode, it is similar to comparing an amateur sports team to professional teams. You get the advantages of continuous audio feedback, and you have static operation for hovering over targets without losing the signal; what you don't have in this Pinpoint mode is all the other support circuitry that a good All-Metal mode has such as the automatic threshold and ground tracking functions. Because this pinpointing function is thus not as stable as that of an All-Metal mode detector, opting to hunt while holding down the Pinpoint button will not be effective. You will have to constantly release and reset the Pinpoint button because of the changing environment. It is quite effective, however, during the short time normally required for pinpointing.

The other type of detector is the **Discrimination** or **Motion** detector which does not give continuous audio feedback. The detector effectively hunts silently in Discrimination mode until it identifies and signals a target. One of the advantages of the Discrimination mode is that it frees the operator from all the distractions that comes with the All-Metal Mode by not responding to everything it encounters. The detector pre-screens everything it analyzes before announcing an item it interprets to be a good target. The user is able to pick and choose which targets should respond and which targets should not respond, such as iron.

In order for this type of detector to operate correctly, the searchcoil must be in motion because discrimination detectors introduce filtering to minimize the ground signal. This filter must be in motion to be effective which requires the coil to be moving as it discriminates or identifies target metals. When you hold the searchcoil perfectly still above a target with a discrimination detector, it loses the signal.

A Discrimination (Motion) detector operated in a "Zero" Mode is essentially detecting all metals ("zero" discrimination), but this is misleading because of the nature of the discrimination filters. When you are using a Discrimination mode of any kind you can never experience a true All-Metal mode because the motion detector always maintains some amount of filtering to eliminate the response of ground and other small perturbations. A true All-Metal detector on the other hand has no discrimination filters, allowing it to signal all metals. On most Discrimination detectors, iron may be the lowest conductivity target identified on the Target ID scale, but even lower on a scale than iron are the electrical and magnetic properties of the ground.

Only a true All-Metal detector (i.e. no discrimination filters) can respond to the entire range of electrical and magnetic properties. *A Discrimination detector with an "All-Metal" mode can never be a "true" All-Metal detector*; this mode should more properly be termed "Zero" discrimination as there is always some discrimination occurring in a motion detector.

You can determine whether your detector is a motion or non-motion type with a simple test. Sweep a coin or other target under the searchcoil to produce a response. When you hold the target perfectly still under the searchcoil, a motion detector will cease to respond. This type of machine requires the searchcoil to be in at least a slight amount of motion to detect a metallic target.

---

### Target Identification with Motion Detectors

A detector's target ID refers to its ability to identify a target. *The conductivity, permeability, thickness, size, shape, and orientation of the target all play roles in determining where it will read on its Target ID scale.*

Every piece of metal has a certain electrical characteristic and a certain magnetic characteristic. The electrical characteristic is *conductivity*. The magnetic characteristic is called *permeability;* a magnet will attract such metals. These two characteristics dictate how metal will distort the magnetic field transmitted by the searchcoil.

The most highly conductive materials, such as pure silver, have no magnetic properties at all and are known as purely conductive *non-ferrous* metals. When the magnetic field from a detector's searchcoil bombards a purely conductive metal, eddy currents form on the surface and produce a secondary field that reflects back. In other words, that piece of metal acts like a mirror, reflect-

## TARGET SIGNALS: Conductivity versus Permeability

This top illustration depicts the magnetic field generated by a metal detector's searchcoil.

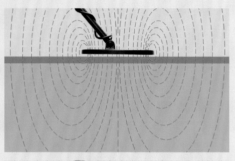

### Conductive Target

This center illustration depicts the distortion of the magnetic fields when it encounters a highly conductive target such as a silver coin. This purely conductive target produces currents that reflect the field almost like a mirror.

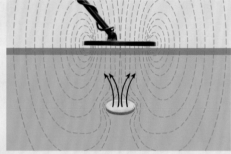

### Magnetic Target

This lower illustration depicts the distortion of the magnetic field when it encounters a magnetic (ferrous) metal item. This object pulls in the field (versus bouncing it back) through itself, creating a response that is the exact opposite of the highly conductive coin.

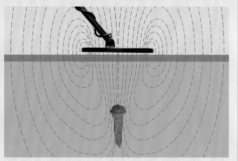

ing what has been transmitted against it. What is received back is basically a mirror image of the field that was transmitted *(see illustration above)*.

An extremely thin conductive metal will allow some of the magnetic field to pass through it; the thicker the conductive metal, the more it will perfectly bounce the magnetic waves back. Thick, highly conductive metals that most strongly reflect the magnetic waves back to the searchcoil will register highest on the Target ID scale. Pure silver is the most conductive metal of the treasures you will usually encounter.

The other extreme example is a metallic object that has very low conductivity but is very magnetic or *ferrous* (i.e. iron). Rather than trying to reflect the magnetic field, a magnetic item funnels the field through itself and out the other end *(see illustration on the opposite page)*. An iron bolt in the magnetic field will draw in the magnetic fields from the coil and create a distortion the exact opposite of the purely conductive silver. These ferrous (magnetic) metals show lowest on the Target ID scale.

*What does all this mean?* Again, electrical conductivity and permeability (magnetic characteristics) are the two major factors that determine how the object will distort the magnetic field (i.e. conductive metals will reflect the field and magnetic metals will draw the field inward). The third mechanism that occurs is *energy dissipation* or energy loss. This happens when eddy currents on the target's surface interact with the metal's resistance and actually begin dissipating energy in the form of heat. The higher the metal's resistance (i.e. the lower the conductivity) the greater the energy dissipation. Very little energy is lost in highly conductive metals such as silver. All metals have a certain amount of energy loss associated with them. *A metal object's target ID is determined by a ratio of energy dissipation to field distortion.*

The levels of electrical conductivity of various metals are shown on displays or meters on metal detectors. Scientists measure the levels of conductivity in Siemens per meter (S/m) with an ohm-meter by measuring how easily electrons move through a metal object. Iron is on the lower end of the conductivity scale along with stainless steel. The electrical and magnetic characteristics of metal, coupled with its energy dissipation are again key factors in determining how a metal object registers on the detector's target ID scale. (See chart on the following page to see how conductivity and permeability both come into play to help rank items.)

In addition to the three scenarios described above, Target ID is also determined by several other factors:

**ELECTRICAL AND MAGNETIC PROPERTIES OF COMMON MATERIALS**

| Material: | Conductivity $\sigma$ (S/m) | Conductivity Ranking | Magnetic Permeability $\mu_r$ |
|---|---|---|---|
| Silver | 62.9 x10$^6$ | Excellent | 1 |
| Copper | 59.8 x10$^6$ | Excellent | 1 |
| Gold | 41.0 x10$^6$ | Good | 1 |
| Aluminum | 35.4 x10$^6$ | Good | 1 |
| Zinc | 16.9 x10$^6$ | Fair | 1 |
| Brass | 15.7 x10$^6$ | Fair | 1 |
| Nickel | 14.6 x10$^6$ | Fair | 250 |
| Bronze | 10.0 x10$^6$ | Fair | 1 |
| Iron & Steel | 10.0 x10$^6$ | Fair | 400 (typical) |
| Platinum | 9.5 x10$^6$ | Poor | 1 |
| Tin | 9.1 x10$^6$ | Poor | 1 |
| Lead | 4.8 x10$^6$ | Poor | 1 |
| Stainless Steel * | 1.4 x10$^6$ | Poor | 1 (typical) |
| Sea Water | 4.0 | Very Poor | 1 |
| Fresh Water | 0.001 | Extremely Poor | 1 |

\* Non-Magnetic

• **Target thickness**—The thickness of a metal object plays a huge role in its Target ID reading, far beyond any minor effect due to the alloying of metals. The thicker a conductive object, the greater its ability to conduct larger eddy currents that reflect more of the magnetic field. The material's inherent conductivity and its thickness together are the primary factors determining what the "effective conductivity" or effective Target ID will be. Even though large pieces of silver register highest on the scale, an equally pure piece of silver hammered paper thin will not register the same.

• **Target Shape and Orientation**—For ferrous objects (e.g. iron and steel), the shape and orientation of the target can have a significant effect on the Target ID. For example, a thin steel washer or flattened bottle cap lying flat in the ground can produce a high Target ID reading, similar to a coin. This is because the object's horizontal orientation is presenting a large surface area to the searchcoil, thereby allowing eddy currents to flow on that large

The shape and thickness of a metal object is much more important in determining Target ID than its metal alloy. These 10k gold items (actually composed of 75% silver content) found by an *ACE 250* detectorist showed on the left side of his Target ID scale. The 1865 medallion (made into an earring) showed on the *ACE* scale under foil. The gold ring at right hit below the nickel symbol on his detector. Their target reading was more heavily influenced by their size and shape versus their gold to silver alloy ratio.

surface and reflect the magnetic fields. This same steel washer or flattened bottle cap when resting vertically on edge is no longer presenting a large surface area. Rather, it is presenting a long, narrow path which channels the magnetic field inward through the object (same as the iron spike shown in the illustration on page 40). As a result, the steel washer or flattened bottle cap oriented vertically will produce a low Target ID reading of iron. This same effect can occur for most any piece of iron—such as a piece of broken plow blade—which, when flat can produce a high Target ID, and when vertically oriented will produce a low Target ID of iron.

In summary, Discrimination detectors with Target ID capabilities allow you to focus on the metals you want to detect and ignore the metals you don't want to detect. This time-saving capability revolutionized the metal detector industry when it allowed searchers to pick and choose targets. The drawback to Motion detectors with discrimination is that the detector must continually analyze all targets that are encountered. The signal that measures magnetic field distortion is extremely susceptible to mineralized ground, making Discrimination detectors more challenged by adverse mineral conditions (and wetted salt sand) than All-Metal (Non-Motion) detectors.

The magnetic properties inherent in all soils factor into the true reporting of Target ID. In even the most inert (pure) ground conditions, the ground signal skews the accuracy of the Target ID to a certain degree. Of course, Target ID is extremely accurate in air tests without the presence of ground mineralization. In inert ground, Target ID is again very accurate but steadily declines as the amount of mineralization increases. White, dry beach sand, with no magnetic black sand or other conductive minerals, is also an excellent area for accurate target identification.

Many detector Target ID scales report on a 10- or 100-point scale. Some high-end Garrett GTI models also report on a 24-point scale. They are all reporting the same physics concerning the ratio of field distortion versus energy absorption. The 100-point scale systems offer better distinction between target readings than a 10- or 24-point scale.

The reality is, however, that ground minerals and other environmental factors will produce the same percentage of fluctuations in the Target ID reading, regardless of the number of points in the Target ID scale. For example, if the ground is creating a ± 10% fluctuation in the Target ID, then a target which reads 4 to 6 on a 10-point scale will likely read 40 to 60 on a 100-point scale. In this situation, the 100-point scale is not providing any more information than the 10-point scale. (The use and benefits of 100-point scales will be discussed further in the section called "Digital Target ID" later in this chapter.)

----

### Signal Processing

The fourth essential component of a metal detector is the way in which it analyzes received signals to determine target information. All detectors, regardless of their technology, transmit an analog signal and must determine how it interacts with a metal target.

Once those signals return to the detector through the search-coil, the technology of the machine's signal processing comes into play. Older units and even some less sophisticated detectors still on the market perform their signal processing and analysis via analog circuitry. By the mid-1980s, *microprocessors* were being incorporated into metal detectors. This immediately eliminated the variability and drift inherent with analog components and filters. Microprocessors use digital processing, which is more absolute, thus offering greater consistency and reliability. The introduction of microprocessors also permitted simpler adjustability. Instead of several knobs to adjust, the microprocessor often permitted the use of touch pads and LCDs that offered greater adjustability, repeatability and flexibility without the variations of analog circuitry.

The next jump forward was *digital signal processing (DSP)*, comparable to a microprocessor on steroids. This powerful, high-speed math machine took even more of the filtering and signal processing away from the analog circuitry to a digital system that is more consistent and accurate. DSP detectors are generally more expensive and among the most sophisticated detectors available. Don't be misled by brands with microprocessors that simply process signals digitally (and claim to be DSPs) versus a true digital-signal-processor instrument. Analog circuitry and microprocessors alone simply cannot process the same amount of signals as fast and as reliably as a metal detector with DSP.

———

**Advanced Audio Features**

There is another level of target identification and signal processing worthy of discussion. The audible signals emitted by a detector vary based upon design features and True All-Metal (generally Non-Motion) machines versus Discrimination/Target ID (Motion) detectors. Many veteran relic hunters consider it crucial that they hear subtle changes in amplitude and subtle changes in conductivity. The names given to these features vary by manufacturer, but for this text we will refer to these options as **Proportional Audio** and **Tone Roll Audio**.

- *Proportional Audio*—This feature is analogous to the operation of a True All-Metal Mode detector, in which subtle nuances (or changes) in a target's amplitude can be heard by the user. Many modern detectors—including Garrett's *ACE* series and the *GTI 2500*—translate a target's audio in basic binary audio response. Computers operate in a binary language of code written as either 1 or 0, where something is either on or off with nothing in between.

Binary audio response of a target indicates the peak response of the target. This information gives the detector operator a good indication of the target's conductivity but no other information regarding the target's shape, size or orientation. Some advanced detectors (such as Garrett's *GTI* series) go a step further to visually profile or identify a target's size.

True All-Metal Mode detectors (including the *GTI 2500* and *AT Gold*) offer even more target information by allowing the operator to hear the *signature* or *envelope* of their target. In this case, the detector is providing the proportional audio, or actual audio response, of the complete target. With some technology, this can translate as small targets having a softer audio signature and large targets having a stronger audio signature.

Proportional audio also brings a target's shape into play. For example, a relic with a strange protrusion on one side can be better distinguished. The subtle nuances you are able to hear with such proportional audio can help the trained ear better process the sound of the target to properly characterize and identify it. In comparison, a binary audio detector will give only one strong beep or ding for the entire target.

For deeper targets, proportional audio will also help indicate the depth of the target. Binary audio only gives the same beep (it either sees the target or it does not) with no indication of depth. Binary audio system thus generally include some form of target depth indication for the operator.

Audio amplitude is proportional to the target's amplitude. The length of audio duration is in proportion to the shape of the buried target. In addition to True All-Metal Mode detectors which allow the operator to hear proportional audio, there are Discrimination/Target ID detectors on the market with Proportional Audio features that act in translating audio signals much in the way that the All-Metal Mode machines do. Examples of such Discrimination/ Target ID metal detector with Proportional Audio are Garrett's *AT Pro* and *AT Gold* machines.

Another benefit of a detector with proportional audio is the advantage of speed or *recovery time* when processing multiple or adjacent targets. Recovery time is also referred to as *reactivity* by some detector manufacturers. Faster recovery time allows the operator to hear multiple targets faster than most binary audio systems have been programmed to allow. It is again the subtle nuances (or variations) of target sounds that allow the user to distinguish the fact that two different targets may be laying in close proximity or that a single target may be oddly shaped.

It is important to understand the recovery speed of your detector is such target-laiden areas. Practice on buried targets in your test plot by placing several coins and other items in the ground at a shallow depth. Space them several inches apart and practice swinging your coil over these targets at varying speeds and from different angles until you are successful in "reading" each target. You might notice that a coin and a bottle cap combine into one signal at faster speeds. By slowing down, your goal is to successfully hear first the bottle cap and the coin as two different sounds. Some detectors permit the user to adjust the recovery speed for areas where multiple targets and target masking are an issue.

• *Tone Roll Audio*—This feature can also be referred to as *Phase Roll Audio* or *Pitch Roll Audio*. Tone Roll Audio addresses the shortcomings of binary audio tone ID system in relation to a target's conductivity or tone. By comparison, Proportional Audio addresses the shortcomings of binary audio in relation to a target's amplitude.

With binary audio, simple targets such as coins produce only a single-tone beep or ding. This is fine for such basic targets but there is a loss of potential target information when it comes to more complex discoveries. Relic hunters in particular are commonly faced with more complex iron targets that can be misinter-

# AUDIO TARGET SIGNALS: Standard Binary vs Proportional

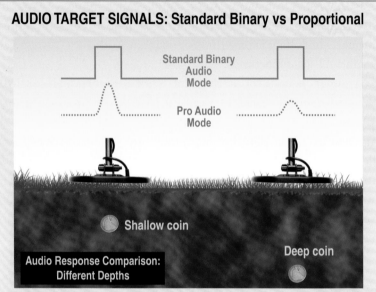

**Example 1:** Notice the differences in binary audio versus proportional audio in the two target scenarios above. The detector with binary audio gives a solid, consistent beep for both the shallow and the deep coin. In contrast, the proportional audio detector provides a stronger signal for the shallow coin and a softer signal for the deeper coin. The actual profile, or signature, of the target's response is heard, thereby providing more information. (These illustrations depict standard and proportional audio options on a Garrett *AT Pro*.)

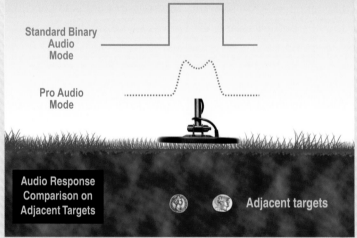

**Example 2:** These two adjacent coins would produce one strong signal from a binary audio detector. With proportional audio, a rise and fall of audio response allows the user to interpret the multiple targets.

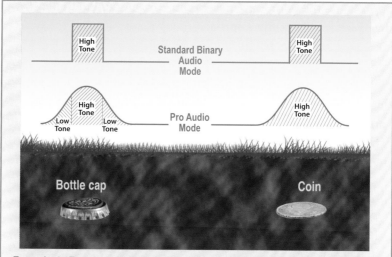

**Example 3:** For many detectors with binary audio, bottle caps, steel washers, etc. sound like good targets, producing a high tone response. This is because the bottle cap's shape and flat surface resembles a coin which tricks the detector. With a detector with the *Tone Roll Audio* feature, however, the bottle cap will produce a very distinctive response with multiple tones. As shown, the bottle cap will produce a distinctive Low-High-Low response as compared to the coin's High-only response.

preted by binary audio detectors. Prime examples are bottle caps, steel washers, some flat nuts, and various other iron objects that can present themselves in the same fashion as a coin.

To further illustrate this point, think of the surface of a bottle cap. It is generally round, flat and similar in appearance from above as a coin and would offer a similar signature. Binary audio detectors report the strongest (best) signal when calculating and reporting on a target. In the case of such a bottle cap, the target's peak, or zenith, is the read the detector receives as the searchcoil passes above the flat top surface of the bottle cap or washer. The detector therefore takes this best read and may report back a good conductive object that reads like a coin *(see illustration above)*. The relic hunter then proceeds to dig what turns out to be just another washer or bottle cap.

Tone roll audio offers the detectorist the opportunity to avoid this worthless digging. The Target ID changes as the searchcoil approaches the bottle cap, passes directly over it and then departs the target. During the approach, field patterns from the search-coil pass through the volume, or side, of the bottle cap. The initial sound produced will be a low tone or typical grunt sound caused by iron. Passing over the bottle cap, the field patterns slam into the flat surface area and the sound changes to a high tone or bell-tone sound often caused by a coin. As the searchcoil departs the bottle cap, the field patterns again pass through the volume, or side, of the cap and produce another low tone.

This is heard in quick succession as low, high and low tones *(see illustration)*. This variance of tones will be enough for the trained ear to discern that the target is more likely a piece of iron than a coin. In contrast, the binary audio reports only the strongest signal (taken while above the bottle cap) and reports a conductive target similar to a coin. The varying phases or pitches of audio thus offer the detectorist far better target information.

Some advanced detectors allow the user to shift the audio range of the mid-tone sound and to hear the discriminated iron as a low tone. By doing so, you can "move the needle" so that the low-tone is nothing you want to dig but you will want to dig everything now from the mid-tone sound on up (since you have moved the needle). The Iron Audio feature on Garrett's *AT Pro* and *AT Gold* are examples of metal detectors with this user-adjustable option.

------

### Description of Metal Detector Features

Your decision in purchasing a detector should be driven by the features you desire. Some metal detectors will allow you to make adjustments with knobs or dials while others feature push-buttons. The following list describes some of the key features you should consider before making a purchase. Some of these you might find to be "desired;" others you may considered to be "required:"

• *Discrimination Mode*—This indicates a detector's ability to decipher between desired targets and trash targets. This is usually a switch, dial or push-button selection that allows the user to tell the detector what items to "accept" and what items to "reject." This allows hunting in trashy areas without detecting and digging every piece of junk metal. For this reason, a detector with discrimination modes is considered to be a "required" feature by most detectorists. A disadvantage of any detector employing a Discrimination Mode is that it achieves less depth than one with an All-Metal Mode.

• *All Metal Mode*—A True All-Metal Mode detector provides the greatest possible depth and sensitivity. It also provides continuous audio response of the target to discern subtle characteristics of the target such as size, shape, etc. An All-Metal mode machine can be at a disadvantage—or virtually useless—in very trashy areas due to excessive target responses. *(Refer back to the All-Metal versus Discrimination section in this chapter for more details.)*

• *Notch Accept/Reject Discrimination*—This feature on many detectors enables groups of metals to be accepted or rejected by notching them in or notching them out. In Chapter 4, the dangers of using notch discrimination to remove unwanted "trash" targets such as pull tabs will be illustrated. Even with the elimination of ring pulls, you will also be eliminating any gold rings that have the same conductivity as these ring pulls. Many detectorists will opt to eliminate some iron targets on the left side of the scale, even knowing that they are also potentially missing some good relic targets.

Notch discrimination is particularly useful if you are searching for a specific type of target and wish to eliminate all other metals—thus increasing your ability to find the desired target metal. Searchers at an organized hunt searching for specific prize tokens can notch out other unwanted targets in order to speed their search for such tokens. *(See discrimination notches and other detector features on the control panel image seen on the following page.)*

• *Automatic Ground Track*—This feature may also be referred to as "automatic ground balancing." Such detectors more or less maintain optimum ground balance against mineralization in order to prevent the need for continuous adjustment of dials

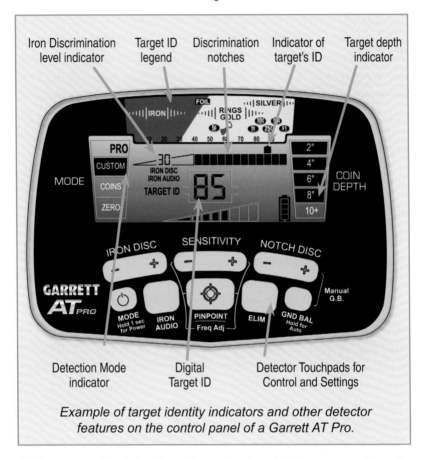

Iron Discrimination level indicator    Target ID legend    Discrimination notches    Indicator of target's ID    Target depth indicator

Detection Mode indicator    Digital Target ID    Detector Touchpads for Control and Settings

*Example of target identity indicators and other detector features on the control panel of a Garrett AT Pro.*

during operation. The Garrett *GTI 2500* and *AT Pro* use automatic ground tracking or "Auto Track" to allow manual ground balancing to compensate for various ground mineralization conditions.

• *Sensitivity*—This feature simply increases the depth of detection. Generally, you will want to get as much depth as possible as you search for older, deeply buried objects. Turning down the sensitivity can be beneficial in certain situations, however, such as the presence of power lines or other objects creating electrical interference; high ground mineralization; or areas of high concentrations of rubbish.

• *Threshold*—Many of the less expensive detectors operate in what is known as "silent search" or a silent mode. As you step up into the higher-end machines, they frequently operate with a threshold tone which is used in the All-Metal mode. Although detectors with threshold adjustments can be turned down to silent while in All Metal mode, it is recommended that you always operate your detector with a minimum level of audible sound.

The use of threshold (also called "hum" or "tuning") allows you to hear the audio increase sharply whenever a desired target is encountered. With experience, you can also judge the size of a target and hear whether your detector is properly tuned or not.

The proper level of threshold must be maintained in order to pick up all good target sounds. When the detector's threshold is set too high, a faint signal is masked and only the peak of loud signals are just audible above the threshold. When the threshold is set too low, faint target signals can not be heard above the hum. When the threshold level is set to a level where you can hear just a minimum audible hum, both faint and loud signals can be heard through your headphones.

• *Volume*—This allows you to set the volume to your preference according to the prevailing external environment (i.e quiet or noisy) conditions.

• *Variable Tone ID*—On some detector models, different types of metals produce different audible tones. Garrett detectors, for example, emit a distinctive Belltone ring whenever a target of high conductivity (such as a coin) has been located. Targets of lower conductivity, such as iron, create a sound with a lower pitch while targets of medium conductivity produce a higher-pitched sound.

• *Tone Adjustment*—This refers to the ability to adjust your detector's audio to a preferred pitch or tone. Increasing the tone will generally raise it into a higher treble range, while decreasing the tone will lower the pitch to more of a bass tone.

• *Imaging (target size and depth)*—This Garrett exclusive feature allows the user to view the size of a target and its indicated depth on the detector's LCD screen. Imaging indicates up to five different target sizes ranging from a item smaller than a coin to larger than a soft drink can.

## DIGITAL TARGET ID TEST

TEST TARGETS

| Detector Used: | Garrett *AT Pro* (in Pro Mode) |
|---|---|
| Searchcoil: | 8.5" x 11" **PRO**formance DD (stock coil) |
| Air Test Method: | Targets were passed perpendicular (flat) to coil at 4" distance |
| Ground Test 1: | Targets were resting flat at 4" depth in neutral (non-mineralized) soil |
| Ground Test 2: | Targets (where possible) were buried on edge (vertical) at 4" depth in the same neutral (non-mineralized) soil used in Ground Test 1. |
| Ground Test 3: | Targets were resting flat at 4" depth in a moderately mineralized soil |

**Results:** A numeric Target ID feature adds to the detectorist's knowledge of a target's potential identify. This data also illustrates how the exact same target produces different target values based upon many conditions, including the amount of ground mineralization, target depth and the orientation of the target in the ground. The numeric Target ID on iron objects often bounces around and varies widely based on the size and thickness of the iron object being scanned. Numeric target identity is also less consistent for targets which were buried on edge and smaller objects buried in highly mineralized soil.

The point is to become familiar with the types of targets you seek and how the existing ground conditions in your hunting area and the target's orientation can affect this Digital Target ID (also known as VDI on some brands). Because these numeric meters vary by manufacturer and even models of the same brand, learn the machine you will use.

## DIGITAL TARGET ID TEST: Example of Target Value Variance

| Target Item: | Test ID (Air) | Test ID (Grd 1) | Test ID (Grd 2) | Test ID (Grd 3) |
|---|---|---|---|---|
| Small iron square nail | 17–20 | 23–28 | 24 | 18–32 |
| Tin foil (small, crumpled piece) | 45 | 45-46 | 42–46 | 49–73 |
| Gold Coin, Thin (French 5 franc) | 47 | 45-47 | 40–45 | 77–85 |
| 14k Gold Wedding Band (smaller size) | 47 | 47–49 | 45–53 | 56–80 |
| Bronze Coin, Roman (thin, small) | 48 | 45-53 | 45–53 | 82–85 |
| Nickel, Shield | 50–51 | 51–53 | 53 | 52–75 |
| Nickel, V (Victory or Liberty Head) | 52 | 51-53 | 53 | 48–63 |
| Nickel, Buffalo and Modern Clad | 52 | 52 | 53 | 50–64 |
| Gold Nugget, small | 53 | 53 | 53 | 76–95 |
| Lead Ball, Small (buck and ball load) | 53 | 53 | 53 | 89–91 |
| Silver Hammered Coin (thin, fishscale) | 60–61 | 58–62 | 53–63 | 75–86 |
| 14k Gold Wedding Band (larger size) | 68 | 68 | 63–72 | 65–76 |
| Musket Ball, .69-caliber | 68–70 | 66–69 | 66–69 | 73–85 |
| Eagle Button (brass) | 68–70 | 67–71 | 43–57 | 76–80 |
| Minié Ball, Civil War, .58-caliber | 69–70 | 65–71 | 67–70 | 80–85 |
| Bronze Coin, Medium (U.S. dime size) | 70 | 68–71 | 72–78 | 77 |
| Buckle, Small Brass | 73 | 72–74 | 62–77 | 64–75 |
| CSA Button (larger brass) | 74–76 | 72–74 | 77–79 | 75–77 |
| Penny, Modern Clad (zinc) | 75 | 75 | 72–76 | 77–86 |
| Bronze Coin, Thick | 75 | 75 | 76–80 | 77–82 |
| Penny, Indian Head cent (copper) | 76 | 76 | 77–78 | 76–82 |
| Breast Plate, U.S. | 78 | 77–78 | 76–80 | 77–78 |
| Belt Plate, U.S. large | 79 | 79 | 75–81 | 79–80 |
| Roman Silver Coin, small (c. 100 AD) | 80 | 80 | 79 | 77–85 |
| Dime, Roosevelt (clad) | 80 | 81 | 82 | 82–90 |
| Dime, Barber | 81 | 81 | 83 | 80–89 |
| Dime, Mercury | 81 | 81–82 | 79–80 | 80–85 |
| Penny, Large Cent | 81 | 81 | 83 | 78–85 |
| Quarter, Barber | 84–85 | 85 | 85–91 | 85–88 |
| Quarter, Washington (silver) | 86 | 87 | 87–91 | 84–91 |
| Quarter, Washington (clad) | 85 | 85 | 85–88 | 86–91 |
| Half Dollar, Kennedy (clad) | 89 | 90 | 87–88 | 91–93 |
| Silver Dollar, Morgan | 93 | 92 | 99 | 92–93 |

Note: The most consistent number is shown for each entry. A range of numbers indicates that the Target ID varied as the searchcoil passed over the target from different directions, particularly on items lying on edge in the ground. Mineralized ground, uneven ground and uneven searchcoil swings also greatly affect the consistency of numeric target identification. Note that larger target size/thickness creates a more consistent Digital Target ID versus the target's high or low conductivity.

- *Digital Target ID*—This two-digit system reports a target's conductivity on a scale of 1 to 99. As compared to simple notch identification, the two-digit number which appears on the LCD screen is more precise, allowing you to more accurately distinguish one target from another. The least conductive pieces of metal will register closer to 1 while the most conductive targets (such as a thick piece of silver) will register closer to 99.

This feature should be studied in your test plot to understand what numbers correlate to particular targets. It should be noted that the target's orientation and environmental conditions such as ground mineralization and electrical interference can skew the accuracy of the numbers which are reported by the detector. *(See test section on pages 54–55 for an example of Digital Target ID.)*

Many detectorists find the 1 to 99 scale easier to commit to memory than the various notches that are reported on other scales. The Digital Target ID adds helpful addition target information but is less depended upon by searchers who prefer to trust their ears when using an All-Metal Mode detector or a machine with Tone Roll Audio and Proportional Audio features.

- *Surface Elimination*—This feature is designed to let the detector ignore objects buried in the first two to five centimeters. In theory, you are only detecting the deeper and thus older metal objects while skipping over the modern trash items that are near the surface.

- *Salt Elimination*—When hunting on a beach or in any area with high salt content, this feature will help eliminate interference caused by wetted salt.

- *Coin Depth Indicator*—This meter helps you judge the depth of a coin-sized target. Large objects and extremely small objects will usually not be indicated accurately. Manufacturers generally opt to optimize depth reporting on a coin-sized object since this is the size of the most frequently-sought items: coins, medallions, bullets, rings, etc. Due to the coin-sized optimization of such depth indicators, large objects such as a drink can will be reported shallower than their actual depth. In other words, a large target may show to be about four inches deep on the detector's indicator but you end up digging it six or more inches deep. Tiny objects will be reported to be deeper than their actual depth.

• *Frequency Adjustment*—Many higher-end detectors allow the user to operate at different detection frequencies to eliminate outside interference. This is particularly useful during organized hunts or in situations where you find yourself hunting in close proximity to other metal detectors. The change of frequency is minimal, designed only to prevent disturbing your search and does not affect target detection capabilities. A frequency adjustment option on a metal detector does *not* indicate that it is using multiple frequencies simultaneously.

• *Battery Level Indicator*—Some detectors will give an audible electronic signal indicating the level of the batteries. A detector with a graphic display or meter is more useful in the field; you can remain aware of the batteries' level and avoid being caught with a "dead" machine.

---

### Purchasing a Metal Detector

Always try to *purchase a detector that best suits your particular hunting needs.* Where you will most often hunt and what targets you will most often seek help determine which metal detector is best for your needs. Since relic hunters are sometimes content to dig all targets on a site, they focus on a machine that offers them the most depth of detection.

• *Are you planning to search an area of the country known for "hot ground?"* A Multi-Frequency (or PI) detector will be of the greatest benefit to those hunting in Virginia, some parts of Georgia and the Pacific Northwest or other areas of the country known to contain highly mineralized ground. For other areas where the soil is fairly neutral, relic hunters desire some discrimination to eliminate the peskiest small iron nails or other fragments that may litter an old site.

The ability to compensate for variations in ground conditions is a key factor. If you will hunt a variety of terrains, there are high-end discrimination detectors that also have True All-Metal modes. This allows you to hunt deep but switch to some form of discrimination where needed. People who routinely hunt in mineralized soil will benefit from a pulse induction model and the use of a Double-D searchcoil to punch through the challenging terrain.

- *Will you be working inner city areas, freshwater streams or along the coastline?* The previous discussions on Single versus Multiple Frequency detectors cover some of the pros and cons of each detector type in relation to various environmental situations.

- *Are you planning on a specialized type of treasure hunting?* Gold prospectors, surf hunters and wreck divers should be aware of the demands required by these particular styles of hunting. The multi-frequency machines that best suit such hunting are generally more expensive and thus require more consideration the necessary investment is made.

- *Are you looking for a good, all-around detector to use during your travels?* If your answer is "yes," read reviews on detector brands that are in your price range and seek out a manufacturer with a good reputation for quality. The Internet is a great place to research and learn about detectors. The Internet can also be a confusing place to get biased opinions on detector brands because of the volume of discussion groups and sites that are driven by commercial interest. Be aware that some online advisors seek nothing more than to drive you to a particular dealer or importer. That said, you can find quality detectors in each price range. One of the best pieces of advice therefore is to *decide which particular features are most important to you.*

- *Do you want a detector that is very lightweight?* Some detectors can become quite heavy after consecutive hours of searching. One helpful feature on some detectors is a detachable battery pack that can be mounted on your hip to alleviate some of this weight.

- *How easy is changing the detector's batteries?* Batteries can run low in the field. Many detectors have battery covers that easily slide back, requiring no special tools for quickly replenishing your power supply.

• *Does the detector offer different searchcoils for hunting flexibility?* Most detectors are sold with a mid-sized searchcoil that is good for most hunting conditions. You might desire a Double-D coil for mineralized ground and also a smaller "sniper" coil for searches in tight spots. The more coils that are manufactured for your detector, the more hunting flexibility you offer yourself.

• *Is a training DVD included for quick learning?* The printed owner's manual included with your new detector is essential, but an instructional video provides an entirely different opportunity to understand your instrument. Many people can grasp a concept that is demonstrated on a video much faster than by comprehending the printed words in a manual.

• *What advice do other detectorists have for you?* Join a detecting club in your area and talk to people about their hunting experiences. But, when receiving advice, always *consider the source.*

• *What is your budget?* For most people, there is a limit to how much money they can spend. Some new detectors can be purchased for less than $100 from retail stores. There is also a saying that goes, "You get what you pay for." In other words, you will pay a little more for a detector of quality manufacture with excellent features. On the other end of the spectrum, there is no sense in spending more than $1,000 on the fanciest detector if it far exceeds your hunting needs.

Decide *where* you want to hunt and *what* you hope to find. This will narrow your detector choices. A final piece of advice is to *consider the warranty and manufacturer's reputation* for producing reliable equipment. A bargain detector is not a sound investment if it is not engineered to stand up to the type of field work you have planned.

———

**Learn Your Detector!**

Once you have purchased the detector that best suits your needs and your budget, take the time to learn it thoroughly. Spend hours with it digging in a local park or playground to become more familiar with how it responds to good targets versus junk targets. Dig everything at first until you become more adept at understanding what it is telling you about a target. There will always be new model detectors on the market that claim to be better at producing various types of targets. Even if your machine does not stack up against the "latest greatest" thing being offered, yours can hold the advantage. How? Simply by your familiarity with it.

An old bird dog may not be as quick as the new pup in the field but it has experience. Similarly, you will understand how your detector reports targets. Taking a new machine that you've had little time to understand to a Civil War site might be frustrating as you watch others dig more around you. When you get to hit a hot spot, make sure your time will not be wasted as you try to learn a new machine.

# CHAPTER 4

# DETECTING TIPS AND DISCRIMINATION

If the seasoned detectorist finds this chapter to be somewhat basic, that is exactly its purpose. As with almost any sport from golf to fishing, you tend to develop your own style, your own swing, your own "something" that fits you. This is not meant to imply that one's particular detecting or target recovery method is incorrect; rather, it is intended to offer helpful advice to those who are less seasoned.

---

### Understand What Your Detector is Telling You

There is nothing wrong with good luck, but you must first understand your detector. If you have just acquired a new detector, start by reading its manual and watching any DVD that was included. The more you learn about your metal detector, the more effective you will be in the field.

*Start at home with "air tests"* by passing various treasure targets in front of your coil to familiarize yourself with where exactly they "hit" on your detector's target ID scale or how they sound on an All-Metal machine. Air tests are important for understanding how your detector responds to various targets; they are not meant to imply how deep these targets will be detected. Practice with your discrimination modes to see how well various items are rejected. Some detectors may not detect targets in the ground nearly as deep as they did in air tests. The ground can have significant affects on detection depth.

It is great practice to *create your own test plot* by actually burying several targets to see how they sound in the soil and where they register on your target ID scale. This should include several coins or artifacts as well as a bottle cap, a pull tab, and iron junk metal. Bury each item about four inches deep, making sure to space them a good foot or so apart. Create a map or use some marking system to keep track of the precise location of each target item. Practice scanning each of the targets while listening to and studying all of your detector's signals.

Your test plot should include several challenging situations that are often encountered. Create a "target masking" challenge by burying a rusty nail together with a modern clad nickel in order to practice setting discrimination without losing the good coin target. A nickel is a good mid-conductivity target for testing purposes. If your iron discrimination levels are high enough that the nail/nickel combination is eliminated, you would likely also be missing small targets of gold, bronze or lead that were nestled amongst iron trash.

Bury another coin target (such as a quarter) flat in the earth at a 4-inch depth and then bury another of the same target standing on its edge at the same depth. This scenario will help illustrate the different signals that an identical target can produce based upon its ground orientation. Ground conditions can also affect how these same targets are picked up by your detector. Use your test plot during periods of extreme drought to check detection depth. Conversely, try soaking the ground with a water hose to see how detection depth is affected in moist ground.

––––––––––

**Tips on Proper Scanning**
*Adjust your detector* so that the searchcoil swings comfortably just above the ground's surface. If your stem length is too short,

you will find yourself leaning forward and you will end up with a sore back. Stand up straight and extend your arm naturally while holding your detector. Move the searchcoil slightly forward of your body and adjust the stem until your searchcoil hovers just above the ground. Hold your detector with your dominant hand, leaving your less dominant hand free to carry your digging tool.

When you pursue a treasure signal, you can use the less dominant hand to dig in soft soils while continuing to hold onto your detector with your dominant hand. Where you are able to do this in fields with softer soil conditions, your target recovery time will be improved. You will find it more tedious to lay your detector down, dig, pick up the detector to rescan the excavated soil, and so on. Of course, some soils are so rugged that you will be unable to dig without setting your detector down.

CORRECTLY ADJUSTED STEM LENGTH
This detectorist is able to maintain good posture with his searchcoil extended before him and hovering just above the ground. He will remain more comfortable after long hours of searching.

STEM LENGTH TOO SHORT
This detectorist will soon have a very sore back from having to lean forward in order to keep his searchcoil hovering just above the ground.

POOR SEARCHCOIL SWINGING TECHNIQUE will result in decreased treasure discoveries. This animated photo series illustrates why you should always swing your coil level to the ground. You will pick up the deep relic shown in the middle but targets at the same depths on the outer edges of your swing area will be lost if you allow the search head to swing upwards.

CORRECT SEARCHCOIL SWINGING TECHNIQUE. In this animated photo series, the same metal detectorist is able to pick up all four relics at the same depth by using good form in his searchcoil swing. Always keep the searchcoil level with the ground surface to achieve the maximum depth while searching for targets.

*Turn on your detector's power while holding the searchcoil a foot or two above the ground.* Do not turn on the power while your coil is in close proximity to metal. Your detector may attempt to "tune it out" or discriminate this particular metal type. After powering your machine on, lower the coil and you're ready to begin hunting.

*Keep the searchcoil level as you scan* and always scan slowly and methodically. Scan the coil from side to side and in a straight line in front of you with the searchcoil just slightly above the ground. Do not scan the searchcoil in an arc unless your arc width is narrow (about 24 inches) or unless you are scanning very slowly. This preferred straight-line scan method allows you to cover more ground width in each sweep and permits you to keep the searchcoil level, especially at the end of each sweep. This method reduces skipping and helps you uniformly overlap the areas you have scanned.

Level swings help reduce the degrading effect of ground mineralization. Because of its conductive and magnetic minerals, the ground always creates a response that can reduce your detector's accuracy and detection depth. It is therefore very important to maintain a level swing with a consistent searchcoil height to achieve optimum performance. Where the ground varies in elevation or has a rugged contour, your searchcoil should follow the rises and falls of the ground at a consistent height.

*Overlap by advancing the searchcoil approximately 50% of the coil's diameter at the end of each sweep path.* You want to sweep an area thoroughly because depth penetration is less at the very edge of your searchcoil than in its center. Occasionally scan an area from a different direction, particularly if you get an erratic or suspicious target signal. Unless you overlap your swing, you will skip patches of ground as you sweep forward. For smaller sites you intend to work over thoroughly, cross back over the area from a different direction and see what your detector finds this time.

Be careful not to raise the searchcoil above normal scanning level at the end of each sweep. When the coil begins to reach the extremes of each sweep, you will find yourself rotating your upper body to stretch out for an even wider sweep. This gives the double

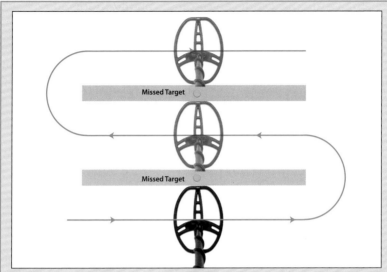

CORRECT OVERLAPPING OF YOUR SEARCH COIL SWING will prevent skipping of good treasure targets. The illustration *above* depicts a detectorist who is advancing while swinging the searchcoil back and forth, creating patches of ground that are missed by the coil. Two good coin targets have been missed by not overlapping the searchcoil swing.

*(Below)* This illustration shows the same detectorist overlapping his swing by about 50% of the searchcoil's diameter as he moves forward. This method will slow your advance but prevents you from missing good targets in the gaps created by the method shown above. Use a larger searchcoil to cover more ground as you advance. Both coin targets would be detectable in this method.

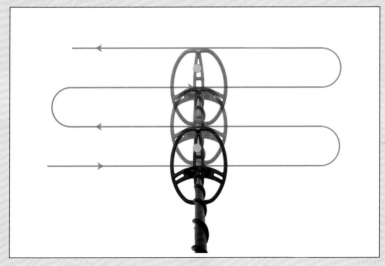

benefit of scanning a wider sweep and gaining additional exercise.

As you scan the searchcoil over the ground, *move the coil at a rate of about two to five feet per second.* Refer to your detector's owner's manual to determine the recommended scanning speed for your instrument. Don't get in a hurry, and don't try to cover an acre in ten minutes. In your mind, you should always imagine that what you are looking for is buried just below the sweep you are now making with your searchcoil.

---

### Ground Balancing Your Detector

As the VLF models continued to improve in past years, microprocessor circuitry offered new advantages to the relic hunter. Automatic ground control or ground balancing was introduced, in which the detector's circuitry scanned the ground and automatically set a level of ground rejection based upon the degree of mineralization encountered.

Prior to automatic ground balancing, the operator was required to manually ground balance his or her machine as different ground types were encountered. Where the soil was relatively constant, the ground control could be set fairly easily to handle the level of iron particles present. This task became more cumbersome in areas where mineralization levels shifted as the hunter progressed along his route. In such areas, the automatic ground tracking of a VLF was constantly analyzing and adjusting to the mineralization swings. With manual ground balance machines, the user was constantly stopping to manually ground balance as the ground content changed. In either situation, optimum search time was lost due to almost constant retuning of the instruments.

Even detectors with automatic ground balance features will encounter problems in more difficult soil conditions. For this reason, many seasoned relic hunters prefer higher-end detector models which allow the user to adjust the detector's ground balance as conditions change. The two most common user-initiated ground balance features are Auto Ground Track (sometimes referred to as "Auto Trac" or "FastGrab") and Manual Ground Balancing. In either method, the goal is to have the metal detector cancel the unwanted ground signals while leaving the signals from buried targets intact. These techniques that calibrate to the actual soil conditions will result in deeper target detection, more accurate target information and quieter detector operation.

With **Auto Ground Track**, the user generally moves to a spot of ground where no metal signals are evident. He or she then presses a control panel button and proceeds to raise and lower the search-coil to the ground—from about a 6-inch height down to about an inch above the ground—until the unit stabilizes. This up and down motion of the coil during ground balancing is referred to as "bobbing" or "pumping" by some manufacturers. The detector automatically tracks the ground mineralization and adjusts to the conditions during this bobbing action.

With **Manual Ground Balance**, the detectorist goes through the same process but uses control panel touchpads to shift the balance to his or her preference. Manual ground balance is an advanced technique that obviously requires practice to perfect. This technique is often used by prospectors or relic hunters who are working an iron-laiden area where there is no clean ground for the detector to sample in a more automated ground balancing mode.

Garrett's *AT Gold* detector includes an exclusive **Adjustable Ground Balance Window**™ feature. This allows the user to spread the ground balance setting in order to be simultaneously ground balanced to a range of values, thereby smoothing out the machine's audio against subtle ground response variations.

With any ground balance method, the process should be repeated whenever drastic shifts in the ground mineralization are encountered. Due to the varying methods available on different detector models, you should carefully review the machine's owner's manual for specific ground balance instructions.

———

## Discrimination: The Pros and Cons

The main goal of most relic hunters is to dig as many good relics as possible while cutting down the amount of trash metal. One of the more frequently asked question of VLF users is," How much discrimination should I use on my machine?" The answer you would hear from many is, "None!"

Those opting to employ zero discrimination are best served by a detector with a True All-Metal Mode or one that has advanced audio characteristics such as proportional audio. You will simply dig more trash items without the ability to hear some of the target's signature, or characteristics. On an important or previously productive site, however, some hunters are okay with digging every last item—just to be sure that nothing good is missed.

Others do not have the time, patience or desire to dig every last item. A good rule of thumb for relic hunters who wish to eliminate some junk targets is *keep your discrimination to a minimum.* Select a specific item to eliminate. For example, if small, rusty nails are abundant on an old home site you are working, scan several of these nails to obtain their Target ID reading. Add just enough iron discrimination to eliminate only these nails. Your detector will still signal other iron items larger or thicker than what you have just notched out.

Remember that there are many good early American and Civil War artifacts that were composed of iron or an iron alloy—guns, bayonets, tools, spurs, harness buckles, etc. An excessive amount of iron discrimination thus eliminates your chance of finding such desired items. Aluminum foil, pop tops, pull tabs, bottle caps and other metal fragments can be similarly frustrating to relic hunters. Target ID readings for these items can vary considerably, from just above iron to fairly high conductivity.

Using notch discrimination above the iron range is therefore increasing your odds of skipping good items. For example, searchers who eliminate aluminum pull tabs may pass right over a good 14k gold ring because the conductivity of such a gold piece is seen by a detector as being similar to aluminum.

In the end, we all desire to dig less trash items and maximize our recovery time. The following sections offer specific tips and techniques on some commonly encountered challenges.

---

### Overcoming the Target Masking Problem

The science of target identification with Single Frequency Discrimination detectors was discussed in Chapter 2. The target metal's conductivity, permeability, thickness, size, shape and orientation in the ground all play a role in determining where the item will register on your Target ID scale. The target's proximity to adjacent targets (particularly iron) can also greatly affect how your metal detector reports *or fails to report* the item.

Targets of mid- to high-conductivity can be hidden by heavy iron presence or the relic hunter's use of too much iron discrimination. Iron objects create a camouflage effect on the good treasure targets that lie below. This camouflaging effect is known as target masking. Some detectorists also use the phrase "iron masking," but since this term in used on some detectors to describe their iron elimination mode, I prefer the term "target masking."

Experienced detectorists investigate target signals carefully from multiple directions. The sound of one good target signal that is accompanied by the sound of junk metal is always worth another few seconds. Sweep the searchcoil back over the area from other directions, walking around the target area in a circle. If a good

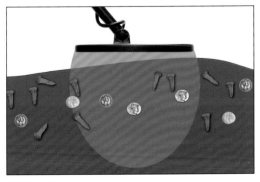

TARGET MASKING can be caused by several issues. Large size searchcoils of concentric configuration produce a large area of energy. In this illustration, multiple large iron nails will produce a camouflaging effect on the good coin targets below. The use of heavy iron discrimination will eliminate not only the nails from detection but also the desired targets.

target is partially masked by iron or is lying vertically in the ground, the target response might be very limited. A hazard of ignoring weak or irregular signals is that good targets that are deeply-buried can become inconsistent near the limits of detection depth.

Target masking is certainly an issue in the field, but there are solutions to help overcome these situations. **Among the target masking solutions you can test:**

• *Use a DD searchcoil to improve your ability to separate targets.* A conventional searchcoil with a concentric figuration produces a detection field below the coil which could be considered as a bubble of electromagnetic energy. The shape of this area *(as illustrated below)* would look something like an upside-down snow cone. By comparison, the detection field of a DD searchcoil is a narrow strip that runs the length of the searchcoil.

This long, narrow detection band produced by a DD searchcoil is more precise for separating adjacent targets. Your chances of distinguishing multiple targets in close proximity are far better with the knife-like detection field of a DD versus the bubble-like detection field of a concentric coil.

• *Invest in a detector which has ample resolution for discriminating unwanted targets.* Some detectors have as few as one Target ID segment that is dedicated to "Iron." You will obviously eliminate all

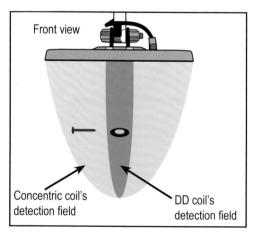

Front view

Concentric coil's detection field

DD coil's detection field

Searchcoil configurations can greatly assist with target separation in trashy areas that can be caused by several issues. A Double-D (DD) searchcoil offers a much narrower detection field than a concentric searchcoil. In this illustration, the narrow field allows the searcher to easily distinguish this good target from the adjacent iron target.

iron by notching this segment out. Good targets below or masked by a larger iron piece will thus be eliminated. Other detectors offer you a wider range, or more resolution, in the iron category.

Detectors that are well-suited for relic hunters will have such a wider range of iron segments for notching or will have a knob for dialing in just the desired level of iron elimination. Another feature available on some detector models is the ability to discriminate the unwanted iron and yet still hear its presence. Some users prefer to hear the low-pitched signals from discriminated iron because they know that good targets lying at the detector's range limit in mineralized soils sometimes produce low amplitude, low-pitched signals. This special iron control feature is referred to as Iron

## THE USE OF IRON AUDIO (IRON VOLUME) FEATURES

Scattered iron objects in the ground can mask good targets and even create "ghost signals" that appear to be a good target. Garrett's *AT Pro* has an Iron Audio feature which allows the user to hear discriminated iron (normally silenced) in order to know the whole picture and avoid being tricked into digging an undesired target.

Iron Audio also allows the user to adjust the mid-tone's range to include all targets above the point of discrimination. The user is effectively adjusting the cut-off between Low-tone discriminated trash targets and mid-tone targets. *(See illustrations below. These images depict the U.S. version of the AT Pro.)*

Normal division of low, mid and high tones on the *AT Pro*. Iron Audio is set to OFF.

| (Low-Tone) | Mid-Tone | High-Tone |
|---|---|---|
| 0 | 35 | 75 | 99 |

With the iron discrimination set to 20, all targets below 20 are silent with the Iron Audio OFF.

| ← Silent → | (Low-Tone) | Mid-Tone | High-Tone |
|---|---|---|---|
| 0 | 20 | 35 | 75 | 99 |

With the Iron Audio feature ON, the targets below 20 are now heard as a low tone and the mid-tone is expanded down to 20.

| (Low-Tone) ← | Mid-Tone → | High-Tone |
|---|---|---|
| 0 | 20 | 75 | 99 |

Audio or Iron Volume on different models. *(Refer to the example chart on "Iron Audio" for a demonstration of this feature as it works on one sample detector.)*

* *Use a smaller Super Sniper searchcoil for areas with heavy concentration of iron or other trash metal.* This size coil will examine smaller spaces where good coins might lie between pieces of junk metal. Smaller sniper coils also allow your detector to search close to metal fencing, sidewalks and foundations where rebar can negatively affect larger coils.

* *Turn down the sensitivity of your detector.* Although your fear in doing so is losing detection depth, you will also be decreasing your detector's reaction to the iron in troublesome spots. The natural tendency for a detectorist is to run his or her machine on the highest sensitivity to achieve the greatest depth. This will actually work against you in areas where electrical interference or ground mineralization creates a great deal of falsing or chatter. The optimal setting will vary from site to site. Learn to make adjustments to help your detector decipher targets without chatter.

* *Use your test plot to learn more about the effect of target masking.* Bury several good targets at about six inches deep. Then, plant nails and rusty iron targets above your target. Practice sweeping over the good target in All Metal mode and then with various discrimination settings. You will find the good targets harder to find in a discrimination mode, and they might not register at all.

To understand the effects of masking, use an iron nail and a coin of mid-conductivity (such as a clad nickel) to conduct your own air test and ground tests. A mid-conductivity coin such as a nickel will emulate the way in which other small targets of similar conductivity (gold, bronze, lead, etc.) will react.

Pass the nail in front of your searchcoil (making sure there is no other metal worn on that hand) and note the Target ID. Then pass the coin in front of the coil and note its much higher Target ID reading. Third, pass the coin and nail in front of the coil with the nail overlapping the coin. Note that the two overlapping targets have a combined conductivity that is much lower than the indi-

## SNIPER COIL USE TO OVERCOME TARGET MASKING

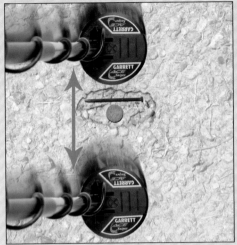

ALTER THE DIRECTION OF SEARCHCOIL SWING to help overcome the target masking effect. As depicted in these illustrations, a good coin target laying adjacent to iron might be largely masked from one coil sweep direction.

*(Figure 1)* The detector may give alternating signals (unable to separate the two targets) or only an iron signal (unable to determine that a good target is present) when the searchcoil passes over the coin and nail from this direction.

FIGURE 1

Walk around the unknown target (about 90°) and then swing the searchcoil from a new direction to check target response. As the searchcoil moves forward it passes over the nail only *(see Figure 2)*, and the Target ID gives an iron reading.

FIGURE 2

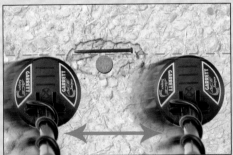

Continue sweeping over the target area and move the coil back toward the lower edge of the target response area. As the coil moves away from the iron nail and over the coin *(see Figure 3)*, the metal detector now offers a good signal from the coin. By physically separating the conflicting signals, the detectorist is able to determine that a good target is present.

FIGURE 3

vidual reading of the coin and *yet slightly greater than the reading of the nail by itself.* The point of this demonstration is that you should only introduce enough discrimination to notch out the nail by itself. The slightly higher combined conductivity of the two targets will still be detected by carefully employing minimal iron discrimination levels.

The combined effect of these two metals will produce varying results on varying detectors. Some will see the iron item and, in an Iron Discrimination mode, will not signal a target at all. This is generally the case with a detector that collectively notches iron items under one segment. When this notch is rejected, the detector then rejects any and all iron targets. Detectors with more selective iron discrimination will produce some type of target signal. This might be an erratic cursor that bounces between notches because of the two different types of metal being in close proximity.

Be aware that with many metal detectors, *any target more conductive than iron will produce a "good" target sound.* This does not guarantee a good target will be unearthed. Iron and aluminum, for example, will combine to produce a reading that is a little better than iron. The use of notch discrimination must therefore be carefully monitored. Once a notch is rejected, all items within this range will be ignored. Metal detectors with older style technology (i.e. dial controls) do allow tuning that permits determining where to drop out iron items. This same flexibility is offered by newer, pushbutton-style detectors with wide ranges of discrimination.

Try placing the iron and silver items on the ground in close proximity. Use an All-Metal or Zero Discrimination mode to sweep around these two objects. Note how the iron item affects the identification of the silver item as you approach the target from different angles with your searchcoil. Try switching from a large searchcoil to a smaller size coil to determine how this can improve your ability to detect the good silver target.

• *Utilize a slower search speed with shorter swings in an iron-heavy area.* Your metal detector's "recovery" speed is slightly longer after it encounters a negative item such as iron. Anytime a metal detector encounters a target signal, there is a certain degree of time before the machine recovers. Detectors with quicker recover speeds present lesser risks associated with iron objects masking out good treasure targets. If you are scanning an area rapidly, when your detector signals iron items you may be passing over good items in the split second before your detector recovers. Some detector models offer variable scanning speeds, but in general *slow down* when you are working against iron rubbish in a good spot. Shorter-width swings also reduce the number of targets your searchcoil will encounter.

• *Learn to recognize the false signals that non-motion detectors will occasionally emit.* Ground mineralization is one of the key causes of this effect. You can determine a false target by making repeated swings with your coil over an area that is giving erratic or short sounds. A good target will produce a solid, repeatable response on most instruments. Non-motion machines will detect a metal target even if the searchcoil is hovering over the target without being moved.

Sometimes, a true target that is very small or deeply buried may produce a good signal from only one direction. This is why veteran detectorists often explore suspicious signals by circling the spot and swinging their coil from different directions to seek a repeatable, solid signal. Again, be aware that even good targets can become inconsistent if they are deeply buried near the limits of the detector's depth capability.

• *Test your detector's recovery speed by conducting an air test with a coin.* Pass the target back and forth in front of your searchcoil to see how well it continues to offer a clear target signal at varying speeds. Muddled audio responses let you gauge your detector's recovery speed.

• *Use a depth multiplier to find larger, deep targets without the interference of surface "junk" metal.* Such two-box configurations are operated in All-Metal mode and are ideal for deeply-buried items of moderate to large size. Small, shallow objects which can camouflage good items with a standard searchcoil are simply not detected. The Garrett *TreasureHound Depth Multiplier* with *Eagle-Eye*™ Pinpoint, however, includes a smaller front coil for accurate pinpointing of smaller objects with the touch of a button.

• *In an important area with high junk concentration, use the All Metal mode of your detector to first find and dig out the iron trash.* This is, of course, more time-intensive. Yet, important archeological sites that must be thoroughly searched might require such measures. Once the surface trash is cleared, however, the camouflaging effect of the iron will open up the ground for the detector to seek any good items below.

---

### General Metal Detecting Tips

The following techniques are basic recommendations that can benefit *all* metal detectorists, regardless of whether the treasures sought are coins, jewelry, caches, artifacts or anything else.

• *Use headphones with your detector.*

The faintest, deep target signals are often hard to hear. This is especially true if you are hunting in a windy area such as the beach. You are better able to concentrate on your search with headphones since you ignore external sounds. Your machine will also be silenced to people around you in public areas. The use of headphones can extend your detector's battery life by not sending signals through the built-in external speaker.

There are a wide variety of commercially-available headsets. Consider the areas in which you will hunt as you contemplate the headphone features. Select headphones with adjustable volume control and a long, spiraling flex cord. This stretchy cord helps prevent your headphones from being pulled from your head as you are digging a target. Those headsets with thin, straight cords can easily become snagged on tree limbs, vines and other outdoor obstacles which can damage or even snap the wires.

Some detectors offer the option of wireless headsets. These can be used to help prevent such tangling of wires and the nuisance of your head being forever attached to your metal detector as you dig targets.

• *Use discrimination to eliminate only the targets you are willing to bypass.* With a true All-Metal, non-motion detector, you will obviously detect all types of metal. The advantage of a discrimination detector with Target ID capability is that you are able to focus on the metals you wish to detect and ignore the metals you do not want to detect. The risk that comes with this metal discrimination advantage is that certain good targets are potentially missed.

For example, an iron-discrimination mode will prevent many rusty metallic items from registering on your detector. Certain interesting artifacts, such as square nails or harness buckles, will be discriminated out at the same time. Pop tops, pull tabs, bottle caps and aluminum foil are all bitter enemies of the metal detectorist. Here again, there is a danger inherent with simply notching out these items with accept/reject controls. Certain gold rings, fibula and coins register just the same on target ID scales.

It is up to you to determine how much discrimination to employ based on what you hope to find. The method of rejecting certain iron targets varies by detector. This might be accomplished by using Accept/Reject notches or by selecting a preset "Relics" Mode. Other machines allow the user even finer control of the iron discrimination level via incremental pushbutton or control knob adjustment levels.

The illustrations on the two following pages show a variety of targets from low-conductivity iron to high-conductivity silver. Note that foil and pop top trash can be found across a wide range of the Target ID scale. Detectors that include a Digital Target ID with a conductivity scale from 0 to 99. Such foil and pop tops may register on one of these digital scales with numbers that range from the high 30s to the low 80s. In that same wide range, there are plenty of desirable targets that can be found. Choosing to apply discrimination against any of these trash targets comes with the risk of losing the desirable targets which share a similar conductivity (such as small gold items, certain coins and jewelry).

## DISCRIMINATION OR ELIMINATION?

Most relic hunters are careful when using discrimination. Foil, pop tops, drink can tabs, shredded aluminum and other litter in the mid-conductivity range have similar Target ID readings as small gold, some jewelry and even small relics.

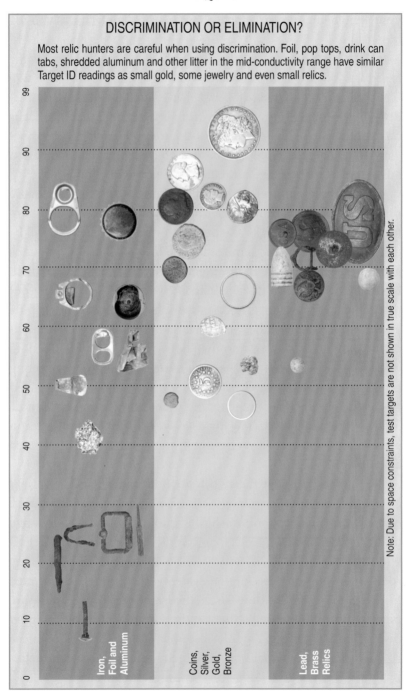

Iron, Foil and Aluminum

Coins, Silver, Gold, Bronze

Lead, Brass Relics

Note: Due to space constraints, test targets are not shown in true scale with each other.

## CHARACTERISTICS AFFECTING TARGET ID

The sample targets on the facing page were scanned on a Garrett *AT Pro* metal detector in a Zero discrimination pattern. This chart illustrates the fact that conductivity is only one factor in determining where a target will register on your detector's ID scale. For example, the silver and gold targets shown in the chart on the facing page vary based on their size and thickness (i.e. thin silver coins will register lower on the Target ID that a thicker silver coin). Target ID conductivity is displayed in a variety of meters, graphic interfaces and numerical systems on different detectors.

Be aware that these same targets can also register differently based upon factors that include: the target's orientation in the ground, the amount of ground mineralization present and changes in the ground surface's level or the user's searchcoil swing method. (Refer to the Digital Target ID test presented in Chapter 3.)

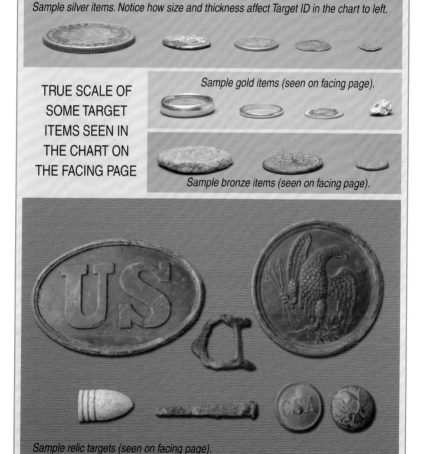

*Sample silver items. Notice how size and thickness affect Target ID in the chart to left.*

TRUE SCALE OF SOME TARGET ITEMS SEEN IN THE CHART ON THE FACING PAGE

*Sample gold items (seen on facing page).*

*Sample bronze items (seen on facing page).*

*Sample relic targets (seen on facing page).*

- *Field test a new detector at a location that has been productive for you in the past.* Improved technology or even different searchcoils might afford you deeper detection depth or better discrimination than detectors you have used in the past. Civil War hunters know that an extra couple of inches of detection depth can open up an area once considered "hunted out."

- *Prepare for the ground conditions where you will search.*

Most manufacturers are shy about offering an answer to the question of, "How deep will this machine detect?" There are really just too many variables. The size of the searchcoil, ground mineralization, moisture, ground compactness, target orientation, target metal conductivity, detector design and frequency, sensitivity settings and skill of the detectorist are just some of the many factors that come into play concerning how deep your detector can penetrate in a specific hunting environment.

If you are planning on hunting the sea coast, you should be aware that wetted salt sand generally causes problems with Single-Frequency (VLF) detectors. Many detectorists opt for a PI detector for hunting the surf and the wet beach sand. Single-Frequency motion detectors with salt elimination or an ability to ground balance, however, can be used effectively. Their abilities are further enhanced by adding a DD searchcoil and turning down the sensitivity to help stabilize the unit's operation.

Another challenging area is any geological area of past volcanic activity where there is a heavy distribution of iron-laden minerals such as magnetite, laterite and hematite. *Black sand*—an accumulation of slightly magnetic heavy minerals most often encountered in mountain-area streams—is primarily composed of pulverized magnetite. Black sand can cause interference with VLF detectors and a loss of depth. In rare instances such as on some beaches in Italy, detectorists can be challenged with both salt water and black sand combined.

Again, Multi-Frequency (or PI) detectors excel in these adverse conditions. On Single-Frequency motion machines, detectorists should adjust their sensitivity settings to help cope with such negative effects of mineralization or experiment with their discrimination levels. Another Single-Frequency remedy is switching to a smaller size searchcoil. Switching into the All-Metal Mode will generally restore lost depth, but additional trash targets make for a more difficult hunting style, especially for less experienced users.

Inland hunters are equally challenged at times with the effects of mineralized soil. High concentrations of iron oxide or granular particles of the previously mentioned black sand minerals are encountered at times. Such conditions can lead to false signals and greatly reduce detection depth. Mineralized stones containing magnetite or other conductive elements are known as "hot rocks," and they can also create havoc with your detector. To overcome the effects of hot rocks, many detectorists utilize Multiple-Frequency detectors or lower their discrimination and/or sensitivity.

In the absence of heavy mineralization, *damp ground improves conductivity and search depth.* Therefore, a productive plowed field may yield even deeper targets after a few days of soaking rain showers. Conversely, freshly plowed fields of inconsistent dry soil reduce detection depth. Your discovery yields should improve after allowing plowed ground to settle for at least several weeks.

• *Retune your searchcoil while pinpointing to tighten your search.*

One lesser-known trick can be used on some detectors to help you pinpoint smaller, elusive targets. Metal detectors which have a Pinpoint or Treasure Imaging button are using an All-Metal mode when you depress this pinpoint function. By "retuning" your searchcoil to your target, you can change the audio field to report only the peak audio response of the target.

Such retuning does not change the size of the detection field that your searchcoil is generating. Instead, the rise and fall of the audio response field has been narrowed to highlight only the peak audio response. In short, you must move your searchcoil much closer to the direct center point above the target object in order to generate an audible response.

This retuning process is quite simple for detectors that have a pinpoint button. First, pinpoint your target as you normally would by holding down the pinpoint button and maneuvering your coil above the target to the point where you receive the strongest target response signal. Then—while continuing to hover directly above this target—quickly release the pinpoint button and immediately press the button again and continue to hold down the pinpoint button. By doing so, you will have retuned the audio field against the target metal to generate only the peak audio response. As you continue to hold down the pinpoint button and carefully position the coil above the target area, you will find that your signal is coming from a much tighter pinpoint area.

Again, you have not altered the detection field but merely the audio field. It will appear, however, as you move the searchcoil over the target area after retuning that you have cut the detection area in half during this special pinpointing process. If the target audio disappears completely by retuning, you may be dealing with a very small target or one that is on the fringe of detection depth.

This retuning method obviously requires some practice. Place a coin on the ground and practice until you can clearly see how the concentration of the target's peak audio response allows you to pinpoint the item more precisely.

# CHAPTER 5

# RESEARCHING PRODUCTIVE SITES

Productive relic sites can often be found in abundance within short driving distances of your own home. Vance Gwinn of Eastland County, Texas is quick to share that fact. He first began using metal detectors more than 30 years ago at age 19 to satisfy his quest for artifacts of early history. "I was always good at it and I've always enjoyed looking for history," he admits.

During those years of detecting, he has amassed quite a collection of coins and relics from a wide range of history. He still spends about as much time researching *where* to hunt as he spends in the field. "I spend a lot of time in the libraries now," he says, "but as a kid I was always curious about where things happened long ago. I was probably one of the few who would visit the retirement homes and just talk with the old folks about early history. They were happy to make conversation with me as a youngster and you wouldn't believe the places they would describe in great detail. That was how I learned about some of the long-forgotten swimming holes, picnic areas and fairgrounds that have been very productive for me with my detectors."

Vance has ample properties to search as time permits, simply because of the friendships he strikes with landowners and the trust he gains from them by respecting their property. The time he spends conversing with the older citizens of his area often points him in new directions. About 20 years ago, he first learned of a place where the local Easter Pageant was held annually between

Vance Gwinn works the tall grass around an abandoned home of a ghost town with his *GTI 2500*.

The images seen below are a sampling of his various treasures, including ornamental jewelry, an eagle button, rings, tokens and Mercury dimes. Old coins and jewelry often come with the territory as you hunt productive relic sites.

Eastland and Cisco. Reenactors staged a three-day presentation of Christ's suffering each year around Easter and many citizens gathered to watch the performance.

They brought lunches, spread out their blankets and enjoyed the fellowship for multiple days each year. As expected, they lost many keys, coins, rings and other keepsakes during the many years the pageant was staged on the property. "Once I began detecting the Easter Pageant grounds, it was an awesome experience," said Vance. "With every swing of my searchcoil, it was *bang, bang, bang* on targets!"

During his first two years of hunting these grounds, he scooped up "piles" of lost jewelry, coins and keys. After the second year, Vance was chatting with the elder land owner about how much he was enjoying his searches on the pageant ground. "That's when the man told me about the 'old' pageant ground that was located in a different spot," he said. "The original pageant ground had been used back in the 1930s and '40s."

As he expected, the original site held plenty of items of older origin. "My finds were so good on the old site that I used string to do a grid and cover the area thoroughly. I cleaned up on rings and coins." Vance was thrilled to find the original gathering site and his diligence in talking with his elder about the old times paid off.

Another old-timer tipped him off to the site of a 1930s-era community concession stand that had been long forgotten. In addition to old coins and 15 rings found at this site, he recovered a World War II bracelet which had a couple's names inscribed on it. Vance eventually tracked down the couple, who were very grateful for his efforts to return a keepsake they had lost many decades earlier.

Vance has worked his way through a number of detectors over the years, using models made by Garrett, White's and Bounty Hunter. In December 2009, he moved up from his Garrett *GTA 1000* to a high-end Garrett *GTI 2500*. "I really like the Imaging and surface elimination features," he says, "because it saves me a lot of unnecessary bending over for worthless targets." He put his new GTI to the test immediately in conjunction with his latest research.

Researching old sites pays off, literally. Vance Gwinn found two coin caches within a week while relic hunting with his new *GTI 2500* during December 2009. *(Left)* This old can contained mostly foreign coins and a 24-inch gold chain. *(Right)* Vance's mini-cache, secreted inside a ladies compact, held a Barber dime, two Indian Head pennies and four V-nickels.

It took only days for his efforts to be rewarded with not one but two caches within a week.

The first was in an old olive-drab-color can which was about the size of a Prince Albert tobacco can. The can was buried about ten inches deep within a large can that was almost rusted away. Inside, Vance found a 24-inch gold chain and 45 coins, most of them being German, Swiss and French. Three of the French coins were made of gold and were dated from the 1930s. Vance and his buddy Jerry Eckhart guess that a World War II soldier may have brought the coins back to the States for his child, who decided to hide his foreign treasures.

Days later, Vance had the great fortune to find a second, smaller cache in a "hunted-out" area. This mini cache consisted of only seven coins locked inside a two-inch diameter ladies compact but they were impressive coins to find: four V-nickels, a Barber dime and two Indian Head pennies. Needless to say, Vance is not a big believer in areas that are completely "hunted out."

————

**Research Sources**

European metal detectorists have a greater chance of happening upon nice artifacts and old coins that do North American searchers. The simple fact is that more conflicts and more centuries of civilization took place on this continent. Still, the European hunters who are more consistently successful in their artifact quest are usually the ones who have done their homework before heading into the field.

The need for proper research is that much more important in North America where relic hot spots are found by chance far less often. Civil War battlefields are now protected national parks and the private lands near these areas have, in many cases, been worked for years. The coveted buckles and weapons continue to grow in value among collectors as the numbers decline.

The best sites might prove to be in the least likely of places. Modern development may have bypassed the oldest areas of a community where the first settlers lived. It is important to understand the conflict you are searching for. Understand the weapons that were used, the range of the weapons and the tactics that were employed. The secret to finding a good detecting area for artifacts is the research efforts. Much of my research involves locating battle sites. There are, however, many sources you can utilize based on the particular time period you have interest in.

• *Civil War sources.* The War Between the States has had more books written about this conflict than any other period of American history with the possible exception of World War II.

One of the most useful places to start is a compilation known as *The Official Records* (or OR's for short). This 128-volume set of Civil War source book was started in 1880 shortly after the war by Lieutenant Colonel Robert N. Scott to preserve the entire history of this conflict. Battle records, letters and maps were compiled from both sides to complete this exhaustive study. Its full title is *War of the Rebellion: A Compilation of the Official Records of the Union and Confederate Armies.*

Fortunately, one does not have to spend a small fortune to obtain a set of these prized books. When I lived in North Carolina years ago, I had to sign in to the special collections room of a local library just to peruse these volumes. The once-mandatory library visits have even been negated by the fact that the Official Records can be searched and read via the Internet. For example, Ohio State University has placed the complete version online at *http://ehistory.osu.edu/osu/sources/records/* for researchers. Cornell University also houses the OR's at *http://digital.library.cornell. edu/m/moawar/waro.html* or the complete set of OR's can also be purchased on CD-ROM.

Civil War relic hunters know that finding productive sites takes quality research. One of the primary collections of Civil War reports is the 128-volume series known as the *Official Records of the Union and Confederate Armies* (or ORs for short).

Another key source for Civil War hunters is the *Official Military Atlas of the Civil War*, available in either printed or electronic format. This companion to the OR's was compiled with more than 1,200 entries, from detailed drawings and official maps of engagements and campaigns.

The Civil War was one of the first engagements of the world to be thoroughly documented by combat photographers. These men went into the field and shot photos of soldiers, battles, camps and the aftermath of many significant battles. By closely studying some of these prints, you might be lucky enough to spot a landmark of some sort that can point you in the right direction.

• *Local history books* often offer the best detail of the area you plan to search. Visit libraries to review state and county history books for the oldest accounts of the conflict. Unit histories and personal accounts such as diaries that were left often offer the most detailed info on camps, marches, routes, etc. Family histories may have important details regarding a battle that official records simply ignored.

Once you have recovered artifacts from a site, you will often find yourself embarking upon a new research project—to identify some of the finds. Fortunately, there are dozens of quality reference books available to identify everything from belt plates to bullets to buttons. Seen above are just a few of those available which can be used to identify Civil War finds. (Some recommended titles are listed in chapters 12 and 19.)

Most county libraries will have a "local history" or genealogical section that includes reference-only books. Although you will not be allowed to check them out, the information you need may be something you can quickly photocopy or snap with your digital camera. Local history collections will often provide information from the earliest settlers about where the communities churches, market places, fairs or skirmish areas were located. In Civil War territory, information may be found on where troops camped, trained or had minor engagements in the local area. Some of these may contain rough, hand-drawn maps that will help to locate important areas.

- *Regimental histories.* These collections follow the movement of specific companies or regiments as recorded first-person by one of the participants. Whether you are studying frontier wars, a revolution or the Civil War, unit-specific books will generally offer the most significant details of troop movements.

- *Maps.* Study the earliest maps drawn of a battle area or site that you are studying. Read letters and battle accounts to find

This live oak tree is more than 300 years old. In the 1880s, it stood near a four-way intersection where two stagecoach trails crossed. An iron ring at the tree's base was used to secure horses while travelers rested. Jerry Eckhart studied old maps to locate this crossing point, where his friend Vance Gwinn was able to recover 1800s-era relics and coins.

landmarks that might still exist—river crossings, roads, mountains, schools, churches, etc.

Brian McKenzie and I often take the earliest map we can and scan it into Photoshop. I then find a modern county map that includes roads, railroads, creeks, etc. and scan that also. By using layers, the maps can be electronically superimposed on top of each other. Some old maps are only crudely drawn. Others are surprisingly accurate in terms of the course of rivers and landmarks that still exist. You can add a third layer to this mix by doing a screen capture from one of satellite maps of this area. Internet search engines such as Google, Bing, Yahoo and others offer road map views as well as satellite images of the spot you are researching. Some even offer bird's eye views of the address you've typed in which have been captured with digital imaging equipment. Zoom in until you have the prominent landmarks on your screen before capturing.

Then, add the satellite map as another layer to your file. You can now determine if the area you wish to search is now covered in farm land, forest or even a lake. If your county has published plat maps of this area, you can even add another layer with the plat maps to find out who currently owns the land on which you wish to conduct a search.

Remember that creeks and rivers often change their courses over centuries. I've been disappointed before to find some Republic of Texas battle areas are now below the waters of a lake that has been dammed up in the past 100 years. Where troops fought along a creek or river may now be in the middle of a farmer's pasture due to some flood of long ago that rerouted the body of water.

• *Internet map sources.* Early maps are true treasures that can lead you to long-forgotten plantations, forts and battle areas. Several specific sites will be covered in this chapter, but relic hunter Brian Pennington shared two of his favorite sites that are worthy of review for rare American maps.

The University of Alabama's Historical Map Archive (*http:// alabamamaps.ua.edu/historicalmaps/*) contains old maps for all 50

# MAPPING AN HISTORIC SITE FOR RELIC HUNTING

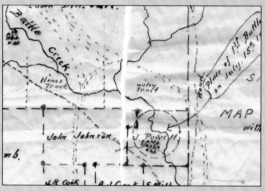

*(Left)* While working to pinpoint an early Native American and Texas frontiersmen battle site, I located the earliest map I could of the precise location.

Next, I located this area on a modern Internet roadmap of the area and then switched to satellite view. By doing a screen capture *(below)*, I was able to study the modern terrain.

*(Above)* The next step was locating a modern county plat map from the local land office on the Internet. Notice the red boundary lines surrounding "A-632" land. They still match up fairly well with the 90-year-old map of this property seen in the top image.

Finally, Brian McKenzie stepped in to composite all of these maps on layers in a Photoshop document *(right)*. He drew the modern property boundaries in green, a pipeline crossing in orange, the original path of a creek in black and the modern plat map's interpretation (not true to actual creek course) of the same creek in red.

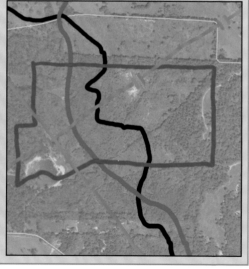

United States, as well as other regions of the world by specific time periods. As an example, in Europe, a searcher can open a variety of maps on France from more than a dozen different time periods. In some cases, the online maps may be of enough quality to be useful; in other cases, you can at least determine how to purchase a copy of the original.

Regional maps can be found at the Library of Congress website's special Map Collections area  (*http://memory.loc.gov/ammem/ gmdhtml/*). Map collections for military battles and campaigns include the American Revolution and the Civil War.

• *Old newspapers.* County and state libraries often maintain microfilm of the earliest newspapers that were published at the time of the battle you are studying. Few of these are well indexed so unfortunately you may be forced to put in the hours of simply scrolling through hundreds of frames of newspaper to find accounts of the action you are studying. For smaller battles, I have turned up a number of detailed accounts over the years by simply putting in the time. Sometimes it has been an official account that was only partially quoted in textbooks. In other cases, I have found eyewitness accounts of an action in the form of a letter to the editor in which a participant described the battle.

• *Travel guides and outdoor books.* Other sources to use when you are traveling are the countless brochures and travel guides to any local area. These often give maps to all local historic areas of interest. In some cases, you can obtain permission from the current owner of the land to search.

Other productive sites can be found by reading local camping, hiking or general outdoor activity guides. In some communities, there are "rails to trails" projects where old railroad lines have been converted to hiking or mountain biking trails for the benefit of community exercise areas. Look for hiking guides to such trails which point out where old stations, stores or hotels were once located along the rail lines.

• *State-specific treasure guides.* Some metal detector dealers sell books that list all the historical areas of interest, battle sites, campgrounds and rumored lost caches that can be found within a given state. Keep in mind that these authors are usually only listing the best known areas. There are still plenty of other areas that can be found only be a dedicated researcher. Such state-specific information can also be found on the Internet without spending the extra money on books. Be wary of regional "treasure maps" that claim to point you directly to known treasure areas; if such sources were credible, the treasure would have been found long ago.

One state-specific book I've utilized for my home state of Texas is called *Why Stop? A Guide to Texas Historical Roadside Markers*. This book lists by city and county more than 12,000 roadside markers which help pinpoint historic sites.

Internet map collections can often house rare maps which can guide you to early settlements, plantations, skirimish sites or other points of interest in your region. County collection may have different maps for each decade. Studying the older maps against the newer one might show a settled area that is now a ghost town.

- *College libraries.* I have spent many hours on university campuses pouring over private collections and microfilm while studying a battle or campaign. In some cases, I've found dissertations in which some student working on his or her masters degree studied a subject thoroughly. These papers are often never published but may be filed away with a local college library's archives. Some of the special collections rooms will require you to visit during normal business hours on a weekday when a staff member is present.

Some major universities house the personal papers of important frontiersmen or local heroes. Within these collections are often letters written to that person by local citizens of the day. More often than not, these individual letters are *not* properly indexed and can only be found by chance as you carefully pour through page after page within boxes of personal collections.

- *Periodicals.* Subscribe to metal detecting or treasure hunting magazines to learn more about the type of relic hunting you are interested in. In the United States, there are general treasure hunting magazines such as *Lost Treasure* or *Western and Eastern Treasures* which are published monthly for detecting hobbyists. These publications feature articles on coin hunting, wreck diving, prospecting, competition hunting, relic hunting, ghost town searching and cache hunting in almost every issue.

Other publications such as *American Digger* and *Treasure Depot* are published every two months or every quarter and deal almost exclusively with relic hunting. Some of their features cover relic hunting in Europe and other countries, although their primary focus is generally on Civil War and early Americana relic hunting. Another more recent e-magazine dedicated exclusively to the search for artifacts is an electronic magazine called *Relic Hunter*, which carries stories on relic recovery in North America, the UK and Europe. Using the Internet, visit *http://www.relic-hunting.com* to view issues.

Civil War hunters have literally thousands of books to turn to for source material, as well as many magazines devoted to the subject. These include *Civil War Times Illustrated, America's Civil War,*

*Blue and Gray Magazine, Civil War, Confederate Veteran, North South Trader's Civil War* and numerous special issues devoted to this conflict. Various clubs and societies organized to preserve Civil War history publish their own periodicals and these journals can be an excellent source for networking.

Throughout the world, there are dozens of other magazines devoted to coin hunting and relic hunting in specific countries or regions. France, England, Russia, Spain, Australia, Germany, Poland, and the Netherlands are just some of the countries with metal detecting periodicals specific to their locales. Any of these magazines can contain articles which can help your site research.

• *Personal contacts.* You've probably heard the advice dozens of times before to talk to the area's old-timers. This still rings true. They may have heard stories from their father who was told things by his grandfather about where battles happened or where soldiers camped out. Some of these may turn out to be tall tales or just people repeating what they've been told. Other times, the word of mouth might be as good as gold.

Farmers know what they've seen or what their plows have turned up. Garrett Brumit related a story to me about talking to one particular farmer who claimed to routinely find Civil War minié balls on parts of his Georgia land. He even mentioned that

Hundreds of metal detectorists fan out to search the fields for Roman artifacts during a 2009 rally held near Torreneva, Spain.

many of the bullets were the "slick kind" that did not have the traditional rings on them. Garrett was naturally excited, hoping that these were the smooth Confederate Enfields that Civil War hunters so highly seek. At the same time, he had long since learned to hold a certain amount of skepticism to such claims that locals often make. To his surprise, this farmer casually walked over to his truck and reached into his glove box. He picked up a handful of bullets that he and his son had recently scooped from a pasture.

Holding out the slick Confederate Enfields, he calmly asked, "Are these those slick bullets you're talking about?"

• *Attend treasure hunting shows, organized hunts and rallies.* Veteran hunters are often willing to share some of their research secrets if you take the time to talk with them. Study the techniques of other hunters when you attend organized hunts or rallies. Where do they begin searching a particular terrain? Take note of their pinpointing and recovery techniques as well.

Become involved in organizations that cater to your relic hunting interests. For example, those who have attended DIV (Diggin' in Virginia) as either a searcher or a volunteer simply can't help but learn from the experience of those who attend. Pre and post-search meetings are a great place to absorb knowledge. I have attended rallies and organized hunts in the U.S., England, France, Spain and Italy. With each one, I learned how to be more productive in the area by chatting with the local hunters.

Find a hunting buddy or group that you search with on a regular basis. Two or three trusted friends can cover more ground than one when you are scouting a site. Research efforts are also doubled or tripled. What you may be giving up by sharing your hot spots with others can pay off in the end. They may in turn gain access to other great spots and invite you along somewhere that you might have never found on your own.

• *Internet forums and genealogy research sites.* Thousands of relic hunters turn to the Internet for the latest news and to see what other people are finding. Some of these are specific to types of hunting and some are metal detector manufacturer brand specific.

Many offer you the place to post photos of your unknown finds for others to offer their opinions or expertise on its identity.

Genealogy web sites can be another fruitful source for research. The *USGenWeb Project* is one such source. This large group of volunteers compile genealogical research for every county in America. Their data is pulled from family records, census data, church papers, local maps, town histories and numerous other sources. New information is added all the time. Start by visiting *http://usgenweb.org* and then select the state you are interested in researching. Your search can then be further refined by selecting a specific county, town, region or even family name records.

Another useful site is *www.hmdb.org* which is the *Historical Marker Database*. The volunteer group which organized this site has broken out data by U.S. states, by other countries, by conflict or war name, and other useful categories such as "Forts, Castles." This database stores photos, articles, map coordinates, inscriptions and other data related to historical markers and commemorative plaques that relate to historic events.

Search engines such as Google are powerful tools for locating documents to help you locate good sites. Be as specific as possible when entering your search criteria in order to narrow down your results. British-born Irish mathematician George Boole created an effective database searching technique which has become known

*(Left)* Non-specific Internet searches can yield hundreds of thousands of results. The use of a Boolean search (using the words *and, or, not* or the "+" symbol) can narrow or broaden your search results.

as a *boolean search*. Boolean logic to broaden or narrow your search results consists of three logical operators—the three words *or, and, not*. Use of the word *and* (or the "+" symbol) narrows a search by combining terms. Use of the word *or* broadens a search to include results that contain either of the words you type in. Using *not* will narrow a search by excluding certain search terms.

More specific results can be located by placing quote marks ("...") around your search phrase. You can also string together multiple items to narrow down your results (i.e. "Denton County" + "military camp" + "Republic of Texas"). Such specific searches will pull in only entries that pertain to all of the desired topics.

Google and other search engines also help you to retrieve old maps of the area you are interested in researching. By selecting the "Images" tab on Google, for instance, you can look for web pages that contain images instead of only text. Many college libraries have now scanned in historic maps and other documents that will appear as images.

• *Historical societies.* County and regional groups often exist whose goal is to preserve local heritage. Visit their office to study their map collection. Spend time talking with some of the senior members. Consider joining the society to give talks and to learn about new areas of interest that are discovered. Offer to work with them to research older properties and to provide some or all of your finds to their local history displays.

• *Travel to the areas you are interested in.* I've talked with plenty of my fellow Texan searchers who take periodic trips to Louisiana, South Carolina and other Civil War areas to scout in the vicinity of history-rich areas. In some cases, they have made contact with someone who owns land in such an area. Other times, they simply plan a week or more in one region and take their maps and notes. Then, they approach landowners near a site of interest and hope to gain access to prime hunting ground. (More on effective ways to approach landowners will be discussed in this chapter.)

• *Use your eyes.* It is not always possible to secure permission to hunt old homesteads or farms long distance. If you are vacationing in an area with old history where you plan to use your metal detector, simply drive around and look for old buildings. Look for structures that are obviously much older than those surrounding it. Ask the neighboring homeowner who owns the run-down building next door and if it would be okay to do some detecting in the yard. If you come across a building being renovated or torn down, ask the foreman if it would okay for you to detect a safe distance away from any of the workers. The older the building, the better your chances are to find early coins and relics.

- *Printed or Internet real estate guides.* These can be valuable both in your local area and while you are traveling. Use sites such as *realtor.com* to conduct advanced searches on a particular part of a town. You can search for homes 51+ years old and then narrow down the ones which are most interesting. These sites also offer specific direction for reaching the properties that are for sale.

Knocking on doors to obtain permission to hunt a yard is a daunting endeavor for some. You might be surprised, however, to find how many homeowners will give you permission if they are interested in seeing what you can find. Offer to give them some of what you find or at least show them your finds.

Robert Jordan, a local treasure hunter with whom I have hunted many times, has made friends with a couple of people who work on Housing and Urban Development projects. His contacts keep him apprised of old homes they are planning to tear down.

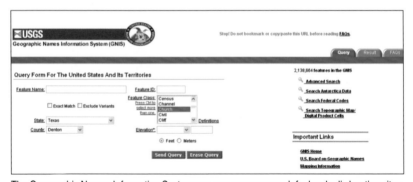

The Geographic Names Information System can narrow your search for local relic hunting sites.

Robert gains their permission to search sites immediately before and just after old homes are razed for new construction. His collection of old coins and relics continues to grow as he works over these improvement properties before the new homes begin construction.

- *Geographic Names Information System (GNIS).* The United States Geological Survey (USGS), in cooperation with the United States Board on Geographic Names, developed an online database known as GNIS for short. Simply visit *http://geonames.usgs.gov/domestic* (or Google "GNIS") to reach the home page. From the main page on USGS, you will need to click the "Maps, Imagery and Publications" tab to find a link to the Geographic Names database.

Then, click on the tab for "Search Domestic Names" and then click "Search" to begin your query. The next page is "Query Form for the United States and Its Territories." Beside State, I selected Texas and then my own local Denton County without refining my search any further. The query results came back with 881 named sites which included churches, schools, airports, historical sites and shopping areas. By backing up and selecting "School" from the Feature Class, I narrowed my search field to 122 school sites in the county. By entering "Church" from the Feature Class, my results were narrowed to 136. Each site is then specifically pinpointed with longitude and latitude coordinates that can be entered into a GPS receiver or mapping program to locate the spot.

---

### Tips on Being a Better Researcher

- *Never consider your research to be complete.*

I'm a walking testimony to this because I am a publisher's worst nightmare. I absolutely never "finished" writing a book until the publisher had completed all editing. Until that manuscript has gone to press and is out of my hands, I never pass up the chance to try to find just that one more key item to add to the project.

Your relic site research should be the same way. You simply never know when you will stumble upon a letter, a map or some document that sheds important light on what you are studying.

- *Keep your research organized.*

This is often easier said than done, particularly if you are working on more than one subject at a time. Try to use electronic folders on your computer to organize your notes into coherent structures that will make sense later. If you have a file cabinet, label your folders based upon subject, maps, letters, etc.

- *Make full copies of sources when you are the library.*

I'm often tempted to scribble quick notes at the library of just the info I specifically came to research. Numerous times, I have gone back to a source wishing I had copied the entire page or had spent more time on that item. What was once insignificant can change later; take the time to photocopy the entire page or the entire report you're reading (time and spare change permitting).

Actually, you really don't even have to spend money these days. Most cell phones have a camera built-in that is more than adequate to take pictures of the page or pages you need copied. Do not violate copyright laws by posting these online or reprinting the information without permission and proper citation. Remember, it's just for your reference. Be sure to observe the rules in your library concerning use of cameras or recording devices.

Some libraries only allow their staff to copy original documents. For example, in the Texas Archives in Austin or the Center of American History on the campus of the University of Texas, I have to flag specific sets of pages for the staff to copy. Due to staff limits and page counts, these pages are often mailed to you— sometimes many weeks later!

———

### Approaching Land Owners for Permission

Many of the best relics come from private property, whether it is large tracts of farmland or small lots in the city. For some people, approaching a total stranger to ask for permission to hunt their land is not a desirable challenge.

- *First impressions are the key.* Most of the time, permission is granted based upon your appearance, delivery and sincerity. It is important that the landowner feels your intentions are good and that you will truly respect their private property. Do not approach the owner as a group; one person is much less intimidating. It might be to your benefit, however, to bring a child with you if you have a son or daughter in your hunting group. You can explain that you hope to find various historic items that will help your child better appreciate early history.

Start by explaining why you think their land might contain some historic items. Show or describe your research efforts to reveal your knowledge of the area. The property owner might be interested to learn history of their property which they were not aware of. If you start by saying that you hope to find coins, jewelry or something else of value, you may get a quick "no." You have just made the owner curious as to what you believe to be on their property. By explaining that you are searching for historic artifacts from a certain period, they will likely be more interested in seeing what you might find. Offer to return any of their personal items that might be unearthed during your search.

Think about the best time to approach a landowner to seek permission. For example, if you knock upon a farmer's door in the evening you might find him to be less than open-minded to your ideas. You should realize that the farmer could have been working his fields, livestock or property since long before dawn and is likely preparing for bed. You would be better served to meet with the farmer during the morning hours when he is not exhausted from the day's chores.

Those landowners who give you a firm "no" may very well have been hounded by detectorists in the past who left them with a bad impression of the hobby. Be courteous to the landowner regardless of the answer you receive. A "no" can sometimes be turned into a "yes" if you are polite. I approached some landowners about hunting a battlefield I suspected to be on their farm. Before asking about metal detecting, I first explained my interest in history, my

previous writing experience and my desire to prove some historically important points about the battle. They knew of the battle,
and we talked for a while about what they knew of it and what
kinds of artifacts their grandparents had found in the past. Eventually, I brought up the fact that I wanted to bring several people
equipped with metal detectors in order to conduct my search.

The landowners agreed and for the first search, I brought only a
few people along. Once we found a relic that garnered everyone's
interest, they were open to our group returning to hunt a second
day. We carefully filled in all of our excavation areas and kept the
gates to the field closed to prevent livestock from escaping. We
also hauled in quite a bit of junk metal from the field. The farmers
seemed pleased that we had cleared shotgun shells, pop tops, beer
cans and various iron rubbish from their land.

• *The manner in which you conduct yourself will help determine if
you are to be invited back to private land again.* Show the owners what
you have found on their property. Trust will be lost if they feel you
are acting nervous or trying to hide what you might have found.
Respect the laws in your country by offering the landowner their
rightful share of your finds. Even if a percentage is not specified in
your country, it will be a generous act to offer them some interesting coins or relics.

Nigel Ingram of England routinely offers his services to search
for any lost farm implements in the future as a means of thank-
ing the landowners for allowing permission to detect their fields.
Other detectorists offer small thank-you gifts to the landowners at
holiday time as a showing of their gratitude. Such offerings often
go a long way in opening doors for future hunts.

By all means, make sure that everyone in your hunting group
hauls out their trash and properly fills in every hole. Failure to follow the most basic rules of treasure hunting will almost guarantee
that you will never be invited back again.

Offer to show landowners or their visitors how your metal
detector operates. They often have interest in what you are doing,
and you might just get someone else interested in your hobby!

*(Above, left)* This old right-of-way path cuts through rural areas of England and has been used by pedestrians for centuries. Note the darker green color of the old path where Nigel Ingram and Henry Tellez are recovering a target. *(Above, right)* The author inspects an old British coin he has recovered near this same path.

- *Scout for other search sites in your spare time.* Look for evidence of habitation by walking the fields during the "off season" when crops do not allow you to hunt a farm. Europeans often refer to this as *field-walking*. In North America, you obviously need permission from the landowners before venturing onto private property. In rural areas of England, however, privately owned land is still required to contain public right of ways through them. Local settlers may have walked across the fields to a school or church for many hundreds of years. The landowners in these areas put up a special gate if they have livestock that might escape. You are not allowed to metal detect along these public paths without obtaining permission from the land owners. Field-walking along these public right of ways, however, can help you spot clues which point you to a potentially good hunting area. You can then contact the owners of these fields for permission to search.

- *Stay alert for excavation or construction areas in history-rich regions.* Modern progress often unearths pieces of our history. Just as the farmer's plow can bring artifacts within reach of your searchcoil, construction digging can bring new life to a previously heavily-worked area. Do not trespass on such areas; rather, find out who is in charge and gain the proper permission. Your search time will likely be in the evenings once construction has been completed for the day. Your time will obviously be limited as the site's construction progresses so be prepared to search as soon as the ground has been cleared and you have been given permission.

Partner with a local historic group to improve your chances of searching a construction area during the early excavation period. Be willing to donate your finds to a local museum. It is not always about trying to fill your personal relic case. Offer your time to help preserve local history. You can fill an album with photos of the artifacts you recover.

Remember that hunting in the field for relics is the payoff. Your success will likely be a direct result of how well you've done your homework prior to hitting the field.

# CHAPTER 6

# PREPARATION AND FIELD SAFETY

### Organize Yourself for the Hunt

At some point, you must lay aside your laptops, your photocopies and your note pads in order to learn how good all of your research has been. Let's face it: only your metal detector can really measure the success of your research work. Still, even armed with the best of research and the best feeling of confidence in your heart, you can be—and probably will be—disappointed at times.

You might be very close to the site but still not productive on that first hunt....don't give up. Go back and study what you've found and look over your maps and notes again. Do things match up? Perhaps you're only hundreds of yards away from the right spot; or maybe you need to hit the books again.

Relic hunting is most enjoyable in the fall and pre-spring months when the weather is more conducive to long days of field work. Since the hunting season poses obvious dangers to anyone metal detecting out in the forest, try to plan your times before deer or other hunting seasons commence or just after the December holidays. In the deep south, temperatures can climb back into the 50s during January and February, offering pleasant weather with little ground cover in the fields.

The cooler months mean that there are less weeds and undergrowth to inhibit your searches. It also means fewer ants, ticks, spiders, mosquitoes, and snakes to contend with. Farmers generally plow their fields in the fall to plant winter crops and again in the early spring to prepare their soil for the new spring crops. Even places that have been heavily hunted can become quite productive when the soil is turned over in the fall and spring.

Some great relic discoveries in the United States and in Europe have been made literally within paces of back roads and even highways. In the open fields, most items are within reach of a good detector's searchcoil. Heavier artillery items will sink deeper into the soil over time but minié balls and buckles can be found at very shallow depths in some areas. It is important to prepare yourself with the proper recovery tools for the conditions you expect to face in the field.

Die-hard relic hunters will go out in all kinds of weather any time of the year, braving heat, cold, rain and all sorts of unpleasant conditions. It is important to properly equip yourself for the weather and field conditions you will enter.

The more you've been in the field, the more you will appreciate the value of being prepared. The old Boy Scouts motto rings true, especially for those who plan an excursion for relics into the deep woods. Once you've maneuvered hills, creeks, briars and all other obstacles, the last thing you want is to have to trudge back to the truck or to town to retrieve some forgotten item.

Keep a relic hunting checklist with your detector supplies. Go over your list before your hunt, allowing yourself enough time for a trip to the store or to your local detector dealer to pick up anything that you need. The farther you must travel, the more crucial this list will become.

I keep a duffel bag packed with my basic detecting necessities: gloves, pinpointer, spare searchcoil, digging tools, rags, a ball cap, sunscreen, bug spray, relic box, and other such necessities. Even with these basics always on the ready, I still run through a mental checklist the night before as I prepare for a full day in the field. In order to save time, I pack a small cooler with water bottles and drinks so that I merely have to dump ice over them in the morning. I also prepare a bag with a sandwich, snacks, fruit and anything else I'll need to get through a long day of hiking and digging.

## RELIC HUNTER'S FIELD DAY CHECKLIST
*(Don't leave home without these things!)*

### DETECTOR GEAR
- ○ Primary metal detector
- ○ Backup metal detector
- ○ Headphones
- ○ Backup headphones
- ○ Pinpointer
- ○ Spare batteries
- ○ Control box rain cover-up
- ○ Spare detector parts (searchcoil nuts and bolts, lower shafts, etc.)
- ○ _____
- ○ _____
- ○ _____

### RECOVERY ITEMS & TOOLS
- ○ Sturdy digging shovel or spade
- ○ Hand digger or pick
- ○ Pocketknife or probe
- ○ Screwdriver, wrench (repair tools)
- ○ Weed sickle, pruners
- ○ _____
- ○ _____

### CLOTHING / PROTECTION
- ○ Hat or cap
- ○ Sunglasses or safety glasses
- ○ Jacket/coat (seasonal)
- ○ Digging gloves (2 pairs or more)
- ○ Extra socks
- ○ Hiking boots
- ○ Backpack or belt to hold tools
- ○ Waders
- ○ Rain gear
- ○ Dry clothing or extra layers
- ○ _____
- ○ _____

### PERSONAL CARE
- ○ Sunscreen
- ○ Food / snacks / fruit
- ○ Water / juices / energy drinks
- ○ Pain reliever / Ibuprofin
- ○ Bug spray
- ○ First aid kit / eye wash
- ○ Any necessary prescriptions
- ○ Cooler with ice
- ○ Folding chair
- ○ Itch cream (bug bite relief)
- ○ Sunburn relief cream / aloe vera
- ○ Toilet paper
- ○ _____
- ○ _____
- ○ _____

### RELIC RECOVERY ITEMS
- ○ Zip-loc bags for relics
- ○ Treasure pouch for finds, garbage
- ○ Trash bags to dispose of garbage
- ○ Towels, soft brush (item cleaning)
- ○ Containers for finds
- ○ Wrapping paper / cloths
- ○ _____
- ○ _____
- ○ _____

### ELECTRONICS
- ○ Digital camera or video camera
- ○ Cellphone or laptop computer
- ○ GPS unit
- ○ Spare batteries, memory cards
- ○ _____
- ○ _____
- ○ _____

*Add to this list based upon your personal preferences. If you will be camping on location, consider a second list for tent, campfire and general camping supplies needed.*

Generally, I like to have everything set out before I go to bed. This includes my cooler, food, detectors, shovels, backpack and bag of supplies. When the alarm goes off, I can simply grab a quick bite of breakfast, some coffee and hit the road without the mental turmoil of pondering what I've left behind this time.

Your needs for a day of relic hunting may be different from the next person's needs but I'm willing to bet that at least three-quarters of the items on anyone's checklist would overlap. The previous page offers a relic hunter's checklist of basic items that should be included before hitting the field. You can copy this one or create your own, adding your particular necessaries.

Without running down the entire list, here are a few items that are worthy of further discussion:

- *At least two pairs of sturdy gloves.*

Protect your fingers from blisters while digging and from nasty cuts on jagged pieces of rusty iron as you sift through the soil. Gloves are also very desirable in overgrown areas where you must hack through briars and thorny brush.

- *Your preferred detector and a backup detector.*

The worst possible scenario is to be in the midst of a highly productive hunt and have your detector expire on you. The more years you put into hunting, the more likely you are to have "stepped up" into another model. Don't be so quick to dispose of your previous favorite. While your new machine might be more productive, it pays to always have a backup machine in your vehicle just in case your favorite decides to play out on you in the field one day.

- *Spare batteries or a recharging option.*

Carrying a spare detector is insurance against things going wrong with your primary machine. Carrying extra batteries is another form of insurance you should include. Some detectorists prefer rechargeable batteries for their detectors. In this case, you can keep an extra set recharging off your car's lighter while driving to the site. There are even batteries that can be refreshed using nature as a solar recharger. If you prefer standard alkalines, just be sure to keep some extras in your backpack or vehicle.

- *Carry a selection of searchcoils.*

Situations may present themselves in the field where the coil you planned on using might not be the best. For example, if you happen upon the remnants of an old homestead, you might find the area to be highly littered with nails and other small scrap iron. Your largest coil, though effective for depth and for quickly covering large areas of open field or forest land, can become frustrating in such an area. Small sniper coils can help distinguish good targets from bad where target masking is an issue. Smaller coils are also more maneuverable in tight areas among rocks and roots. If you have encountered areas of high ground mineralization while using a concentric coil, try switching to a DD configuration coil.

*(Above)* Relic recovery tools, such as these sold in the UK, are available in numerous sizes from many different manufacturers.

*(Left)* Small, specialty diggers can be carried in multi-compartment backpacks, used by many relic hunters for long days in the woods. Be sure to include snacks, water, your relic recovery box, first aid kit, bug spray, optional searchcoil, camera and other gear to avoid the need to hike back to your vehicle.

- *Extra clothing for changes in weather.*

Dress so that you will be comfortable in the weather you expect but keep additional items on hand to be fully prepared. This should include an inexpensive rain poncho that folds down to a compact size. Knee pads can save your skin from cuts and bruises if you will be kneeling on rocky ground or digging in brushy areas with briars. In warmer weather, you will want a lighter T-shirt for comfort or even a light, long-sleeved shirt to protect your arms from sunburn and scratches.

In cold weather, dress in layers that can be removed as mid-day temperatures rise. Ventilated jackets will help allow the moisture from sweat to escape if you become too warm. Extra foot gear can be kept in your vehicle if you find the need to switch. I often bring a pair of rubber hip waders just in case I find that I will be wading through creeks or sloshing through muddy fields. The alternative of spending hours in wet socks and waterlogged shoes is not desirable. Wet feet can quickly lead to blisters. Comfortable tennis shoes, hiking boots or snake boots should be selected based upon what will keep your feet the most comfortable and what will offer the most protection based on where you will be hunting.

- *Don't forget sunglasses and a protective hat.*

Protect your eyes from the bright sun whether you are hunting in the mountains, in the pastures or at the beach. The intense reflection from sun off a snow-covered ground can seriously hamper your vision without a good pair of sun shades. I tend to wear ball caps for most hunts but these are less practical in the warm weather when you will be working under the direct sun. Wide brim hats not only offer shade for your eyes and face but serve well to save your neckline from excessive sun exposure.

- *Sunscreen, insect repellent and pain reliever.*

You should apply liberal amounts of high SPF sunscreen for a full day in the field, even on those overcast, windy days—when sunburn sneaks up on you. Trust me: I may tan well during the summer but I burn quickly without the sunscreen.

Mosquitoes, chiggers, ants, hornets, wasps, poison ivy, poison oak, ticks and dozens of other woodland pests can really hamper your search efforts. The biting and stinging pests will make their presence known right away. Ticks, red bugs, chiggers and other minute crawlers require a thorough scrubbing and inspection after vacating the forest and pastures in warmer weather.

There are many brands of insect repellent but the ones that are generally accepted as being the most effective include the active ingredient Deet or permethrin to repel these tiny critters. *Off! Deep Woods for Sportsmen* and *Cutter Max* are two brands which contain 100% Deet for maximum protection. For those who are concerned with such concentrations of Deet, there are plenty of brands which contain lower doses of this ingredient (many ranging from 20% to 40%) such as *Cutter, Sawyer Controlled Release* and *BugOut*.

Another recommended brand is *Repel* with Permanone. Bug repellents with lower doses of active ingredients, however, will required you to reapply more often to maintain maximum protection against bug bites in the field. During the warm season, it is advisable to treat your hunting clothes the night before or at least

Steer clear of bee hives and hornet's nests, such as this one spotted in a Georgia forest. Yellow jackets have been known to pursue those who disturb their nests in the forest.

several hours before you enter the woods. After spraying your clothes, fold them up and store them in a bag overnight to allow the repellent to fully soak in.

Wasps, yellow jackets, bees and hornets can quickly ruin a good hunt. Yellow jackets often make their nests in the ground or in low bushes. Those who have run afoul of yellow jackets advise you to flee as soon as you feel the first sting. Once a yellow jacket nest has been disturbed, these flying menaces attack with a swarming fury. By the time you feel one hit you, it is likely that an entire bunch of yellow jackets is buzzing toward you. My daughter once stepped into a bush and her leg was quickly peppered with numerous painful stings. Hornet's nests can often be spotted suspended from a tree. The best advice is to simply steer clear of their area.

Carry a first aid kit in your backpack or in your vehicle with lotions for bites, bandages for cuts and ibuprofen for headaches and other pains. There are commercially available kits or you can simply assemble your own to include antibacterial solution, lip balm, cleansing swabs, a disposable flashlight, tweezers, scissors and the like.

Snake boots are a good idea for hunting during warmer months in forests and other areas where poisonous snakes are a concern. These reinforced boots are designed to protect feet and lower leg areas where a snake's strike is most likely to land.

In the warmer months, many relic hunters wear snake boots to protect themselves from snake bites in areas where the serpents are dangerous. Most major sporting goods outlets sell snake boots, particularly during the early fall as the hunting seasons approach. The cheapest option is strap-on snake guards that resemble shin guards worn by soccer players. The lace-up or slip-on full boots are more expensive (many selling for more than $100) but do offer the best full-leg protection against snake bites. Look for bargain prices on snake boots in the off season.

- *Spare batteries or a recharging option.*

Carrying a spare detector is insurance against things going wrong with your primary machine. Carrying extra batteries is another form of insurance you should include. Some detectorists prefer rechargeable batteries for their detectors. In this case, you can keep an extra set recharging off your car's lighter while driving to the site. There are even batteries that can be refreshed using nature as a solar recharger. If you prefer standard alkalines, just be sure to keep some extras in your backpack or vehicle.

- *Control box cover-up.*

Most metal detector control boxes are not designed to be waterproof. An inexpensive accessory known as a control box cover or an environmental cover-up can save you from an expensive repair or replacement. These cover-ups have clear panels on the front to allow you to fully view the controls of your machine while protecting your expensive electronics from rain, dust, dirt or unexpected drops in the mud.

The other option, of course, is to invest in a metal detector with a control housing that is fully protected from the environment.

- *Weed sickle or pruning gear.*

Some of the best productive areas are ones that are normally bypassed because of thick undergrowth, tall weeds or excessive thorns. Be prepared to deal with such obstacles by carrying a weed sickle in your vehicle, a pair of pruners or even a gasoline-powered brush trimmer. This extra labor, utilized by some of the more serious hunters, can pay for itself if you find a hot spot that is badly overgrown. By mowing down tall weeds and small brush, you will gain additional search depth by allowing your searchcoil to sweep closer to the soil.

———————

### Relic Hunting Safety

Your health is a prime concern as you enjoy the outdoors. In addition to bringing along first-aid items, use due diligence to avoid potential dangers.

- *Keep a careful eye for snakes in warmer weather.*

I'll be the first to admit I'm not a big fan of snakes. My favorite one, in fact, is skinned and wrapped around a pair of my boots. As a kid, I spent a lot of time fishing and hunting around my grand-father's 40-acre lake in East Texas—one that he had dug out and dammed up in 1959 for his retirement home.

My grandparents' German shepherd ran afoul of water moc-casins or timber rattlers a time or two. These hearty dogs can often survive the bites but become very ill and suffer from a leg swollen to several times its normal size. My grandfather and I killed our fair share of the moccasins around the lake by baiting out snake traps—an idea of his to tie a trot line hook to a heavy rock or brick on the edge of the shore. We then ran the hook under the dorsal fins of a perch and left him flopping in the water's edge overnight.

Shortly after sunrise, we would take one of the boats around the lake to check the snake traps. Granddad would maneuver the boat up the weedy banks while I stood on the bow with one of my "snake-charmers"—usually a .22-caliber with hollow point bullets. If the fish was still flopping near the bank, we moved on. If you could see the rock but no fish there was almost always a large water moccasin lying nearby in the weeds which had swallowed the perch whole and snared himself on the sharp trot line hook.

It is not always easy *to distinguish whether a snake is poisonous or non-poisonous. There are several key ways*, if you so choose to take the time to notice. The most commonly referenced way to tell a

# A SAMPLING OF SNAKES YOU COULD ENCOUNTER

This page shows just a small sample of some of the North American snakes you might encounter in the field while relic hunting. This Mexican ridge nosed rattlesnake *(above, left)* is poisonous but the equally fearsome-looking bull snake *(above, right)* is not.

*(Left)* This eastern coral snake is very poisonous. A saying to help remember this snake from the non-poisonous scarlet king snake *(seen below)* goes: "Red and yellow, kill a fellow. Red and black, friend of Jack."

Pygmy rattlesnake: poisonous.

This water snake *(above, left)* is non-poisonous but intimidating nonetheless. Notice how well the poisonous copperhead *(above, right)* blends in with the forest floor covering.

*Snake photos by Gary M. Stolz and Robert S. Simmons, U.S. Fish & Wildlife Service.*

"good" snake from a "bad" snake is by the *shape of its head*. Poisonous snakes usually have a triangular or arrowhead-shaped head such as those of the viper family. Be aware that this does not ring true in all cases. For example, an eastern hognose snake can flatten its head when frightened and appear to be a poisonous snake. The very poisonous coral snake is an exception to this rule as well.

A second trait of poisonous snake identification is *the shape of its eyes*. Most poisonous snakes have a vertical or elliptical pupil (the black part in the center of the eye) which look almost catlike. The pupils of harmless snakes are round and are centrally located in the eye. Another way to identify a poisonous snake is *the presence of a pit*, or hole, between the snake's eyes and nostrils. Non-poisonous snakes lack these specialized sensory pits which help

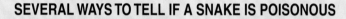

## SEVERAL WAYS TO TELL IF A SNAKE IS POISONOUS

Non-poisonous garter snake. Note its rounded, centered pupils. While this snake has a nostril opening forward of its eye, there is no additional sensory pit.

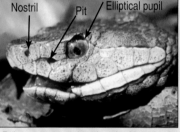

Poisonous copperhead snake. Note that its pupil is vertical and looks more like a cat's eye. The sensory area or "pit" on the side of its head indicates a venomous snake.

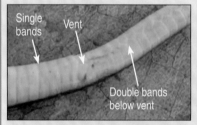

Scale arrangement on the underside of a snake near its tail is another way to tell a harmless snake from a poisonous snake. (I recommend this method only on snakes you have already killed.)

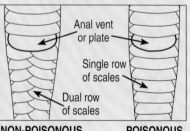

**NON-POISONOUS SNAKE**     **POISONOUS SNAKE**

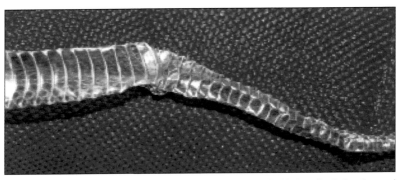

This snakeskin, found in the author's backyard, clearly shows double banding below the anal vent—indicative of a non-poisonous snake.

pit vipers sense warm-blooded prey in the dark.

Another sure way to tell a poisonous snake from a non-poisonous snake is one not known to as many people. My grandfather built Civilian Conservation Corps (CCC) towns during the Great Depression of the 1930s. Most of his work was in extremely rural areas of Texas where snakes were commonly encountered. After we would kill a snake, he would roll it over and show me the best way to identify if it was harmless *by its scale arrangement.*

The underside of a venomous snake has a single row of scales extended from its anal plate. The lower section of a non-venomous snake's underside will have two rows of scales from this vent to the tip of its tale. Naturally, this method does you little good with a live specimen but it's a sure-fire way to tell what it was after you kill a snake (particularly if you have been bitten and are not sure yet if it was poisonous). Snake skins you find in the forest can also be identified with this method—double rows for most non-poisonous snakes and single rows on the tail's underside for the poisonous snakes. An exception to this rule is the deadly coral snake, which has double rows of scales below the anal vent.

Even living in the outlying Dallas-area suburbs today, snakes continue to slither into my life. I've killed at least 12—mainly rat snakes with the occasional small copperhead—in my own yard in the past three years. The point of this digression is to *always be aware of your surroundings* when it comes to snakes.

Waterways, swamps, heavy forest, rocky desert terrain and even city parks can present a deadly surprise for you if you fail to exercise the proper caution while searching. If you've ever been digging a target in the woods and happen to catch that slithering movement close by from the corner of your eye, you know the unpleasant feeling.

Let your searchcoil be your snake prod as you move through heavy brush or thick leaves in warmer weather. Your eyes are your best defense, though. Do not become preoccupied with scanning distant areas in the forest while you are walking. Keep a sharp lookout in your immediate area. Don't believe someone who tells you that you shouldn't worry about snakes in the cooler months. I've nearly stepped on a thick water moccasin sunning himself in the middle of winter while I was deer hunting on a day when the late morning temperature crept above 50 degrees.

Most snakes can be avoided by simply being aware of your surroundings. When you do encounter one, try to ease away and avoid the situation.

* *Beware of animal attacks.*

Wild animals should be avoided but expeditions through backwoods areas can occasionally bring you face to face with creatures of every descriptions. Most animals will scurry away unless you happen to surprise a mother with young ones that feels challenged. Wild hogs can be particularly dangerous if confronted. I have often come up freshly rooted areas in the forest where hogs have been recently; fortunately, I have not come face to face with such beasts while detecting.

Bears are a serious concern in some parts of North America. George Wyant of Montana had a close encounter with a black bear in 2009 that was reported in his local newspaper. He was able to escape without injury but he now admits to carrying a firearm with him to prepare for such a future brush with danger.

You should avoid attacking or provoking a startled animal unless it is your last resort. I was startled once while hunting in Kentucky to look up and see a large, snarling dog approaching me over a hilltop. The nearest home was several hundred yards away but he was apparently coming out to warn me to stay back. I gripped my shovel tight, prepared to smash it against him only as a last resort. I remained calm and did not raise my voice to further agitate the angry canine. Instead, I slowly continued sweeping my searchcoil while slowing turning to move in the other direction. By simply maintaining my steady pace in the other direction, the dog gradually calmed and curiously followed at a distance for a while. You can bet that I kept one eye on his movements as I slowly exited "his" territory.

Cattle will generally move out of your way as you approach. Avoid quick movements or loud noises that can spook a herd into stampeding. Always secure any gates or fences that you pass through while hunting. Landowners do not appreciate detectorists who bother their livestock or offer them the opportunity to escape. These are two quick ways to insure that you will never be allowed back on their property.

On one occasion, I was confronted by a menacing bull that did not turn the other direction as I approached his area. Instead, he began moving steadily toward me, perhaps to prove his dominance over his harem. For some reason, I slowly unplugged my headphones to bring my *GTI 2500's* external speaker into play and turned up the volume to full. I then placed my shovel blade on the large searchcoil and the detector immediately began to clatter with a loud overload signal. Whether or not this was really a good idea against an irritated bull, the loud rattling did the trick this time. He abruptly turned tail and raced away.

- *Keep hydrated and be aware of your own fatigue.*

A long day of hiking, climbing, carrying your extra gear and continually digging targets can leave you as sore at the end of the day as a good workout. Before you hike away from your vehicle, take a moment to stretch your muscles and limber up. Take short breaks during the day if you feel yourself tightening up.

One of the biggest dangers you can face is overdoing it in hot and humid weather. Be sure to take plenty of water breaks to keep your body hydrated. Drink more fluids in warm weather than you normally would. Carry water with you, particularly if you will be hiking great distances from your vehicle. I prefer to wear either a backpack or a hunting vest in which I can carry a large bottle of water to sip on. Others often wear camelback water supplies in their backpack (akin to those used by cyclists and joggers) that can be sipped on while hunting.

As one who sweats easily in the sun, I know that it is vital to replace the liquids in your system to keep your body cool. Hard, dry ground and rocky soils force you to work hard to dig down for targets. On more than one occasion, I've been excited in a productive area and worked far longer than what was good for me in temperatures above 90 degrees.

When your body becomes overly fatigued and dehydrated, you may develop a bad headache. Pay attention to this warning sign. Find a shade tree, pull up a chair or cooler to sit on, and consume liquids until your headache dissipates. I generally reach for some type of aspirin and try to rest long enough for my body to cool down again. If your fatigue and headache persists after such a rest period, call it a day. You'll thank yourself later and those targets still in the ground will probably still be there tomorrow.

# CHAPTER 7

# TARGET RECOVERY AND SCOUTING TIPS

**Relic Recovery Tools**

The implements used by relic hunters to unearth their treasures vary based upon soil conditions. Keep in mind that there is a direct relationship between the speed with which you can recover your target and how much time you can spend hunting a good area. The most commonly used diggers for such recovery work are solid metal shovels and hand-held digging knives. While the discount stores offer plenty of bargain shovels for around $10 or so, you may quickly be disappointed by the "value."

Red-clay and rocky terrains will put strain in more than just your back. They can quickly bend or snap a bargain shovel if enough force is being applied to it. A short-handled pick or sturdy entrenching shovel will power through this nasty clay but will also dig a less precise hole. Be cautious of shovels with plastic or hard rubber handles which can also be bent or broken. It will cost you a little more up front but in the long run you will be better served to spend the money on a solid metal (including the handle) relic recovery shovel.

Many metal detector dealers carry such specialty shovels. There are also a number of sites and manufacturers on the Internet who sell a nice variety of spades, picks and diggers. Read reviews about various recovery tools on detecting forums to see which tools are favored by detectorists. Your own trial and error is, of course, the best way to discover the ones that work best for you.

Many of these are tapered to allow the tip to dig deeper without making such a large hole and creating clean-cut plugs to replace. Some shovel makers who cater to relic hunters feature heat- treated and tempered steel diggers that have sharpened sides or serrated edges to help cut through nasty roots in the forest. Look for a kick plate or pegs on either side to help power through roots and tough ground. The goal is to dig as small a hole as possible to recover the item and to be able to fill it back in quickly.

In addition to such a full-size shovel, it is a good idea to carry a smaller, hand-held digging tool. Such a compact item should be solid metal or steel in composition. Many find that saw-edged diggers are particularly useful to slice through vines and roots while digging an elusive, deep target. When not in use, this instrument can be sheathed on a waist belt holder.

In addition to digging tools, you should wear a treasure pouch, apron or some other special bag in which you can collect both your treasures and your trash. Use a zippered pouch or compartment to best protect against the accidental loss of your recovered treasures while you are in the field. Your bag or apron should have at least two pockets made of waterproof plastic or with plastic pocket liners. Quite often you will be digging in areas that are wet. The damp soil accumulated on recovered targets can cause the contents of non-waterproofed pockets to leak through onto your clothing. You can also protect your clothing (and your knees) with comfortable and adjustable waterproof knee pads.

Gloves are a necessity for serious relic recovery work where you will be doing excessive digging, particularly in rough areas with briars, roots and rocky soil. Reinforced gloves will protect your fingers from nicks and cuts and potential infection from broken glass, sharp rocks, rusty iron and jagged artifacts. Most garden centers, hardware stores or discount centers will carry a wide variety of gardening and work gloves. Personal preference, comfort and durability of the gloves must be considered.

I've tried standard cotton garden gloves, which are generally cool and comfortable in warm weather but they tend to wear out quickly when you dig with your fingers. I've also used some of my old tight-fit scuba diving gloves but these also became shredded after a couple of relic hunting trips.

Leather or reinforced work gloves for farm and ranch work or construction tend to be more solidly built for the long-haul. I generally prefer tight-fit gloves (with reinforced fingers or no-slip surfacing) that still allow easy use of detector controls. If your main concern is preventing blisters during excessive spadework, open-fingered mountain-biking gloves are quite comfortable.

Because prices and durability in work gloves vary, choose what best fits your budget while offering the comfort and protection you desire in the field.

---

### Improving Your Relic Recovery Time

Your methods for excavating targets will vary based upon your location. In areas where you want to minimize damage to grass and its roots, you will use a more careful technique. You are obviously less concerned, however, with how you a dig a target hole in a plowed field, in the forest or on the beach.

The beginner will often dig larger and deeper holes than necessary while recovering a treasure target. He or she will also often struggle to find their smaller targets. In order to recover more targets during your limited time to hunt, it is important to improve your target recovery time. Less time searching for a pinpointed target equals more search time.

- **Practice more precisely pinpointing your target.** Use your test plot to practice your pinpointing technique. If you spend a minute recovering a small target versus struggling for four minutes, you have thus added three minutes to your search time. In the process of shortening your recovery time, you will be digging smaller holes and causing less damage to the soil.

Being symmetrical in design, *concentric searchcoils* pinpoint a target more easily for beginners. Practice in your test field to find where the center of electrical energy is located. With most concentric coils, this should be directly beneath the center of the two windings—although this center point can vary just slightly. The old "X marks the spot" method works just fine, moving the coil left and right and forward and backward above a target to locate the strongest signal point.

Shallow targets can be a little tougher to precisely pinpoint because they are producing a stronger signal. Try lifting the searchcoil a few inches off the ground to reduce the target signal intensity and pinpoint again. Another way to reduce the target signal intensity is to retune the searchcoil by narrowing the audio response field (refer to the end of Chapter 4 for this technique). Either of these methods can help you to greatly define the digging area for your target.

Pinpointing puts your detector into an All-Metal Mode to precisely locate a detected target's location. Most manufacturers focus on pinpointing coin-sized objects since the majority of items sought (rings, buttons, bullets, coins, etc.) happen to be coin-sized. Because the electronics are focused on coin-size items, be aware that your detector's depth indicator will lose accuracy for items significantly larger or smaller than coin size. *Items smaller than a coin can thus be found shallower than indicated. Similarly, items larger than a coin will often be found deeper than indicated.* In other words, a large item (a large buckle or cannon ball) might show to be at about four inches but will actually be found at six inches or more.

Although the symmetry of a concentric searchcoil naturally makes pinpointing a little simpler to learn, *Double-D coils by their design can improve the accuracy of your pinpointing.* You might find Double-D (DD) coils trickier for pinpointing when you begin but the old test plot can help perfect your skills. Refer back to the Chapter 2 illustration of this coil's D-shaped design. The coil's hot spot is that very narrow strip down the center where the TX coil and RX coil overlap each other.

There are several methods of pinpointing with a DD coil. First, there is the obvious method using the detector's pinpoint but-

Pinpointing with a DD searchcoil is very simple once the technique is mastered. As the coil is pulled away from the target, note the sharp drop in both audible and LCD meter response. In this case, the target will be located near the center tip of the DD coil (denoted by the "X" in the image).

ton. A second option will be referred to as the DD "wiggle" technique. Quickly locate targets *without using the Pinpoint button* as follows. Continuously swing the searchcoil side-to-side using fast, narrow swings of 2–4 inches (i.e. wiggle). While continuing this side-to-side wiggle, slowly move the searchcoil sideways toward the target's suspected position until the audio response produces a consistent, symmetric beat. This indicates the lateral left-to-right position of the target. Then locate the target's front-to-back position by rotating around 90° and repeating the same process.

A third DD pinpointing technique is to pinpoint off either the searchcoil's tip or tail. Press and hold the Pinpoint pushbutton during this technique. Sweep the searchcoil side-to-side to center the target (the point where the strongest audio response is heard and the maximum LCD pixels on the top row are displayed). Then, pull the searchcoil slowly toward you, noting the target signal.

Once the target signal drops off (both audibly and on the LCD meter), shallow targets should be located immediately in front of the searchcoil's tip. Deep targets will be under or just inside your searchcoil's tip. This is because the conical shape of the searchcoil's detection field begins bending in slightly as the depth increases. You can reverse this pinpointing technique to pinpoint off the DD coil's tail; in this case, push the coil away from you. The audio and LCD meter will place the target just off the searchcoil's tail. Whether you opt to push or pull the coil to find the drop-off in response, you should be able to dig a very tight recovery hole. The depth of the hole should be as indicated by your detector's depth indicator. In the absence of a depth indicator, you can estimate the depth with the coil lift method to gauge target response drop-off.

A fourth DD pinpointing technique employed by some DD coil users is to stand the coil up on its edge during the pinpoint process. You have thus reduced the size of the coil's hot spot to a very narrow area and you can again speed your target recovery time.

Whether you opt to search with a DD, mono or concentric searchcoil, you will dig smaller recovery holes as you improve your pinpointing ability. Take note of the heavy-duty relic shovels carried by the veterans: many have opted for narrow blade shovels that dig tighter recovery holes. The less soil you dig, the faster you will have your target in hand—if your pinpointing is accurate.

• **Work on tightening your excavation area.** In the perfect scenario, you will flip over your plug and either find the target lying in the bottom of the hole or just in the base of the soil you have overturned. By misjudging the depth of your target—whether you have dug too shallow or have overturned an excessive amount of earth—you will waste more time trying to find the item.

What do you do if you are using a detector that does not or cannot indicate true target depth? For those using Multi-Frequency (PI) detectors which do not have target depth indication, your precision at gauging target depth will improve as your ability to understand target signals improves.

First, precisely pinpoint the target as you normally would. Then "size" your target by slowly lifting your coil above the ground to gauge its relative size and depth. If you are coin hunting and have a nice silver response you believe to be a coin, you will loose this signal as you gradually lift the searchcoil higher. If you continue to get a strong response even after lifting the coil about six inches off the ground, you're certainly dealing with a target larger than a coin. By practicing this "coil lift" method in your test patch on targets that you have planted (where you know their exact size and depth) you will be able to reasonably judge your target's depth.

Metal detectors with Coin Depth Indicators do a nice job of showing you the approximate depth of coin-size targets, which is the size they are specifically calibrated to pinpoint. You therefore know just how deep you should dig. *Again, be aware that the actual depth of targets which are larger or smaller than coin size will vary in accuracy.* A tiny relic the size of a tiny gold nugget will be found a little shallower that the detector's indicated depth. Similarly, a coin standing on its edge in the ground will be reported shallower than its actual depth due to the smaller target area it presents.

Your ability to effectively dig the proper depth of your excavation hole will but speed your recovery time and prevent you from damaging a nice relic by running your shovel through it.

Andy Sabisch recommends a practice method he learned while attending an Alaska Treasure Seekers Club hunt near Anchorage. He and other detectorists tried their luck at pinpointing a target which was taped to the bottom side of a piece of cardboard. With each attempted pinpointing, a pin was pressed through the cardboard. Upon flipping over the cardboard, the club gauged who had actually come the closest to precisely pinpointing the target. Andy recommends using a similar cardboard pinpointing target at your home test plot to work on your technique.

- **Quickly determine whether your target is in the removed plug or still in the ground.** Swing your searchcoil over the excavated soil and the target hole to determine whether you have unearthed your target. *If you have lost all target response, chances are that your item may have dropped down deeper into the hole you've dug.* If you don't have a pinpointer to probe the hole, remove more soil and swing your coil over it again.

Use your searchcoil to first determine that you have removed the target from the ground. If the item is small and difficult to see, utilize a hand-held pinpointer to scan the pile. In the absence of a pinpointer, scoop piles of soil with your hand and pass them in front of your searchcoil.

• If you don't find the target in the additional dirt you've dug, *the target may be on its side in the large original chunk of earth you removed.* Spread out this soil with your foot or shovel and sweep it with your coil. If you still can't find the item and have been searching with discrimination, switch over to All Metal Mode. Your item may have slipped against an iron object that is now masking the item's presence.

• *Be aware that the hole you've created can cause false signals if you are searching with threshold tone.* Your detector has been ground balanced to the soil you are searching and it is now suddenly facing a void of this soil content (the empty space you've created).

Once you have recovered a fair number of targets, all of the above information will be second nature to you.

*Another consideration is how to actually dig for your target.*

• **Plug method recovery**—Use this technique in areas of manicured yards to minimize grass damage. Some of the old Civil War campgrounds or field hospitals were once located in what is now a developed area. If you are given the opportunity to hunt in a neighborhood where artifacts might be found, do not hasten your own exit by leaving visible evidence of your work. Property owners will be more likely to allow you to return if you do not leave unsightly brown patches of dead grass. Hunting manicured yards is obviously preferable in the cooler months when grass damage is less visible.

Make a plug in the ground by pushing your spade down around the area that you have pinpointed. Flip the plug over and scan it to see if your target is inside the plug. If the plug offers no response, scan over the hole and the ground around the hole. Usually, if you have dug the plug hole to the depth that the target was indicated, the target should be easy to recover. After retrieving your target, carefully push the loose soil back into the hole and replace the plug.

By completely digging up a plug and turning it over, you will kill the grass by cutting through all of the roots. This method is not effective where manicured green grass exists. In these areas, do not completely cut through an entire plug. Use your spade to cut through the roots around only three-quarters of your plug. Then, carefully roll the plug back to one side on a cloth or piece of tarp to catch the loose soil. Make sure that one side of the grass roots remain uncut. After retrieving your target, scoop the loose soil from the cloth back into the hole and carefully roll the plug back into place. By not completely severing all roots, you will allow the good ones to take over and the grass should remain green. Practice will help you perfect this technique.

• **Field recovery**—When relic hunting on farms or in the forest, it is less necessary or practical to dig such clean plugs. (It is still imperative that you properly fill in all excavation areas.) Simply dig the amount of earth needed to reach the target depth. Scan the removed dirt and the hole. If your detector indicates that the target response is still in the hole, dig deeper and repeat the process. Once you can get a target response from your pile of dirt, gently push it around with your foot or shovel and then scan over the pile again until you can locate the target. Experienced detectorists can speed through this entire sequence in mere seconds for the majority of their recoveries.

Veteran detectorists recover many targets without laying their metal detector down. *(Upper left)* Mark Hallai of Belgium uses his left hand to dig a scoop of soil from his pinpointed area. *(Upper right)* He then scans the excavated soil to determine if the target has been removed or is still in the ground. If the signal remains in the hole, he will take another scoop with his shovel and repeat the process as necessary.

• **Small object recovery**—Sometimes, you might dig up a very small target that is nearly impossible to spot. In the absence of a hand-held pinpointer, use your detector's searchcoil as a pinpointer. Once you've narrowed down the area where the target remains, scoop handfuls of dirt and pass them directly in front of your searchcoil about an inch or two away. (Make sure to not wear any metal objects such as a ring or watch on the hand passing the dirt in front of the coil.) Continue scooping and inspecting dirt until the detector responds. Then, carefully sift through the dirt in your hand until the item is located. If you sift through the soil until nothing remains, you've obviously dropped the little item and must start again.

Finally, *always double check all holes* to make sure you haven't missed a secondary target or fragment. Your backpack or treasure pouch should include special protection for a delicate relic you may find. Smaller items can be packed into cotton and placed in an old 35mm film canister or empty pill bottle or wrapped in a soft cloth or handkerchief. *Do not make the mistake of placing a fragile relic into your treasure pouch where it can be damaged by other objects during your search day.*

---

### Relic Recovery with a Pinpointer

Although hand-held pinpointers have been around for years, many metal detectorists have not learned their true value. Those who have used a well-designed treasure pinpointer will often tell you they would not go into the field again without one.

Even veteran hunters will be challenged at times to find small targets. During the European rallies I have attended, I have watched quite a number of people sifting and scanning the clods of earth in the plowed fields to find their targets. Dry farm

A quality pinpointer can help with the recovery of small items and also prevent damaging the target. The author points to the area his *Pro-Pointer* indicates a target to be located *(upper left image)*. When the signal is narrowed to this clump of earth *(lower images)*, the soil is carefully broken up by hand to reveal this post-medieval button— found during a UK hunt.

A *Pro-Pointer* helped find a second artifact in this recovery photo. The archaeological team had successfully recovered a musket ball from this deep hole (about 12.5"). A final sweep of the hole by the author revealed another target in the side wall. Careful excavation revealed a second musket ball *(below arrow)*, seen still embedded in the side wall.

soil falls back into the hole almost as quickly as you dig it. Some become quite frustrated or even give up when a small object proves to be elusive. After such detectorists are offered the chance to use a good pinpointer, they often are left wondering how they ever lived without one!

During a relic recovery, I prefer to remove a plug of soil slightly larger than the pinpointed area to avoid striking the object with my shovel. I also prefer to excavate slightly deeper than the target's pinpointed depth to remove it from the ground in the initial dig. Then, I scan the excavated sod and often find that the target signal is now in the removed soil. If not, I sweep my searchcoil over the hole. If the target is still in the ground, I dig another scoop of soil and scan over the excavation pile to insure that the object has been moved to the surface. At this point, I use my Garrett *Pro-Pointer's* side-scanning ability and scraping blade to quickly root through the soil to pinpoint the object. I always use my pinpointer to make another sweep of the recovery hole as well. You will often locate a second target by double-checking the area.

Small coins, buttons and musket balls are often well camouflaged by the soil color in which they are buried. The use of a

## HUNTING TECHNIQUES: Retuning Your *Pro-Pointer*

The Garrett *Pro-Pointer* can be retuned to pinpoint smaller, elusive targets. By "retuning" to your target, you are changing the audio field to report only the peak audio response of the target. In other words, the pinpointer must be moved closer to the object before it will respond.

1. Slowly scan toward the target until the *Pro-Pointer*'s response increases to the full/constant alarm.

2. Then, without moving the detector from the target, switch the power off and then quickly back on again in order to highlight only the peak audio response of the target.

3. Now, continue scanning towards the target to find its precise location. Repeat this power off/on cycle to further narrow the audio response as needed. After you have finished, you can return the *Pro-Pointer* to its normal detection by simply switching the power off and back on again while holding it away from any metal.

hand-held pinpointer can greatly speed your recovery time with such items and help prevent damaging them. A pinpointer will also help you dig smaller recovery holes and can identify multiple targets in close proximity. Pinpointers are also handy for scanning tight interior areas such as walls and ceilings, where coin and jewelry caches could have been stashed in old homes.

Franco Berlingieri of Belgium suggests a "quick-find" technique that he has developed for pulling a small item from a large pile of excavated soil with his Garrett *Pro-Pointer*. He places his *Pro-Pointer* flat on the ground above the spot where his detector indicates the target to be. Then, he twists the pinpointer in a clockwise circle until it begins vibrating and audibly alarming. Where the audio and vibrate alerts become the strongest, Franco stands the *Pro-Pointer* up to use its pinpointing tip to precisely locate the small treasure object.

Your treasure recovery methods and the tools you choose to use will vary based upon the terrains you encounter. Just as your ability to locate treasure with your metal detector improves with practice, your ability to quickly recover targets without damaging them improves with repetition.

The final step in target recovery is the need to *fill in your excavation hole.* Do not leave unsightly and potentially dangerous holes in the property where you hunt. You should always leave your hunting ground in better condition than you found it. Bring a treasure pouch or bag to collect the garbage metal that you dig. Land owners will be more apt to allow you to metal detect on their property again if they see the pop tops, tin cans and other debris you haul away.

---

### Field Signs: Make Your Practice Pay Off

Scouting an area of land for productive detecting areas is even more important than the time you spend on recovery techniques. You can't worry about recovery times on what you can't find.

Specific tips and techniques will be given in various chapters that relate to specific genres of relic hunting. There are, however, some basic pieces of advice that are beneficial to almost any types of artifacts you seek.

• *Conduct an area "recon" of your site.*—Before beginning to metal detect, you should do a reconnaissance scout with your eyes to look for clues. Broken bits of pottery in a field are great indicators of an old homestead or village. If you have studied enough pottery shards to know much about them, they can also be key indicators at to the relative age of items you expect to find in this field. This is not to say that you should walk the whole field looking for clues before you start detecting; keep a keen eye out for visual items *at all times.*

Take note of the height of plants and vegetation in areas where old settlements were once located. The color of the soil will look different where it has been mixed with layers of old rubbish. Look for long rows of old trees that don't seem to have grown in such a formation by pure chance. These might lead you to the remnants of an old foundation, wall or collection of large stones that were once part of a homestead or early structure.

In some areas, oyster, clam or mussel shells were used for roads, paths and around early structures. Anything that seems out of place—from such crushed shells to areas of scattered rocks or even patches of plowed soil that appear lighter or darker than the rest of the field—is worthy of further investigation. Finding such signs does not guarantee that your metal detecting efforts will be successful but they certainly can be of value.

Once you have located such promising signs, conduct a search of the area to pinpoint hot spots. For a large field, you can sweep the entire perimeter of the area in hopes of locating a crossing point. Then, work two diagonal sweeps across this rectangle in the form of an "X" shape through its center. This is obviously not to be considered a detailed search of a large area but it is a quick way to sweep a zone without spending too much time. If you find a nice coin or artifact, then you can conduct a more thorough grid search by walking lanes up and down through the area. The abundance of iron, such as old square nails, is often the first sign that you have happened upon an old camp site or early homestead.

- *Use a search grid on a productive area.*—It is difficult to truly "hunt out" a battlefield, camp site or other area of concentrated artifact finds. Some of the best finds are made by those who return to work over a hard-hit spot once again. If your usual detector is not finding anything else on a site where you have previously done well, try a larger searchcoil or a Multi-Frequency detector if you have previously hunted with a Single Frequency instrument. Many relic hunters keep at least two or more machines in their arsenal for different circumstances. You can also return to this area shortly after a good soaking thunderstorm, which will saturate the ground and make it more conductive for your searchcoil.

Kelly Rippey of Brentwood, Tennessee, took a new, higher-end detector than he had previously used to one of these hunted-out sites near an old homestead. He was thrilled to turn up several Indian Head and wheat pennies, plus a small dirt-filled bottle dating to the 1860s. Inside this tiny bottle was a coin cache which contained an 1863 Indian Head penny, an 1868 Shield nickel, an 1858 Flying Eagle penny, an 1853 Seated Liberty half dime and an 1854 $2½ Liberty gold piece. Rippey is thus a firm believer that you can never call a place completely hunted out.

The need for overlapping your searchcoil during your swings has been discussed. Given a large battleground or relic-productive area, however, it is less likely that you have completely covered every acre, even using such a consistent overlap method. Archaeologists work "lanes" when they cover an area of interest to insure that no ground is inadvertently skipped. With some simple wooden stakes and twine, you can accomplish the same thing.

Drive stakes into the ground about 100 feet apart from each other on a site where you have had previous success. Start at one stake and move slowly across the field while making sure to completely overlap each swing. Upon reaching the other stake, move to the opposite side and return back to your starting point while carefully sweeping and overlapping your swings on the opposite side of the string. To truly work each lane thoroughly, archaeology searchers actually *work the same lane from each direction* one or more times. At this point, you can move the stakes and the string to a new point that will just allow your coil to slightly overlap one of the lanes you have just scoured. Continue this process across the hunt site and see if your extra efforts don't produce a few more items in this "hunted out" area.

Crime scene searchers use *zone patterns* similar to the method described above to thoroughly search an area whose boundaries have been clearly marked. Each of the zones can be covered by the above *single straight line or strip pattern* method. Most relic hunters using such a grid technique in the field do not opt to use string or stakes. The strip pattern is natural due to the fact that the coil must be scanned from side to side.

A more thorough variation of the single straight line method is the *double straight line pattern*. In one of your grid areas, search the area with overlapping swings as you walk north to south. At the end of each lane move about three feet over and return in the opposite direction, swinging your coil in enough overlap so that no ground is missed. After completely sweeping this grid in a north to south and south to north fashion, cover the entire grid a second time using an east to west and west to east alternating lane sweep. By covering the entire grid from two different directions, you increase your chance of finding a target that is lying on edge or being masked by another item.

In the *contracting circle pattern*, the searcher works in an ever-decreasing circular pattern. Begin at the outside of an area and search about a three-foot wide pathway in front of and to each side of you as you slowly walk around the decreasing circumference of the circle toward the center of the search area. Overlap previously searched paths by about eight inches as you move inward.

Charles Garrett has taught this method to crime scene searchers using a tree and a 100-foot rope tied to the searcher's waist. The searcher then walks around the tree, searching each concentric circle with the metal detector—all the while maintaining a taut rope. There is little likelihood that this search could miss a metallic object in an area, as long as the rope remains taut. Each successive circle becomes smaller until the tree is reached. If the object is not found during a first search, the area should be searched in the *opposite* direction. This method can be used in an open area by driving a stake into the ground and tying a piece of twine from it to the searcher.

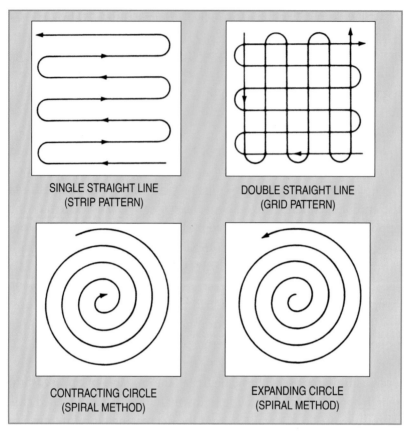

SINGLE STRAIGHT LINE
(STRIP PATTERN)

DOUBLE STRAIGHT LINE
(GRID PATTERN)

CONTRACTING CIRCLE
(SPIRAL METHOD)

EXPANDING CIRCLE
(SPIRAL METHOD)

Conversely, the same tree or stake in the ground can be used as a starting point. The person with the end of the rope tied around their waist should walk in an *expanding circle* out from the tree to the edge of the search area to fully cover the grid. There are other grid patterns that can be explored that may work successfully for you. The point of any of these is to fully cover the area in a productive relic site.

• *Search near natural water sources.*—Troops generally camped near creeks and rivers furnishing a fresh water supply both for themselves and for their horses. Start near the water source and move out toward areas that look like natural camping areas. Higher ground afforded strategic advantages for lookouts and for firing upon an advancing enemy.

In other cases, commanders took their men away from such high ground to foil the enemy's scouts. The sides of hills could be dug into for defensive positions and as protection against cold winter winds. Infantrymen may have camped in groves of old trees away from the elevated areas for similar protection but they would still likely be relatively close to a water source.

• *Non-natural indicators.*—Campgrounds were also made on old farms or near the remnants of old homesteads where rock walls could serve as barriers to gunfire. A house that was standing during the Civil War may well have been used as a field hospital or a command post. If this property was used for any length of time, relics may be found in a wide area surrounding the spot where the old home stood.

Trenches dug during the Civil War can still be found in almost the condition as when they were first used. Scan such trenches thoroughly to find items that were undoubtedly lost by soldiers who took shelter beneath the upper rim of these trenches.

• *Use maps to determine potential search areas.*—Because battlegrounds may not always be accessible for searching, think about surrounding areas that could be productive. Study maps both from that period and modern maps to better understand the local territory. Look for natural crossing points over rivers and creeks which troops would have used long before modern paved roads existed. Where might soldiers have stopped to rest en route to the final battle site? If you were marching through the same terrain, think about the most likely paths to either surprise an enemy or to avoid marshy areas, rough terrain and other obstacles that would impede your hiking ability.

• *Return to productive areas for another search.*—Larger items such as swords, cannon shot or rifle barrels produce a stronger audio signal in a True All-Metal Mode or with a detector that has proportional audio. Lengthy items can be traced audibly by those who have developed such an ear or have an imaging function on their detector. After such large items have been removed from an area, try scanning it again with your sensitivity increased. Smaller bullets, buttons, coins and other items may have been disguised by the bulky items that were lying in the ground near them. Pay attention to the faint signals that may indicate a deeply buried item.

• *The "nastiest" areas can sometimes be the most productive.*— The easiest work is covering the plowed fields and open pastures in relic country. It takes the more diehard type to get after the tough areas, but it can be very productive. Wooded areas can be productive if you are willing to take on the extra challenge of swinging a coil in areas that are, by nature, more prohibitive. In the winter months, forested ground does not freeze as quickly as the soil in open fields thus allowing you a slightly longer hunting season before ground freeze adds an extra element of challenge.

The easy areas will have had the most searching done on them. Get down in the creek bed and scan the water. Also scan the sides of the creek walls along its banks. This is best done in the cooler months when you have less chance of snake encounters.

When you're working a good site, ignore nothing. This might mean scanning into a cactus patch or crawling into a thicket of briars. The thrill of the hunt can carry you into areas that you would

Good finds sometimes await those who make the extra effort to move fallen logs in a hot spot or "hunted out" area because of what you might find under them.

not normally care to venture into. Sometimes great finds can be made if you take the extra effort to move fallen logs and other brush that obstructs your search. Most searchers work around such obstructions without taking the time to move them aside. In a hot spot area, you should leave no ground unsearched.

Your recovery tools are even more important in the forest, where you will often have to chop through tree roots to get at a strong target signal. This is where strong steel tools with sharpened edges will enable you to cut through the roots and undergrowth without destroying your recovery tools. Smaller sniper coils should be carried along to maneuver into the worst of underbrush areas. Larger coils will allow you to cover more ground but might be too large to effectively swing in briars, underbrush and rocky areas.

While searching along Battle Creek to pinpoint a Native American battlefield in East Texas, I followed that creek a long distance through the worst of conditions. At points, the briars were so thick they pulled my hat from my head, snared my searchcoil and ripped at my arms. I always figure, nothing ventured, nothing gained. You don't know what's in there until you crawl in and explore it.

• *Put your own common sense to work.*—Put yourself in the shoes of someone who stood on this same spot hundreds of years before. Look for natural trails or passes through rough terrains. Imagine where a hunter would stalk his prey or make his way toward a water source. Look for elevated areas or natural clearings that would make a good campsite or field hospital area. Study the area and consider where you would go if you were dropped into the same situation. Where would you take cover in a fire fight? Where would you carefully conceal yourself to ambush an approaching enemy? Is there a natural ridge line where someone might fire down upon approaching cavalry scouts?

Sometimes you just have to follow a feeling. If your gut tells you to veer left toward a certain rock or take a turn right and up an embankment, just go with the thought. Sometimes your mind is subconsciously processing something that seems to make sense.

Some of the best relic sites are the ones least accessible to the general public. By taking that path less traveled, your odds can be increased.

Although many of these zigs turn out to be wild goose chases, you may surprise yourself once in a while with a great find.

• *Take advantage of the weather.*—Fishermen will tell you that a falling barometer is a good time to hit the lakes. My granddad had his own 40-acre lake in East Texas that he dammed up in 1959. He kept a barometer on the mantle above his fireplace and glanced at it daily. As a storm front approached and the barometric pressure began to drop, he knew it was time to take a break from chores. "Come on, boy, grab your fishing pole and let's get on the water," he would say. "The bass will be biting this afternoon."

Detectorists know that weather also works for and against their luck. A good rain can improve a detector's performance in terms of a little better depth (due to the increased electrical conductivity).

During extreme drought, the soil becomes very hard as it contracts from the lack of moisture, and detection depth is reduced.

• *Log your finds to assist with future searches.*—It is good practice to keep a relic hunting log book just as scuba divers or sky divers keep a log book of their trips. As a relic hunter, you will find that patterns develop. Jot down the date, place hunted, types of relics or coins recovered, your hunting partners and other vital information concerning each day's hunt. If possible, draw sketches of the areas hunted that day on your journal page.

I carry a little tablet and pens with me in my backpack at all times to make note of hunt locations, conditions, hunting companions and finds. If you've brought along a map or GPS, make notes of find areas and look for patterns. Keep your notes and refer back to them on subsequent visits to the same property.

When you find yourself trying to pick a new place to hunt in the future, try reviewing your log book. Take note of which areas of a field or old camp site were the most productive. You may find patterns emerging that will help you pinpoint the most productive areas of a new piece of property when you are allowed to hunt it. Perhaps one search area netted some nice items but you found that the weeds were tall or that heavy brush made swinging your coil difficult. Perhaps a return visit to this site in the winter months would be lucrative when weeds and brush have died down.

For historic sites, keep specific details on the targets you recover. Include depth of discovery and exact location in case there are future efforts to document the history of this site. There are several brands of software available online for purchase that will help you organize your finds into logical notes that you can search on your computer in future years.

––––––––

### How to Handle Your Recovered Items

There is a natural rush of excitement as you pull a Civil War or early colonial relic from the ground. Such items are often covered

The author examines his finds on a Georgia Civil War site. Small tackle boxes, such as this fly-fishing box lined with cotton balls, are an excellent way to protect your recoveries in the field.

in mud or heavily encrusted with soil. Your natural tendency will be to immediately start wiping off and cleaning the item to see more of its detail. Rubbing the dirt off the relic or old coin is almost as damaging as using sandpaper on it. The abrasiveness of the dirt can quickly ruin the value of a rare coin, button or buckle. The best course of action is to safely pack away your finds to review later with a proper cleaning method.

Small items such as minié balls or buttons should be packed into cotton and closed in a small container such as an old 35mm film canister. Larger items such as buckles should be closed up in heavier Zip-loc bags or other containers with the remaining soil still on the item. Do not try to rub away all of the dirt in your haste to inspect the item. There is plenty of time for this later.

Treasure pouches and aprons are a great place to collect small relics but make sure that they will not rub against other items and trash that you have collected. Your important finds should be zipped or secured in a special area that will prevent them from falling out of your treasure pouch as you continue to bend and dig through the day. Inspect your apron or pouch closely for tears or holes before you suffer the agony of losing a "found" item.

Rare relics, gold coins, jewelry and other valuables that you recover are simply worth the extra minutes to secure them properly. This might mean a trip to the car or removing your backpack to zip them safely into a smaller interior pocket that is housed within a larger compartment.

Your main goal should be to leave the field safely with each of the relics and coins that you have worked so hard to find. Unless something is an obvious junk item such as a pop top, rusty fence nail or other undesirable element, hang onto it for later study. Some unknown items can later prove to be a nice addition to your collection. For example, Robert Jordan dug a dirty button on the 1839 battlefield where Cherokee Chief Bowles made his last stand. Robert carefully tucked it away, although I heard at least one searcher comment that it was a more modern button. We later found that this was a bullet button that was indeed from the period of this battle. Simple lesson: do not discard an item based on the speculation of another searcher unless you are absolutely trusting of their opinion. Many a searcher has sifted through his unknown finds pile later only to have someone else explain what the item is.

Refer to Chapter 23 for a discussion on how to clean and preserve the various types of metal artifacts that you recover. Having spent ample time on metal detector and target recovery basics, we will next examine some of the specific types of relic hunting that appeal to my fellow history hunters.

## RELIC HUNTING TIPS FROM CHARLES GARRETT

Charles Garrett has been searching for relics and caches for more than 60 years and he has manufactured his own brand of metal detectors for more than 45 years. He has written numerous articles and books on treasure hunting tips and techniques. Garrett was recently asked to share a few of his thoughts on becoming a better relic hunter.

*(Left)* Charles Garrett holds a Federal Eagle breastplate while pointing to a U.S. belt plate he found. The "S" shows a bulge where it was damaged by a shot which struck the back side.

- **Don't believe that good relic hunting sites are "hunted out."**

Modern treasure continually replenishes itself as people continue to loose coins, rings, necklaces and personal items of all types. In time, they will become the relics of tomorrow. As far as working an historic site from early America, such as one from the Civil War period, I firmly believe that you can never work out a site.

Why? For starters, many artifacts work deeper into the ground than even a good metal detector can find. Traditional archaeological digs on early sites produce items of all sizes, many from great depths. Metal detectors today are better that what we had in the early days. They will search deeper and they are more sophisticated to handle some of the challenges you can encounter in the field.

I had the opportunity to search some Civil War relic sites in Tennessee years ago. I was there to attend a regional organized treasure hunt. After the event had ended, Dorian Cook and I were invited by a few other detectorists to do some relic hunting in the area. Dorian was a skilled Civil War searcher who had recovered thousands of Civil War relics from at least 14 different states. We had done some detecting together in Louisiana in the past and Dorian and I both jumped at the chance to join this group in Tennessee.

The area we hunted was apparently an old campsite of some Union forces. It had been hunted before but it certainly was not hunted out. Everyone in our group came away with some Minié balls and other nice recoveries. This was where I dug my first buckle, a Federal plate that was in pretty good condition.

While you are relic hunting, your mind's subconscious can speak to you and help you notice things. Train your mind to look for natural indicators of a good place to search. I've often changed direction while scanning for no apparent reason other than gut instinct just because something looked good or appeared to be a natural protection area. I've been rewarded many times with good finds for making such a gut instinct change of direction.

- **Good location research will often lead you to good sites.**

I can't emphasize enough how important it is to conduct the proper research to find good relic hunting sites. More often than not, the most productive sites are the ones that have been the least publicized and therefore least visited by tourists or detectorists. One of

Charles Garrett holds up a gold British military insignia piece he recovered from an old fort site. Before him are some of his favorite Civil War and frontier wars artifacts recovered in past hunts.

my more productive relic hunts was around the remains of an early English fort site used in the late 1700s to defend against French troops. This particular military complex, named Shirley Heights, was located on the island of Antigua in the Caribbean. By 1781, Britain had lost of all her West Indies colonies with the exception of Antigua and Barbados. Sir Thomas Shirley, Governor of the Leeward Islands, much effort into defending these two islands because of their great sugar-producing value.

Three areas of ruins from the old Shirley Heights fort remained when I visited the island years ago. Because this site was not widely known, it had been detected very little if at all. There was also very little tourist trash (cans, pop tops) for me to contend with. I was by myself and I literally worked from dusk to dawn to make the most of my limited time.

This varied collection of military relics was found by Garrett around a 1700s-era British fort site.

By the end of the week I had accumulated some 500 artefacts. These included hand-made lead gaming pieces, coins, musket balls and all sorts of projectiles, uniform buttons and two gold officer's cap emblems, one of them a gleaming beauty. My preferred metal detecting method was in the All-Metal mode with my sensitivity set to detect as deeply as possible.

Some of the most interesting artifacts were those that were handmade out of materials the soldiers had readily available, such as lead. These men did not have much wealth in these days. They just often made things out of lead in the Old World days. Many of these things have little value today to most people but to me they are still very interesting treasures.

[Author's note: John Howland of England reviewed photos of some of the buttons and other ornamental pieces found by Charles Garrett which had company numbers. Among those infantry units he identified were the 49th (Herefordshire) Regiment of Foot, the 54th (West Norfolk) Regiment of Foot, the 67th (Hampshire) Regiment of Foot, the 89th (Princess Victoria's) Regiment of Foot, and the 96th (Queen's Royal Irish Regiment) Regiment of Foot. Records show these units deploying specifically to Antigua or the Caribbean between 1783 and the early 1800s.]

- **Study the local terrain for natural hiding places or fortification areas.**

During one relic hunting excursion in the northwestern U.S., I was accompanied by two of my good hunting buddies, Roy Lagal and Charlie Weaver. We were searching areas where the U.S. Army had battled Native Americans during the late 1800s. As we climbed into the hills with our detectors one day, we came upon a site that had obviously been cleared out. There were also a number of large boulders where people could have easily taken cover during a battle.

We saw this as an area of natural fortification where bullets or arrows would be deflected when troops were under fire from an opponent. We searched this area thoroughly and were rewarded with a large number of bullet cartridges, Native American artifacts and various iron relics that were obviously lost by Army soldiers. This natural defensive area made for productive hunting and we happily split the results of our combined search.

Among the relics found by Garrett at the British fort were what appear to be game pieces which were hand carved from chunks of lead by bored soldiers. The center and far right items on the bottom row are early lead dice. The one on the bottom right appears to have been only partially completed. The other die was completed and carved dots can still be seen to represent the numerals. The inset pictures to right show three other sides of this die (numerals 1, 2 and 6).

I also study local terrain to determine where artifacts would most likely be lost, hidden or naturally deposited by the effects of rain, erosion and time. That is how I started my scanning of that 1700s-era English fort site on my first day. There had once been a moat that surrounded this fortification and an old dirt mound about six feet in height was still present. This, I decided, was the best place to start. Sure enough, I had my first signal atop this hill in little time and it was loud! The target, pinpointed at about eight inches, was a virtually pristine British Monmouthshire 57th Regiment shako plate (cap ornament).

Scan old trees and stumps for battle artifacts. During one of my European excursions, we obtained permission to hunt on private property that backed up to a famous 19th century battleground. Each member of our group found musket balls this day. Noting one particularly large old tree stump, I ran my detector around the rotting old stump. Sure enough, the detector sounded off and I began to hack into the stump. We retrieved a number of smaller lead balls, believed by our group to be pistol shot. In an area of heavy shooting, it is only natural that trees will catch their fair share of flying metal.

- **Exercise care while recovering your treasure targets.** The story of my recovery of a gold officer's cap emblem near the Shirley Heights fort is a prime example. It was on my last day of hunting and dusk was approaching. Near the remnants of an old stone wall, I picked up a good signal and began to dig. The ground was very tough and I had to use a pick to chop through the soil. I was exhausted after more than 12 hours of hunting in the sun with only a sandwich break. In my haste to find the source of this signal before dark, I destroyed my treasure. Upon the last swing of my pick, I saw a glimmer of gold and knew that I had chopped right through it. The gold cap emblem was smashed by my own retrieval pick!

I'll never forget this "haste makes waste" lesson. Since that time, I have always made it a point to use a quality pinpointer to prevent damaging a coin or artefact with my shovel.

- **Equip yourself for the conditions you are likely to encounter.**

I generally favor larger searchcoils because I am always hoping to find buried caches and deeper items. I switch to a smaller coil in areas where I need to maneuver around

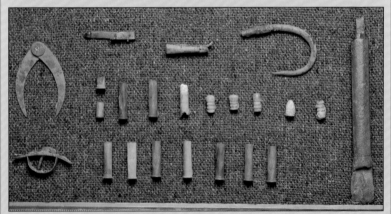

These rifle cartridges and other U.S. Army relics were recovered by Garrett and his companions while hunting an area where Native Americans and clashed with government troops. The rifle barrel section seen at right is believed to have been converted by the Indians into an animal hide scraper.

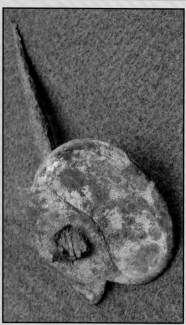

Perhaps the most striking artifact (literally) of Charles Garrett's collection is this breastplate which has been shot through by a wooden, iron-tipped arrow. A piece of the original wood remains where the tip pierced this unlucky soul.

rocks or other obstructions that may be present. Multi-frequency metal detectors may be required in more challenging terrains. When you are hunting in a known mining area, you will have rocks with all types of mineral content to work with that can challenge a VLF detector.

- **Be aware of the dangers of more modern military artifacts.**

Years ago, I made a hunting trip to an area near Koblenz, Germany. Some of our German friends were proud to show us various World War II German Army artefacts they had discovered with their metal detectors. We returned to one of these areas and our team recovered an estimated 2,000 pounds of artefacts. We dug countless bullets and ammunition clips as well as helmets and even hand grenades. Such military artefacts should be treated with great caution. When in doubt about discovered ordnance, notify your local authorities versus attempting to dig it up. European antiquity laws have become stringent regarding exactly how such discoveries must be reported. Always follow your country's law regarding treasure recovery.

- **Don't be in a hurry to get to a "better place" to search.**

Work the area you are standing in thoroughly before rushing to some other spot that might hold treasure. When I am hunting old farms or homesteads, I won't hesitate to search around the remnants of old structures, abandoned wells or even an old corral. My mind wanders to some cowboy breaking in a young horse who was thrown and may have lost an old silver coin in that corral.

Take the time to pursue those signals that are good enough to just make you wonder. Some signals are clearly good targets; others are clearly junk. Then there are those which are inconsistent. Many of these are often worth checking again or even digging just to make sure. I prefer to use an All Metal Mode unless there is simply so much junk present that it is not practical. In rural areas, I always prefer to dig a signal just to see what it is. Sometimes those iron signals are nice relics such as old tools or broken pieces of weapons.

My final piece of advice for relic hunters is one that I've passed along quite frequently over the years. ***Jump on an opportunity right away when it presents itself.*** I can't begin to tell you how many times I've kicked myself over great treasure hunting opportunities that I've let get away from me. My wife Eleanor and I found the stone wall ruins of an old stage coach stop one evening near dusk. We had no time to detect this day, but planned to return again before our trip ended. Well, it didn't happen.

People may offer to let you hunt on their property. If you wait too long to take advantage of an offer, the property might change hands or the landowner might have a change of heart. *The lesson here: don't wait!*

The caretaker of an old castle in Spain we visited offered to let me come back sometime and do some thorough searching. Knowing how things often worked out, I decided to at least scan a few minutes before we had to leave. In the end, we did not make it back there but I did make a great recovery during that short time of searching: an ancient crossbow point. For once, I was proud of myself for seizing the moment!

Charles Garrett searches the British fort site with one of his early *Beach Hunter AT3* model detectors.

# CHAPTER 8

# RELICS FROM EARLY HISTORY

Long before the spring sunshine has finished melting the icy remnants of a harsh winter, underseas explorer Scott Mitchen is donning his dry suit, scuba gear and metal detecting equipment to search for ancient treasures. A native of Wisconsin, Scott has literally made a business out of exploring shipwrecks and recovering treasures. His work has been featured on television programs and in print all around the world.

The treasure that Scott is most excited about lately literally dates back thousands of years and is being recovered in the northern United States. His team began discovering ancient copper artifacts in a river during the summer of 2006.

He has since logged hundreds of hours diving and snorkeling these frigid, and sometimes icy, northern waters in the months that followed. The copper tools include spearheads of all sizes, fish hooks of the earliest design, hide scrapers, and numerous awls, pointed tools used for boring holes through leather or wood.

"What this site does is change the way history has been taught to us," Scott relates. Working with the Garrett *Sea Hunter* and the *Infinium LS* underwater metal detectors, he continues to discover more of the ancient tools. It was not until November 21, 2007, that his relic detecting really hit the jackpot.

The weather in the northern plains was 35° but a dry suit and determination led Scott to an important copper spear. "Upon rotating the artifact, my eyes opened widely and my mouth gaped," he wrote. "This particular copper spear tip still had the wood inside its socket! I realized this was an extremely rare find. We would be able to date this piece if I could keep the wood in place."

Scott contacted Garrett Vice President Vaughan Garrett, who agreed to help with the carbon-dating process. The laboratory results returned with exciting news—the wood from Mitchen's spear was determined to be 3,400 years old!

Scott's company, International Explorations, has since been hard at work on books and a TV series covering his expeditions. In the meantime, he has continued to work this historic site. To date, he has literally turned up hundreds of pieces of this ancient copper. Scott likens the old riverbed to an ancient copper highway upon which every dive he makes is "like a step back in time."

---

### Really Old Relics

Metal detectors have played a role in unearthing much of what we now understand of ancient history. In America, explorers such as Scott Mitchen continue to turn up evidence that people lived in this area long before Christopher Columbus and other explorers arrived and even thousands of years before the Native Americans.

Spear points and bone tools found near Clovis, New Mexico, date back 13,000 years. Is is believed by many scientists that the earliest North America settlers came from Asia, hiking across a land corridor that once existed between Siberia and Alaska. Archaeologist Dennis Jenkins continues at this time to work in central Oregon caverns recovering artifacts which radiocarbon dating has placed at 14,300 years of age.

Arrowhead hunters find such ancient artifacts in caves, along early water sources or where farmwork has plowed up bits and pieces of early cultures. Native Americans began using bows and arrows about 2,500 years ago but spear points were chipped from stones for many thousands of year prior to that time. The quality of some of the early tools is simply amazing, considering what

*(Left)* Treasure hunter Scott Mitchen holds a pair of copper spears from 1500 BC to 3500 BC that he found underwater with his Garrett *Sea Hunter Mark II* metal detector.

*(Below, left)* Scott often dives for ancient artifacts in rivers and lakes long after the winter season sets in.

*(Below, right)* Scott has also recovered coins and relics from more "modern" sites, such as 17th century pirate ships. These coins were photographed on an underwater Caribbean site.

*Images are courtesy of International Explorations, Inc.*

Scott holds some of the ancient copper culture tools he has just recovered from a river.

limited resources early man had to work with. Arrowhead hunters who search on private property for Native American artifacts tend to have the best luck after a hard rain. In plowed fields, the rain will beat down the loose soil enough to expose pottery shards and the tips of stone tools or arrowheads where they are prevalent.

The earliest European artifacts that can be found on North American soil date back more than 500 years, brought over by the early Spanish explorers. Bob Spratley of Florida, now retired, spends his days metal detecting for just such early treasures.

He has found scale armor, Spanish buckles and buttons dating to the 1500s and earlier. Bob hunted Florida waterfront property in 2008 on which legend said that the Spanish once had an outpost. At the end of a full day of fruitless detecting, he finally picked up a "weak and very deep" signal. He eventually dug out four triangular-shaped rusty shields. When he emailed photos of his finds to a Florida archaeological conservationist who specialized in Spanish military artifacts, he was told that these were medieval scales used prior to chain mail armor in the 14th Century and earlier. Bob was told that these were likely the rarest and earliest metal relics ever found in Florida.

The Spanish explorer's site lay on private land that was being sold to a developer, so Bob returned to work the area thoroughly in the two weeks he had before the site was lost. In that time, he detected and dug a sword hangar, one sword strap buckle, iron buckles, six doublet buttons (circa 1350–1565), copper aglets (used by Spaniards on the end of leather garment laces similar to those found on modern shoelaces), several more armor scales, and a Spanish double quarto coin dating from 1474–1516 which was minted during Ferdinand and Isabella's rein.

Bob also sifted the soil from a small stream near the outpost site and collected dozens of rare Venetian glass multi-layered chevron trade beads. Once construction began on this site, Bob was successful in obtaining permission from the building contractor to metal detect the dirt excavated from his previously productive area. Because the soil he had hunted was not adequate for build-

These prehistoric Native American stone tools were found by Vance Gwinn while searching in caves in Texas and Alabama.

This Bronze Age axe head was found at about ten inches depth by British detectorist Ian M. with his *GTI 2500*. It is now on display in the Durham Cathedral. Archaelogists who examined this 6.5" by 2" wide axe head have estimated it to be from about 1500 BC.

These ancient Celtic buckles—made of iron, bronze and copper—were dug by detectorists in the Czech Republic. They date from about 100 BC to the 15th Century. *Courtesy of Traco International.*

More Celtic artifacts detected in the Czech Republic, including ancient iron tools, a sword and other weapons. They date from about 300 BC to the 10th Century. *Courtesy of Traco International.*

ing, it had been removed by heavy equipment and dumped at another location. Bob and his hunting partner Bob Rembisz had to work the excavated soil areas for months before they finally found some piles of soil containing more Spanish artifacts.

They were able to recover more Spanish buckles and buttons dating to the 1500s and earlier before final leveling work of the site ended all future metal detecting. Bob then began the daunting task of researching and identifying all of their Spanish artifacts. He learned that similar scale armor had been found in Aztec, New Mexico, in 1920. By contacting one of the archeologists who had investigated these New Mexico artifacts, Bob found that his Florida recoveries were virtually identical. Each shield was cut from a sheet of metal according to a pattern. Each was drilled for two rivets that attached the shield to a leather or cloth vest.

Bob continues to study the origin of his armor, since the Spanish settlement of Florida did not begin until 1565 under Pedro Menendez de Aviles. One possibility, Bob believes, is that the armor could be from an unknown voyage by the Spanish that was never recorded because the explorers might have become shipwrecked. The true story may take more years to be finally figured out, but at least the artifacts have been saved and preserved for future generations.

Bob enjoys showing his early history to different organizations, including high school history clubs. "I generally give a 50-minute presentation on Florida's Spanish history and allow the students to hold some of the artifacts as I explain them," he said. "My primary goal is to get them interested in history because they are our future. They can help change the current ill will that exists between archeologists and metal detectorists. People who use metal detectors can help show others the good that can be done with finding history."

Bob credits his intense research for his success in finding the earliest Spanish artifacts of Florida. He has been metal detecting for more than 40 years. "My first 20 years of detecting were in Virginia, where I started hunting on school yards, like most folks

Large doublet buttons (ca. 1350–1565) which Bob dug near the scale armor.

Spanish double quarto coins (ca. 1474–1516) which Bob dug near the scale armor.

Sword hangar buckle (upper left) and various other Spanish buckles that Bob Spratley has dug near the Spanish armor.

*All photos courtesy of Bob Spratley.*

*(Above)* This Spanish medieval interlocking chain armor recovered by Bob dates to the 1500s. This scale armor is one of the oldest artifacts of European creation dug in America.

do," he said. A Vietnam veteran, Bob became interested in hunting for Civil War relics around Virginia but he later migrated to Florida to hunt for Spanish treasure. San Augustine, Florida—first settled in September 1565—is the oldest city in the United States settled by European explorers. His searches generally range from South Carolina down to Vero Beach, Florida.

Bob's primary targets for his research and scouting efforts are coastal outposts and beach shipwrecks. The majority of his hunting is done by boat "because rivers and streams were the highways of the early areas which I hunt. I bought my boat in 1964 and have literally worn out trailers and motors during my years of searching with it."

Bob often travels up and down coastal creeks in search of key spots to detect. He keeps a sharp eye out for pottery shards, Indian artifacts and other signs of life in places that appear to have been laid out for settlement. Once he finds such a spot, he scours it to see if it compares well with the historic information he has studied. He has found French and German artifacts on overgrown islands along the intercoastal waterways, sometimes hacking through the brush with a machete to get to the artifacts.

While taking a break to eat his lunch on one such intercoastal island, Bob happened to notice two large trees in close proximity. His gut instinct told him to search between them and following his intuition paid off. Scattered between the two old trees were silver coins dating back to the 1600s. "I can just imagine that some early explorers must have strung a rope between the trees to hang their clothes to dry," he said. "The coins I found must have dropped from their clothing just as they would from modern clothes lines."

His research and scouting along South Carolina streams led him to the site of one of the earliest French outposts, one that had not been recorded in the area history books. These small structures were usually built within earshot of a main fort. "If enemies or pirates were spotted, the outpost would send a runner to the main fort or fire off a signal cannon to warn them," he explained. Bob's proof of the age and existence of this early French

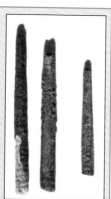

*(Right)* These copper aglets were used on the ends of leather garment laces by the Spanish explorers who landed in Florida.

*(Below)* New construction caused much of the soil on this Spanish site to be excavated. Bob and his companions worked the area where the soil was dumped and found these nine Spanish buttons and 75 buckles.

*All photos courtesy of Bob Spratley.*

*(Above)* A French pike and a 1600s Spanish dagger *(below)* found at a 1565 massacre site in Florida.

*(Below)* Spanish silver coins from the site on a Florida beach where French and Spanish conquistadors clashed in 1565.

outpost can hardly be questioned: among the relics he pulled from the site are, trade beads, Catholic icons from the 1600s, the small signal cannon and a foundation cornerstone rock for the outpost which is dated "1566."

He advises detectorists to take notes on where artifacts are found and in the research which led them there. "I use metal detectors to find the metal objects on these sites," Bob stated. "I also dig and sift the soil for other artifacts to prove what was there. I'm just as interested in what I find as learning how it got there."

Bob has used a wide variety of metal detector brands during his decades of searching but he now prefers operating with a True All-Metal Mode on a Multi-Frequency detector. "A good relic hunter only hunts in the All Metal Mode," he related. "Gold and silver can be attached to iron by way of coquina and you would miss it entirely. So a detector that does not discriminate is worth its weight in gold to the knowledgeable person."

Evidence of this advice is Bob's discovery of a long-lost African slave ship which was wrecked in 1773 near San Augustine with a heavy loss of life. He began digging a heavy concentration of iron relics from the ship—hammers, chisels and other items. The finds soon turned to silver religious medals, which he was able to use to determine that the lost ship was the British slave ship *Dove*.

Another of his significant finds was locating the spot where early Spanish settlers of San Augustine had slaughtered rival French explorers in 1565 who were trying to make their claims on the New World territory. The French had been shipwrecked by a hurricane that destroyed all seven of their ships. Years of re-searching coastal inlets and detecting in coastal sawgrass finally paid off for Bob and his companions—Bull Durrance, Jimmy Koenig, Robann Koenig and Bob Rembisz—in the past two years.

They found that the inlet known today as Matanzas ("Point of Slaughters") was mapped in the early 1600s almost one quarter of a mile from its current location. Bob and company consulted other maps, both modern and by late 1600s cartographers, during their work. "Searching the beach for such artifacts depends on the wind,

More of the coins recovered by Bob and his companions from the 1565 site.
*(Above)* Spanish silver coins.
*(Right)* French gold, silver and copper coins.

*(Above)* A brass French military payroll coin known as a jetton. Dated 1563, it was recovered at the 1565 French massacre site.

*(Right)* Copper jettons from one of the French payroll barrels.

*(Below)* Bob Rembisz, one of Bob Spratley's hunting partners, holds two silver coins found at the massacre site.

A small signal cannon and the dated 1566 corner stone from a French outpost Bob found near Port Royal, SC.

167

tide, beach erosion, hurricanes and northeasters," Bob wrote. The team's persistence resulted in their eventual location of the area of the 1565 slaughter.

This is evidenced by the early artifacts they have dug. These include silver, gold, copper and brass coins that date to 1563, a beautiful white cross carved from white coral, Spanish and French buckles, buttons and other artifacts such as a large French pike and dagger. Their goal remains to find the true mother load treasure, the French payroll for the 1565 fleet. Bob and his friends believe it was buried ashore in the coastal area where the French fleet was destroyed by the hurricane.

He has had some success with this quest. In 2009, a northeaster tore up a remote section of Florida coastline and exposed some of the French explorer's payroll. Bob believes the copper and brass coins were contained in a deeply buried barrel. He plans to continue working the Florida coast in the wake of future violent storms. Their churning force creates a brand-new detecting opportunity for his detecting team.

There is little doubt that Bob Spratley and his companions will continue to turn up more of the earliest artifacts from the first European settlers of America. His is truly a case of an avid metal detectorist unearthing ancient American history before modern progress bulldozes and paves right over it.

Bob Spratley has found some of the oldest artifacts in Florida from the original European explorers and settlers of the 1560s. He is seen here wearing one of two Spanish Sacred Heart pendants he has recovered. This one was valued by an appraiser at $35,000.

*(Below)* Some of Bob's most recent finds in late 2010 with his *Infinium LS* metal detector include a pair of 4-reale cobs from 1619 and a 1550 French coin found near the Florida coast.

# CHAPTER 9

# EUROPEAN ARTIFACTS

Relic hunting in Europe can be quite profitable. Although the laws for collecting such items (commonly referred to as "artifacts" by Europeans) vary widely by country, some of the governments pay detectorists handsomely for their finds in an effort to keep historic treasures from disappearing forever from the public eye.

In 1989, the Middleham Jewel was auctioned at Sotheby's of London for £1.3 million. Surprisingly, this 15th century treasure had not been considered to be a protected "Treasure Trove" artifact and it slipped from the grasp of the English to the highest bidder. The British public was disappointed to find that the unique jewel had been allowed to leave their country. Some ten years later, the Yorkshire Museum in York raised £2.5 million to buy back the exquisite Gothic pendant.

The so-called Middleham Jewel, believed to have been owned by King Richard III, was found by Ted Seaton of England with a Garrett metal detector. He was searching along a well-worn footpath near Middleham Castle in North Yorkshire, England, where King Richard III had been raised. Seaton was preparing to quit searching on a rainy day when he detected a faint signal. He dug down 14 inches and pocketed the item, assuming at first that it was a lady's compact. Seaton was quite shocked when he began cleaning the 69-gram medallion to see its detailed golden surfaces and a 10-carat blue sapphire. This pendant measures 6.6 cm tall by 5.9 cm wide and contains intricate religious engravings on both sides.

Ted Seaton's golden relic is just one of countless stories that have played out in the UK and Europe over the past decades as the metal detecting hobby has continued to grow in popularity. In 2009, British detectorist Nick Davies found a pot in a farmer's field which was filled with more than 10,000 Roman silver and bronze coins which date between 240 AD and 320 AD. The value of his Shrewsbury Hoard has not been announced but Mr. Davies will likely collect a nice check from the British Museum in due time. In April 2010, detectorist Dave Crisp located an enormous hoard of more than 52,000 Roman coins buried in a large jar about a foot deep in southwestern England. The cache weighed about 350 pounds and dates to the rule of Marcus Aurelius Carausius, a Roman officer who seized power in Britain and northern France in the late third century. The value of Crisp's Wiltshire Hoard will likely be assessed between £1 and £3 million.

The most valuable European find to date is the 7th century Anglo-Saxon Staffordshire Hoard, which was discovered by British detectorist Terry Herbert in July 2009. More than 1,800 pieces were unearthed in all, ranging from sword pommels to gold jewelry. Together, the artifacts of the Staffordshire Hoard contain more than five kilograms (eleven pounds) of gold—three times the amount found in 1939 at the Sutton Hoo burial site in Suffolk—and more than five pounds of silver. The value of Herbert's treasure find was valued in November 2009 at £3.285 million, and the profits will be split between the lucky detectorist and the landowner.

Another spectacular find was made recently in Scotland by a novice 35-year-old detectorist named David Booth. Employed as a chief game warden for a wildlife safari park near Stirling, Scotland, David had just purchased a Garrett *ACE 250*. He initially spent a little time practising around his house and garden to begin understanding its capabilities. Five days after purchasing his *ACE*, David drove to a field he had decided would make an interesting spot for his first real treasure hunt.

After parking his car, he turned on his detector in its All-Metal (zero discrimination) Mode. "I was still learning how to use the

David Booth *(above)* was making his first true field search with his new ACE 250 when he made Scotland's most important Iron Age find in more than a century. These five gold "torc" necklaces *(right)* are more than 2,000 years old and will earn David a very significant finder's fee from the National Museum of Scotland.

machine and thought it was best to dig everything for the first ten hours or so," he related. He had advanced only seven paces from his vehicle and had spent less than five minutes swinging his coil when he heard a signal that would forever change his life.

Since his *ACE 250's* Target ID indicated this object to be gold, David began to dig carefully with a garden spade. He made a large circle around the spot he had pinpointed and then switched to a hand trowel as he dug closer to the source of his signal. "It was between six and eight inches under the ground," he related. "As I uncovered the first piece of the hoard, I was stunned. I immediately knew that it looked like something important. However, I did wonder if I could possibly be that lucky on my first trip out."

David had indeed found an incredibly rare hoard of five gold treasure pieces that were grouped tightly together—three intact necklaces and two fragments of another. These four golden neck pieces, referred to as "torcs," were of a Southwest French style annular torc design. They are each of a gold and silver alloy with a touch of copper in their mix. These ribbon torcs, believed to be of Scottish or Irish creation, had been twisted from sheet gold with hinge and catch clasps on their ends.

Excited beyond belief, David took the muddy artifacts home and rinsed them carefully. "It was only when I got home and did some research on the Internet that I was fairly sure they were Iron Age," he noted. David locked the ancient treasures in his gun safe for the night and then took them to his safari park the next morning. He emailed photos of the gold necklaces to the National Museum of Scotland (NMS).

Within hours, NMS representatives had arrived at David's door. The museum's principal Iron Age and Roman curator, Dr. Fraser Hunter, would admit that he nearly fell off his chair when he first saw the photos. Experts have thus far estimated the date of David Booth's hoard to be between 300 and 100 BC. The decorative ends of the looped golden torcs have fascinated Scottish historians. Each terminal piece is made from eight golden wires looped together and decorated with thin threads and chains.

This hammered Roman bronze coin, circa 117–138 AD, has an approximate value of $1,200.

This rare Roman silver coin from about 379 AD has an approximate value of $5,000.

These tiny Greek staters (1/24th of a full stater) were hammered around 6 BC.

This pristine condition Greek hammered coin depicts the face of Alexander III. It is 2 cm (.75") in diameter and was created about 323 BC.

These tiny silver Greek coins, found in Sicily, each weigh about .8 grams and measure only .8 cm (less than .5") in diameter. They were hammered from bronze dies around 500 BC.

This silver Celtic coin, circa 100–50 AD, was found in a farmer's field near Lyon, France.

European detectorists dream of finding vast caches of ancient coins—and many do! This lucky *GTI 2500* searcher found an iron pot filled with early Celtic silver coins.

This craftsmanship suggests that the metalsmith had learned his trade in the Mediterranean and had combined his style with that of the local customs. Ian Ralston, a professor of archaeology at the University of Edinburgh, suggests that early Scottish tribes and other Iron Age people in Europe may have been more interlinked than previous research had suggested. Subsequent analysis by archaeologists at the site of David's find produced the remnants of a wooden roundhouse, suggesting that this jewelry hoard was perhaps a votive offering to higher powers or had been cached beneath an old homestead during a time of war.

Scotland's Treasure Trove Unit, based at the National Museum of Scotland, investigates all such metal detector finds. Since ancient times, the common law of Scotland has been that such treasure trove belongs to the Crown. Such rare jewelry will certainly become a national treasure for the public museums, and David Booth will be compensated with a reward equivalent to the market value of the find. His "Stirlingshire Hoard" could fetch more than £460,000 (about $725,000 U.S.).

---

### Common European Finds

Europe is a unique hunting environment in that you can literally dig coins and artifacts spanning thousands of years and from various empires in the same plowed field. There are modern areas of France, Spain, England, the Netherlands, Germany and many other countries where Celtic, Greek and Roman people had all previously lived thousands of years ago.

Charles Garrett advises those who wish to detect in Europe to "be mindful of the restrictions in each country and province as you travel with your detector." Garrett has found ancient Roman and Greek coins and artifacts from French, German, Scottish, English and Italian cultures during his own European excursions.

Multiple volumes have been published on the ancient Roman coinage which can be found with metal detectors. Other Europe-

*(Upper right)* Ancient Roman fibula brooches with intact clasp pins—such as these found in England—are a treasured European relic recovery.

*(Below, right)* This crossbow fibula measures 9 cm (3.5") in length and would have been worn by a Roman centurion, a high-ranking officer in charge of at least 100 soldiers.

*(Below)* A silver fibula—such as this crossbow fibula broach, circa 1000 BC, found in France—is a rare find.

*(Right)* A variety of buckles, fasteners and harness rings found near an old village outside of Moscow by detectorist Maxim Burmistrov.

*(Left)* These bronze and copper oval rings were found by French detectorist Regis Najac. Some of the rings were part of armor vests for battle while others were part of harness gear for horses. The yellow arrow points to a bronze Gauloise button (circa 150 BC), the first loop of an ancient belt loop.

an artifact identification books are dedicated specifically to items such as buckles, buttons or military artifacts. I'll touch briefly on some of the exciting potential finds.

- *Brooches and Buttons*

Metal buttons, used as practical fasteners and for decoration, date back to at least the Bronze Age (2100 to 700 BC). The majority of metallic buttons recovered by European detectorists are of more recent origin—generally dating from the 18th to 20th centuries. During the Bronze Age, conical bronze buttons of about 2 cm in diameter were used in contemporary dress. Decorative Celtic pieces made from wrought iron and bronze, with elegant Greek-influence designs, are found that date back to the Iron Age (1200 BC to 400 AD). Such pieces of Celtic influence are found mainly in France, Spain, Belgium, England and Ireland.

Early Celts used a variation of the button known as a bronze "toggle," a fastener of varying shapes used to secure a cloak. Such Celtic toggles have been found in rectangular, square, triangular and butterfly-shaped forms. Early Saxon and Viking people even used bronze hook fasteners for their clothing. By the mid-13th century, a guild of button markers was established in Paris and decorative fasteners made of pewter, brass or bronze were more commonplace. The elite even acquired more pricey fasteners formed from silver or gold. By the 18th century, copper had become one of the primary metals used in casting common buttons.

Bronze brooches, known as *fibulas*, date back to the pre-Roman days in Europe and can be found in all areas of Europe. Fibula is a Latin term to describe a fastener. Many such brooches were lost due to a damaged or broken pin, making the discovery of a fibula brooch with an intact pin particularly special. Roman fibulas, generally between three to eight cm in length, were mainly made of bronze although detectorists can find simple iron brooches and the occasional silver or gold fibula. These early fasteners were cast as a solid piece with a hinged pin that was used to fasten a heavy woolen cloak. Women used brooches to fasten tunics as well as cloaks.

The gold and saphhire Middleham Jewel, found by a Garrett detectorist, is one of the most valuable pieces of European jewelry ever recovered with a metal detector. The front of the pendant *(left)* depicts the Trinity scene while the back shows the Nativity.

*(Above)* This bronze Roman ring, which contains a small hematite stone on top, dates back approximately 2,000 years.

*(Above)* These 2,000-year-old bronze rings, recovered by Belgian detectorist Franco Berlingieri, each bear the owner's personal insignia, which could be used to officiate a document.

The author snapped the photo *(right)* of a 7th century Saxon brooch shortly after it and a skull were discovered during a September 2009 rally near West Hanney in England. The copper alloy brooch contains gold and is studded with garnets and coral. Some have speculated that the value could be assessed at £50,000 or more.

Among the more ornate brooches that can be found in Europe are *plate brooches,* which are often larger disks that contain more intricate designs that could include beads, glass inlay, painted colors or special designs. Others were crafted into the form of turtles, snakes, rabbits and other figurines. By the 3rd century BC, fibulas known as *crossbow brooches*—resembling a highly arched bow with a long catch plate recessed for securing the pin—were in use. Other types of fasteners such as rounded fibula, ring brooches and even Roman-era straight pins are often excavated in Europe.

Buckles of brass, bronze and silver may be found in all types of designs and sizes by European detectorists. They were used equally for securing pants and blouses and as ornamental pieces on shoes, uniforms and even hats. Fasteners are commonly found that date from more modern times on back to the Roman period.

- *Rings and Jewelry*

Rings, necklaces and other ornamental bodywear often indicated a person's wealth. Rings from the Roman era were often made or iron or bronze and may contain expensive precious stones or glass ornaments. Silver was used more and more by the 7th century as the European gold supply dwindled. By the Middle Ages, medieval rings in Northwest Europe were often very plain and were made from bronze, brass or copper. *Signet rings* were used to stamp personal seals into important documents or correspondence.

Rings were used for a wide variety of purposes in ancient Europe. They were not only worn as decorative signs of the owner's wealth but were given for signs of affection, medicinal, religious, political, ceremonial and mourning purposes. Such bands might include memorial inscriptions, verses or special symbols.

- *Military artifacts*

The earliest tools of warfare were swords, daggers, knives, axes and similar weaponry. European detectorists search avidly for uniform pieces and other collectible military items. Uniform buttons, commendations medals, brass buckles, bayonets, ammunition belts and helmets are sought from the conflicts of World War

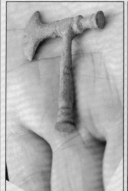

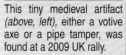

This tiny medieval artifact *(above, left)*, either a votive axe or a pipe tamper, was found at a 2009 UK rally.

These Merovingian belt parts *(above, right)*, which date between 500 to 800 AD, were found in the Pyrenees Mountains by a French detectorist.

*(Right)* A Garand rifle, two German Mausers, a Belgian rifle and two old Belgian revolvers were all found by *GTI 1500* user Danny Reijnders.

*(Above)* World War II artifacts recovered by Charles Garrett during some of his European metal detecting trips. The items seen include a German Army helmet *(left)* a British helmet, bayonet, knife sheath, a magazine of bullets, a first aid kit and a smoke bomb.

II, World War I, the medieval period and from battles that were waged across Europe over thousands of years.

Rifle balls, musket balls and other lead bullets are more modern finds, ranging in date of use from about 1500 through the 1860s. Guns with rifled barrels have fired pointed lead bullets since about 1780, and the sophistication of bullets has progressed since that time. By the 1870s, centerfire cartridges which housed the bullet, gunpowder and the percussion cap were in use. The ammunition and the calibers ranged widely by the 1900s and many different military ammunition artifacts from World War I and World War II can be found across Europe.

———

### Europe as a Detecting Destination

For those of us who live "across the pond," it is possible to contact detectorist clubs in other countries before traveling to Europe. There are also several groups and individuals who organize detecting adventures to search the fields of England. Information on these tours can be found on the Internet or in some of the metal detecting periodicals.

Speaking from experience, I can say that traveling with your metal detector is not a problem if you are visiting Europe. You will obviously need a current passport, and you should learn the antiquity laws of the country or countries where you intend to hunt. Your detector can be disassembled and packed into a larger suitcase with clothing packed around it for protection. I know of others who have flown with their detectors disassembled in their carry-on bag and have not experienced problems with security checkpoint screening.

I do not, however, recommend carrying a hand-held pinpointer in your carry-on bags. My *Pro-Pointer* was the subject of much scrutiny when an x-ray screener spotted it in a Spanish airport. Such items that might be mistaken for a weapon on an x-ray machine are best stowed in your checked baggage!

Lightning does strike twice in some cases. Just a few hundred yards from where the West Hanney Saxon grave and brooch were found during a 2009 UK rally, another discovery was made in September 2010. *(Above)* Areas of archaeological importance are quickly roped off as the digging proceeds on an ancient building site. *(Right)* Rally organizer Peter Welch holds a Roman artifact as a BBC crew films the dig.

European gold. *(Above, left)* A tiny gold Celtic stater found by a Canadian searcher at the 2010 UK rally near West Hanney. *(Above, right)* A Dutch detectorist using an *AT Pro International* detector unearthed this tiny, ancient gold pendant in a plowed field.

*(Right)* Searchers at this 2010 UK rally scour a ridge and furrow stubblefield for coins and artifacts.

Your best bet for visiting a foreign country to detect may be to sign up for an organized rally. The rules of such rallies vary by country with those of England being perhaps the most liberal. Searchers there simply report in at the end of the afternoon with their finds to a tent where local authorities examine and record the discoveries. The majority of the finds are logged and returned within hours to the searchers. Finds deemed to be of great significance are retained by the officials but the finder will eventually be rewarded with a fair market value for the artifact or coin.

During 2009 and 2010, the Weekend Wanderers fall UK rally was held on a large farm near Oxford that once was an area settled and traveled by Romans, Celts and Saxons. In 2009, a Saxon grave and ancient brooch were unearthed. Just hundreds of yards away in an adjacent field, I was digging a musket ball during the 2010 rally when I noticed a commotion across the ridge and furrow field. Shortly after I arrived at the scene, it was roped off as two detectorists dug deep to uncover an ancient building deep beneath the stubblefield. British film crews showed up and began filming the excavation. Two silver staters and a Roman artifact found on this site were significant enough to warrant more interest for the strong, deep signals the pair were picking up with their detectors.

In due time, the full story of just what was unearthed on the New Hanney farm this day will be told. The bottom line on hunting on European soil is that you just never know what valuable relics lie waiting below the surface in any given field.

# CHAPTER 10

# COLONIAL AND FRONTIER RELICS

Relic hunters who live in or visit the area of America's original Thirteen Colonies have the opportunity to find rare artifacts from our nation's founding fathers. The Thirteen Colonies were British settlements along North America's Atlantic coast which declared their independence in the American Revolution and formed the United States of America. This territory ranged from Georgia in the south to what is now Maine (then part of the Province of Massachusetts Bay) to the north. The original Thirteen Colonies were Delaware, Pennsylvania, New Jersey, Georgia, Connecticut, Massachusetts, Maryland, South Carolina, New Hampshire, Virginia, New York, North Carolina and Rhode Island. The Republic of Vermont declared its independence from Great Britain separately from the Thirteen Colonies, and also proclaimed its independence from New Hampshire and New York.

Richard Murphy of Easton, Maryland, truly enjoys finding pieces of colonial American heritage. Although he only purchased his first metal detector, an *ACE 250*, in 2008, he was quick to make nice recoveries. He became so interested in the sport that he soon moved up to a more advanced machine, the *GTI 2500*. During his first year of detecting, he unearthed more than 250 silver coins, more than 1,000 Indian Head pennies, at least 60 colonial-era coins, and relics that range from early musket balls to British buttons and even three Civil War buttons. His rarest Indian Head penny dates to 1877, the second lowest mintage in the series.

*(Left)* Richard Murphy holds his rare 1793 Chain Cent, found on a Maine school yard that was once a late 1700s-era farm.

*(Right)* This image shows the obverse and reverse of a 1793 Flowing Hair Chain Cent that is in better condition. These were the first regular coins struck by the federal government on its own machinery. During the first twelve days of March 1793, a total of 36,103 Chain Cents were struck. Designer Henry Voight engraved the die for this rare coin, which features a Liberty Head with Flowing Hair on the obverse and a linked chain device on the reverse with the words "United States of America." Criticism of the wildly flowing hair and the use of chains in Voight's design caused this design to be quickly abandoned.

Today, only ten or so Chain Cents are known to exist in mint condition, with a dozen in AU (Almost Uncirculated) and perhaps three dozen in XF (Extremely Fine) condition. During the 1793 minting of this coin, four different steel dies were used. Richard's Chain Cent was created from one of the dies in which the word "America" was abbreviated to "AMERI," making it extremely rare. Chain Cents are considered by numismatics and detectorists to be among the rarest and most highly desired of all United States coins.

His favorite coin find to date is a true rarity from 1793 that he found on the grounds of an old school yard in 2010. Richard said, "I was on my way home from work one afternoon and saw a construction crew tearing out a section of playground of a mid-1900s school. I stopped and got permission to detect where they were digging up the grounds. That afternoon I found some Wheat pennies and a couple of silver quarters from the early 1900s."

Richard's interest was peaked by the fact that some of the silver coins he found predated the school's first construction in the 1950s. "That evening, I went home and researched the area," he said. "I found out that the school was built on top of a farm that dated back into the late 1700s." He returned with several buddies and a renewed interest to see what older coins he could find.

"After about thirty minutes of hunting, I got an 'iffy' signal from my Garrett *GTI 2500* at about 8 to 10 inches deep," he wrote.

"I dug down and uncovered the Holy Grail of American coppers, the 1793 Chain Cent. It had a mintage of 36,000 coins and I have read that less than 2,000 of these Chain Cents have survived to this day. To top it off, I found the rarest variety of the Chain Cents, the AMERI S-1 variety."

As Richard was digging for this colonial target, he at first unearthed a small cast iron hook. "It was no bigger than an eraser head, but I knew this couldn't be my target," he related. "I was hunting in Relics Mode and my target reading had been jumping between copper and the 50-cent mark, so I knew this was not the signal I was getting." He quickly used his *Pro-Pointer* to determine that the stronger signal was still two inches below the iron hook.

Among the earliest coins Richard has found are King George coppers, American large cents and British half pennies. "I prefer to find old coins, but some of the relics I run across are simply great," he related. "I have found three Civil War buttons in the past three months, one being an Ohio Militia state seal button. I particularly enjoy digging the early copper coins that are skipped over by some detectorists who simply ignore copper readings."

He advises other coin and relic hunters to investigate those "iffy" signals that often turn out to be good finds. "Another of my favorite found coins was an 1833 Cape Bust half dollar, which had a square nail laying in the ground right on top it. It was another of those 'iffy' signals, but I always dig the 'iffy' ones."

Richard works on an 1,800-acre vineyard, where he has access to search many of its fields. "Around here, there is a lot of nitrogen used in the fields for fertilization which burns the surfaces of the coins we find," he says. "Modern clad coins disintegrate quickly in this soil." Richard thus prefers searching fields without such high nitrogen presence in order to find more well-preserved coins.

The farms and Maryland vineyards where he hunts have been productive, in turning up colonial items. Among these are 1772 Carlos III Spanish reales, many flat buttons, some British buttons with nice backmarks still present and 1700s-era colonial shoe buckles. His area, of course, is rich with history. "I have also hunted

(Above) Some of Richard Murphy's colonial finds include these large cents, flat buttons and buckles, all recovered with either his *ACE 250* or *GTI 2500*.
*(Below, left)* Several of Richard's Civil War button finds.
(Below, right) An intact mid-1700s colonial shoe buckle with good details.

(Left) Two of Richard's early 19th century coin finds: an 1833 Capped Bust silver half dollar and an 1843 large cent known as the "Braided Hair Cent."

near the oldest privately-owned ferry in America that is still in operation. It is located near me in Oxford, Maryland (a town founded in 1694). I have also made some nice finds near an old private military academy that was operated in this area."

Richard feels fortunate that "ground mineralization is not bad here on the eastern shores of Maryland. The western shores of the state and the more mountainous areas can be a little more mineralized. Our local detecting club has traveled to Virginia for Civil War hunts, and there we really encountered heavy mineralization."

One of the challenges he now sees in his area is an agricultural move called "no-till" farming in which modernized equipment plants new crops without having to till up the soil. "In the past, the tractors which disked up the ground literally tilled up a whole new crop of relics and coins that could be found with our detectors," he says. "The fact that our area has gone to no-till farming means that we do not have this luxury any more."

The area is still rich with history and good finds are made by those who take the time to research the better search areas. Richard studies old maps, pores through early colonial history books and make contacts in his area to search farms and historic homesteads. He also scouts fields for evidence of brick and ceramics. "On older sites, we find a lot of light-colored red brick," he shared. "I also keep an eye out for big trees growing in a field or tulips growing out in remote areas as good sites to search."

Richard questions whether he can ever top his recent recovery of the rare 1793 Chain Cent. Still, he admits, "it will be fun trying to do so. You just never know where a great find will pop up."

--------

### Locating and Hunting Frontier Posts and Homes

Early settlers worked farms separately, but banded together as a community. During most of the 19th century, there was also unrest between the settlers and the Native Americans. Frontier posts were built to help protect settlers from Indian attacks as they worked their farms. In Texas, I have visited the site of many old pioneer forts. Some hosted Texas Ranger companies during the Republic years. Others were simply fortified residences that bore the name of the landowner.

The site where such an outpost stood may have very little left. The walls were probably made of logs that have long since deteriorated. What can still be found on the site are bullets, coins, and various metal artifacts. The trouble is locating the site. This is where you must turn to your research. Early maps may give the general area where a fort once stood, but it is often not precisely pinpointed.

Your field work comes into play in pinpointing the area where old homesteads or frontier posts once stood. There are both natural and non-natural indicators you should become familiar with as you scout for potentially productive old sites.

• **Rubble and foundation remains.** Look for piles of rubble that remain from a fallen chimney or squared stones that may have once served as chimney stones or as part of a building's foundation. These large stones were often a foot or two square in size. If you find a group of flat stones together on a hill or in a pasture, you may have located the remains of an old building's stone floor.

Keep a sharp eye for brick, limestone or shale fragments in fields or along old roadways. Limestone and shale were used as building blocks of early dwellings before brick was commonly available. The presence of an abundance of such flat rocks scattered on the ground can be an indicator of former inhabitations. Mixtures of brick and stone on a site can indicate where people have lived for many centuries. It is important to be familiar with the stones native to the area you are searching; those that are not native can be a sure sign of an old building site.

Early bricks can be either bright red, black or a brownish color. Those that contrast most sharply with the present soil are easier to spot than non-native rock remnants. Where you can find patches of stone or broken glass in a plowed field, look for the heaviest concentration of it. Begin a spiral pattern working out from the heaviest concentration of remains until you begin to find artifacts. The farmer's plow will often have scattered the items.

Be prepared to cut brush in a heavy thicket if the land owner will allow you to do so. Heavy brush often grew up from the rich ash minerals after a cabin or frontier fort burned down.

• **Abandoned roadways.** America's road infrastructure was not well developed before the mid-1800s. Instead, they were essentially clearings through the forest over which horses, wagons and even troops made their way from settlement to settlement. As the more well-traveled paths became significant means of moving from place to place, efforts were often made to improve the roadways with stones, crushed coal, corncobs, crushed oyster shells along the seacoast and even wood planks in the northern states. European countries constructed more permanent cobblestone highways by the 1500 to 1800 period.

Any obviously long-abandoned path or roadway discovered in the forest is worthy of exploration. As you hike along an old road-

The author hunts along the remains of an early roadway in a Georgia forest. Federal troops hiked along this road in 1864 en route to a nearby Civil War battle. Although fallen trees and brush almost obscure the old roadway, its path is still visible between the embankments.

## Native American Trade Goods Found With a Metal Detector

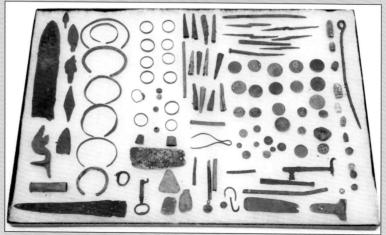

One avid relic hunter from the upper Northwest visited the Garrett factory in 2007 and shared his latest relic case *(above)*. These artifacts were all recovered with an *Infinium LS* detector on private property in the northwestern United States. He says the artifacts date back prior to 1870 and were found on what appears to be an old Native American camp or rendezvous site. These relics—primarily iron and copper—include arrowheads, fish hooks, knives, flat buttons, rings, flintlocks, tweezers, keys and brass bracelets.

"Most of what my hunting partner and I found are called trade goods," he explained. "Early Anglo explorers would trade copper and iron tools, jewelry and knives to acquire what they wanted from the Native Americans." The narrow, cylindrical artifacts seen above are what he calls "tin tinklers." He related, "The Indians rolled up little pieces of copper and hung them from their dresses, so that they made tinkling noises when they danced."

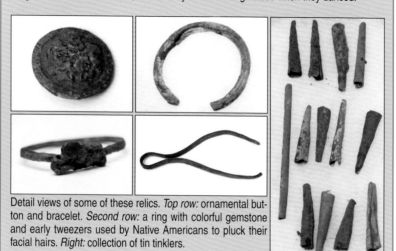

Detail views of some of these relics. *Top row:* ornamental button and bracelet. *Second row:* a ring with colorful gemstone and early tweezers used by Native Americans to pluck their facial hairs. *Right:* collection of tin tinklers.

way, there are many natural and non-natural indicators of areas worthy of scanning.

- **Earth mounds or depressions located on or near the roadway.** Search around unexplained mounds that you find and roll aside any large rocks that seem to be out of place. Scan under and around them, watching for snakes, scorpions and other varmints that might be hiding among the rocks.

- **Areas around creek crossings, such as bridges or bridge remains.** Look for an area that appears to be a natural rest stop for wagons, horses or pedestrians. Most early settlements were also constructed near natural streams or river confluences. Travelers could bathe, draw drinking water or allow their horses and livestock to drink. Sawmills and grain mills used the water power before the age of steam engines.

Deep water areas of streams were also used for recreational swimming. You should also look for steep-banked areas along bends in the river where homes or forts could be built with commanding views of the area—while being safely located above the potential threat of floodwaters.

- **Intersections or junctions of two or more roads.** Such early crossings were often a spot where people met or where stagecoaches or riders paused to rest. Naturally, items of interest would have been lost over many decades at such intersections.

- **Non-native trees that are growing near the roadway or a short distance away in the forest.** Atypical trees near old paths can include pear, apple, chestnut or cherry. Trees that would not grow in an area by chance are sure signs that early settlements stood nearby. In East Texas near where my grandparents lived, they showed me several orchards of non-native species such as peach trees that were planted long ago by the early Indians who first settled that part of the state.

- **Unusual or non-native plants and flowers growing along the roadway or nearby in the forest.** Blossoming and fruit-bearing vegetation such as rose, lilac, lilies, raspberry and forsythia or vegetation such as myrtle or periwinkle can be spotted in dense

## Native American Stone Artifacts Found by Relic Hunter

Native American arrowheads and other artifacts are a cherished find for many metal detectorists. Such items can often be found while digging a metallic target or can be spotted while searching an area where Indians once camped or hunted. Vance Gwinn, for one, enjoys making excursions specifically to hunt for Indian relics.

He has recovered crude, prehistoric stone tools from caves in both Alabama and Texas. During 2009, he spent time working an Indian camp located on the shores of a central Texas lake. With water levels lower during a drought period, Vance was able to dig and sift the soil through screens with good results. Some of his finds on this page reflect the ingenuity that Native Americans employed in designing their tools and weapons.

This artifact case includes various sized arrowheads used for hunting, fishing and fighting. The smallest arrowheads may have been used for hunting birds or fish. Note the round Indian bone button and the long, thin bone needle (left side of case) used for sewing skins and poking holes in leather.

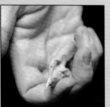

More of Vance's recovered Indian artifacts *(clockwise from upper left).* A corn grinding stone with rocks that could have been used to crush the corn.

*Above center:* stone marbles.

*Above, right:* hand tool for punching holes in leather that is grooved to fit an individual's fingers.

*Left:* another case of recovered arrowheads and tools chipped from various stones.

patches near old homes. Day lilies can be spotted during their bloom with large flowers of white, orange or yellow color. These plants are drought and heat resistant, making them very adaptable to all kinds of conditions as early settlers sought pretty vegetation to dress up their homes.

• **Pathways or driveways that lead up to the roadway.** Some old paths may have become deer trails. These animals find fruit trees or other foliage near an old home site and continue to visit the area to feast on the edible vegetation or fruits in the area. Watch for well-worn animal paths leading in the forest; they can sometimes lead you toward the remnants of an old home.

• **Openings in stone walls that had been constructed along the path or roadway.** In New England, stone walls can still be seen that lead for miles into the forest. I have also explored along such old stone walls in Kentucky in Civil War areas. In the early 1800s, such dividers were often constructed by slave labor to separate one piece of property from another.

The neatly piled stones may also have served as defensive positions during the Civil War or in some frontier skirmish. Such rock walls may have once been topped with wooden rails which have long since rotted away or have been used for firewood. As you scan along one of these walls, picture in your mind how many early farmers or hikers may have stopped to rest or nap in the shade of the rocks. Coins, jewelry and various personal relics that spilled out of their pockets can be found. Others who lived on the property may have found the stoneworks to be an ideal place to hide a coin cache.

• **China or pottery shards along the road.** Relic hunters pay close attention to pieces of pottery found along early paths, just as they use stone and brick to sniff out home sites. Heavy rains and erosion can expose shards of china, bottle glass fragments, brick rubble or clam shells that are indicators of human presence.

Experienced diggers can begin to identify the age of an old home site by the types of pottery shards and other non-metallic remnants that are found. Spotting these scraps while scouting can

Linda W. of Mountain View, Wyoming was "in digger's heaven" when her uncle granted her the okay to search his historic ranch. "This area is noted for the Overland Stage, the Pony Express, the Mormon Trail, the 49ers' original trail and many more people who traveled west. Many of those folks stopped here in our area to stay a day or more, getting ready for the next adventure westward." Linda's Wyoming relics cover a wide range from the 1800s into the early 1900s.

in turn lead a hunter toward a previously undiscovered site.

One notable decorative technique of the 18th and 19th centuries was known as *transferware*, a method based on transferring a pattern printed on tissue paper with wet ink from a copper plate with engraved design to a ceramic surface. The ceramic piece was then heated to fix the pattern and affordable decorative pieces thus became available for citizens of average means. Colors of such pieces vary from black, brown, red, green and blue, with brown being less expensive and blue being the more expensive color of ceramics. Detectorist Sergei from New York explains how to distinguish china shards of the pre-19th century plateware from more modern fragments. On his *www.metaldetectingworld.com*, he states, "Since the china shards of modern plateware often do not have crazing [fine crackling] on glaze, you can still distinguish the 19th century shards from the 20th century ones by the following characteristics:

1) Presence of the same simple and one-colored pattern (similar to Transferware) that appears on most china shards.

2) Dark color of edges where plateware cracked, or where glaze is worn off.

3) Partial appearance of the manufacturer's coat of arms (if you are lucky to come across a central part of the plate's back side)."

• **Nearby meadows or openings in the forest along the path**. Such open patches where trees were obviously cleared long ago may indicate a field for crops or may be worthy of scouting for signs of ancient dwellings.

• **Large "first-growth" trees.** Old homesteads usually had at least one significant sized tree for shade that was left standing when the smaller trees and underbrush was clear to build the house. In many areas, an unusually large old oak can be found in the forest. These are worthy of scanning and for visual scouting to locate old cellar holes or the rock remains of an early foundation. Along with rock walls, these large trees made great natural resting spots or landmarks to hide caches. Many an old coin or early cache has been found around the base of the largest old trees found in the forest.

———

### Interesting Frontier Finds

The "frontier" has a different meaning in different parts of the United States. While the upper northeast part of the country was well settled many hundreds of years ago, other areas of America were still uncivilized frontiers little more than a century ago. Some of these states simply did not exist during the American Revolution, the War of 1812 or the Civil War. That is not to say that such areas are void of great relics.

On the contrary, there are different pieces of American history found in some of these states that are fascinating in their own right. Gold rush boom towns, early explorers, wagon trails and Indian War sites are just a few examples of events and actions that deposited relics that are still waiting to be found. Infantry buttons, cavalry insignia, musket balls, gold coins, cannon balls and other great relic finds have been unearthed from former frontier military posts throughout the West.

• **Arrowhead Hunting.** Some relic hunters using detectors got their interest in the hobby from hunting for Indian arrowheads in earlier years. Such artifacts are occasionally encountered on frontier sites while digging metal targets. Many arrowheads are simply spotted ("bird-dogged") by relic hunters while they are in the field. For example, Keith Cochran has an impressive collection case of arrowheads and Indian artifacts he has encountered during his years of searching in Georgia.

Arrowheads, spear points and Indian pottery pieces from Paulding County, Georgia, found since the 1990s by Keith Cochran while relic hunting. The large piece in the center was an early Indian knife and the axe-shaped black piece below it was used to bore holes through wood.

The practice of collecting arrowheads is prohibited on state and federal lands in Texas because of conservation efforts. It is legal, however, to collect arrowheads on your own property or on private property with the owner's permission. The Antiquities Code of Texas (redefined as the Texas Natural Resource Code of 1977) provides the legal documentation of how to legally hunt. Always consult and obey your own local regulations.

Hunting for relics on land or submerged in any bodies of water controlled by state, counties, river authorities and cities is prohibited. Those found collecting or digging in such areas without a proper permit risk imprisonment or fines.

• **Colonial Coins.** The American Revolution separated the new United States of America from Great Britain. As a sovereign nation, the U.S. would soon begin issuing its own formal currency. The first U.S. minted coins were issued in 1792 and were known as pattern coins. The following year, copper coins went into production, followed in 1794 by silver coins and in 1795 by gold coins.

*(Left)* This rare 1789 George Washington inaugural pin was found by Terry C. of Kingston, Rhode Island, in 2010 with an *ACE 250.* "About five inches down out pops what I thought was a large piece of copper," he admitted. "I carefully wiped off a little dirt to see the GW in the oval." Terry quickly realized that he had found one of the rare first president's inaugural pins which he had seen on auction sites fetching high prices.

*(Right)* These 1787 colonial coins are just two of 13 early coins that Tom F. recovered in Virginia with his Garrett *Grand Master Hunter* detector. Such colonial coins were in circulation before America officially began minting a national coin in 1792.

Prior to the United States officially minting its own national currency, business was conducted using a wide variety of coins, tokens and medals which were struck both inside and outside of America. Collectively, all such coinage created and distributed in America prior to officially produced coins are collectively known as *colonial coins*. The Massachusetts and Maryland colonies were producing silver coins during the 1650s.

The first silver coins struck in America were known as New England Schillings. Struck for three months during 1652, these schillings were quickly replaced by a newly-designed silver coin known as the Massachusetts "Willow Tree" coin. Massachusetts "Pine Tree" and "Oak Tree" silver coins refer to two other tree design variations of silvers that were struck in this colony during 1652. There were also privately minted coins, such as the Lord Baltimore coins struck in 1659 to help stabilize Maryland's economy. Such colonial coins are very rare today and can command exceptionally high prices on the numismatic marketplace if they are in good condition.

Imagine the thrill experienced by East Coast detectorist Matt Carr when he found a six-coin cache of colonial coins from the 1780s. He had returned one Sunday in the fall of 2009 to a homestead where he had permission to hunt and where he had previously dug three large cents. He located six early copper coins stacked together in one target hole: two 1787 Connecticut coppers, a 1788 Machin's Mills copper, a 1788 Vermont copper, a 1787 Hibernia copper and another Hibernia copper with an illegible date.

## COLONIAL AND FRONTIER RELICS GALLERY

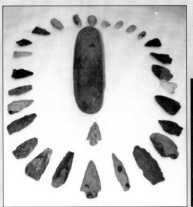

Dave Thatcher shared several of his East Coast finds. *(Left)* Some Indian artifacts of the Shawmut Indian tribe of Warwick, Rhode Island, and *(below)* various clay pipes Dave has found while metal detecting.

*(Left)* These are just a few of the colonial era belt buckles Dave has dug in Rhode Island while metal detecting around old foundation sites.

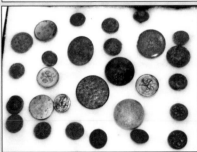

*(Above)* Eagle broach and wise owl pendant Dave found by digging into an old privy.

*(Above and bottom right)* Assorted buttons from the colonial and federal period Dave has found while working old Rhode Island foundations. The gold dress buttons were worn to show social standing and wealth. The shiny black buttons to right were made from a semi-precious stone called Jett. Most of these buttons were found using his old *Beach Hunter AT-4*.

*(Left)* An exploded piece of a 24-pound cannon and an 18-pound cannon ball found at the Hope Furnace & Foundry in Rhode Island, circa 1765–1814.
*(Below)* Obverse of an early Fugio cent.

*Courtesy of David Thatcher.*

Colonial coins found by David Thatcher. Left: a 1787 New Jersey copper. Center: a 1722 French Sou 9-denier coin. Right: a 1787 Fugio cent coin, one of 26 David found.

*(Above)* 19th century sheet music holders found by Dave Thatcher.

*(Above)* An assorted box of buttons Dave has found while detecting on 18th and 19th century foundation sites.

Pennsylvania detecting buddies Tom Ference and Steve Evans have made relic recoveries during the past decade in their area. They do ample hunting on early home sites but also research important sites along an old road built by the British in the 1750s. Trading posts, taverns and military camps popped up along this major road that led west toward Philadelphia and Washington. *The finds photos on this page and the next are courtesy of Tom Ference unless otherwise noted.*

*(Above)* A large, brass sword belt buckle.

*(Left)* A tomahawk, belt ax and shoemaker's hammer.

*(Below)* Colonial era musket balls.

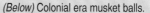

*(Above)* End of a blown-off gun barrel with site attached.
*(Right)* Ramrod holder and gunpowder "charger."
*(Below)* Indian peace medals, ca. 1720–1740. Often made of silver, these medallions were given to North American tribal representatives as tokens of friendship.

*(Above)* Two buttons and a token from the William Henry Harrison presidential campaign of 1840. *Courtesy of Steve Evans.*
*(Below)* A colonial barrel spigot.

*(Above)* A recovered large iron pulley wheel used to move "flatte" rafts loaded with troops and equipment across a river crossing during the French and Indian War in the 1750s.

*(Below)* Grapeshot, iron lock, a stirrup, a fort door latch, an artillery hammer and a claw hammer.

*(Below)* Selection of silver finds: an officer's cuff link, a 1723 reale coin, an Indian trade ring and a butterfly charm.

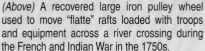

*(Below, left)* Wagon parts and a carriage ring believed to be from a cannon.
*(Below, right)* 1830 Republic of Mexico silver 8 reale author found on fort site in Arkansas.

## Coastal Colonial: Digging the Early American Plantations

Dan Frezza and his father, John Frezza, have been serious relic hunters for many years. In Dan's cases, the passion has been there nearly 20 years. In his father's case, the digging bug bit him even sooner.

Although Dan now lives in Virginia and has spent a considerable amount of time relic hunting in his new home state, he estimates that roughly 75% of his vast relic collection has been recovered in the eastern areas of North Carolina.

"I lived for many years in North Carolina," he said, "and even some people there are unaware of how much early history took place in the current area of the state. We had the original Lost Colony in the late 1500s on Roanoke Island, off the North Carolina coast. Some of the early colonial settlements were located in present North Carolina, which was part of Virginia in the early days."

Dan is quick to point out that the early coastal plantations in his former home state are rich with history. Edward Teach, better known as Blackbeard the pirate, even spent time along the Tarheel State's inlets and coastal plantations.

The Frezza digging team has spent many years hunting early home sites, plantations, skirmish sites, forests and field with great success. John Frezza firmly believes that the most fruitful hunters are those who possess great patience and who have a gift for reading a site to sense where its likely hot spots will be.

In some cases, Dan and his father have found oyster shells or porcelain shards in a wooded area. Other clues have been odd-looking small depressions in the ground or the discovery of small brick piles in a thicket of trees. "When we are hiking over an area to scout it out, I am always on the lookout

*(Above)* Veteran relic hunter John Frezza holds a recovered colonial shoebuckle. *(Right)* His son Dan Frezza in the field.

Some of Dan and John's buttons dug at North Carolina colonial home sites. *(Left)* War of 1812 era 2nd Light Artillery button. *(Second)* A very rare early 1790s diplomatic button. *(Third)* An Intertwined USA button, issued by the Continental Army in the 1770s, with state specific North Carolina initials. *(Right)* An 1820s era Rifleman's button with 16 stars.

for encouraging signs," said Dan. "I have spotted Native American arrow points, bits of pottery, or even clay pipe stems in the field. Where you find this kind of evidence of human existence, put your metal detector to work checking that area carefully."

An abundance of iron targets also helps Dan to pinpoint colonial home sites. "Whether I'm hunting with my dad or a buddy, we check around the pockets of iron in hopes of digging some brass items," he explained. "If we begin hitting bricks as we're digging these targets, then we often dig test holes to get below the plow layer. Sometimes you can detect deep iron that is work digging for. As you dig deeper, stop and swing your searchcoil and listen for better signals."

Sometimes the foundation remains of 1700s homesteads are deeply buried in cultivated fields, making it important to follow

Dan excavates at a colonial home site and pauses occasionally to let his buddy Beau Ouimette scan for coins and relics in the removed soil.

*(Right)* At another site, Dan is digging around the brick footer of a 1720s colonial home's chimney footer. Note the soil layers of his excavation. The top layer is the "plow layer," which has been tilled by farming. The lighter soil layer just below is undisturbed soil, in which bits of old charcoal can still be seen. The reddish layer below that is actually remaining chimney footer brick. Note the bits of dug pottery.

*(Above, left)* Dan digs out brick around the chimney foundation. *(Above, right)* This case holds items recovered from the chimney. Among the coins, flat buttons, pipe stems, bone buttons, and utensils are pottery pieces that Dan has partially reassembled.

the brick trails and deep iron signals with a shovel. Sometimes, Dan and John find remnants of a brick wall, a partial chimney, or even a stone foundation once they dig some test holes. The sandy soil they often dig in coastal areas of North Carolina makes such deep excavation fairly easy digging.

"The beauty of detecting and digging these old colonial sites is in the wide range of artifacts that often come out of the same area," Dan said. "It is said that in this early dual society, people were a little bit religious and a little bit man, meaning military. Some of these old farm homes can contain buttons and other military items from several different generations of rural veterans. So, you may find Revolutionary War, War of 1812, local militia and even Civil War relics on the same site."

Equally exciting and equally wide ranging in dates and types are the coins that can be found on plantation land dating back to colonial times. British, French and Spanish coins are not uncommon finds, as well as the earliest American copper coins that eventually came into circulation.

*(Left)* An early kepi button found by Dan, this is an 1820s general service infantry button.

*(Right)* A 1-pc. silver washed 1830s general service militia button.

*(Above)* This unique, die-cut Eagle plate contains a back side tongue and is thought to be from the War of 1812 era. At left is a Hillsborough Military Academy 1-pc. button. Although hard to see, the letters "HMA" are at the top, along with "NC" at the bottom. At center is an early North Carolina sunburst button. At right is another type of Hillsborough Military Academy, which was attended by one person who lived on this land, Ivy Forman. After finding the HMA buttons, Dan found through research that Forman, while in the Confederate Navy, accepted the surrender flag of the USS *Congress* during the Battle of Hampton Roads.

*(Above)* Some of Dan and John's favorite colonial site button finds. Top buttons from left are: a pewter script I button from early 1800s; a Tudor Rose cufflink *[The Tudor Rose design was used as one of George Washington's hallmarks and was adopted by the British Navy]*; a Civil War era eagle button; and a late 1700s Navy button. Second row, moving upwards: a 2nd Regiment of Artillery button; a Continental Army USA button from Revolutionary War period; a Georgia state seal Civil War button in center; a 1-pc. silver-plated Infantry button from the 1840s–1850s; and a very worn 1-pc. eagle button. Lower four buttons, from left: a British Navy Rev War button; an Intertwined USA North Carolina Continental Army button; a War of 1812 artillery button; and, above it, another well worn eagle Artillery button.

*(Right)* Various items found by Dan while scouting a field for a colonial home site. Seen in this pile are Indian arrow points, British-issued Tudor Rose cuff links, clay pipe stems, a two-holed button made from a seashell, pieces of Indian pottery, and a colonial buckle.

More of Dan's colonial finds. *(Left)* A U.S. infantry button from the 1820s–1830s. *(Center)* A 1779 one-reale from a colonial house site. *(Right)* A 1798 Flowing Hair large cent.

*(Left)* Small 13mm flat button dating to 1820s with the U.S. motto E Pluribus Unim above the eagle emblem.

*(Right)* A Jacksonian era button commemorating George Washington as President, a very rare 13mm flat button of which few have been dug.

Proof that some iron targets are worth digging. *(Above)* A cleaned 6-pound solid shot cannon ball dug by Dan on a Revolutionary War site at a 15-inch depth with his *AT Pro*. From his research, he believes this to be a British artillery piece fired from one of General Banastre Tarleton's cannons.

*(Right)* Dan holds a Hotchkiss artillery shell he has just found with a Garrett *AT Gold* while hunting a Civil War river site. *(Lower)* The partially exploded shell—with some of the original matrix and lead case shot still in it—after being cleaned.

*(Above)* Finds from one colonial plantation made by Dan and John include flat buttons, brass hardware, shoe buckles, a variety of buttons and coins, and bullets.

*(Below)* This wide array of coins came from a North Carolina colonial site. The cut coin to right is a counterfeit piece of eight, a copper coin painted to pass for silver in colonial times. The cut coin in center is an authentic silver piece of eight, which has not deteriorated in the ground. The larger coins to the right are large cents that date as early as 1798. The small silver coin with a hole to the left is a Spanish silver half real. In the center is a U.S. three cent piece. The darker coin in the upper left is a King George copper and the dark coin to its right is an early French coin.

# CHAPTER 11

# TRACES OF TWO REVOLUTIONS

Some experienced relic hunters just have an uncanny knack of being able to see what others can not. It is beyond luck and although certainly an acquired skill, this ability to "see" signs is hard to teach others.

Spencer Barker from Columbia, South Carolina, is almost reluctant to admit that he has a certain focus that some others simply do not reach. "I don't consider myself to be a great detectorist," he says. "I think more than anything else, I just pay attention to some of the small details that fly right past others."

Spencer has been an avid relic hunter for decades but in the last six years, his services have been called upon quite frequently by professional archaeologists to pinpoint significant Revolutionary War and Civil War camps and battle sites. During these recent years, he has spent thousands of hours as a so-called "archaeology technician," whose abilities with a metal detector are trusted to help locate sites where historians wish to unearth some of America's early history.

Various universities and companies have employed him to seek out sites of interest, and their desires more often than not have been fulfilled. One of his steady employers has been the University of South Carolina, for whom he has located several key American Revolution sites they wished to excavate.

"I generally provide detector surveys of their sites," he explains. "Sometimes, it's many acres of land where I go through criss-cross

Spencer Barker quickly collected these pieces of evidence of previous inhabitation while scouting a remote area with a survey team. In the upper left is a prehistoric Indian relic. The blue colored pottery likely dates to the late 1700s or early 1800s. The blue piece of glass was originally black or green in color before being burned in a fire. Also seen are early pieces of brick work and many white clay pieces of early pipes. Note hole in bottom of pipe bowl on the piece in the lower right corner.

patterns to narrow down the better prospective sites. I don't feel that I really have great skills, but some people just don't pay close attention to the signs that are there."

An obvious clue to previous habitation can be the shards of pottery, glass, pipe stems and other remnants visible to the naked eye in plowed fields or forest land. While leading one group, he was once asked why he felt that a certain area held good prospects. "I walked out into that field, and within ten minutes, I returned with pieces of pipes, broken glass, and late 18th century ceramics that I spread out on a manila folder to show them," he said.

Because some properties are tougher to navigate than others, Spencer often turns to detail maps and GPS to locate the desired search area. "When it comes to finding an interesting area to hunt, I like to study troop movements and research early records of a particular area," he says. "I have spent a small fortune on research books. My favorite for the South Carolina area is the Robert Mills Atlas, which was published in 1825. It contains many

*(Right)* This Revolutionary War brass shoe buckle was found by Spencer on a battle site. It is rare for an older buckle like this to still retain much of its inner iron works, which are usually rusting away.

*(Below)* The Spanish reale was still legal tender in the United States until the 1850s. Spencer found this one reale, known as a "bit," on one of his Rev War sites. Cut from the larger full reale, two bits was equal to a quarter.

*(Above, right)* This is a side plate to a British-made Brown Bess musket which was manufactured in 1770.

rare, historical maps by districts which I have used to locate old cabins or plantation homes that were mapped in the early 1820s."

Spencer looks for changes in the natural terrain as he scouts a piece of property. "I look for changes in the vegetation. I often see changes in the terrain or in the elevation that are important to me. The proximity of water is also important for locating camp sites or old home sites. Even my best hunting buddy tells me, 'You see things I don't always see.'

"I'm also looking for things that just didn't happen on their own. Four years ago, I walked into an area where something was changed. It just happened to be in a pine forest that may have been pasture land many decades ago.

"In a pine forest, everything pretty much looks like a pine forest where the timber industry has taken over with their farms. But, the vegetation in these pine forests can have drastic changes that can be spotted. In many of these areas, it often appears to me that something happened here at one time. Then, I'll turn on my metal detector and see if I can begin picking up objects. The archaeolgists have recovered thousands of artifacts off this site, which was located on public land that had already been open to detectorists in the 1970s and 1980s before it became a protected area.

"Rev War and Civil War artifacts can be found on the same land because they sometimes camped on the very same sites. So, you work an area and find relics from the late 1700s on up to the early 20th century on top of each other."

Although Spencer puts in a fair number of hours on paid archaeological projects each year, he still finds plenty of time to enjoy his personal relic quests. "I've done my share of dirty work with the professionals and have helped with the excavations from time to time," he said. "But when I'm on my free time detecting for Civil War or Revolutionary War sites, I stick to detecting."

One of his tips is to search areas slated for repair or construction. Earth moving equipment often relocates soil from the higher elevations and places it in the lower areas to create the desired level of construction. "Most of the coins and artifacts that would have been at the 6 to 12-inch depths are moved in the process," he related. Years back, he happened upon a construction area in downtown Columbia and returned at 4:30 p.m. as the workers were preparing to knock off for the day.

Spencer asked for permission to detect for old coins in the loose soil, knowing that the concrete for new sidewalks would be poured the next day. He was also one of several relic hunters who had the opportunity to search an area being prepared for a new mall in his area. "This location had once been a plantation site with several slave cabins," he wrote. "After earth moving equipment scraped the land during the day, we would search in the afternoon and into the night. We found Civil War artifacts such as U.S. and Confederate uniform buttons, minié balls, artillery projectiles, and assorted gun and sword parts. Other finds included coins dating back to the mid 1800s, flat buttons, marbles and watch fobs, and silver and gold rings."

In one 12-month period, Spencer searched seven construction sites in central South Carolina, some being more productive than

This gallery of early Americana relics found by Spencer Barker date back as far as the Revolutionary War era of the late 1700s. Typical finds from this period are various size round musket balls, one-piece buttons and cast buckles, all found on South Carolina sites.

others. His finds again included minié balls, Civil War buttons, coins and two early buckles—an 1845 militia waist belt plate and an 1881 Mills sportsman's belt plate.

Aside from chasing bulldozers, Spencer and his closest detecting companion have a few favorite search sites in the countryside of South Carolina. They remain quiet about their search areas in respect to the landowners. "It's not that we're being greedy or anything of that sort," he explains. "It's a bond you form with certain property owners, a trust. If you talk too much about where you went to hunt or what you found, it can create problems for the landowner. I've seen cases where landowners have suddenly been badgered by dozens of eager detectorists, or even worse, they found trespassers searching for relics.

"When we get permission to hunt on a large piece of land, I can usually walk it or ride through in a truck to decide on the best areas to start using our detectors. I also make certain to have the landowner's permission. There have been times when a son or relative has stopped us on private property to question what we were doing there. You must be able to convey to them that you have the proper owner's authority to be where you are." Spencer adds that when things appear to be tense with a relative who doubts their permission, they simply pack up and leave in order to keep the peace and be able to return again later once things have been validated by the landowner.

"It's not worth fighting a battle if you end up losing a war," he says. He values his reputation with the people who are kind enough to allow him to search their land. "One landowner really wanted to have a Confederate souvenir," he said. "He followed me while I searched his Georgetown County, South Carolina, farm. Before long, I dug a block "I" infantry button from the South. I had dug some of these before, so I just turned and handed it to him. He couldn't have been any happier.

"My friend and I have certain places we enjoy hunting several times a year," he added. They routinely turn up colonial coins, minié balls, musket balls, buckles and other military artifacts that

Spencer dug this 1746 Spanish one reale (reverse side shown) in the South Carolina Low-country.

He found this 1845 militia waist belt plate on South Carolina construction site and straightened a minor bend.

1881 Mills sportsman's belt plate Spencer dug on another SC construction site.

Spencer found half of a South Carolina palmetto buckle which may date back to the pre-Civil War era.

Front and back side of an early breast plate found Spencer at a Union camp site where an old home once stood. Its age may date to the Revolutionary War. Note that sand has bonded with the patina on the front side. This plain design plate has a three hook fasteners on its reverse.

His first-ever military button find was this CSA button.

## Early South Carolina Servant Tag Found

Spencer's hunting buddy dug this rare slave tag in South Carolina in 2010. It is No. 457 of the issuance year of 1805 from Charleston. Such identification pieces were sequentially numbered for tax purposes and were only valid for one year. New tags were then issued each year in order that proper taxes could be levied on plantation owners.

Such copper tags were issued by the city of Charleston and Charleston Neck from 1800 to 1865 for the fee of $2 per tag. The shapes varied from round to diamond to square cut with four corners. Each tag was holed at the top and was required to be worn by the hired servant during his or her period of servitude. The various occupation for the laborer was stamped on the tag. These included servant, porter (one who carried luggage or supplies, as on the above tag), carpenter, fruiterer (fruit picker), seamstress, cook, fisher and drayman (cart driver).

The number of authentic servant tags that have been found are relatively few, and they have thus become quite collectible. Spencer warns that there are many counterfeit slave tags on the market and that any city of origin other than Charleston should be doubted.

date to the Civil War and Revolutionary War periods. Spencer's finds and several of his articles on hunting techniques have been published over the years in *North/South Trader* and *Western and Eastern Treasures* magazines.

His first passion in relic hunting has always been Civil War sites. Some of the finds he and his hunting pal have made over the years have been noteworthy. His buddy recently dug an 1805 slave tag in the Low-country area of South Carolina. The porter tag was numbered 457 for the year, and its place of issuance was stamped as Charleston.

Spencer's wife Teresa also became interested in detecting and the couple were hooked on relic hunting from the start. During one of their earliest hunts, Teresa found a 1st Regiment of Artillery button. Spencer's atlas handiwork once led him to a 1700s-era home site that produced a remarkable find. He dug a rare South Carolina buckle worn by an early militia leader that may go back to the War of 1812.

"When I dug up this buckle, my buddy just about passed out," he said. "We knew instantly how rare it was." His target was about four inches deep. Upon brushing it off, he immediately spotted the distinctive shape of a South Carolina palmetto tree on its face. It was his first Confederate belt plate, the tongue section of a silver-plated tongue and wreath buckle. The fact that its owner had worn it long before the Civil War gives this artifact even more value. Although he has been offered top dollar for this find, Spencer has declined to part with his most prized relic recovery.

"I learn something from everybody I go out into the field with," he acknowledged. "Working with the University of South Carolina folks has provided a wealth of knowledge for me. It improves my relic hunting because they've helped me become better educated on relics. I'm willing to bet the average relic hunter has tossed away plenty of 'tree iron' trash that is truly a relic."

---

### Revolution in the New World

The United States of America arose from the struggle of the original Thirteen Colonies (Delaware, Pennsylvania, New Jersey, Georgia, Connecticut, Massachusetts, Maryland, South Carolina, New Hampshire, Virginia, New York, North Carolina and Rhode Island) to break free from British control. The leaders of the American Revolution rejected the authority of the Parliament of Great

Britain to govern them overseas without representation and therefore created their own provisional government in 1774. The British responded by sending armed troops to re-impose direct rule but the newly formed states joined together in 1775. The Second Continental Congress issued its formal Declaration of Independence in 1776, which was adopted on July 4.

The ensuing revolution raged in America from 1776 through 1783 before a peace treaty was signed in Paris which gave the United States all land east of the Mississippi River and south of the Great Lakes, with the exception of Florida. More than 200,000 Americans participated in the American War for Independence; some 4,435 Americans perished and another 6,188 were wounded.

Peace did not last in the U.S. as England came calling again with another war early in the 19th century. During the War of 1812, which continued into 1815, more than 286,000 American served. Some 2,260 were killed and another 4,505 were wounded.

Relic hunters who live along the East Coast have more access to older areas of civilization. Even in some of the larger cities, people can find revolutionary war artifacts when clearing or plowing is done. In some areas, newer settlements have formed over the older ones, meaning that artifacts can be found in layers with one generation right on top of another one.

Early American buttons found in South Carolina by Spencer Barker, circa 1810 to 1830.

Robert Silverstein of New York happily displays the Revolutionary War buckle that his good research led him to find near a very old tree.

Join local clubs to gain access to some of the better colonial hunting grounds. Those who find good hunting places often don't talk too much about them, but the more relic hunting connections you establish the more likely you are to be invited along when an interesting piece of property opens up for a small hunting group. Revolutionary War sites have special meaning for searchers who wish to find their own keepsake from the period when a nation of patriots fought for their dreams of independence.

Robert Silverstein of New Windsor, New York, feels "very fortunate to live in a very historical area for the American Revolution. I like to hike into the woods and look for outlines of old stone foundations of early settlers' homes." One of the areas he hunts is where George Washington encamped with thousands of his troops from the fall of 1782 through the spring of 1783.

For one such area, Robert visited a local town hall to investigate records of troop movements and encampments. Then, he and his hunting partner Dan ventured into the woods in search of clues of old camp sites. They found the remnants of old stone walls, faint foundation outlines of old stone buildings and a forested area with numerous trees he estimated to be more than 300 years old.

"I quickly evaluated the area and looked for a small clearing that might have been a central gathering spot outside of the few remnant stone outlines of homes," Robert recalled. "I kept saying in my head, 'If I was a soldier in this makeshift encampment, where would it be most comfortable for me to spend time sitting and talking?' I switched on my *ACE 250* and put it on All Metal. I like to start with All Metal and then when I get a hit switch it to Coins or Relics to try to get a better feel for what my beeps are telling me. Then if I get a strong signal I hit pinpoint."

The first hour of searching turned up nothing of interest, so Robert hiked an eighth of a mile up a little path in search of better prospects. He came upon an old dirt road about eight feet wide with a stone wall flanking either side. "About 100 feet away from the end of the road off to the side was a huge tree, which I would estimate was 400+ years old. I knew that the tree would have been here during the encampment, even if only a much smaller version of itself."

Robert proceeded to search around the giant tree and he soon had a strong signal from between two rocks sticking up out of the ground near its base. "I knew I hit something, but I had to dig out the rocks first," he said. "As I lifted the first big piece of slate out of the ground, I immediately saw a corroded horseshoe. Could this be from an officer's horse? I immediately knew this wasn't manufactured and definitely was the work of a blacksmith. I was happy that my Garrett found something, but being an American Revolutionary War buff, it didn't get my heart pumping.

"I realized that this actually might be a sentry post at the beginning of the road into the encampment. I kept looking at this huge old 400-plus-year-old tree in front of me by the side of the stone pillar, and knew that this probably would have been a great spot for soldiers to lean their brown Bess guns on, or rest up against" Robert then began sweeping in a circle about six feet out from the tree and he soon had another strong signal.

" I found what I have been searching for," he related. "My homework paid off. I found an original American Revolutionary War buckle! Some soldier probably sitting with his back up against the tree 227 years ago, chucked it out."

---

## Relics of the American Revolution: 1776–1783

*(Above, left)* A French 12-pound cannon ball and a French 4-pound cannon ball *(above, center)*, both from Fort Ticonderoga, New York, with the French Fleur-de-Lies cast into them. *(Above, right)* A British 6-pound cannon ball with the Broad arrow cast into it. All three relics were dug by Corky Huey and George Juno of Columbia, SC. *Courtesy of Charlie Harris.*

 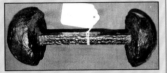

*(Above, left)* Bar shot, from approximately 12-pound cannon ball size halves from Fort Independence and Outwork of Fort Washington. *(Above, right)* Another bar shot of approximately 6-pound cannon ball size halves from Yorktown, Virginia. Both relics dug by Corky Huey and George Juno of Columbia, SC. *Courtesy of Charlie Harris.*

*(Above)* An 8" solid brass side of a Revolutionary War horse bit. All work was done by hand as evidenced by the file marks. *Courtesy of Charlie Harris.*

*(Above)* Steve Evans of Pennsylvania has found many cut Spanish silver coins on early American sites.
*(Left)* Steve's 18th century luggage trunk plate could be easily mistaken for a military cross belt plate.

More finds by Steve Evans. *(Above, left)* A very rare George Washington cuff link button showing his likeness. *(Above, right)* Colonial coppers. These King George I and KG II half-pennies are both English (Brittania) and Irish (Hibernia) coins.

Joe Dinisio from Maryland also shared some of his Revolutionary War era detector finds. These items were found near the site of a Baltimore area iron foundry. Built in the late 1750s, the factory furnished cannon and shot for the revolution.

*(Above, left)* British and Connecticut coppers and large cents. *(Above, right)* Shoe buckles and flat buttons. *(Below)* Three cannon balls Joe recovered near the foundry site.

## Texas Revolution Sites

A second revolution took place on North American soil more than five decades after the American Revolution. The Lone Star State of Texas joined the United States in 1845 but control over this southern territory was heavily contested in the decades prior to Texas joining the Union. The flags of France, Spain and Mexico had flown over Texas before its Anglo citizens finally tired of the tyranny of Mexican President Antonio Lopez de Santa Anna.

On October 2, 1835, a defiant group of 18 settlers rolled out a lone cannon with a flag whose motto was "Come and Take it." Mexican soldiers were engaged and the Texas Revolution was on. In the six months that ensued, Mexican Army troops and the Texas Army battled. Control of the key town of San Antonio passed back and forth until the fall of the Alamo on March 6, 1836.

Six weeks later, a rag-tag force of 930 Texans achieved a stunning victory against numerically superior Mexican Army troops led by General Santa Anna himself. General Sam Houston led Texas cavalrymen, artillerymen and infantrymen silently across a coastal plain near the San Jacinto River. They caught Santa Anna's troops taking a siesta and threw them into a complete panic with only 18 minutes of close fighting. Two more hours of combat raged before order could be restored. The battle became a one-side massacre as vengeful Texans slaughtered Mexican soldiers by the hundreds as payback for the hundreds of Texans who had perished at the Alamo and who had been mass executed at Goliad.

The capture of General Santa Anna following the Battle of San Jacinto secured Texian independence for Sam Houston's troops. Today, the battleground is a protected state park from whose plains rises a marble obelisk that stands taller than the Washington Monument. Yes, things are always bigger in Texas, as they say.

Relic hunters cherish any artifacts that can be recovered from the Texas Revolution. Why? This is the only state of the Union which was a sovereign country for a decade, a country with its own army, navy and a fabled frontier force of mounted lawmen known as the Texas Rangers. Republic of Texas buttons and other militia accoutrements are quite rare and thus valuable to collectors. The key battle areas such as the Alamo, San Jacinto, Goliad and the like are obviously protected state properties which are forbidden detecting grounds. The only legal chance to hunt such sites is by taking part in state approved archaeological expeditions.

There are, however, plenty of Republic-era relics to be found to those who are diligent in their research. Mustering areas, Texas Army camps, Mexican Army campgrounds, skirmish areas, Texas Ranger camps, river crossing points and other sites can be found. Dr. Gregg Dimmick has gone to great lengths to document many such camps in the past decade.

Gregg is deeply involved with the Texas Parks & Wildlife Department on historic Texas Revolution projects such as the battle of San Jacinto. He has also traced the retreat of the Mexican Army after this battle as the remainder of Santa Anna's forces made their way back toward Mexico during the summer of 1836. In his 2004 book *Sea of Mud*, Gregg presents a well-documented study of the camps he and his associates have worked.

A pediatrician from Wharton County, Texas, Dr. Dimmick took up metal detecting his quest to find Mexican Army artifacts from the Texas Revolution. When his first detecting efforts came up short of good finds, he realized that he must do some serious research into archival documents if he was to be successful. His research and continued efforts began to turn up artifacts. He and fellow detectorist-turned-advocational archaeologist Joe Hudgins located one of the Mexican Army's retreat camps and produced a number of artifacts.

As Gregg and his teams began finding more camps, they spurred the interest of serious Texan historians. Their unearthed collections of artifacts soon surpassed the collections held by both the Alamo and San Jacinto. Members of the Houston Archeological Society and the Fort Bend Archeological Society joined to help with some of the excavations.

### Finding Historic Texas Camps

Bobby McKinney of Rosenberg, Texas, has been quite productive in the 33 years he has been relic hunting in the Lone Star State. A certified scuba diver, he first became interested in metal detecting after reading stories about people digging for Spanish treasure on the beaches. His early detecting quest lead him into surf hunting along the Texas Gulf coast and Mexico finding lost jewelry and coins. However, his attention soon turned to searching for lost relics of Texas' past history.

His oldest treasures have been found while hunting old camp sites that date back to the Civil War and to the Texas Revolution. Even though the number of Civil War actions occurring in Texas were few, there were plenty of soldiers stationed about the Gulf Coast who left evidence of their presence during the 1860s. "Many of the big plantation owners called for small groups of Civil War soldiers to camp on their plantations to help guard their crops and homes," Bobby explained.

He and his hunting companions have gained the trust of a number of land owners along the Texas Gulf Coast during the past few decades. "Some of the ranches we hunt are up to 40,000 acres in size," he said. "There are some camps on these ranches we have hunted for 20 years. Even today, we can go work one of the larger camp sites and still find good relics."

"There are a number of indicators of early settlement I look for in the field," he related. "Many cisterns from the 1840s to 1860s are still standing. Find an old cistern and your chances are good of finding military buttons or old coins. I also look for brick scatters in the field or stands of very old oak trees. Another good sign is domestic flowers such as lilies growing up in a pasture. There was obviously something there at one time."

Bobby has found a number of old coins, some around the sites of old taverns that pre-date the Texas Revolution. One such 1826 tavern site produced coins dating to the 1780s, Republic of Texas buttons and Confederate military buttons. He knows of an old Brazoria County home where a cache of Republic-era money wrapped in leather and hidden in a wall with an 1820s period sword was uncovered.

One of his hunting secrets is to visit a productive site after a lightning storm. "We found out by pure chance many years ago that there was a pattern in the effect that lightning has on the ground," Bobby stated. "It seems to nullify the soil's chatter and anything metallic in it just seems to radiate. Things a foot deep can seem loud. I had known that moisture help detector signals penetrate deeper but the effect of lightning's energy was surprising to me. The ground becomes completely quiet around here and the targets become more distinct. You have to go out quickly after a storm, though, because this effect only lasts about a half day."

Bobby's best Civil War find is a Texas state-specific sword belt plate which is considered to be quite rare with only two other

Veteran Texas relic hunter Bobby McKinney *(seen above)* shared these photos of cisterns that date to the mid-1860s and earlier. He has found many relics around these pioneer water sources. "These standing relics of the past point out the presence of an early occupational site and are great areas to metal detect for early artifacts," Bobby shared. The early cistern seen in below left photo marks the homesite of Mirabeau B. Lamar, second President of the Republic of Texas. It is located on the bank of the Brazos River off Front Street and Ransom Road near Richmond, Texas.

known examples to exist. In 1987, he researched the coastal forts that were manned by Civil War troops in his area. The one that interested him the most was a Gulf Coast Confederate fort located at the mouth of Caney Creek in Brazoria County. During 1864, Union artillery gunboats which ran along the coast regularly bombarded the soldiers who manned this little-known fortification.

"After researching where the old Caney Creek fort was located on old maps, I drove down there to scout the area," Bobby said. "During the time of the Civil War, this post had been located about a mile from the beach. In the century that had passed, erosion and modern development had caused the beach to move all the way up to the fort site on the creek. So, I reached the point on the beach where I believed it to be located and just started scouting. I walked a mile to the east of the location and found nothing.

"Then, I hiked about a quarter mile to the west and suddenly I was finding Parrott shells, artillery fragments, canister fragments, fuses and other relics all over the beach." At the time, few people probably had any indication that such a coastal Civil War outpost existed in the area. Bobby spent many hours working the fort site with his metal detectors, digging artillery relics, Confederate buttons and numerous artifacts. His largest shell weighed 120 pounds, contains a fuse dated 1862, and required two feet of digging in the sand to unearth. He wrote a book called *Confederates on the Caney* which describes his successful relic hunting efforts in this 1860s fort site area. Due to heavy erosion, the area of this fort has now subsided into the Gulf of Mexico.

In addition to Civil War relics, Bobby enjoys searching for camp sites that date back to the Texas Revolution. His research, sweat equity and proficiency with metal detectors has proven to be equally beneficial in locating early 1800s relics. The terrain he hunts varies widely from sandy beach areas to plowed plantation fields to rugged, brushy woodland areas. Bobby thus keeps five different metal detectors in his arsenal for the different challenges he encounters.

"I just favor a certain detector for certain conditions," he explains. "In some cases, I prefer a machine that is very sensitive and gets great depth. I have an older 1979 detector that offers me an unlimited number of tones when I'm working a very trashy area. Then I have a Tesoro Silver Sabre which I like for buttons and bullets because it is hot on brass and lead. I also have an old Garrett BFO model which is great for relic hunting that I have used to find cannon balls and bayonets. I generally carry several of my detectors with me because of the different ground conditions. There are times when one machine will pick up things another one will not."

Although Bobby has yet to find the great Spanish treasure along the coast that first engaged his interest in treasure hunting, he has found his share of nice Spanish coins. At the time of the Texas Revolution, the coins that might have been in use between the Mexican and Texas Army included Mexican, Spanish and U.S.-minted coins.

Old Velasco, the site of the signing of the Mexican surrender following San Jacinto, was founded prior to 1831 and is located on the east bank of the Brazos River at its mouth at the Gulf of Mexico. Between the Texas Revolution and the Civil War Velasco and the port of Quintana (located on the other side of the river) served as summer resorts for wealthy plantation families, and the area was heavily fortified by the Confederates during the Civil War.

Bobby has searched around old Port Velasco and turned up quite a few good finds, including Spanish reales and early naval buttons. One was from the Continental Navy, which predates the U.S. Navy's creation in 1785.

Bobby and his friends have metal detected on archaeological projects which have recovered significant Texas Revolution artifacts. His research of Republic of Texas records shows that the Texas Army's purchasing agents acquired vintage U.S. Army surplus which most likely included uniforms of a pre-1830 era. "This would account for the variety of 1820s U.S. buttons found in some Texas Army campsites," he wrote. Bobby also assumes that some Texas volunteers entered service wearing their own regional uniforms, as militia buttons from other states have been excavated from Texas Army sites.

Mexican Army artifacts recovered from pre-Republic-era sites similarly show that their soldier wore both newer Republica Mexicana style uniforms and a mix of older style uniforms with numbered buttons. Mexican soldiers also wore various insignia on their caps, collars, hats and helmets, in addition to such cartridge box insignia as flaming bombs or bugles. Early belt plates were of either oval, rectangular or two-piece plate designs. Texas Army uniforms by 1839 began to include a belt plate which featured a raised star of five points. Such rare Texas plates remained in long use, as evidenced by the fact that some Texas local plates have been found on Civil War sites in other states.

The tireless work of Bobby McKinney and some of his fellow Texas detectorists has helped to paint a vivid portrait of the military accoutrement worn in the early Republic years. Some of the relic photos he shared for the following gallery are a fine tribute to their efforts.

## Relics of the Texas Revolution: 1835–1836

*(Above)* This 7-inch brass howitzer shell was found in a Mexican retreat route in Wharton County. Note that the Mexican artillerymen scratched some marks into the shell. *Courtesy of Bobby McKinney.*

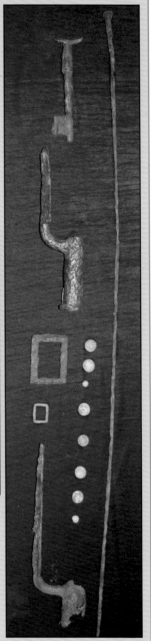

*(Above)* The front and back of a Mexican Army bugle plate from a cartridge box. Companies were distinguished by such emblems. This recovered emblem belonged to a soldier of a Grenadier company, a reserve force company which was part of a Mexican battalion.

*(Right)* These artifacts were found near a Texas Revolution battle area by a relic hunter several years ago. Shown are a musket ramrod, a large iron key, two bayonets (likely Mexican Army), musket and pistol balls, a shot pouch buckle and a larger harness buckle.

Texas Revolution relics found in Mexican Army camp sites. *(Left)* Brass canister found in a on the San Bernard River in Wharton County. *(Center)* Brass heel plate found at Thompson's Ferry in Fort Bend County. *(Right)* Flaming bomb insignia from a "Sea of Mud" encampment. This brass belt plate was worn by a grenadier or artilleryman.

More Mexican Army relics dug in retreat camps in Wharton County. *(Left)* Stamped out copper fan dug on the San Bernard River. *(Center)* BDL No. 6 button from Battalion de Lina Number 6 (Battalion of the Line No. 6). *(Right)* Republics Mexicana staff button found in General Urrea's camp on Turkey Creek.

*(Left)* Mexican breast plate of the Guerrero Battalion (BGo) found at Mexican Camp at Thompson's Ferry near Richmond, Texas.

*(Right)* A Confederate 26-pound cannon shell which was found with others at the Fort Manhasatt magazine site near Sabine Pass. Notice the wood fuse plug.

*(Left)* Mexican cartridge box bugle plate dug in Brazoria County. *(Middle)* Mexican button of the 1st Battalion found in Wharton County camp. *(Right)* Rectangular brass cross-belt plate with clipped corners and a scrolled letter "M". This Mexican breast plate may have belonged to the Moreles Battalion.

*All images courtesy of Bobby McKinney.*

Mexican Army buttons found by Bobby McKinney, from left, are: Republica Mexicana staff button found at retreat camp on San Bernard River in Wharton County; 11th Battalion button found at Fort Velasco; artillery button found in Mexican camp at Thompson's Pass in Fort Bend County; star burst button found at Thompson's Ferry; and a numbered button from the old 6th Battalion (later part of the 1835 Aldama Battalion) found at the same ferry.

More of Bobby's Mexican Army buttons include *(left)* an 11th Battalion button which was dug at Goliad, Texas, and *(right)* flat buttons found at a retreat camp in Wharton County.

Found Republic of Texas buttons include *(left)* TMC (Texas Marine Corps, circa 1839) button found near Crosby, Texas, on a San Jacinto River plantation site; *(center)* a Republic of Texas staff button, circa 1836, from a Fort Bend Co. plantation, and *(right)* a Republic of Texas infantry button found on an early plantation site in Brazoria, Texas.

More early Texas finds *(from left)*: a Republic of Texas Marine Corps hat star (first two images courtesy of John Culberson); a Republic of Texas Army hat star, found in a Republic fort site in north central Texas; Republic of Texas Dragoons insignia (examples have been found in Brazoria Co. and Bueno Vista, Mexico, where ex-Texas Army volunteers served with General Zachary Taylor); Texas Army button circa 1840 (dug in a Mexican War site near Bueno Vista, Mexico); and Texas Navy button circa 1840 found near Port LaVaca.

Early buttons recovered in Texas *(from left)*: a New York Militia button from Civil War era found in Texas Army camp in Brazoria County; Continental Navy button (pre 1785) found in Texas Army camp in Brazoria County; Eagle on cannon naval cuff button found at Port Velasco in Brazoria Co.; Eagle with shield Navy button found in Texas Army camp in Fort Bend Co.; and Eagle on anchor cuff button found at Port Velasco.

*All images courtesy of Bobby McKinney.*

## Texas Army Camp Finds

Finds made at Fort Velasco (present Freeport, Texas). To left is a powder flask with the motif of a dog holding a rabbit in its mouth. Above center is a black English musket flint. To right are a musket trigger guard, spur piece and musket balls.

*(Above)* A brass spur with strap slots found in Brazoria County.
*(Right)* Powder flask found in Galveston County.

*(Above* Musket parts found at site of Post Bernard, the first armory established in 1836 for the Republic of Texas.

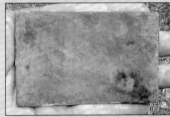

*(Right)* Rectangle belt plate found in a Texas Army guard camp, Brazoria County.

*(Left)* Bobby McKinney points to a dug Mexican Army bayonet.

*(Right)* This clip corner belt plate was found at Goliad, Texas, with the initials JC. It is believed to have belonged to one of the Texans under Colonel James Fannin's command who was slaughtered in the March 1836 Goliad Massacre.

*All images courtesy of Bobby McKinney.*

More early Texas button finds *(from left)*: U.S. coat button from Texas Army camp in Fort Bend County and U.S. Infantry button from Texas Army camp in Brazoria County.

Small oval plate dug in a Mexican Army site.

This clay pipe was eyeballed along the banks of the Brazos River near old Quintana, Texas.

The area near this old plantation cistern in lower Brazoria County produced relics including coins, a spur, flat buttons, a cannon ball and numerous minié balls.

Spanish 8, 4 and 2-escudo coins found at site of Jane Long's tavern in old town Brazoria.

This 1801 Spanish reale was found in the old town of Brazoria.

Spanish 1789 4-reale found at Fort Velasco after 2001 tropical storm Allison.

1834 Mexican 8-reale found during excavations at San Jacinto.

1778 Spanish 1-reale *(left)*, 1781 Spanish 2-reale *(center)*, and 1816 Spanish 1-reale *(right)* found in 1836 Mexican Army camp at Thompson's Ferry.

An early cognac bottle found near a cistern at site of old Velasco.

*All images courtesy of Bobby McKinney.*

## Alamo Artillery Piece Returns for 175th Anniversary

*(Above)* This bronze cannon was returned to the Alamo in September 2010 through the work of Rick Range and Raymond Cruz.

*(Above and inset)* The cannon can be seen in the front yard of the old Alderbrook estate in this early 1900s photo.

Not all revolutionary artifacts on display today were recovered with the use of metal detectors. Some can be admired by museum visitors thanks to the research and sweat equity of dedicated historians. Such is the case of a special cannon which was recently returned to the Alamo in San Antonio nearly 175 years after the historic siege of the Texas Revolution.

This bronze four-pound artillery piece was sent from San Antonio around 1880 to Philadelphia, where new owner Howard B. French kept the tube on display in front of his country estate, Alderbrook. It was not until 1986 that Texas collector J. P. Bryan learned of the Alamo cannon's existence and was able to buy it from a Philadelphia dealer.

The cannon was shipped back to Texas and sold at auction to benefit the Texas State Historical Association. The late John McRae of Ponder, Texas, purchased the cannon and had a carriage constructed to hold it. After the passing of Mr. McRae, Rick was able to track down the family and convince them to put it on display at the Alamo once again.

Gregg Dimmick and Jan Devault of the Friends of the San Jacinto Battleground Association stepped in to take ownership of the artillery piece. Under the direction of

Jim Jobling of the Texas A&M Conservation Research Lab, the cannon was properly conserved for the Friends group before being delivered to the Alamo.

Rick, Raymond Cruz, Gary R. Wiggins, Jim Strouhal and Paul Pyle handled the delivery of the cannon, which is now on display inside the Alamo Church. Further investigation is underway to prove that the cannon in indeed one that was used by the Alamo defenders in 1836. Range adds, "It would be the only surviving bronze or brass barrel cannon. The rest of the Alamo pieces are all iron."

Rick Range has also uncovered other artifacts which were likely used by Alamo defenders. Among them is an iron sword that was found during demolition work on the Long Barracks at the Alamo in the early 1900s. A Mexican worker found the sword in the rafters during the demolition work and removed it. After his death in the 1950s, his son later sold the sword to a collector for a very modest amount—likely oblivious to the potential value of this revolutionary relic.

Daughters of the Republic of Texas member Adina De Zavala, a granddaughter of the Republic's first vice president, was instrumental in saving much of the historic Long Barracks from complete demolition. In 1908, De Zavala went so far as to barricade herself inside the north barrack of the Alamo for three days to protest the destruction. History would prove that she was correct in believing the long barracks to be a significant area of the March 1836 Alamo fighting.

Another interesting item is a cannonball made entirely of lead that was reportedly unearthed in the 1930s by a contractor working on a plumbing project in the Main Plaza (La Plaza de Las Islas) located in front of the San Fernando Cathedral in downtown San Antonio.

The 18-pound artillery ball—which physically weighs 16.125 pounds—bears evidence of numerous hammer strikes. The ball appears to have been poured into a cup-shaped hole in the ground and hammered into a round shape by hand. Rick reports that it is conceivable that Colonel William Travis may have fired it from an 18-pound cannon the Texans had received at the Alamo shortly before the arrival of General Santa Anna's troops.

Due to its caliber size and weight, its unique form of manufacture, and the specific location of its recovery, this unusual lead cannonball may have been the only one of its kind at the Alamo. Rick thus feels it could be the shot that Travis fired toward town from the 18-pounder on February 23, 1836, the day that Santa Anna arrived and ordered the red flag of "no quarter" to be raised on top of the San Fernando Church.

*(Above)* The Alamo cannon as it appeared with patina before recent conservation efforts to preserve it.

*(Above)* Rick Range believes this solid lead cannonball may have been fired by Colonel Travis' Texans at General Santa Anna.

*(Left and below)* A Texan sword found in the rafters of the Alamo's Long Barracks during work in the early 1900s.

# CHAPTER 12

# CIVIL WAR
# RELIC HUNTING

American Civil War relics, hunted for decades by avid detectorists, will likely continue to be among the most highly sought targets. Some may be surprised to read about the various corners of North America in which they are unearthed. Take Minnesota for example.

Dave Foss and his four brothers (Guy, Gary, Scott and Kevin) have all been bitten by the relic hunting bug. Dave's older brother Scott, an *ACE 250* user, has been at it the longest, since the early 1980s. "He's the one that got me interested in metal detecting," Dave said. "I started out by picking up one of my dad's old detectors and upgraded soon."

Dave's first old coin find was a 1915 Barber quarter, "and I got hooked." In rural parts of Minnesota, he and his brothers have recovered many such old coins along rivers and other areas that were popular picnicking spots. His favorite coin is an 1862 two-cent piece that he found while hunting an old home site in a farm. "There were old lilac bushes growing where a home had obviously stood a long time ago," Dave recalled. "As old as this coin was, I found it buried under leaves literally sitting right on top of the ground. Minnesota is not really that old, since it didn't become a state until 1858, so I was thrilled with an 1862 coin."

The Foss brothers have spent many free hours during the past two years researching and hunting a productive Civil War area. During the early spring of 1863, President Lincoln stationed thousands of Federal soldiers in Minnesota to protect the settlers from threats by hostile Indian tribes. Many of these soldiers camped near the Minnesota River until they marched out on campaign months later. Dave and his brothers researched old maps, compared them to modern plat maps and then acquired the permission of a farmer to search his pastures.

One of Dave's favorite Civil War finds was made purely by chance while he was out searching with his young son. "A rain shower came up and we headed back for the car," he related. "My *GTAx 550* was still on as I walked with the coil near the ground. Before we reached the car, I got a loud signal when I wasn't even swinging the coil." Dave and his son stopped long enough to investigate the source and dug a U.S. belt plate in good condition.

His brother Kevin Foss actually made the first interesting find on the Civil War camp-area property—an 1855 large cent that pre-dates Minnesota's statehood. Dave was so excited to begin hunting the farmer's land during their first year on the property that he had to use a hammer and chisel to break through the frozen ground. His determination paid off in the form of his first Civil War era button find.

Dave has learned to dig all targets on this 1860s camp site. "I put my detector in the All Metal mode and dig everything," he says. "We may pull up hundreds of square nails, but I've found an iron skeleton key and other interesting pieces that I would not have otherwise found." Other rare relics have been unearthed while digging such iron signals. Mike Foss recovered a projectile point during one excavation while his brother Scott happened upon a nice arrowhead while pursuing an iron relic signal.

The Foss brothers have also dug numerous 3-ring minié balls, round musket balls and an Eagle breast plate in recent months. Their appreciation for the early history of Minnesota and its part in the Civil War continues to grow with each visit to the plowed fields. Dave, for one, is hopeful that his family is able to continue searching the old camps for many years to come.

## Early American History Dug in Minnesota

These are some of the Civil War relics Dave Foss and his brothers have recently found while hunting a Union campground in Minnesota. Among the minié balls and round shot are a Federal box plate, eagle breast plate and two Native American artifacts unearthed while digging target signals.

*(Left)* This 1915 Barber quarter was Dave's first old coin find, the one that helped him become excited about relic hunting.

*(Lower corner)* An 1855 large cent found by Kevin Foss near the Civil War camp site.

*(Below)* Obverse and reverse of Dave's 1835 two-cent piece, a coin older than his own home state of Minnesota.

Michael Bennett searches through the stubble of a Virginia cornfield. *(Inset)* The author found this Civil War button from a New York company in this same corn field.

---

### Artifacts From "The War Between the States"

The issue of slavery drove many Southern states against the Federal Union in the late 1850s. The election of President Abraham Lincoln in 1860 was the final trigger, as Southerners feared that Lincoln would abolish slavery. South Carolina declared in December 1860 that it would secede from the Union and before Lincoln took office in March 1861, seven states had declared their secession from the Union. They established a Southern government, the Confederate States of America, on February 4, 1861.

The eleven Confederate States were South Carolina, Alabama, Mississippi, Florida, Georgia, Louisiana, Texas, Tennessee, North Carolina, Virginia and Arkansas. Sympathizers from other states such as Kentucky and Missouri joined the Confederate cause during the war. Several slave-holding Native American tribes supported the Confederacy, giving the Indian Territory of present Oklahoma a small but deadly civil war of its own.

More than 3,250,000 Americans served in the military during the Civil War. Of every 1,000 Confederates serving, 150 were wounded and 112 of every 1,000 Federal serving were hit. At least 258,000 Confederate soldiers died during the war with 94,000 perishing in battle. Another 360,222 Union soldiers were killed with 110,070 falling in combat. The scores of other deaths on both sides were attributed to sickness, deaths in prison and various other causes. All told, more than 618,000 Americans died during the Civil War—a casualty rate that exceed the nation's loss in all of its other wars from the Revolution through Vietnam.

Civil War interest stems from the fact that at least nine of my great-great and great-great-great grandfathers fought for the Confederacy. They joined companies from their home states of Texas, Louisiana, Mississippi and Alabama. My great-great grandfather Henry James Yancy Kolb was wounded in the 1862 Battle of Glorieta Pass in New Mexico. Armed with a .69-caliber Enfield rifle, he later fought in Louisiana during the 1864 Battle of Pleasant Hill. Henry Kolb was fighting alongside his two brothers Harmon and James when a minié ball struck and killed Harmon. The same bullet also wounded his brother James.

Civil War relics can be found all across the southern states and in practically every state east of the Mississippi River. They periodically turn up even in far northwestern areas of the U.S. that might surprise some. Not all states, of course, had battles or skirmishes fought on their soils but Civil War era bullets and buckles have been found in just about any area of the country where veterans of this conflict eventually settled.

People began collecting relics almost as soon as the smoke had cleared from the battlefields. During the Civil War, residents near present Washington, D.C., came out to examine the Manassas battlegrounds and to pick up souvenirs left by the first major battle between the Confederates and Federals.

The man credited with being the first to use a metal detector to search for Civil War relics is the late William G. Gavin, who passed away in early 2010. He had taken a course on mine warfare training in 1943 while attending the United States Military Academy at West Point. He learned to use the Signal Corps Radio 625 Metal

Detector, and in 1946 he purchased one of the first commercially available gold detectors, which was manufactured by a company called Goldak, Inc.

Bill Gavin convinced a former West Point classmate (and later Brigadier General), Henry H. Bolz, to join him on November 25, 1946 for a hunt on private property near the Cold Harbor battlefield in Virginia. His first Civil War relic was the rusted liner of a Confederate cartridge box which contained a single Enfield bullet. He continued to hunt Civil War areas before being deployed to Germany for four years. He resumed his Civil War relic hunting in 1952 and during the following year he was officially appointed to perform archeological work on National Park Service properties.

During the years that followed, Bill Gavin had free rein to hunt any national park Civil War battlefield of his choice. Anything the National Parks Service did not want to keep was his. Needless to say, he unearthed artifacts that most could only dream of: rifles, canteens, bullets, 14 plates in a single day on one hunt, artillery shells, buttons and Confederate and Union relics of all description. His 1963 book, *Accoutrement and Plates North & South, 1861–1865*, was the first book entirely devoted to identifying belt buckles and cartridge box plates of the Civil War.

Most of the significant battlefields have long since become state or national parks which are obviously closed to any relic hunting endeavors. Less conspicuous are the countless campgrounds, field hospitals, training camps and skirmish and rendezvous sites of Union and Confederate soldiers. Many of these have long since been forgotten about or were never inscribed on an official map.

Quality research of the contemporary documents from this conflict can lead you to such a site that in many cases may never have been searched with a metal detector. These places are oftentimes located on private farms whose history has been passed down for generations.

Relic hunters have worked some of the prime hunting grounds for many decades in their quest for Civil War relics. Some places that were once considered to be hunted out have become produc-

This Civil War relics case from Brian Pennington displays recoveries from an 1862 mustering site in Newbern, Alabama. It includes a butt rifle plate, a toe piece, a broken knapsack piece, an eagle button, a Louisiana state button, a Howard College button, two thimbles, a rosette and five scabbard tips.

tive again in recent years as metal detector technology increases the detection depth. Hot soils in states like Virginia and Georgia once challenged the best VLF detectors and prevented searchers from looking deep into the soil. Thanks to Multiple Frequency detectors with Double-D coils, some of these areas have proved to be quite productive.

Most of these artifacts have had nearly 150 years to be covered over by the ground and settle. Many such good finds routinely are covered at depths of 12 to 18 inches depending upon the soil content where they were lost. Rocky soils tend to trap such metallic relics at shallower depths while the sandier soils allow the pieces to settle much deeper.

Many of the search techniques previously discussed come into play due to the variety of terrains in which Civil War relics can be found. That said, here are some general tips which can be applied. More specific case studies can also be reviewed in the chapters which cover campsites, farms, homesteads, battlefields and underwater searching.

- *Be prepared to search deep.* Some of the best finds still remain in areas that have been hunted previously. Be prepared to scratch it out by going deep to find those artifacts that have been passed over by less diligent searchers. In sandy and loam soils, the good artifacts will have naturally settled deeper. A larger searchcoil will allow you to cover more ground and to detect deeply. Use headphones to listen for the faint whisper of a good signal.

County soil conservation agents can offer information on the average depth of topsoil ends and where the subsoil begins in your area. As the soil becomes more dense, most relics will stop settling past that point.

- *Be prepared for mineralized soil.* Anyone who has searched the hot soils of Virginia or in certain parts of Georgia will tell you that a standard Single Frequency detector has limited abilities in this mineralized ground. Switch to a Multi-Frequency unit to penetrate this ground and use a DD coil to help cancel out the negative effects of the hot soil. It is also essential that your detector is properly ground balanced to avoid losing detection depth.

- *Plot relic locations for areas of concentration.* In many cases, relic hunters will return to productive areas again and again to continue pounding out the elusive, deeper targets. It is therefore important to record your finds, particularly on larger tracts of land where you have found different areas of concentration.

Modern global positioning system (GPS) handheld receivers have become more affordable with higher quality of accuracy. There is a growing worldwide hobby called geo-caching where GPS users hide small caches of goodies and log the coordinates into Internet sites for others to find. Vacationers can thus pull up geo-caching sites to locate precise areas in almost any spot in the world enabling them to hunt for the hidden caches.

Relic hunters who utilize GPS consider it less of a hobbyist's game and more of a secret weapon for returning to good sites. Older GPS units, produced prior to 2000, had accuracy to about 300 feet of a precise spot. More recent differential GPS (DGPS) units employ the Wide Area Augmentation System (WAAS), which utilizes two additional satellites that broadcast environmental corrections from a number of fixed ground stations in the United States. This technology effectively provides locations accurately within 10 feet.

Relic hunters can thus return to a productive area in rural areas and immediately place themselves within about 10 feet of their earlier locations. A find journal with additional notes can help put you precisely on a spot by noting distances from fixed objects (rock formations, a distinctive large tree or a structure). There are a number of helpful Internet sites that recommend various GPS models for relic hunters and offer techniques on the use of such instruments for metal detecting. An Internet search for "gps mapping + metal detecting" will point you toward various sites that offer tips on the use of GPS technology and relic hunting.

Successful fishermen have used satellite positioning to navigate their boats to known fishing sites on the open water for many years. The relic hunter, properly armed with terrain maps and good research, adds yet another level of sophistication to his or her hunting by utilizing GPS receivers to return precisely to good spots in distant fields and forests. *Interpreting History from Relics Found in Rural Civil War Campsites* by Poche Associates contains an excellent section on GPS use for creating waypoints, logging coordinates of Civil War relics and in comprehending the clusters of logged relic data.

• *Utilize artifact reference books to understand exactly what you have found.* There are many good published sources and Internet sites for identifying Civil War artifacts. Chapter 19 offers a sample list of good book titles to use for identifying buckles and buttons. In addition to those titles, here are just a few Civil War reference books that have been recommended by veteran Civil War relic hunters. Note that some of these are out-of-print titles which may be difficult to locate.

Campbell, J. Duncan and Michael J. O'Donnell. *American Military Headgear*. Alexandria, VA: O'Donnell Publications, 2004.

Coggins, Jack. *Arms and Equipment of the Civil War*. Wilmington, NC: Broadfoot Publishing Company, 1990.

Crouch, Howard R. *Civil War Artifacts: A Guide for the Historian*. Fairfax, VA: SCS Publications, 1995.

———. *Historic American Spurs. An Identification and Price Guide*. Oakpark, VA: SCS Publications, 1998.

———. *Horse Equipment of the Civil War Era*. Oakpark, VA: SCS Publications, 2003.

Dammann, Dr. Gordon. *Pictorial Encyclopedia of Civil War Medical Instruments and Equipment. Volume I*. Missoula, Mont.: Pictorial Histories Publishing Co.

Dickey, Thomas S. and Peter C. George. *Field Artillery Projectiles*. Atlanta: Arsenal Publishing Co., 1980.

Harris, Charles S. *Civil War Relics of the Western Campaigns, 1861–1865*. Mechanicsville, VA: Rapidan Press, 1987.

Jones, Charles H. *Artillery Fuses of the Civil War*. Alexandria, VA: O'Donnell Publications, 2001.

Melton, Jack W. Jr. and Lawrence E. Paul. *Introduction to Field Artillery Ordnance, 1861–1865*. Kennesaw, GA: Kennesaw Mountain Press, 1994.

O'Donnell, Mike. *U.S. Army & Militia Canteens, 1775–1910*. Alexandria, VA: O'Donnell Publications, 2008.

Phillips, Stanley S. *Excavated Artifacts from Battlefields and Campsites of the Civil War, 1861–1865*. Lanham, MD, 1974.

Phillips, Stanley S. *Excavated Artifacts from Battlefields and Campsites of the Civil War, 1861–1865. Supplement 1*. Lanham, MD, 1980.

Sylvia, Stephen W. and Michael J. O'Donnell. *Illustrated History of American Civil War Relics*. Orange, VA: North South Trader's Civil War, 1978.

---

## Hunting With Fort Donelson's Relic Couple

John and Nikki Walsh fell in love with Civil War history and, along with this shared passion, each other as well. They met in 2002 while participating in Civil War reenactments. "Nikki was quite a trooper," says John. "I have to admit I was impressed with this girl who hauled her own gear, prepared her own period food and slept on the ground the same as the rest of us."

In addition to taking part in reenactments, John had been relic hunting since he was a teenager. "My mom bought me my first metal detector and I started as a coinshooter," he said. "I grew up in southern Illinois, where my first historic sites to hunt were those from the French-Indian wars. In time, I came to understand history and got more interested in relic hunting."

Nikki grew up in Marion, Illinois, only about an hour away from John's hometown. Although they graduated high school the same year in the same area, they did not meet until their shared love for Civil War history brought them together in Tennessee in 2001. They were married in 2004 and the couple are now raising two sons in Dover, Tennessee, where their shared interest in history is part of their daily lives. Although John works as a respiratory therapist, he and Nikki also run Fort Donelson Relics, a Civil War collector's shop located near the national battlefield.

Nikki joined John for a relic hunt near the Vicksburg battlefield and her first efforts were quickly rewarded. "I dug a .69-caliber fat boy 3-ring drop and I was hooked," she related. "My favorite find was here at Fort Donelson and it was a .69-caliber Dimmick minié ball. We've researched this battle thoroughly and have found that only two soldiers fired this particular gun at Fort Donelson. They were from the 66th Illinois Sharpshooters and they used the Dimmick rifle, which was made in St. Louis. That .69-caliber Dimmick is the only one I'm aware of that's been dug around here." Although Nikki's Dimmick is a fired bullet, dropped versions of this bullet have been known to fetch $800 from collectors.

The Walsh couple has collected countless bullets, buckles, buttons, shells, artillery fragments, camp gear, cannon balls, and other

## Fort Donelson Relic Hunting Couple

*(Above)* John Walsh stands beside some of his cases of dug relics in the couple's store, Fort Donelson Relics. *(Right and below)* Nikki Walsh display some bullets she has dug while field testing a new metal detector near Fort Donelson. They include a round ball and five partial buck and ball loads.

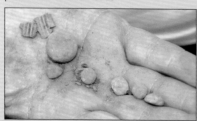

*(Above)* Carved minié balls from one of John's collection cases at the couple's shop.

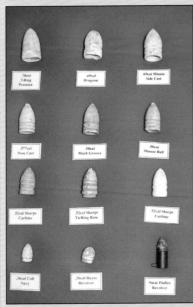
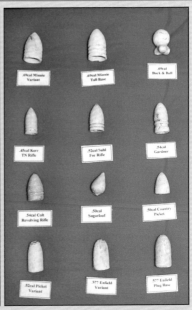

*(Above)* These various size and manufacture minié balls from one of John's cases illustrate the wide variety of bullets he has found in Tennessee.

*(Above and left)* Tree iron trash or treasure? This ring found by Nikki was actually once part of a Civil War sword. Experience in relic identification pays to avoid tossing such an uncertain find.

*(Left)* This .69-caliber Dimmick rifle bullet found by Nikki is from one of only two such rifles known to have been used at Fort Donelson.

*(Above)* Group of round balls, minié balls and buckles dug by Nikki near the main day's battle near Fort Donelson.

Civil War artifacts in their past eight years of hunting together. They continue to work various hot spots on private properties surrounding the Fort Donelson area, as well as detecting trips they periodically take to other historic sites.

John and Nikki have become well known in the relic hunting community in part because of the large seeded relic hunts they have organized in past years. Hundreds of detectorists have descended upon Dover for the Fort Donelson Relic Hunts. Hosting such events is no small task. For one of the most recent hunts, the couple personally planted more than 12,000 relics on private property. Hunters paid an entrance fee to join in the relic hunt and everything they found was theirs to keep.

"We acquired thousands of Civil War period relics," explained Nikki. Many of the items were fired or dropped minié balls but they also planted certain choice items, such as state-specific buttons, artillery shells and even belt plates. It was not surprising even for some of the hunters to dig up period relics that had not been planted prior to the organized hunts.

John's deep interest in Civil War history is obvious when he speaks about the various commanders and companies that were engaged at Fort Donelson. He is currently compiling an exhaustive book on artifacts from this key engagement. It will document the companies, the weapons and the thousands of artifacts that have been unearthed from the 1862–1863 period in his area.

Nikki is no slouch on Civil War history, either. In the field, she is quick to precisely identify most relics and bullets to the caliber or manufacturer as they are dug. During one of her hunts, she found a piece of tree iron—a discarded relic that another hunter likely mistook for a piece of pipe fitting. It was, in fact, the artillery fuse piece from a 3.8-inch Hotchkiss shell. Nikki detected in the vicinity of the tree and soon dug a fragment which was the perfect fit for the iron nose piece to the shell where the fuse had belonged. "You would be surprised at the really nice relics that some hunters toss aside simply because they don't know what they've found," she said.

(Above) Nikki found this 3.8-inch Hotchkiss artillery shell fuse that had been discarded by another hunter and then proceeded to dig the nose piece to the shell—a perfect fit.

(Above, left) Confederate Borman shell and solid shot 6-pound cannonballs dug by Nikki plus two Bormann time fuses (one punched by its gunner with a less than 1-second delay). (Above, right) This Walsh-found case of Dimmick minié balls varies in size from .45 to .69 caliber and includes a bullet mold and two sprues.

(Above) Discarded canister plates found by John Walsh and a 6.6-pound canister round reconstructed by Dennis Nunnery of Camden, TN. (Right) The author and Brian Pennington show their finds and fatigue from mid-day August heat digging at Fort Donelson.

(Left) Various Fort Donelson Civil War finds made by Brian Pennington during our hunts with Nikki Walsh.

(Below) Fort Donelson finds by Steve Moore include a horse tack buckle, a flattened .44-caliber pistol ball, other round balls and two minié balls, including a Shual 2-ringer.

They are often surprised by some of the people who acquire a fascination with relic hunting. They have even taken country star Hank Williams Jr. out detecting several times, including digs near Fort Donelson.

During a summer 2010 visit to Dover, Brian Pennington and I accompanied Nikki for relic hunting on private property where portions of the Fort Donelson battle once raged. The area we hunted was where the Confederates commenced an assault on Union troops during the early morning of February 15, 1862, in their attempt to break free from a stronghold to flee toward the road which led toward Nashville.

The area is heavily forested among rock-infested rolling hills that led toward a Union artillery position. The late August heat and humidity generated exhausting digging conditions but the wide variety of relics still present made it well worth the sweat. Liberal doses of deep woods insect repellent with Permanone did not prevent our later suffering from seed tick bites. I was relieved to not encounter any copperheads in the warm weather, although I did walk face first into numerous spider webs as I kept a wary eye on the ground crossing creeks and twisting through underbrush.

Nikki, Brian and I found minié balls, buck and ball loads and pistol shot scattered throughout the acreage. Two hilltops in particular showed held ample remnants of both fired and dropped shot. Nikki had previously dug a cluster of nice Shual carbine 2-ring miniés near one hill. During this hunt, she proceeded to dig more miniés and five buck and ball load pieces.

---

### Diggin' in Georgia

One in nine Americans fought in the Civil War of the 1860s and an estimated one-quarter of them were wounded or killed. Of all the participating states, Georgia provided the second-highest per capita of soldiers with 112,000 men. In addition to the famous Atlanta campaign led by Union General William Tecumseh Sherman, the state is also home to the second bloodiest battle of the Civil War—Chickamauga. A total of nearly 550 skirmishes and battles occurred within the state and four of the dozens of national historic parks dedicated to the Civil War are in Georgia.

With this kind of history residing within the state, I was naturally thrilled when the opportunity arose during 2010 to do some detecting in Georgia. Brian McKenzie, Bill Kassellman and I set out from Texas to field test some new detectors in the hot red soil around the Dallas, Georgia, area. Located in Paulding County, this area saw large numbers of Confederate and Union troops on four occasions, most notably the 1864 battles of New Hope Church and Pickett's Mill. Both battles—occurring between May 25 and 27—resulted in Confederate victories against Sherman's forces.

Our hunting companions on various days included Paulding County local relic hunter Keith Cochran, area resident Steve Beck, Spencer Barker from South Carolina and Butch and Anita Holcombe. Butch is an avid relic hunter who served as a freelance writer for detecting magazines for years until he and Anita decided to begin publishing their own relic hunting magazine in 2005. Since launching *American Digger Magazine*, the Holcombes have since turned their hobby into a full-time periodical dedicated to sharing the stories of their fellow diggers and collectors of America's heritage.

Anita Holcombe handles the administrative tasks for the magazine, helps take photos of finds at relic shows, and enjoys taking part in the digs when time permits her to do so. Her first relic find, on a construction site in Georgia where a new Lowe's store was being built, was "a fat Yankee three-ring minié ball. I still have it in the curio cabinet." Anita's favorite relic find was a Jeff Davis hat badge recovered during an organized hunt in Virginia.

Butch's love for detecting dates back to the late 1960s, when he and his dad built a Heathkit metal detector from a kit. He says it "worked tolerably well for the times, but the hot soil of Georgia made for limited finds. My first find was a fired Confederate bullet, which I still have in a special case, despite my having found over 10,000 Civil War bullets since then."

His first accoutrement plate (i.e., "buckle") was a Georgia State Seal cartridge box plate, of which only 1,000 were ever made. "It is still my most valuable find, and I can actually narrow it down to a brigade of Georgians—the Republican Blues of Savannah, GA—who were pulled from duty on the coast, and shipped to the battlefields of North Georgia," he related. "They were placed on a hilltop as pickets with no real military experience, facing Sherman's most hardened soldiers. The Georgia boys broke and ran, and my box plate was lost at that time. This area during the war was known as Gilgal Church, in north Georgia."

Butch's favorite relic find over the years was a Federal Identification disc once owned by Ithiel E. Town of the 5th Connecticut

The Georgia diggers hitting the forest this day are *(left to right)*: Steve Moore, Keith Cochran, Anita Holcombe, Butch Holcombe and Bill Kassellman.

*(Below)* Anita's favorite relic find is this Jeff Davis hat badge.

Volunteers. Town was the son of a prominent American architect and civil engineer whose architectural design projects included the early capital buildings of Indiana and North Carolina, the original U.S. Custom House in New York City and the Potomac Aqueduct in Washington, D.C. Butch found Town's identification disc while hunting a hospital site near Dead Angle near Marietta, Georgia. Ithiel Park had been working in the field hospitals when he lost his Federal ID disc.

"Dead Angle was also the most interesting place I ever hunted," Butch related. "The Angle itself is now Cheatham's Hill National Park, which is strictly off limits to metal detecting, but all of my detecting in the area was in the Federal camps and advance routes on private land. I discovered a roadbed leading to the battlefield that the Federals had advanced on, and along it quite a few eagle breastplates were found.

"The soldiers, knowing they were headed into a bad fight, had pulled them off their sling straps and tossed them away, because a shiny brass disc worn over the heart was not a good thing to be wearing...it made a great target! I also found several pocket mirrors there. Records claim that some soldiers discovered that by attaching mirrors to their guns at this battle, they were able to see and shoot at the Confederates remaining under cover. It's a great example of relics supporting the written record."

Butch was an avid arrowhead hunter as a youth but his past four decades have been dedicated primarily to finding Civil War relics. He considers the Dallas–New Hope area very interesting because of how common it is to find unfired bullets. "The reason is that it rained everyday for 40 days while the soldiers were here, meaning that their paper wrapped cartridges got wet, rendering them useless," he explained. "Thus, a lot of bullets got thrown away.

"Another interesting thing is the buttons found in Confederate sites down here. The most common are Federal issue Eagle buttons (confiscated by the Confederates). Next are cast brass 'I' Infantry buttons and finally North Carolina buttons. The North Carolina buttons are the most interesting. When the Confederacy requested troops to help turn the tide against the overwhelming Federal numbers, most states complied. The exception was North Carolina, whose governor refused to give up his state militiamen; instead, opting to send uniforms, which were issued to men from various Southern states in General Joe Johnston's army. Thus, North Carolina buttons may appear anywhere. This is why you can't positively identify who occupied an area strictly by what buttons are found there."

Butch has collected plenty of Civil War military buttons in his years of detecting but one continues to elude him—a Georgia state button. "You would think that from all the buttons I've found in all the time I've hunted in Georgia, that I would have come across one by now," he sighs. His Civil War relic hunting quest remains that elusive Georgia button. As fate would have it, the Georgia button eluded him again during our hunts, although he did make the best button find of the week—a cavalry cuff button in nice shape.

Our luck started a little slow but picked up as the week progressed. Butch's old high school buddy, Steve Beck, first allowed us to hunt on forest land in the vicinity of Pickett's Mill near New

(Left) Butch Holcombe displays a cavalry cuff button (above) which he has just dug while field testing a Garrett AT Pro detector. (Below, right) Spencer Barker, Steve Moore, Bill Kassellman, Steve Beck and Butch Holcombe prepare to tackle the Georgia red dirt on private land near site of Pickett's Mill.

(Above, left) The team's ever-ready photographer, Brian McKenzie, was snapped by Anita Holcombe. (Below, left) Bill with another dug minié ball. (Below, center and right) Another bullet is unearthed in Georgia and Bill holding a freshly dug Enfield round.

Hope. The land was recently logged and new saplings were growing up amidst the brush. Although the red iron ore dirt is fairly hot, we found no problem ground balancing our machines in this soil. The trouble with this area was that kids have obviously used the land for partying as shown by the abundance of beer cans and camp fires. There is also an abundance of modern-day rifle cartridges and shotgun shells, some literally littering the ground in places where target practice has taken place. I dug several modern slugs from pistols and one small piece of lead that appears to pre-date even the Civil War period. Everyone else dug a wide variety of modern bullets. The terrain was rugged, choked with briars and fallen logs and various brush. By late afternoon when the rain set in again, we were already prepared to depart. The rain merely confirmed our decision.

We moved to another area near the Pickett's Mill battlefield the following day, scouting private property in a heavy forest. My old college roommate, Ron Montgomery, lives nearby in Rome, Georgia, so I was happy when he decided to join us that afternoon. Ron and I spent many years in the past deer hunting, fishing and hiking the forest with our guns. He was interested in learning more about relic hunting, so I gave him a crash course on using the new *AT Pro* detector that we were field testing this day.

While the operation of a metal detector was a little foreign to him at first, the challenges of the local terrain—rocky, steep slopes choked with briars and ankle-grabbing vines—were old hat. Just as we had chuckled at each other's misfortunes in the forest in years past, we found humor during our Georgia explorations. Poor Bill was the source of much of our amusement as we watched him take a tumble after losing a battle with "trip vines" that snared his foot. Bill also managed to pull a classic "one-legger," stepping into a leaf-covered varmint hole that caused his right leg to plunge deep into some critter's den.

Entertainment aside, we did happen into more productive grounds this day. I dug a small round ball near a pipeline and then moved up a slope to a thicket where dropped and fired minié balls

(Left) First-time relic hunter Ron Montgomery of Georgia was all smiles when his first dug target proved to be a slightly bent Federal eagle button (above).

More Pickett's Mill area finds. (Above, left) The author found these rounds near the spot where Ron dug his Eagle button. (Center) Three pieces to a Spencer round dug by the author near an old Georgia road bed. (Right) Knapsack hook and minié balls dug by Bill.

became more plentiful. Ron surprised me with his beginner's luck. The first target he pinpointed and proceeded to dig was not trash iron but instead an eagle button. Needless to say, Civil War hunting is suddenly very appealing to him!

The following day, Keith Cochran took our group to several of his previously hunted spots in Paulding County. We hiked into the 200 acres his family owns on which the old Georgia road from Cassville to New Hope can still be seen. It was thrilling to imagine how many Union soldiers had hiked through this forest just two days before the big battle near New Hope Church. The woods are heavy with pine and hardwoods along the dirt road that twists up and over a series of steep ravines. One can only imagine how tiring it was to march through these thickets, climbing steep hills with a full load of gear.

Keith and Bill recovered several minié balls and a round rifle ball in the forest short distances from the old roadway. In places, the original roadway can be seen where it veers off the more modern, improved access way through the forest. Brush and fallen logs litter the mid-19th century road where it has fallen into neglect and yet its steep sides still clearly indicate its original course.

As we were heading back to our trucks in the afternoon, I paused long enough to dig an "iffy" signal near the base of a large pine tree just inches from the road. I dug the base to a Spencer bullet that some Union soldier had dropped a century and a half before. When I caught up to Keith to show it to him, he urged me to go back and work around that tree more diligently. Taking his advice, I swept the full perimeter of the tree and picked up another signal that bounced between good target and something in the range of pop top. I decided to dig out the area and see if there was indeed the remainder of this Spencer round. Sure enough, I dug three more pieces of metal: a twisted pop top and, lying alongside it at the base of the pine, two more pieces to the Spencer round.

We followed Keith to another piece of property which lies closer to the Pickett's Mill battle grounds. Bill was the top finder this day, happily overcoming his poor luck in the forest the previous afternoon. In addition to several three-ringers, he dug a brass knapsack hook and a nice Enfield round that was near the base of a tree. Bill actually dug an old tobacco tin near the tree and, while diligently giving the hole a secondary sweep, found that he still had a good signal beneath the tobacco tin. His secondary efforts were rewarded with the good Enfield bullet.

By week's end, everyone had dug enough period relics to feel satisfied and also hungry for that next opportunity to visit such productive sites of the Civil War.

---

## Civil War Hunting in Perryville

On October 8, 1862, the bloodiest Civil War battle to take place in Kentucky happened in and around the town of Perryville after the Confederate Army's defeat at the battle of Shiloh. Confederate troops controlled all of Kentucky east of the Louisville and Nashville Railroad (roughly along today's I-65) by the fall of 1862. Their forces were met by Federal Army troops under General Don Carlos Buell near Perryville on October 8.

Both sides were desperate for water, as a severe drought raged in the area during this time. Much of the fighting was centered near the Chaplin River and on Doctor's Creek, where a Confederate division caught Union troops fetching water. Although more than 72,000 troops were stationed about the area, the actual battle of Perryville involved some 20,000 Union troops and 16,000 Confederates. Men from 21 states fought in this battle and 90 cannons were fired during the day. By day's end, some 1,422 soldiers had perished and another 5,534 were wounded. Among the more famous men fighting here had been General Philip Sheridan and Lieutenant Arthur MacArthur, father of World War II's General Douglas MacArthur.

The battlefield is now protected and operated as a unit of Kentucky State Parks. Visitors to the park can take interpretive driving and hiking tours of the battlefield. Relic hunters have worked the private farms all around this town for years to unearth artifacts from this battle. The key is locating areas where one or the other armies made their approach, retreat or engaged their enemy outside the area of the main battlefield. As with many Civil War battlefields, there are plenty of productive areas on private land just a stone's throw away.

Dave and Linda Edwards offered to let a couple of us from Garrett field test new detectors on private property near the Perryville battlefield. The couple had already found a few productive areas on the farm. Brian McKenzie joined me for four days in Kentucky with the Edwards family to field test machines in this historic area and to document the process with photos.

## Civil War Hunting in Kentucky

*(Above and right)* Dave Edwards is all grins after finding literally a handful of musket balls and minié balls in this Perryville area field. *(Below)* Half of a Parrott shell found by his wife Linda on "Artillery Hill."

*(Above)* General George Thomas was second in command of the U.S. troops during the battle of Perryville. This 1864 photo shows him during a council of war in a Georgia camp.

We found this to a beautiful part of Kentucky filled with rolling hills and lush, green pastures. It is just south and west of Lexington, one of the country's premier horse farm areas where many past Kentucky Derby horses have been raised. Many of the stables in this area are far more lavish than the average home.

Dave and Linda were gracious hosts who had already gone to the trouble to set up a detecting camp on the Perryville farm we were to hunt. Upon reaching the farm, we greeted the tenants at the farmhouse, weaved through the myriad chickens that shuffled about the front yard and headed for the distant pastures.

We were joined in the field by Dave's daughter Deann, his son Michael and Michael's girlfriend Emily. We were excited that our campground was apparently set up in an area where some action had taken place. Michael and his mother Linda had each found musket balls within 50 feet of camp the previous day. We felt spoiled in that the tents were already set up, firewood was split and ready to burn and the Edwards had even built a firepit from the available stones.

We stowed our gear and headed into the field. Dave was first to find a minié ball as he moved up the hill from our camp. We spent a lot of time this afternoon scanning over the fields around the farm in hopes of finding new hot spots. The areas we searched acquired nicknames based on their location or what was found there. A hillside where we dug small pieces of Parrott shell fragments soon became "Artillery Hill." Since Brian and I work for Garrett Metal Detectors, the campground was soon christened "Fort Garrett" and the productive hill above it "Fort Garrett Hill."

I was determined to find some minié balls while hunting the Perryville area, but by late evening I was still disappointed. I had found some interesting relics and a flattened hunk of lead, but not a minié ball in good shape. We took a break to start our campfire and enjoy looking over the day's finds while cooking our dinner.

Dave was eager to continue hunting after dinner, and I quickly joined him. Although it had grown quite dark, our *GTI 2500*s were equipped with a backlight feature to allow us to see the Target ID display on the control box. I carried a small flashlight for digging targets while Dave wore a small head lamp light similar to what a coal miner might wear. I admittedly felt a little odd about night searching until he reminded me, "We're hunting on property with permission. It's just not daylight."

My conscience eased, I settled back to hunting through the darkness and began working up a slope near some small trees. Linda had previously made some discoveries in this area and I found it hard to believe that any area could be "hunted out." In only a short while, I picked up a solid hit while searching in the All Metal mode. I quickly shifted to Relics Mode in the Discriminate, Motion search mode and scanned over the area to double check the reading. Sure enough, it continued to hit solidly in the middle of the Target ID scale—a conductivity reading consistent with lead bullets.

I quickly dug six inches deep and was rewarded with the view of a powder-white chunk of lead showing from the bottom of the hole. There was no mistaking that view—my first minié ball of the night. I happily collected the relic, scanned for a possible second target and then covered up my excavation area. Within a half hour, I had retrieved two more minié balls from the area, one that was buried about eleven inches deep.

The following day, we conducted additional searches around the large farm and continued to find interesting artifacts which ranged from an iron gun tool to horseshoes to flattened minié balls and melted lead. Linda and Dave drove Brian and me to the near-by Perryville Battlefield State Historic Site for a tour of the little museum and the battlegrounds.

We left Kentucky with new interest in the history of the Civil War that took place in this area and great appreciation for the hospitality shown to us by the Edwards family. They will no doubt continue to work the private lands around this area for some time in their ongoing quest to unearth more artifacts from the greatest conflict to occur in their region.

*(Left)* Emily looks on as Michael and Dave prepare the campfire.

*(Below, left)* This collection of some of Dave's Perryville finds include three Parrot shell fragments on the lower row. In the top row are a tool, a flattened musket ball and a rifle part.

*(Below, right)* The author searches with an Infinium near the camp.

*(Above)* More of Dave Edwards' Perryville finds include this piece of lead canister shot and these minié balls and musket balls. *(Below, left)* Dave holds an iron gun tool. *(Below, right)* Steve holds a freshly dug minié ball.

*(Above, left)* Linda is in the field with her *GTI 1500* while her son Michael *(above, right)* sweeps with a *GTI 2500*.

*(Left)* Grape shot, two musket balls and a three-ring minié ball recovered near Perryville battlefield.

*(Below, left and bottom)* Linda holds a knapsack buckle she has just dug.

*(Directly below)* Linda holds a small caliber shell while Michael examines a relic he has just unearthed.

(Left) The artifacts in this display case all came from the hill above our camp. The items in the top two rows include a tent ring grommet, a Kentucky State Seal medallion, a button made in the UK by the Wallace company (circa 1800–1828), three bullets and two uniform rivets. Below the rusted pocket-knife are a spoon handle, buckle, part of a Confederate cavalry spur and, at the bottom, a bayonet scabbard tip.

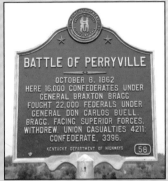

(Above) This Kentucky Department of Highways sign describing the battle of Perryville in 1862 stands along the highway a short distance from the privately owned farm we hunted.

(Below) Another minié ball is found by Dave is just beginning to show from the side wall of his recovery hole.

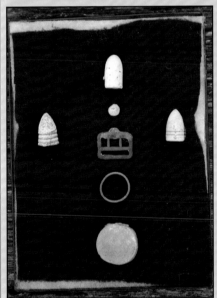

(Above) This Perryville relic collection holds (top to bottom) a smooth Confederate Enfield bullet, a small pistol ball, two minié balls, a suspender buckle, a brass ring and a percussion cap box.

Some of the Perryville Civil War artifacts found by the author include minié balls, musket balls, buck and ball shot, melted lead, iron nails, horseshoes, a harness ring and the head to an iron camp tool.

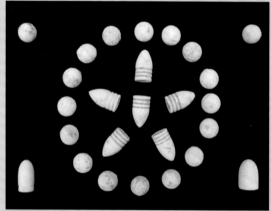

*(Left)* A cluster of CSA bullets Dave recovered from the Perryville camp.

*(Lower left)* An eagle button and rifle ball recovered from the same hole.

*(Below right)* A bayonet, artillery fragment and various relics recovered by Dave Edwards during July 2010 on "Artillery Hill."

## Civil War Hunting Can Be Productive at Any Age

(Left) Lucas Hall proudly holds the Civil War sword he found near his Berryville, Virginia, home one week after receiving a new metal detector for his seventh birthday.

(Above) Closer view of Lucas' recovered sword after it had been cleaned by a local restoration expert.

Don't tell 7-year-old Lucas Hall that he's too young to understand relic hunting for Civil War artifacts. He might just smile and show you some of his recoveries.

This first-grader from Clarke County, Virginia, became interested in metal detectors at age 6. According to his mother, Tina, Lucas became very interested in owning his own detector thanks to a neighbor who had been a relic hunter for some 25 years. The man gave the youngster a few minié balls that he had dug.

Lucas was already fond of the Discovery Channel program "Meteorite Man," which chronicles the efforts of two men in finding meteorites with their metal detectors. The Civil War bullets only further fueled Lucas' desire to obtain a metal detector to search for his own artifacts.

He was naturally thrilled when his parents recently bought him a Garrett ACE 150 for his seventh birthday. His hometown area of Winchester was the site of six key engagements during the Civil War. The Battle of Opequon, or more commonly known as the Third Battle of Winchester, was fought in September 1864, not far from his own home.

More than 40,000 Union troops engaged some 12,000 Confederates in a battle that marked a turning point in the Shenandoah Valley in favor of the North. Clarke County had other engagements during the Civil War and numerous troops camped around this area during 1864.

Lucas, along with his 9-year-old sister Samantha and their father Gary, quickly learned the basics of his new ACE 150 and began searching on private property. During their first days of searching, both Lucas and Samantha were excited to dig their own Civil War minié balls and rim-fire rifle-musket cartridges.

About a week after his birthday, young Lucas and his dad set off on their four-wheelers on a November Saturday with the detector. Gary recalled, "We reached a spot where Lucas said, 'Right here.' So, we stopped our four-wheelers and he began hunting."

Lucas very quickly announced that he had something. As he began digging up a sizable object, Gary was at first skeptical. "It's probably an old fence post," he said as his son began pulling a long object from the dirt. Gary, kneeling down to help Lucas un-

Lucas and his older sister Samantha displayed some of their first finds with their detector, including the sword, various bullets, brass cartridges, minié balls and a musket ball.

earth the item, suddenly spotted a distinctive handle and muttered, "Oh, my gosh."

This young detectorist and his father were stunned as they pulled what appeared to be a Civil War sword from the ground. Although badly corroded from nearly 150 years in the earth, the handle and blade of the sword could not be mistaken.

Gary and Lucas returned home with the prized find and quickly contacted local Civil War historians. Early estimates are that this is a light cavalry sabre model 1840 or 1860 that was likely manufactured in the North. The family hopes that better information as to the sword's origin may be found in time. "I'm dying to know just exactly how old it is," said Gary. About 18 inches of the blade appears to be missing and the family plans to return to the site to search for the remainder of it.

Gary and his kids have gone out relic hunting a few more times since the big recovery. When asked how his sister Samantha is with their detector, Lucas admits, "She's pretty good. But I've dug more bullets." Lucas also admits to caring more about American history since beginning to dig relics. He and his father recently visited the local Civil War museum in Winchester, where he found the artifacts on display to be very interesting.

Young Lucas quickly became something of a local celebrity. His story and a photo of him clutching the Civil War sword appeared in his hometown paper and a reporter from the *Washington Post* soon appeared to write a feature story on this youngster's prized find. Other newspapers have run the story of Lucas' sword, including *USA Today*. Lucas admits that it is "pretty wild" how much attention he has received, both from the media and from his friends at church.

"It's amazing to me how many people have become interested in this," said father Gary. A local restoration specialist has offered to help the family clean and preserve their relic for safekeeping.

Gary reports that he has already received generous offers from Civil War collectors who wish to purchase the rare sword. "We're not interested in selling it," he said. "This is something that I want Lucas to enjoy during his lifetime. He and his sister are home-schooled by their mother and this is a significant teaching tool. What better way can kids learn about American history?"

# CHAPTER 13

# OLD HOMESTEADS AND FARMS

Brian Pennington has been interested in relic hunting since he was a young boy. His interests were further sparked when his grandfather passed away and left him with some of his most prized metal detector finds. When Brian opened the safety deposit box his grandfather had willed him, he was deeply touched by the personal treasures left by a grandfather who helped raise him like a son. Inside were many old coins, pieces of gold, relics and items that Guy Hulsey had recovered in his years of relic hunting.

One of the most treasured pieces Guy left his grandson was a 1.65 pound ball of melted silver that he found with a Garrett detector in the late 1960s. "I have melted plenty of old silver coins and to me the irregular shape and little chunks of silver have the same signature of someone who melted old coins," Brian stated.

Since that time, Brian has amassed an impressive artifact collection of his own. His first big relic hunt was the 2003 North/South Hunt, where "I really got hooked." There, he found half a breast plate, about ten bullets, a couple of eagle buttons, a tompion (the plug for the muzzle of a gun), several button backs and other nice finds. He has hunted Civil War sites and old homesteads from Virginia to Louisiana in the past ten years with much success.

He was thrilled to actually win the Best Find of the North/South Hunt he entered in 2006, which was held near Colonial Heights, Virginia, at Fort Powhatan. "We were hunting near a Yankee cavalry camp, when I made my best discoveries at a spot I believe

Brian Pennington shows the 1.65-lb. silver ball *(above)* found by his grandfather in the 1960s with a Garrett metal detector.

to have been a hut site," Brian says. In one small area, he dug a group of Starr carbines, a kepi buckle and the identification tag of Private George Washburn from Company I, 20th New York Cavalry, under Major General George McClellan.

He particularly enjoys hunting antebellum style homes from the 1800s because of the finds he often makes there. Brian lives in Tuscaloosa, Alabama, a short drive from one of the state's earliest settlements of Greensboro. He is therefore blessed with an abundance of old home sites within his region but he is particularly fond of Greensboro, where he and his wife Connie bought the 1840s era Helton Cottage for a weekend house. "Every time I go to work on the house, I take time to dig," he admits. "This has produced lots of good finds for me."

Some of his hunt sites are the result of his social networking in the area. "Friends I've made will often call me up to tell me about some new place they've discovered," he says. "It's like a domino effect. I actually have people asking me if I want to search their property. It doesn't get any better than that!" One of his contacts is a woman who buys old properties for renovation who allows him to hunt the properties before they are demolished.

Brian enjoys hunting antebellum homes because Civil War era relics can be found just as readily as good non-military artifacts. He dug these items from an old plantation home which is still standing in Greensboro, Alabama. Several of the small pistol balls still have sprues attached, indicating that soldiers were probably pouring them on this home site. This collection also includes an early pewter utensil handle, a heel plate, a sewing dress weight, a gold tie pin, a Spencer cartridge and a personalized name plate. Brian finds such homesteads interesting because of the layers of history that can be found in the same yard.

Various Antebellum home site finds Brian has made. (Above, left) Personalized gold tie pin. *(Above, center)* 1800s-era brass ring. *(Right)* Trade and tax tokens.

*(Left)* Examples of early coins Brian has found on such sites. Clockwise from upper left are: late 1700s half reale recovered from a Mississippi ghost town; 1841-O Seated Liberty half dime found in Mississippi; 1852 silver three-cent coin found in Virginia; and an 1857-O Seated Liberty half dime found in Louisiana.

More Antebellum home site relics found in Alabama by Brian Pennington. This group includes Victorian jewelry pieces, suspender straps, an endpiece from a barber's razor strap, a silver plated thimble, a brass ornament with an Asian design and a Victorian era makeup case. The top center item is an Eley Brothers pinfire shotgun shell from the 1880s.

He finds other sites by driving through the countryside. "I ride the old roads a lot in the winter when there are no leaves on the trees and I can see farther," Brian says. "Then in the springtime I make more drives to look for daffodils and other flowers that are springing up where they shouldn't be—sure signs of an old homestead." To find who owns such properties, Brian usually turns to the Internet for help.

For specific site identification, he relies on *www.platmaps.com* to pinpoint the current owner of a piece of property. "On this site, I select the state to find the latest plat map by county that is available," he says. "Then, I stop by the county plat book service office to buy that map to locate owners' information." He cites local soil and water conservation offices as another good source to acquire local landowner information. He is also fond of the U.S. Geological Survey's site (*www.usgs.gov/*) Geographic Names Information System (GNIS) area. *(To access this site, refer to Chapter 5.)* Brian enters the state and county under search criteria and then adds "plantation" in the "Feature Name" box to pull up historic plantation sites for further research.

Once he begins working a site, Brian scouts for broken glass or the remnants of feather-edged pottery as indicators of early home sites. "The front yards generally have less trash," he relates. "Nowdays, the front yards of some of these old homes have been manicured with nice centipede grass and the good stuff can be real

This old plantation home in Alabama is just one of the historic sites that Brian Pennington has found to hunt thanks to his research and social networking diligence.

deep. Usually, I wait until the winter months to dig yards like this. It can be risky to dig a nice yard in the hot months. It will leave brown spots that make homeowners very unhappy. In the back yards, they are more trashy but at an old place, that trash can be real good." Home sites with sloping hills might even contain an old dump site on the down slope of a back hill.

Brian is always careful to do a visual survey of the land upon arrival before ever starting to swing his searchcoil. "On many sites, you can hunt it for a while and find only modern stuff," he admits. "The good stuff is often layered below the more modern deposits. Many people are not diligent enough to dig through the more recent stuff to get down to the old relics and coins."

Some of Brian's hunting buddies have become proficient in locating more obscure early home sites by studying topographical maps and locating early water sources. While some old maps in libraries may occasionally indicate an old home site or plantation, others are found simply by remote scouting in areas that just seem natural for a settler to have built a home close to a water source. These are sometimes on elevated pieces of land that require hiking through tough terrain.

Brian has found other treasures in his own back yard, literally. It doesn't hurt that he purchased an old "rambling" home that was added onto several times from its original 1840s cottage setup. Right off the back porch, he has detected and sifted soil to unearth old coins, buttons and even a patchbox cover from a musket.

As a final piece of advice, Brian adds that social networking Internet sites such as *Facebook.com* have helped his relic hunting. He connects with buddies there to share relic photos, help learn the identification of certain finds and to uncover new search sites that await him and his detector.

————

### Locating and Working Old Home Sites

Hunting old farms and homesteads can be very productive for many reasons. These sites may contain more than just early coins and interesting lost personal property. Homes that were standing during the Civil War might have been camped on by soldiers or even used as makeshift hospitals or command posts. Below the more modern layers of metallic relics can be earlier pieces of history just waiting to be uncovered.

Old coins, jewelry and military relics may hold greater monetary value to collectors but there are plenty of the more common type recovered relics that have great sentimental value to some detectorists. In some cases, the most basic types of items can become fun collectibles. For example, some detectorists have collections of old 19th and 18th century thimbles representing different periods of our history. Others have collections of rare key that have been dug in all shapes and sizes. Such keys can range from the larger ones used to lock heavy church doors to small casket keys and chest keys. Bronze keys are more common to discover because ancient iron keys tend to deteriorate in the soil.

Crotal bells—also known as jingle bells, sleigh bells, rattles or animal bells—are common discoveries on farmland in the U.S., the UK and throughout Europe. Example of such harness decorations

*(Left)* Danny Norris holds a Barlow knife he dug near an old East Texas homesite.

*(Below)* Don't neglect older homes that are still standing. You never know what great coins and interesting relics might lie right in the front yard!

have been found in England that date back as early as the 13th century. Many of the post-medieval bells were constructed of an alloy of copper and tin. Some crotal bells even carry on their underside a maker's mark, a symbol or the initials of the maker.

Countless other everyday "odds and ends" are unearthed by searchers each day. For some, these metallic artifacts may be considered junk, but to others the ancient household items are treasured just as much as a valuable coin. Such early homestead relics also help to date a site since the approximate age of an artifact can be determined based on its metal type and its crafting method.

Relic hunting on old homesteads often means that you must contend with heavy amounts of iron. You can increase the amount of discrimination by your detector, but you also run the risk of losing small rings, some buttons or good targets that are lying next to pieces of iron. If you decide to use discrimination, try dropping out just the small bits of iron and nails. Scan areas from multiple directions at slower sweeping speeds to approach targets from different angles. This can help reduce the issue of target masking and provide your detector with a better chance of separating the targets.

Smaller "sniper" coils can help you to maneuver through the more iron-infested areas. Be aware that high presence of crop fertilizers can cause your detector to chirp and squeak with false signals. You may have to reduce your sensitivity around an old homestead to help stabilize your machine.

Many experienced relic hunters simply opt to hunt in a True All-Metal mode with a constant threshold to listen to all of the snaps and pops made by the varying targets. Their trained ears are able to pick out the occasional high tone or mid tone of a good target amongst the other grunts and pops of trash items. They then concentrate on digging these higher-pitched sounds that emanate from the chorus of lower tones.

There are a number of audio features that can work in your favor when hunting a homestead site that may contain numerous iron pieces. (Refer to Chapter 3 for details on the pros and cons of different audio features that can aid you in such areas.) Such metal detector features are certainly crucial for hunting through the junk targets that can be expected on a homesite in order to find the "good stuff."

Before such features become a concern, however, you must first find the old homesite which you believe is present. In some cases, you may find old homesteads shown on early maps. In other cases, you may be relying on the memory of an old-timer who describes where an old house was once located. Finding these actual sites, or even unexpected home sites, is an acquired skill that you can sharpen through practice. Here are just a few tips on aiding your search for an early site.

- *Look for indicators of previous inhabitation.*

In the field, old home sites can often be spotted because the soil around the site simply sticks out to the trained eye. The color of the soil will look different where it has been mixed with layers of old rubbish. Plants and vegetation can be of different heights than that in the area. Look for long rows of old trees that don't seem to have grown in such a formation by pure chance. These indicators can guide you closer to look for ceramic, brick or stone remnants from early structures. Keep a sharp eye out for little pieces of pottery, glass fragments or unnatural-looking collections of rocks that could be indicators of an early dwelling.

- *Take note of old trails and paths.*

Keep an eye out for old trails that can show themselves during certain months. David Hugg of Mississippi experienced this in early 2010 as he hunted a field near an early Antebellum home site where he had previously recovered an 1848 large cent. As he detected, his eye suddenly caught a land feature that he had not noticed in his previous year of hunting this area.

Because it was winter, David noticed "a perfect path leading out into the middle of my field and right to the front door of this Antebellum home. The grass was dead, but the clover was growing in just enough to be able to make out the path. I stood in the middle of it and it went as far as the eye could see. I shook my head and couldn't believe I haven't noticed this all along. If it were not for the clover growing this time of year, I would have never known it was there."

David began detecting along the old path with his *ACE 250*. He was soon rewarded with the recovery of a 1906 Barber quarter and then his oldest coin find to date—an 1842 Seated Liberty dime. "I let out a yell you could have heard a mile away," he admitted.

- *Investigate flower patches that seem out of place in the wild.*

Some annuals will continue to return for many decades after anyone has cared for them. Pioneer homes were often decorated with plants that required little watering or attention. Iris were often used along walkways and as borders while four o'clocks were popular by the back doors of homes. It is not unusual to find clusters of these flowers growing long after a home is gone.

One landowner granted us permission to search his multi-hundred-acre property for signs of a battle. He mentioned that there

The site of an old home removed many decades ago stands out from the remainder of the farmland it sits on for two reasons: an abundance of these yellow bitterweed flowers and the presence of several patches of these white irises. (l-r) Ron Rutledge, Lewis Murray and Danny Norris are seen searching around this old home site.

had been an old home removed from one area of his property more than 35 years ago but he could not quite describe where the location was precisely. Even without clear directions from the man, it did not take our search group long to find the site.

Common sense again comes into play as you search for an old home site when you have only general instructions concerning its whereabouts. In this case, it was located on a nice hill a short walk from a natural creek. In addition to a close water source the hill once provided the settlers natural air-conditioning from the prevailing breezes as well as protection against flooding versus the lower creek land below. Although the home had been gone for well over three decades, patches of beautiful white iris stood where they had been planted untold years before. You may have noticed so-called "cemetery iris" growing unaided around early cemeteries in the same fashion.

- *Locate and search near early water sources.*

Water has always been a necessity to support life. Early homes

This abandoned water well is fortunately marked as searcher Lewis Murray carefully maneuvers around it to search for old coins and relics. Note how well camouflaged the dangerous well opening *(below)* has become after years of flowers and weeds growing over it.

and villages were generally built near creeks, rivers, lakes or natural springs where the people, their life stock and their crops could be maintained. As settlers ventured farther away from such natural sources, they dug wells to reach the water table below.

If the farm contains creeks or streams, look for signs of old windmills or watermills that may have been used to grind corn or funnel water for irrigation. Look for old bridges or natural fords across waterways that were used for crossing bodies of water. Streams and farm ponds were once used for bathing, fishing or washing clothes. Coins and other personal objects can be found in and along the water's edge.

Patches of elevated ground offered good drainage to farmers raising crops and may indicate areas where crops were raised in centuries past. Wells, springhouses and stone cisterns found in the forest or on a farm are sure signs of early civilized communities.

Dave Edwards found many interesting relics and old coins on a private cattle farm near Lexington, Kentucky, which contained a spring and an old well. "There was only a round circle of rocks where the filled-in well once stood but near that well I found evidence of at least eight old home sites," said Dave. The property also contained the remnants of an old community spring house where the settlers had drawn their water. He discovered numerous artifacts including old square-cut nails, brass doorknobs and hinges.

"After about 45 minutes, my *GTI 2500* indicated a pop-can-size target at 12 inches," Dave recalled. "I started to dig, using my *Pro-Pointer* after each scoop, until at about 15 inches deep I recovered a belt buckle from Morehead State Teachers College. Researching it later on the Internet, I found the buckle was from the 1920s era."

Dave's favorite find near the old springhouse turned out to be a silver 1877 Seated Liberty half dollar. "It is in excellent condition (EF 40+)," he said, "valued at $185.00. What a great find!"

Relic hunters know that in addition to early artifacts they have the chance to find many such old and valuable coins.

---

### Key Search Areas Around Old Homesteads

There are areas of old home sites and farm properties worthy of searching in addition to springhouses or cisterns. Texas detectorist

Dave Edwards searched this old cattle farm near Lexington, Kentucky, which contains the remnants of an old stone springhouse on the property *(see below)*. In addition to various relics, he recovered this 1877 Seated Liberty half dollar in excellent condition.

Obverse and reverse of Dave's 1877 coin.

1877 Half Dollar Found Here

Jerry Eckhart shared some of his bits of wisdom concerning search sites on old farms and homesteads.

- *Determine where clothes washing would have taken place.*

"Most washing was done behind the house at a distance far enough away from the house so wood smoke from her 'bilin' fire' wouldn't blow into the house," Jerry detailed. Knowing that the housewife would have moved her fire to a point where prevailing winds would blow the smoke away from the house, Jerry checks the prevailing wind direction for a clue. The finished laundry was hung on trees, fencing or shrubs to dry in the days before clothes

The author and other detectorists search the grounds of an abandoned Civil War era homestead. This old Kentucky home was built in 1851.

An abundance of cans, wire and various iron scrap metal often make iron discrimination desirable on such sites.

lines were common. Items of interest to relic hunters can be found below the areas where clothes once dried in the sun.

Jerry has learned that fertile growth areas resulted where the wash water was dumped and also from the fire's ashes. Irises and other hearty flowers may still remain where the flower beds were used to dump the dirty wash water. The dirt and grime in the bottom of the dumped wash pot, of course, often hid the buttons, coins and other items dumped out with the wash water. "I was working a homestead where only a slight vestige of house remained," Jerry related, "but some 50 yards behind the house was a small cluster of four o'clocks. Within five feet of them, I found two overall buttons and a wedding band, all victims of the wash pot."

- *Search the shaded areas around old homesteads.*

Look for very large, old shade trees that would have likely been standing near the homesite when it was occupied many years ago. In the heat of summer, these big shade trees would make a cooler place to visit, to picnic or for kids to play.

In the absence of large trees, families tended to gather on the east side of their home to take advantage of the shade the structure offered from the hot afternoon sun. A home with a complete wrap-around porch would also be most shaded on its east side in the hot afternoon. In the absence of side porches, the back porch was more commonly used by families for casual gatherings—the front porch being reserved for company.

- *Search inside old homes.*

People have cached away money and valuables for all eternity for a variety of reasons. Some wished to avoid taxation, some hid things from their own family and others hid their valuables during times of war or other emergencies.

Metal detecting can be quite productive in older homes that have passed from owner to owner. Wooden floorboards can hide a box of hidden money or other valuables. Veteran detectorists are sometimes called upon by relatives to help search for gold coins and money caches that relatives were unable to locate after their loved one passed away.

Inside a home, caches have been found under loose boards of an old staircase or behind a crossboard immediately above a door frame. Kick boards that run around the circumference of a room could easily have been removed and replaced after something was stashed. Money, jewelry, guns and family treasures of all sorts have been found by detectorists who search old homes.

A general purpose size searchcoil can be effective in scanning wooden structures for cached items. Adjustable discrimination

Barns, attic spaces and basements, such as this old French homestead, can yield great sums of hidden loot and other valuables. Courtesy of Bruno Lallin, Lutéce Détection.

enables you to eliminate the response of the nails that were used in construction. For tighter spaces, switch to a smaller coil or even a hand-held pinpointer to sweep into the cracks and confined areas. Larger searchcoils are effective if your goal is to find caches concealed in walls, floors, ceilings or attics. Try pulling the coil back a couple of inches from the surface to eliminate the response of nails and small iron objects. Larger targets will still respond to such larger coils swept a little farther off the surface.

Adobe walls and log cabins obviously made it easier for someone to carve out a false area in a wall to stash their goods. Do not destroy property in the course of your searches, even if it is an abandoned cabin or fisherman's hut.

Use extreme caution when entering old structures. Beware of snakes, spiders and other varmints that often take up residence in abandoned buildings. Be mindful of the soundness of the structure itself to avoid a crumbling wall collapsing on you or old floor boards giving way under your weight.

Bill Kassellman found this Civil War sword belt plate in an abandoned home. Its owner had converted it to an ammunition belt, to which he had attached this Civil War era shot bag. Inside, Bill found these intact loads of .45-70 rifle cartridges with wooden plugs.

Some old structures may have been hastily abandoned for various reasons. One of Bill Kassellman's metal detector quests took him into a remote area near Huntsville, Texas, where he was searching for an old home on stilts under which a friend had recovered a cache of money. His friend's direction did not take him to an abandoned home that matched the description, but Bill happened across another old building off a dirt country road.

"This place was obviously abandoned many decades ago," said Bill. He was curious enough to investigate the old home. "The front door was so rotten that it literally fell off the hinges when I opened it. The whole house was only about 20 by 20 feet square and it had been split into four rooms. The guy that lived there must have been killed or he could have even died out in the forest somewhere because everything in the old house was still intact."

This particular old building, however, did not provide Bill with great riches in jewelry or coins. The old farmer's overalls in his closet had four to five layers of patches on the knees, indicative of someone who made the most of his limited means. The best treasure of this old home was Bill's discovery of his first Civil War belt plate, an 1857 style sword belt. Sometime after the War Between the States, the former homeowner had converted the sword belt into an ammunition belt to hold more modern bullets.

---

### Searching Farms

Search in and around old barns for relics and coins. Barns were often used in early days for social events such as dancing. Look for old footpaths leading toward nearby pastures or storage areas that might have been heavily traveled in the past.

Relic hunters know that old farms and country homes can be a good place to locate caches, items hidden away from others that had value to the person hiding them. Children often buried their own little hoards of coins or other treasured items. Although their coins might have been only nickels, dimes or pennies when cached away, their modern value can be quite higher with the passage of more than a century.

This Kentucky farm pasture was once the scene of heavy artillery shelling in 1862.

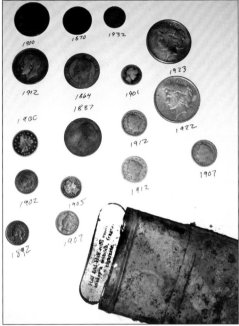

*(Above)* This ornamental Texas saddle star was found by the author while searching an 1800s home site on a West Texas ranch.

*(Right)* Joseph D. recovered this cache of coins, ranging in date from 1864 to 1923, near an old farmhouse where his great-uncles had buried it many decades earlier.

Joseph D. from North Carolina made an interesting cache find while searching where his great uncle was raised in southwestern Pennsylvania. "The property is a farm where he and his brothers were born and grew up," he related. "The farm dates back to the mid-1800s. The house where they were born is boarded up and overgrown but still standing."

Joseph's great uncle related a story of how one of his brothers had a coin collection as a kid and they buried it like pirate treasure near their home. Many decades had passed since Joseph's relative had thought about this old coin cache. After hours of searching around the old farmhouse with his *ACE 150*, Joseph dug a strong signal he picked up six inches deep at the back corner of the house.

He pried out an old Half & Half tobacco tin, as his elder relative excitedly called out, "You found it!"

Inside the tobacco tin were old coins ranging in date from 1864 to 1923. They included: two silver Peace dollars, two Barber dimes, four V nickels, three Indian Head pennies and some foreign coins including three French Napoleon coins.

"It was my first cache. Looking at those coins and remembering burying them with his brother brought some tears to my uncle's eyes," wrote Joseph. "I told him I was happy to find them for him and he told me that they were now mine. He said it with a big smile on his face. Finder's keepers!"

Treasure hunter Bill Mahan once estimated that one in five homes has a cache of some form hidden in or around it. Farmers—who did not trust the city banks before they were federally insured—often tucked away some of their money to pay for supplies in a future year. The majority of people hiding a valuable cache would not want to bury it or dig it in a place where they could easily be spotted. It would be buried with some type of landmark, structure or other indicator nearby for reference and generally would not be buried very deep.

Scan tree trunks and large limbs for spikes or old nails that might have pointed toward a cache site. Such markers may even have an object dangling like a pendulum to point toward a prized burial site of hidden goodies.

Farm gates and property entrances that have stood for many decades can be productive search areas. Those entering the property may have dug in their pockets for a key to open the padlock. In early times, the day laborers may have been paid as they exited the property and old coins might be discovered here.

The farmer's fields of today often cover the remains of long-forgotten villages, homesteads, forts, battlefields or ancient roadways. Cultivated fields offer an ideal search location because of the fertile soil and generally easy digging conditions. Be aware that you must time your searches around the season when the farmer is most likely to allow you to search his fields. Each seasonal plowing loosens the ground and brings new relics closer to the surface that had been beyond your searchcoil's reach the previous season.

Sweep your searchcoil parallel to the new rows that have been plowed. This will allow a consistent height for your coil above the ground. Sweeping against the direction of the rows forces you to raise and lower your coil constantly over the ridges and furrows.

The loose soil of a freshly plowed field needs time to settle into a more consistent state in order to achieve greater detection depths.

Relic hunting around farms and old homesteads requires a certain degree of caution.

- *Use gloves to protect your fingers.* Old home sites are likely to contain rusty iron, nails, wire, broken glass and plenty of other things that can cut your fingers if you sift through the excavation piles bare-handed.

- *Beware of old, exposed wells on these sites.* Some property owners are careful enough to fill in old wells or to cap them with a solid structure that cannot be easily moved by hand. Other wells are left open with only some wire or a simple barrier to impede access.

- *The purple fence posts mean "No Trespassing."* Here in Texas, it is becoming more common to see country fence posts or trees painted purple. This is an alternative to the traditional method of posting "No Trespassing" signs. Traditional signs can and are still used, especially on gates and entrances.

Central Texas detectorist Jerry Eckhart says this purple paint system has been used by farmers for quite some time although the legislation for its use was only passed in 1987. "Many farmers are

Several states have enacted "Purple Paint" laws to help landowners protect their property without the expense of fencing or "No Trespassing" signs which can be torn down. Purple paint can be used to spray fence posts, trees, rocks or other permanent structures at specified distances. Such purple post notices are legally binding methods in these states for owners to enforce their no trespassing wishes.

very protective of their land when it comes to trespassers," Jerry warns. "Purple on the tops of fencing is a warning that the owners might shoot you if you go into their land."

The benefit of the purple-colored markers is to allow ranchers to have an easy and economical way to keep out unwanted trespassers. The landowners are not required to fence property that is adequately marked with purple paint. In addition to avoiding the maintenance, labor and cost of fencing, rural property owners do not have to worry about "No Trespassing" signs being removed, stolen or destroyed.

The purple warning is not specific to Texas farms and ranches. Arkansas has allowed this warning system since 1989. The Missouri legislature passed a new law in 1993 known as the Purple Paint Statute (RSMO 569.145) to help Missouri landowners protect their property from trespassers.

Under Missouri's purple paint law, any owner or lessee of real property can post property with the purple paint marks. These vertical paint lines must be at least 8 inches long on either trees or posts (the statute does not specifically allow the option of placing paint marks on buildings). The bottom edge of each paint mark must be between 3 feet and 5 feet off the ground, cannot be more than 100 feet apart and must be readily visible to any person approaching the property. In Texas, a 2001 statue for purple paint markers additionally states that these markers must be no more than 100 feet apart on forestland and no more than 1,000 feet apart on non-forestland. Missouri's statute provides that any person trespassing onto property marked by purple paint can be found guilty of a first-degree trespassing charge. First-degree trespassing in this state is a Class B Misdemeanor, with potential punishment of a maximum $500 fine and/or a maximum of 6 months in jail.

Landowners can purchase a latex semi-paste form of purple boundary posting paint—to be applied as a semi-paste or sprayed on once properly thinned—at a hardware store.

The bottom line for relic hunters is to always avoid entering anyone's land without permission. Be advised that you might be risking your life if you enter land with purple markers or posted "No Trespassing" signs. Some old-timers shoot first and ask questions later. Consult your state's laws on trespassing to see if purple or some other color markers are acceptable warning systems.

———

### Dump Sites and Bottle Hunters

Settlers generally dumped or burned their own trash at a location downwind from their home to avoid the unpleasant aromas. Wooded hillsides or ravines running down and away from the home were frequently used as dump sites. Relic and bottle collectors alike know the value of sorting through such sites for lost coins, relics and old bottles.

Broken glass and oyster shells are potential indicators of a dump site, these being items that will not have deteriorated over time. Bottle collectors use special tools of the trade to help search through dump sites. Specifically, a bottle probe with an extension pole is used to gingerly press the probe's blunt tip into the soil to "feel" for glass artifacts without breaking them with a shovel. During a trip to South Carolina several years ago, our group hunted relics with Tim Zissett and Joey and Tami Gunnels.

As avid bottle hunters, Joey and Tim never pass up the chance to inspect a dump site or privy area. I watched them carefully and methodically working these sites with their probes and then care-

Tim Zissett uses a bottle probe to carefully poke around for antique glassware at this 19th century South Carolina homestead's dump site.

fully excavating with their shovels and hand tools. Sites like these from the 1800s can contain many styles of bottles not used today and therefore of value to collectors. I continued using my detector to dig some of the signals around one of the dump sites and with care was able to dig a couple of smaller medicine bottles in the process of recovering a metallic target. Great care must be taken to not tap old bottles with your shovel because even a light hit can disintegrate a nice collectible.

Serious bottle hunters will be prepared to dig deep for the oldest glass artifacts. Those who work around old colonial privy and dump sites often burrow into small caverns as they dig for the best items. In such cases, it is important to work in teams, wear head protection and be continually alert for cave-ins of the side walls of your deep excavation areas. Sifting screens can be used to locate nice non-metallic relics as soil is dug from deep in the privy site.

Since many nice iron relics can be found in dump sites used by early settlers, the use of discrimination should be carefully considered. A broken Civil War belt plate, discarded buttons and other objects considered to be trash in the 1860s are true treasures today.

John Bortscher of Edmonton recovered these relics while working a dump site in Canada. He found the old iron tea kettle to be interesting but was obviously more impressed with the pocket watch, which is brass with gold plating.

*(Above)* These recovered bottles include a Chattanooga brown Coke bottle, a pickle jar, a case gin bottle, medicine bottles and a 1700s onion-shaped bottle. *(Below)* Umbrella inks, pottery inks, small Master ink and carved lead ink bottle with its cork still in it. *Images courtesy of Charlie Harris.*

*(Left)* These recovered bottles include a champagne bottle, a huge pickle jar, a condiment jar and an old log house whiskey bottle.

*(Below)* Two leather shoes (brogans) recovered from a Nashville, Tennessee, Civil War dump. Also seen is a badly beat-up canteen half.

*Courtesy of Charlie Harris.*

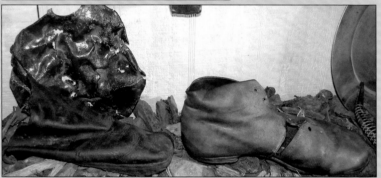

European coins are sometimes found around early settlements. The author found this badly worn 1850s French Napoleon III bronze 10-centimes coin *(left)* near a pre-Civil War Texas ghost town. The image to right shows how this coin once appeared.

This 1860 half dollar was found on a plantation homesite in Brazoria County, Texas. *Courtesy of Bobby McKinney.*

An 1843 five-dollar gold coin and a $2.5 ("half eagle") gold piece found at an early plantation homesite in Fort Bend County. *Courtesy of Bobby McKinney.*

# CHAPTER 14

# FRONTIER WARS AND BATTLEFIELDS

Dave and Linda Edwards enjoying hunting together with their metal detectors on historic sites near their Kentucky home. Fortunately for them, there is no shortage of colorful history in their area. During their first two years of hunting together with their *GTI 2500* and *GTI 1500*, they unearthed more than 3,000 coins and eleven rings.

On one old Kentucky homestead, they managed to find a gold-plated broach, an 1864 two-cent piece, an 1822 large cent, an 1829 large cent and a 1916 D Lincoln penny. Other trips have taken them to sites that hold Civil War history, such as Camp Nelson, a Union training camp for black soldiers in present Jessamine County. Among the interesting relics Dave found there was a .58-caliber Williams Cleaner bullet which, when fired, caused its base section working as a plunger to cause a zinc washer to spread out and clean the bore of a gun.

In Scott County, Kentucky, Linda and Dave obtained permission to hunt the grounds of an old home site that once belonged to the Barlow family, makers of a famous brand of pocketknives. On these grounds, Dave recovered an early belt plate with "puppy paw" clasps that dates to the Civil War period.

Dave and Linda spent their Easter Sunday 2010 in Perryville, Kentucky, near the site of a major 1862 Civil War battle. "The battleground is a 1,000-acre Kentucky State Park, which is off limits to metal detecting," Dave detailed. "Fortunately, we found a private

Dave Edwards searches on the grounds of a horse racing track in Lexington, Kentucky with his *GTI 2500*.

*(Left)* These Civil War era finds are from a Bourbon County, Kentucky home site that Dave and Linda searched. Seen are the two halves of a gun powder flask, a .36-caliber musket ball and a brass button from a New York company known as the Zouaves.

*(Below)* Linda Edwards holds minié balls she has recovered using her *GTI 1500*.

*(Above)* Two cent piece, two large cents, a 1916 D Lincoln cent and an 1800s era gold broach.

*(Left and right)* Front and back side of Dave's puppy paw buckle.

These Confederate minié balls and musket balls were found by Dave and Linda in March 2010. Note what looks like a "face" carved into the top middle rifle ball, likely a buck and ball load indention.

*(Left)* This .58-caliber Williams cleaner was found by Dave on a Civil War site.

*(Right)* Confederate rosette, a decorative piece attached to the harness of a horse.

Good relic hunting sites often produce good coins, as well. These are a few of Dave Edwards' favorites. Top: a 1786 Connecticut copper. Second row: 1907 Liberty Head "V" nickel, 1911 V nickel and an 1867 Shield nickel. Third row: 1934 Walking Liberty half dollar, 1894 silver dollar, 1887 Indian Head penny, and a 1926 Buffalo nickel. Bottom: 1941 Mercury dime.

landowner whose farm is adjacent to the battlefield who allowed us to search his property. Using the *GTI 2500*, *GTI 1500* and the *Pro-Pointer*, we found several minié balls, musket balls, canister shot and a suspender buckle that dates to that period."

The Edwards studied old battle maps of the area and decided that the landowner's property was behind the Union Army's lines. "We believe the minié balls we found are Confederate shots," said Carl. "One of the rifle balls has three little indentions that I thought might have been carved into it to make it look like a face. I've heard that some of the soldiers would do such carvings with their shots just for fun while they were sitting around their camps at night. Another guy informed me that it looks like it is indented from being fired as a buck and ball load."

In addition to relics, the couple often find valuable coins on the old homesteads and Civil War sites on which they search. Dave's favorite coin is a 1786 Connecticut copper he dug on a Lexington horse racing track where he had obtained permission to search.

Dave and Linda research historic areas before they set out to hunt. They politely approach landowners in those areas and explain to them their desire to metal detect. Dave advises other relic hunters to "be persistent and don't be afraid to ask people for permission to hunt their property. Don't ever procrastinate. When you get the chance to hunt a good spot, do it right away before someone else beats you to it."

---

### Native American Artifacts

In the United States, the Indian Wars existed from 1817 through 1898. More than 1,000 pioneers died during the battles from coast to coast and many more early settlers were killed during Native American depredations.

The frontier wars are a subject of great interest to me for several reasons. I have studied the Texan Indian conflicts of the Republic years extensively while writing a half dozen books about the various battles and Texas Rangers companies. I am also part Cherokee, as my great-great-great grandfather Moore married a Cherokee girl in 1848 in Texas. While possessing some Native American blood, I am also interested in my early Anglo ancestors who fought on the other side of the early frontier scrapes. Many of them did not fare so well.

Great-great-great grandfather William T. Sadler, an early Texas Ranger captain, lost his first wife and infant daughter to an Indian attack in 1838 in Houston County, Texas. Great-great-great-great grandfather Jeremiah Garrett was scalped and killed by Indians while working his South Carolina farm. Another of my ancestors, Laban Menefee, was shot through the thigh with a Comanche's arrow while serving with Texas Rangers in 1839. My great-great-great-great grandfather Jacob Kolb was killed in 1859 while fighting in a battle with Cherokees in South Carolina.

Indian "tin tinkler" relic found by the author in Idaho. These rolled brass decorative pieces were strung together and made sounds as they clinked together.

My point in relating the above is not to show prejudice of one side being in the right or wrong but to illustrate the number of brushes our early ancestors often had with Native American tribes in this troubled period of American history. It simply adds an extra layer of interest in my quest to unearth artifacts from either side when detecting on a  frontier battle site.

Among the items that traders marketed to Native Americans were little bells that could be strung together in groupings. These are often referred to as crotal bells or jingle bells. While hunting in Idaho, I found a "tin tinkler," an item which first appeared to me to be junk metal. Charlie Weaver quickly explained that the Indians often rolled and shaped such pieces of brass and strung them out in necklaces that could be worn as decorations or to ward off evil spirits.

Throughout the United States, there are unexplored caves which often served as dwellings for primitive people and later for Native Americans. Early traders, trappers, explorers, miners and settlers also used natural caverns for temporary living quarters. Outlaws also used caves to stash stolen goods.

Native American artifacts are often found on land where the early tribes lived, farmed and hunted. Spear points and arrowheads chipped from stone are prized finds for many, although most of these are recovered by walking fields after a heavy rain or by sifting soil in areas where tribes are known to have lived. Indian camp sites were often made near creeks and rivers, particularly where two streams came together.

Indian sites can produce many other artifacts aside from arrowheads. British, Dutch, French and Colonial settlers all engaged in trading with the American Indians as early as the 1700s. Textiles, beads and ornamental decorations were common items to trade, but the early settlers also used brass, "trade silver," muskets, tools and lead items to barter for goods from the Indians.

---

### Recoveries from a Texas Indian Wars Battlefield

It is particularly exciting for me to metal detect on the fields where some of my ancestors fought in the Texas Indian Wars during the 1830s. Since I am also part Cherokee, I am thrilled to find artifacts from either "side" of these conflicts.

My greatest thrill so far has been working with a number of Dallas-area detectorists to pinpoint the main battlefield of the 1839 Cherokee War in East Texas. Although this effort was fully chronicled in the 2009 RAM Book release *Last Stand of the Texas Cherokees*, I will give a quick recap here.

The book describes the 20-year struggle of the people of Chief Bowles to secure legal rights to the land upon which they settled in eastern Texas. Republic of Texas President Sam Houston, who had once lived among the Cherokees, advocated peace with the Native Americans, and in 1836 he carved out a large section of land covering several modern Texas counties. Known at the time as Cherokee Nation, this land did not go undisputed during the years of the Republic of Texas.

President Houston's successor in office, Mirabeau B. Lamar, was in favor of driving all "hostile" Indians from Texas lands and he made no qualms about enforcing his desires. Chief Bowles and his hundreds of followers were given the choice of leaving in peace or being removed forcibly. Peace negotiations were conducted between Bowles and commissioners representing the Texas government during the early summer of 1839. These peace talks failed, however, and the so-called Cherokee War of 1839 ensued.

The Cherokees, allied with members of twelve other Native American tribes, retreated across the Neches River west of

Tyler. An inconclusive skirmish was fought near dusk around the present town of Chandler. After dark, Bowles and his followers retreated northward to a Delaware Indian village where more than 700 Indians made their final stand on July 16, 1839. They held off the advances of 900-plus Texas Rangers, militiamen and Texas Army soldiers for nearly two hours before being overwhelmed. Chief Bowles and approximately 100 Indians were killed in the Battle of the Neches that day.

Eagle Douglas and members of the American Indian Cultural Society—who maintains the commemorative marker and land where Chief Bowles fell—granted us permission to detect for artifacts on their land several years ago. The condition was that any relics we recovered would be donated to their ongoing preservation efforts. To make a long story short, our searches for period artifacts were fruitless on the AICS land. I returned to my early maps and research documents and soon decided that the main battle must have occurred on adjacent land.

The neighboring land owners gave their consent for our team to search their farm and our efforts were soon rewarded. Robert Jordan dug a .69-caliber musket ball in the forest a short distance from a significant hilltop where a Delaware Indian village had once stood. The land owners were interested enough to allow us to return with a larger group to continue our detecting efforts.

This time, our group of eleven relic hunters was able to home in on the main area of conflict. Paul Wilson was the first to dig two musket balls in close proximity, followed by Bob Bruce with another piece of fired lead. In a short period of time, Rusty Curry, Mike Skinner, Robert Jordan, Joe Wilson, Matt Bruce, Robert Jeffrey, Dave Totzky, Stan May and I had all dug either dropped shot, fired shot or iron artifacts from the main area of conflict.

The bullets ranged in size from .40-caliber pistol balls to larger .69-caliber musket balls. Totzky was the first to dig a complete buck and ball load, consisting of a larger round ball and two pieces of smaller .32-caliber buck shot pieces. Early accounts of the 1839 Neches River battle state that Chief Bowles was struck by at least

(Above) A group of searchers work over a concentrated relic area where the last stand of the Texas Cherokees occurred in 1839.

(Right) The author holds up a flattened .69-caliber musket ball he has just pinpointed on the site of the old Delaware Indian village.

(Below) Battle of the Neches bullets, left to right: another .69-caliber musket ball that impacted something; an intact .69 caliber ball with the tip of its sprue not properly clipped off; an untrimmed .42 caliber ball which also dropped; and a properly formed .69 caliber musket ball.

A complete buck and ball load found on the battlefield by Dave Totsky.

An 1826 large cent found by Bob Bruce.

*(Above)* Relics of the 1839 Cherokee War. The musket balls, pistol balls, buck shot, bullet button and pieces of an iron pot were dug by the author and his companions in March 2009. The arrowheads and Indian pottery were plowed up by the farm owners.

*(Right)* More buck and ball loads dug in November 2009 on the battlefield.

*(Left, above)* The author presents a case of battlefield artifacts to Texas Ranger officers for their museum. Left to right are Lieutenant George Turner, Captain Al Alexis and Captain Kirby Dendy.

*(Left, lower)* Another relic case was given to the American Indian Cultural Society. Left to right are Charles Anderson, Sondra McAdams, Eagle Douglas and author.

one round of buck and ball shot in his back during the closing moments of the battle. My friend Donaly Brice of the Texas State Archives later helped retrieve a militia ordnance receipt from Nacogdoches that clearly shows that the Texans had been equipped with 50 pounds of buck shot just weeks before this battle.

Later that year, I organized two more hunts with Dallas-area detectorists to continue scouring the Cherokee War battleground. We moved down the hillside, where the Delaware Village had once stood, toward the deep ravine of Price's Branch. Chief Bowles and his comrades had held off the Texas Militia, Texas Rangers and Texas Army soldiers for some 90 minutes from within the protective banks of this twisting creekbed.

More fired and dropped musket balls were found in and around this creek. My oldest children, Kristen and Emily, thoroughly enjoyed joining us to help detect during one of our fall outings. The land owners were pleased with the manner in which our hunters buried their excavation areas and hauled out plenty of garbage metal from their farm. We offered them several relics, and in exchange they donated a number of Indian artifacts that their family had plowed up from these fields in past years.

My thoughts turned to preserving the recovered relics so that future generations could benefit from the knowledge that we had uncovered. Combining the Indian pottery and arrowheads with the recovered musket balls, Brian McKenzie and I created two artifact cases to donate. One of them was given to Texas Ranger officers for display in the Texas Ranger Museum and Hall of Fame in Waco. The other was presented to Eagle Douglas and board members of the AICS group that maintains the Chief Bowles land.

Both groups were pleased to receive pieces of history that can be used for future teaching about the early Indian Wars. The relic hunters who passed along their finds for the cases were equally happy to do a good deed. Handing over history to those who truly appreciate it and care to preserve it can be just as satisfying as the moments when you are first digging it from the soil.

―――――

**Battlefield Routes are Key for One Georgia Detectorist**

Keith Cochran estimates that he has found 97% of his relics in his own home area of Paulding County, Georgia, on or near battlefields or along the early pioneer roads leading toward battle areas. Keith can trace his family roots in Paulding County back to the 1840s and his finds in this area have been numerous.

He has found a solid silver pocket watch whose serial number he has traced to manufacture in 1863 by the Wortham Watch Company of Massachusetts. He believes this watch was owned for no more than a year before it was lost in his county during 1864 in Civil War action. He has also found countless minié balls, cannon balls and artillery fragments, two Federal eagle breast plates, many cast "I" buttons, many Federal eagle buttons, two Georgia state buttons, a Texas breast plate, two U.S. box plates, a U.S. belt buckle and a silver Illinois veteran's hat pin.

Keith began metal detecting seriously in 1986, the year he began teaching school. "I used the relics I found when I was teaching history classes," he related. "Learning about the Civil War was more interesting to my students when they could actually see and touch period pieces I had recovered. In those days, I could go out relic hunting with my buddies and dig quite a bit. On any given Saturday, we could dig 40 or 50 three-ringers until we were just tired of digging them."

Keith was forced to take medical retirement from teaching four years ago. As he foresaw the inevitable end to his teaching, he sought a new career that offered him more freedom to deal with his ailments. He turned to his hobby as a new way to help support his family and founded Bonnie Blue Detectors, named both in honor of his wife Bonnie and for the famous unofficial flag of the Confederacy which bore the same name.

He finds detecting sites a little more difficult to find than those which were so plentiful 25 years ago. "Modern construction has covered many of our good hunting areas with concrete," he

## GEORGIA BATTLEFIELD FINDS

*(Above)* One of Keith Cochran's display cases. This one includes an eagle breast plate, a Texas or Mississippi buckle, an Illinois hat badge, two Georgia buttons, three North Carolina sunburst buttons, five cast I's, a two-piece Infantry button, a silver pocket watch from 1863, his son Aaron Cochran's railroad baggage tag, a Memphis reunion badge from 1919–1923, a silver dollar from Kennesaw Mountain, a New York staff button, a silver reale from 1782, an 1856 "O" half dime, a piece of eight from Fort Powhatan, Virginia, a Sunday school pin found in Keith's grandpa's yard, and a U.S. plate from a Georgia battle area.

*(Right)* The tongue and groove breast plate which Keith believes to be from a Texas Civil War company. This was found at a campsite located on his uncle's Georgia property.

*(Left)* Keith Cochran holds a rifle ball dug while field testing a Garrett *AT Pro.*

*(Left, center)* Arrowheads, spear points, a wood-boring tool and Indian pottery Keith has found in Georgia while relic hunting.

*(Left, lower)* Keith and his buddies found eight minié balls in a stump while hunting the South Carolina Low-country. These .58-caliber miniés are still embedded in the wood, which he believes was used by Civil War soldiers for target practice.

*(Lower right)* A Read Parrott shell dug about six inches deep in Paulding County. Keith dug the two Union Hotchkiss shells—evidence of the artillery pounding Atlanta received as General Sherman attacked the town—in an Atlanta yard. One was only inches deep in the soil while Keith had to lay on his chest to dig the other shell from a full arm's length deep. The 10-pound solid shot cannon balls were dug by Keith on a construction site in New Hope while his son Aaron dug the smaller 2 pound, 10 ounce cannon ball closer to their own home.

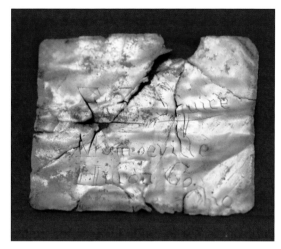

*(Right)* The back to a tin type picture carried by a Union soldier. It was probably believed to be trash and was wadded up. When Keith straightened out this tin type, he found the soldier's ID scratched into it: "E. J. Squire, Monroeville, Huron Co. Ohio."

admits. "Nowadays, I keep track of construction projects and work these areas as excavation begins." Keith dug several 10-pound cannon balls near the New Hope battle area after earth movers had exposed formerly dense forested acreage while clearing land for a new grocery store shopping center.

He prefers hunting in the woods over searching iron-laiden home sites because of an ailment that troubles him. "I have rheumatory arthritis, which makes it tough on my knees," he said. "So, when I kneel down to dig, I want it to be something worthwhile. In the woods, I usually dig a shotgun hull, a bullet or some kind of relic versus the iron targets found around a home place."

Keith also enjoys digging with his boys—19-year-old Phillip and 16-year-old Aaron—who have been relic hunting with their father for years. Both have found their share of relics, including canister shot, Civil War buttons and minié balls dug by Aaron.

Keith, along with his uncle and cousins, have more than 200 acres of forestland on which to hunt in Paulding County. One of the earliest roads in the area runs right through this property. Union troops marching toward the 1864 battle of Pickett's Mill (or New Hope Church as it's also known) tramped right through the Cochran's land. "I don't hunt battle lines," Keith says. "I look for marching routes and hunt those." His Texas breast plate came from a 90-acre tract of land owned by his uncle upon which troops apparently made camp sites. "Out of those 90 acres, I have found all of my relics in four tight spots within only four acres."

With relatives all over Paulding County, Keith is able to scratch out plenty of hunting sites. "They tell me where the old road beds are and where they've plowed up bullets over the years," he said. "The old road beds are my favorite, because I often find bullets lost several yards off the roadways. The soldiers were often forced to march 20 to 30 feet off the roadways because they didn't want the troops to wear out the roads. The heavy wagons could become bogged in the muddy roads, so they limited the troops' use of the road beds during their marches."

Although the relic collections in his home are impressive, Keith believes his best finds are yet to come. "There are many pieces of land in this area that I can't wait to search," he said. Finding the time during the right season is sometimes a challenge. He still manages to work several new sites each year, and more often that not he comes away with satisfactory finds. He also returns to previously productive sites to try new detectors and searchcoils, particularly after timber has been cleared.

----

### A Battlefield That History Has Forgotten

If only Paul Harvey was still around, perhaps he could help fit the pieces together to one West Texas puzzle and give us "the rest of the story." In early May 2011, Brian McKenzie and I returned to some private property in southern Stephens County, Texas, to relic hunt with Jerry Eckhart, his buddy Vance Gwinn, and Jerry's son-in-law, Chuck Mace.

On this land, we had previously recovered many interesting relics from an 1870s buffalo hunters camp (see story, Chapter 17). Since that time, Jerry and his hunting companions had explored across other areas of this vast property and continued to find significant military relics. Among them was a beautiful Model 1851 officer's sword belt plate that Chuck dug. Shortly after the fall deer season had ended, Vance and Jerry hit another hot spot in early 2011 where they each dug a pouch full of brass cartridges. It was some of their other finds, however, which were of more interest: three-ring minié balls, pancaked lead rifle balls, and even a carbine sling batwing attachment.

"We had started thinking some time ago that there may very well have been a skirmish between the buffalo hunters and some local Indians," explained Jerry. "This new site only added to that speculation of an Indian battle."

So it was that Brian and I joined Jerry, Vance, and Chuck in early May—having waited for the county's turkey season to end before the landowner would allow us onto the property. It took only moments for the area to begin producing artifacts. The soil was fairly hot in terms of iron mineralization, but it was also hot in terms of targets. Just paces away from our trucks, Vance and I

*(Above)* A U.S. bridal rosette recovered by Vance in 2011.

*(Above)* This Model 1851 sword belt plate found by Chuck Mace on the property certainly had everyone excited that more significant military relics remained to be found.

*(Left)* Chuck holds out an ornate piece that he has just dug during our May 2011 search of this battleground.

both dug a couple of fired Henry rifle cartridges. Just a few minutes later, Vance dug a damaged U.S. plate near the base of an old fallen tree. It was hard for me to decide which was tougher to take—the calmness this man displays while turning up such great relics or his uncanny ability to continue finding the same!

As the morning continued, so did the finds. Among them were many dozens of brass Spencer and Henry cartridges, and even a rare, intact .50-90 Sharps black powder rifle cartridge. Seven U.S. eagle buttons were turned up during the day, as well as a very interesting ornamental piece that I dug which has a distinctive Texas star imprint. Charlie Harris, who has been called upon over the years to determine the identify of thousands of frontier relics, later told me that he believes it is most likely a civilian made Texas saddle ornament, probably stamped just after the Civil War.

Brass cartridges, musket balls, rivets, minie balls, iron square nails, and a batwing dug in one afternoon by Vance Gwinn in late March 2011 from the battle area.

An abundance of iron trash, added to a fairly mineralized soil content, made proper ground balance and careful use of discrimination very important this day. Our cartridge finds were mixed with more recovered minié balls, buck and ball loads, rifle balls and pistol shot—most of them mushroomed out from impact.

The wide variety of bullet types found, particularly those of smaller caliber, have led us to feel more strongly that some kind of skirmish took place in the vicinity of the buffalo hunters' camp. Jerry has turned up some vague pioneer account references to an early Indian fight in this area, and he hopes to find more definitive references to what actually happened here. Until such documentation turns up, the evidence of what happened, when, and why will be best answered by the artifacts that Jerry and Vance hope to continue recovering.

*(Left)* Some of the finds made by Vance with his *AT Pro* during our May search on the battle site: a U.S. plate missing its lead backing, three eagle buttons, and a .50-90 Sharps black powder rifle cartridge.

*(Below, left)* Texas star saddle ornament found the author.

*(Below, right)* Jerry seen recovering another brass cartridge.

*(Left and inset)* Vance with one of his recovered eagle buttons.

*(Below)* This uniquely shaped brass piece was dug by Vance.

*(Above)* Chuck searching an iron-laiden area of the campground, believed to be a skirmish area. Two of his eagle buttons found this day are shown before cleaning *(above, right)*.

*(Right)* Author displays a brass Henry rifle cartridge he has just dug.

*(Left)* Case of author's cleaned brass, iron and lead relics from this battleground hunt.

# GALLERY OF BATTLEFIELD FINDS

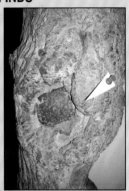

*(Left and right)* Two views of a tree that was cut from the Chickamauga National Military Park in 1889. This trunk has two canister balls and seven pieces of embedded shrapnel.

*Relics on this page are all part of the Charles Harris Civil War Museum; photos by Charlie Harris.*

*(Below)* Wide variety of Civil War artillery fuses recovered from various states.

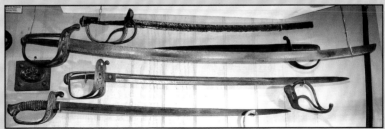

*(Above)* Recovered Civil War swords. Top one is from Virginia and the third down is from Gettysburg. The second one down is a Nashville Plow Works CSA sword that was found sticking out of the ground near Florence, Alabama.

317

*(Left)* Confederate Enfield rifle recovered from the Conasauga River. The x-ray shows that the rifle is still loaded with an Enfield bullet.

*(Below)* Recovered Civil War bayonets, mostly from .58-caliber rifles. Two on the right are from .69-caliber muskets.

*(Above)* Three more tree sections removed from Chickamauga in 1889. At left is a tree section with an embedded minie ball. In center is an embedded canister ball. To right is a tree that grew around a discarded mule shoe.    *Photos courtesy of Charlie Harris.*

*(Above)* At top is an artillery short sword recovered from Macon, Georgia. Two Confederate Bowie knives lost by Rebel cavalrymen at Stones River (Murfreesboro, TN). Brass handle from a sword bayonet recovered from Lookout Mountain, TN.

*(Left)* At top left is a homemade tompion for a Whitworth rifle. Top right is a lead-filled brass star, possibly for a high ranking officer. Lower left is an eagle plate from Dalton, Georgia. The bayonet hole in the center indicates the soldier may have survived this wound but he likely died from the blow through the lower right corner. The lower right buckle has a pistol bullet hole that came through it from the rear. *All photos on this page courtesy of Charlie Harris.*

*(Left)* Also found on a Dalton, Georgia, battlefield, this bullet-holed breast plate is shown with a .69-caliber minié ball—the size that this man was shot with.

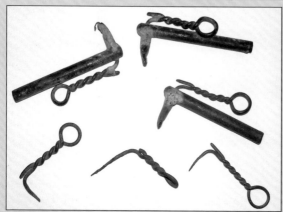

*(Left)* Confederate friction primers—both complete primers and some detached pull wires—recovered from the Savannah River at Augusta, Georgia. These were made of copper and were used to ignite the powder charge in a cannon.

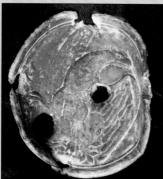

*(Left)* Another Dalton, Georgia, battlefield find. This U.S. eagle breast plate has a .44 and a .36-caliber bullet hole, plus four nail holes where a Confederate soldier apparently nailed it to a tree for target practice.

*Relics on this page are all part of the Charles Harris Civil War Museum; photos by Charlie Harris.*

*(Below)* These 12-pound, 4.56-inch cannister rounds were for use with a 12-pound gun and a 12-pound howitzer. They were recovered from the wagon fire in Sequatchie Valley, Tennessee, piece by piece, then cleaned and reassembled.

# CHAPTER 15

# UNDERWATER RELICS

In only six years of searching underwater with metal detectors, Aaron Schancer had accumulated an impressive collection of rings, necklaces, medallions and other tokens. The Wisconsin native enjoys working the numerous fresh water lakes in his area of the country, particularly well-used swimming areas.

Aaron's friend Doug Chisnell became interested in underwater detecting a little over a year ago and now the two travel together in quest of more lost treasures. "The first thing Doug ever found was a silver 50-cent piece from 1942 with an old Garrett *Freedom ACE* detector," recalled Aaron. "He was hooked on the sport right away."

The friends have taken their detectors cross-country to search the surf along the Gulf Coast in Corpus Christi and South Padre Island, Texas—both popular spring break and summer vacation beach areas. Doug and Aaron both settled on Garrett *Sea Hunter* pulse induction models as their detectors of choice for such searches in the breakers along the coast. Silver chains, gold rings, coins, charms and other pieces of jewelry are common finds as they work the shorelines and surf.

In their home state, Aaron and Doug visit local libraries to study old maps from the 1800s. Once they settle upon an area of interest, they use the original maps and modern GPS coordinates to locate the precise area of some place of interest. One of their recent research efforts helped them to pinpoint the site of an 1877

*(Left)* Doug Chisnell (left) and Aaron Schancer stand before some of the coastal treasures they have recently recovered with their *Sea Hunters*.

*(Below, left-right)* A brass ring from the French trading days found by Aaron in the Yellow River in Wisconsin; a rare Civil War era officer's button found by Doug; and a silver officer's button found by Aaron off a beach in Peru.

*(Below)* Several more of Aaron's *Sea Hunter* treasures. Clockwise from upper left are a silver buckle, an ornate 10k gold ring, a Sterling silver Catholic medallion and an 18k white gold ring from a French designer.

*(Left)* Aaron Schancer recommends a floating sieve for detectorists who search in the surf or chest-high in fresh water lakes. He constructed this one using wire mesh, a wood frame with styrofoam and a cable that attaches to his waist. Aaron dumps each sand scoop onto the mesh screen to insure that all good treasure targets are recovered.

*(Below)* Aaron emphasizes the importance of good research to find quality relic recovery sites. He and his friend Doug studied old 1870s maps of their area, such as this one below, to locate an early French lakeside trading post site.

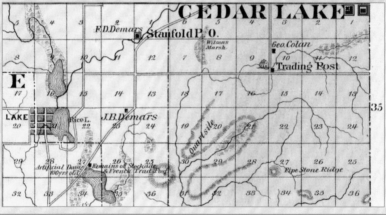

French stockade and trading post which stood on the shores of a Wisconsin lake. "We found it to be a very trashy area but we have never let that stop us," Doug related. "After hours of digging up some clad and some old coins from early 1900s, I got a weak signal and went to digging. I came up with a button from an officer's uniform from the Civil War era." Doug also dug an Indian arrowhead near the site of the old French trading post.

Some of Aaron's more productive beach areas have been in Hawaii and in Peru while he was visiting both places. Both coasts had areas of heavy volcanic rock beaches in addition to magnetic sand. "I adjust the threshold to hear the difference between the targets and the lava rocks," Aaron explained. "Where you find the black sand in places like these, you will find the treasure. They go hand in hand because this heavier black sand traps the treasure from sinking any deeper."

He has retrieved large gold rings from as deep as 17" with his *Sea Hunter* by learning its subtle target identification sounds. "You have to listen for the little tones and really understand how to use your detector," he explains.

"I prefer using the Standard Elimination on the *Sea Hunter* to find items in salt water. I would only use the Discreet Elimination in an area where the targets I find have been fairly shallow. The deeper targets only give you a faint signal but when you pick up one of these faint signals, it will repeat and give you a constant, signal. I also run with Zero Elimination so I don't lose the deep targets."

Aaron admits that pulse induction detectors can be frustrating for beginners. "Some of my friends who have tried water hunting have given up after digging four or five pop tops. I've learned that you simply have to dig pop tops to find many of the good gold rings. That just goes with the territory."

Another water hunting recovery tip that Aaron offers is his homemade sieve for double-checking his sand scoop. Using a flotation device with chicken wire for a screen, he dumps any remaining sand from his scoop onto the screen and simply allows the waves to filter the contents. Any secondary coin or ring he might not have seen will remain atop the wire mesh. Aaron keeps his sieve floater tied to him with a cable so that it is always floating along close by.

His best recommendations for successful water hunting with a metal detector are admittedly pretty basic. "Do your research to find a good area. Be patient as you dig some trash to find the good rings and relics. And, finally, be persistent."

---

### Freshwater Relic Hunting

Most metal detectors can be used for wading into shallow water or streams as long as they have fully submersible search-coils. The danger you risk is in dropping or accidentally dunking any part of the detector that is not waterproof—particularly the control box. If your relic, coin and jewelry hunting will often involve wading into deeper streams, lakes, ponds or other swimming areas, it may be worth your investment to add a fully waterproof machine to your arsenal.

The cost of a fully submersible detector will discourage 90% of relic hunters from investing in such a specialty machine. Single frequency metal detectors in fully waterproof control boxes start at prices around $600 and go up from there. As you look into a waterproof VLF detector, it is worth investigating whether optional coil sizes and configurations (i.e. concentric versus Double-D) can be purchased.

The most popular form of fresh water metal detecting is hunting modern or older swimming holes. Many public swimming areas can be found on modern maps and in community guides, but the lesser known swimming areas will only be found by being from the area or talking to the locals. As a kid, I enjoyed rope swings over creeks and rivers. Today's underwater hunters know that we lost all kinds of coins, rings and other items while launching ourselves from the rope into the water.

Metal detectors that are fully submersible offer the greatest flexibility in hunting such areas—allowing the searcher to work under piers or diving platforms. For deeper water recovery work, the mask and snorkel is traded for either scuba gear or a hookah system. The latter consists of a gasoline-powered engine and a low-pressure air compressor mounted on a flotation device to supply filtered clean air through regulators.

Many good items can be found simply by wading. Search around "treasure traps," objects that prevent coins or jewelry from washing any farther along. Wave action on fresh water lakes—created by the wind, storms and boats—can move objects until they hit a solid barrier. These may be large rocks and boulders or piers and docks where their support pilings enter the soil. Boat ramps are another good sources of finds. These ramps and the lake bottoms surrounding the launch area are generally littered with aluminum cans, pop tops and all sorts of trash. Boaters, however, lose far more valuable items than trash as they struggle to secure or launch their boats, kayaks and jet skis.

Take advantage of drought conditions and low water levels on lakes and ponds during summer months. When you start at the water's edge during these periods, you are often covering areas that would normally be submerged.

There are also plenty of good areas that can be worked on dry land near swimming holes. Concentrate on the sunbathing area where towels are spread out. Fingers become slippery with suntan oil and many rings are lost in the sand or grassy areas near the water. Other productive areas include the parking area near the swimming beach and any trails that lead toward the water or sunbathing areas. This applies to both modern-day swimming areas and trails from swimming areas of long ago.

While most underwater detectorists work swimming areas where coins and jewelry can be found, there is a smaller group of relic hunters who have taken their history quest below the surface.

Some Civil War camps and other battle sites have been flooded for various reasons. While researching battle sites for one of my Texas Rangers books, I found that the 1841 battle of Village Creek area is now submerged below Lake Arlington. On the bright side, I figure one of these days I'll try to find time to investigate it with scuba gear in hopes that many of the relics still remain.

Veteran relic hunter Andy Sabisch points out that the Tennessee Valley Authority dammed the river in Chattanooga for power production and flood control. Along the old riverbanks are Union and Confederate camps, now submerged, which divers have worked with success.

## Saltwater Relic Hunting and Salvage Law

Old World shipwrecks have long fascinated treasure hunters. While many lie in deep waters far beyond the reach of conventional treasure hunting, others were wrecked by storms or reefs relatively close to shore. Recovery efforts were usually made shortly after the losses when possible if survivors existed to help pinpoint the shallower wrecks.

A number of Spanish galleons were lost in hurricanes along America's East Coast during the early 18th century. Building contractor Kip Wagner made the chance discovery in 1948 of seven Spanish silver coins near Sebastian Inlet, Florida. He eventually tried his luck along Florida's coast with a metal detector and discovered dozens more silver and gold Spanish shipwreck coins.

The beachcombing craze soon set in and hundreds of treasure hunters descended upon the Florida shores to search for their own Spanish goodies. From Maine to Texas, the shores of the United States have produced tens of thousands of old coins and other treasures from ships wrecked centuries earlier. Veteran beachcombers know that violent weather such as hurricanes and tropical disturbances can churn up the water and wash previously unreachable items closer to the beach.

My first experience with working a wreck site was in 1984 near Akumal on Mexico's Yucatan Peninsula. My father and I had become certified scuba divers and had taken a family trip to a remote area of the Mexican coast south of the Cancun area. One of our dive sites was a lonely white sands beach with coral reefs lying just offshore.

The dive master knew of an old Spanish wreck that lay just offshore that had been worked for many years. Recreational divers still managed to find relics from this wreck. This ship was the 73-foot frigate-class Spanish merchant ship *Nuestra Señora de los Milagros* ("Our Lady of Miracles"), whose alias was *El Matancero* or "Matanceros." She had departed Spain for Veracruz in November 1740, and was sailing near the Caribbean coast of the Yucatan Peninsula on February 22, 1741, when she crashed into the coral reefs

The author and his father recovered these artifacts in 1984 from a Spanish trade ship which wrecked off the coast of Akumal, Mexico, in 1741. The emerald and diamond-colored beads are glass replicas which were used as trade goods in the Caribbean. The Spanish brass crucifix in the center was obtained from Bob Marx, whose team first found this wreck in 1958.

just off the shoreline. The point along the coast where she was lost was known in Spanish as Punta Mantaceros ("Slaughter Point").

*El Mantancero* had been destined for the colonial port of Veracruz, Mexico, when her crew of 70 was wrecked near Akumal. Her cargo included both registered and unregistered items, such as 100 tons of pig iron and 25 tons of tempered steel wire. She also carried a hefty cargo of household goods for sale, including spoon scissors, knives, buttons, needles, buckles, writing quills, paper, glassware, window glass, walnut and almond oil, and hand tools, plus 750 barrels, 400 casks, 204 cases and 21,200 bottles of brandy and wine.

Treasure diver Bob Marx discovered the wreck of the *Nuestra Señora de los Milagros* in 1958 about 5 miles down the coast from Akumal. He led several expeditions which salvaged the wreck and recovered thousands of artifacts. Instead of vast hoards of Spanish coins they may have dreamed of finding, his team recovered only a few Spanish copper coins and four silver reales from the reign of Philip II (1556–98). They recovered four cannon, a large anchor, 600 silver-dipped brass spoons, more than 3,000 brass crucifixes, more than 3,000 buckles in 20 sizes, more than 300 musket balls, cannon balls, bottles, metal buttons, 140 brass devotional medallions, 500 brass knife handles, 31 pewter plates, ballast stones, and numerous personal items, including a gold pocket watch. In all, more than 12,000 items were recovered from the wreck.

The wreck of *El Mantancero* was well known to the locals when my family arrived at Akumal in 1984. In fact, several of her recovered cannons have been mounted in the rocks near the beach and still point out to sea. The vessel had been mounted with 16 iron cannons, four swivel guns, twenty rifles and ten pairs of pistols for the crew to protect its cargo. The complete story of this expedition was written by a member of Marx's team, Clay Blair Jr.

Marx and his team recovered the lion's share of goods from this wreck but countless small artifacts remain to this day. Divers who visited this remote site in the 1980s hoped to find some of the Spanish crucifixes, religious medallions, pewter buckles and colored glass trade beads. The European-manufactured crosses were exciting to find because many believed them to be made of gold upon recovering them, although they are actually made of brass. The larger variations bore the Latin words *Vitam Praesta* ("Give Us Life") on the arms of the cross on the Virgin Mary side, while the figure of Christ nailed to the cross adorns the other side.

Fortunately for us, the wreck site was located in relatively shallow water—15 to 20 feet—just off the coast. In the nearly 250 years since her loss, *El Mantacero*'s remaining cargo had been washed into the coral and sand from that point up into the shallows. All that was required on our part was donning scuba gear and making beach entries to swim toward the site. We carried small mesh bags to pocket our finds and spent the afternoon poking around any coral outcroppings we could find along the bottom. Dad and

I fanned the sand and dug under coral with our fingers to retrieve items. It has been speculated that *El Mantacero* intended to make a stop in a New World port based upon the quantity of pewter buckles and costume jewelry aboard her.

My father and I recovered hundreds of little diamond- and emerald-colored glass stones, some mounted in metal or ceramic settings. Some had once been mounted like cuff links, while others had been fashioned as buttons for fancy clothes or even to be used as earrings. One diver from of our group was fortunate enough to find one of the brass Spanish crosses in nice condition and many of us recovered some of the rusty pewter and bronze trade buckles. Some 25 years later, while visiting Bob Marx in his Florida home, I was thrilled to obtain one of the 1700s-era brass crosses he had recovered in the 1950s from the *Nuestra Señora de los Milagros*— where Dad and I had made our first wreck dives.

In the decades since, my wreck dives have been of the recreational variety in the Caribbean and off Hawaii over sunken merchant ships or World War II era wrecks. One highlight was a dive made in 2001 between Wilmington and Myrtle Beach on the wreck of a Civil War blockade runner. Such blockade runners are popular wreck sites for Civil War buffs who hope to retrieve Confederate coins, belt plates and other memorabilia from the 1860s. Bob Marx fondly recalls diving on several such blockade runners in 1969 that had been located by amateur divers off Charleston, South Carolina. Many other Civil War blockade runners have been located in recent decades, some containing vast holds of Confederate military supplies and other goods.

Professional salvage and treasure hunting operations spend millions of dollars in their efforts to locate and salvage the world's richest wrecks. Two recent famous discoveries are worthy of mention because of the varying results that legal actions have had upon their hauls.

The Ohio-based Columbus-America Discovery Group found the so-called "Ship of Gold" in 1987 near Cuba. The 280-foot side-wheel steamer *SS Central America* sank in a hurricane in Septem-

(Above) The treasure recovered from the sidewheel steamer *SS Central America* included thousands of $20 gold coins, nuggets and gold ingots weighing as much as 80 pounds. The ship sank with a load of 30,000 pounds of gold prospected during the California Gold Rush.

(*Left*) An artist's depiction of the so-called "Ship of Gold" sinking during a hurricane in 1857.

ber 1857, along with 400 passengers and 30,000 pounds of gold which had been prospected during the California Gold Rush. At the time of her loss, the gold had an approximate value of $2 million (U.S.).

Led by Tommy Thompson, the salvage team recovered more than 5,200 Double Eagle ($20-denomination) gold coins minted in 1857 at the San Francisco Mint. The *Central America*'s cargo also contained privately-made gold coins and ingots, the largest of which weighed nearly 80 pounds. The total value of the recovered gold was estimated at $100-150 million.

In the ensuing legal battle, the Columbus-America Discovery Group argued that the gold on the *Central America* had been abandoned although 39 insurance companies filed suit with claims that they had paid damages for the lost gold. The courts eventually awarded 92% of the gold to the discovery team. The 80-pound gold ingot from the Ship of Gold sold for a record $8 million.

Legal proceedings for a more recent haul of a major treasure ship's cargo did not go as well for the salvors. Florida-based Odyssey Marine Exploration announced in May 2007 that it had recovered 17 tons of colonial-era silver and gold coins from an undisclosed wreck site in the Atlantic Ocean. The shipwreck, code-named the *Black Swan* by Odyssey, had produced more than 500,000 silver coins and 203 gold coins which had a collective value of as much as $500 million.

Spain filed motions in U.S. district court to force Odyssey to clarify the wreck's identification. Legal review proved that the salvage company had actually set out to find the Spanish frigate *Nuestra Señora de las Mercedes* and had found it off the southern coast of Portugal. The *Mercedes* was carrying a cargo of treasury from Spain's South American colonies back to Spain when she sank in 1804 after being attacked by British warships.

Odyssey tried to claim that the treasure was jettisoned chests of silver from an unknown colonial ship. Spanish officials, however, successfully argued that the company had specifically used extant documents to pinpoint the sinking site of the *Mercedes*. In December 2009, a U.S. District Court judge ruled that the *Mercedes* was a naval vessel of Spain, which still was rightfully entitled to the ship's cargo and any human remains. Odyssey has taken the ruling to the Eleventh District Court of Appeals in America, but Spain remains confident that the recovered treasure will be returned as a matter of international law and principle.

Specific treasure laws should be consulted for each state in which you plan to detect. Since the Florida coast has been among the most popular to detect for Spanish treasures, I will relate the basics for this state. All Florida beaches are public domain with the few exceptions being National Parks and a few small stretches owned by hotels.

The rule on the beach is finder's keepers. Florida beaches may be hunted from the dunes to the low tide line, and that includes the beaches adjacent to the 1715 fleet of Spanish shipwrecks. Although beach finds are okay, surf finds have become an entirely different story in Florida. Effective June 1, 2005, Florida did away with its Isolated Finds program, where people could keep their finds as long as the state was provided with details of the recovery location. It is now against the law to keep anything which is more than 50 years old that comes from state waters. Divers and treasure hunters are responsible for knowing these laws. In Florida, state waters include all submerged bottom lands to include lakes, rivers and 3 miles out into the ocean on the East Coast, 9 miles out on the Gulf Coast and 12 miles out from Key West. Some state parks do allow metal detecting with a permit but not federal parks.

This example of the Florida coastal treasure laws illustrates how important it is to understand the beach, surf and state waterways legislation in your area.

————

### General Underwater Detecting Tips

• *Swing your detector parallel to the sea as you approach the water.* Some detectors, particularly Single Frequency (VLF) models, lose their ground balance as their electronics pass from wet salt sand to dry sand and back to wet sand. Ground balance, either manual or automatic, is a vital feature in order to effectively hunt with a VLF in the ocean or along the saturated sand at water's edge.

• *Take special care to keep your detector's control housing dry and out of the water* unless, of course, you are using a fully submersible unit such as Garrett's *Infinium LS*™ or *Sea Hunter Mark II*™ models. Deep surf hunters and wreck divers are best served by one of these two models, which are fully submersible to 200-foot depths. Both models use PI (Pulse Induction) technology, which transmits a pulsing signal that is impervious to the effects of the salt mineralization. PI detectors are thus ideal for use in the ocean for diving to deep shipwrecks or for use in the wet salt sand on ocean beaches.

Regardless of what brand of detector you select for beach hunting, you should carefully study the instruction manual or DVD that accompanied your unit. This will better help you to understand the pros and cons of any discrimination modes, such as Salt Elimination, that might be available on your detector.

Garrett's *AT Pro*™ and *AT Gold* single frequency detectors, which can be submerged to a maximum depth of 10 feet, are less expensive options if you desire to search around shallow swimming areas, lakeside docks and piers, or other target areas in shallow water. The *AT Gold* is appropriate for freshwater hunting, while the *AT Pro*'s ground balance range even allows it to operate in saltwater environments.

• *Single Frequency metal detectors will do well in dry sand areas* and many offer a graphic target display system to help searchers distinguish between potential good targets and trash. Be sure to revisit the discrimination illustration in Chapter 3, because opting to discriminate the pesky pull tabs so often found on the beach may cause you to miss gold rings. The widely-varying composition of gold jewelry—in addition to size or thickness of the piece—plays into each piece's Target ID reading.

| GOLD JEWELRY COMPOSITION AND MARKINGS | | | |
|---|---|---|---|
| % Pure Gold: | Stamp | Marking | Parts per 1,000 |
| 100.00% | 24kt | 24/24 | 990 |
| 91.66% | 22kt | 22/24 | 916 |
| 87.50% | 21kt | 21/24 | 875 |
| 75.00% | 18kt | 18/24 | 750 |
| 66.66% | 16kt | 16/24 | 666 (dental gold) |
| 58.50% | 14kt | 14/24 | 585 |
| 50.00% | 12kt | 12/24 | 500 |
| 41.66% | 10kt | 10/24 | 417 |
| 33.33% | 8kt | 8/24 | 333 |

- *Areas of trash concentration can be good areas to find gold and jewelry.* Casual hunters using more discrimination may be able to pick out some of the coins in such a trashy area but may just by-pass some of the better gold items buried in the sand to avoid digging the junk.

Those who dig jewelry know that by discriminating pop tops, pull tabs or foil, you will absolutely eliminate some gold items. Jewelry covers such a wide range of the discrimination scale due to the wide variety of metals that are alloyed with pure gold to give it strength. A pure gold ring or chain is recognized as being 24kt while a 10k gold item is less than 50% pure gold. Platinum jewelry is often similarly stamped with an indicator of its purity. A platinum piece stamped as either "950/1000" or "950 PLAT" is 95% pure platinum.

- *Use headphones while hunting on the beach or in shallow water.* The practice of using headphones is solid advice regardless of whether you are hunting near the water or not. You will simply hear the faint signals better with headphones and you will hear more of them. Crowds, wind and surf noises at the beach can negatively affect your ability to pick up target signals.

- *Take advantage of tides and treasure traps.* By studying the tides, you will learn that certain times of the day are better than others for hunting the coastline. Nearly twice a day a full tide cycle occurs—two high and two low tides. Low tides are of greater interest to you because the water level has dropped, leaving more beach areas exposed.

Look for tidal pools and long, water-filled depressions where lost items can collect. Both wind and water move beach sand around in a continual process that create natural treasure traps. Coins, jewelry, relics and other debris shift until heavy objects—such as rocks, piers, fencing or other obstructions—impede their progress.

Relic hunting along the beaches or in waterways is a special hunting environment. Consult detecting books focused on surf, sand and submerged searching for more on this subject.

## Tips for Hunting Freshwater Rivers and Streams

In most areas of the United States, there are rivers, streams, creeks or lakes fairly close to any given community. Since such natural water bodies were sources of survival for the area's early pioneers, you can bet that old coins and relics can often be found at these sites. Preparing to hunt moving streams and rivers differs from traditional water searching in some aspects, particularly in being properly prepared to hunt.

Be aware that antiquities laws vary between states in regard to what you can keep from rivers and streams. Make sure you are familiar with your local regulations. One of the big keys to being a successful freshwater relic hunter is your diligence in researching potential hot spots—places where history happened on or near a body of water.

It is then vital that you are properly prepared for the type of water environment you plan to hunt. Brian McKenzie and I joined Beau Ouimette and Dan Frezza in the late summer of 2011 to hunt Eastern theatre Civil War water sites. The rivers we hunted were fairly tame due to the fact that there had been no significant rain events in the previous month.

Beau Ouimette, Dan Frezza and Steve Moore work a river in search of Civil War artifacts.

The group used this kayak for lunch and for hauling extra gear and finds up and down the river.

- *Kayaks or canoes:* We found it quite advantageous to let Brian pull a kayak along nearby to hold his camera equipment, as well as our extra gear, lunch, and beverages. The kayak later served a perfect mid-day lunch table in the river and was most useful for depositing the larger and heavier relics we found.

- *Footwear:* For river hunting, tennis shoes or aqua socks can lead to nasty falls on slick, moss-covered rocks in running water. Many sporting goods retailers sell special felt wading boots for river use. Their special felt soles provide extra traction on slippery surfaces and most have reinforced hard rubber toe protection. Look for wading boots that also include drain holes, pull-on straps, and padded upper collars.

You can wear neoprene dive booties inside such wading boots by purchasing larger size boots. In the absence of dive booties, wear heavy socks inside the wading shoes and then roll the tops of your socks down over the upper collar of the wading boots. This will prevent pebbles or any other sharp or rough matter from working its way down into your boots.

- *Protect your fingers.* Extended searching in water will make your skin more vulnerable to nicks and cuts. Use protective gloves that are reinforced to protect your fingertips but ones that still allow you great dexterity. Basic cotton gloves will not provide the extra protection you will need while handling sharp rock surfaces and rusty iron items in running water.

- *Recovering targets in the river.* Once your detector announces a good target signal, recovering that item in running water can be

Protect yourself and your finds in the water. Pouches should be zippered *(left)* or include draw strings *(right)* to prevent losses. Other key river hunting tools are gloves with reinforced finger protection, waterproof headphones, a prospector's pick with magnetic tip, and knee pads for kneeling on rocky river bottoms during recoveries.

something of a challenge. The metal scoops often used for hunting at lakes and beaches are not appropriate for rocky river bottoms where good targets often become wedged in crevices and under rock ledges.

Beau and Dan both prefer a prospector's pick for river hunting to help pry up rocks in search of targets. Be sure the pick includes a strong magnet on its tip. Use the magnet to pull ferrous targets from the bottom so that you do not have to bend over. Targets that

This underwater recovery sequence demonstrates the use of a mask and snorkel to work deeper pockets of the river. After fanning the silt and small rocks from the pinpointed target area *(upper right)*, the author holds a Confederate Enfield bullet in his gloves *(right)*. Note the lack of patina on this Civil War bullet.

do not stick to the magnet will require the use of your hands. Beau and Dan both use waterproofed pinpointers to home in on the target signal. Then, use your hand to agressively fan away the river silt and small rocks. The water current in a river naturally clears away the silt and debris you have stirred up.

Your target will often be visible after such fanning. If not, continue to fan the area and use your pinpointer, removing larger rocks or debris as needed. For targets that have wedged in layers of rocks or under narrow ledges, carry a dive knife to pry items out of tight spots. A dive knife can also prove to very handy should you become fouled in fishing line or netting.

Use a finds pouch strongly secured to your belt or one that physically buckles around your waist to avoid loosing it in the current. I opted for an inexpensive pouch (less than $10) that came with an adjustable waist buckle, two water bottles with securing bands, and zippered pouches. Be careful to zip your finds pouch closed after dropping in each recovered item! Mesh diving bags with drawstring openings also work well.

Finds made by Beau, Dan and Steve on this day's river work include minié balls, lead sinkers made from minié balls and camp lead, a buckle, a Spanish real, camp tools, an artillery shell, a musket barrel, part of a double-barrel shotgun, a scabbard tip, and more.

## BEAU KNOWS CIVIL WAR WATER HUNTING

Beau Ouimette's home lies tucked away near the historic Potomac River which divides Maryland and West Virginia. The interior decor is impressive but words fail to describe the first view a relic hunter experiences upon descending into his cellar level "man cave" of history.

Decades of relic recovery success adorn virtually every square inch of wall space. Tens of thousands of Civil War bullets are piled in containers and line the chair rail ledge two-deep around the room. Display nooks are arranged with pistols, rifles,

camp tools, scabbard tips, swords, horse shoes, artillery shells, stirrups, bottles and the like.

Display boxes are magnificently adorned with Civil War military buttons and buckles. As far as Civil War plates, Beau has found more than 120 so far. These range from the standard issue U.S. belt and box plates to state-specific variations from New York, Ohio, Maine and Alabama.

While a great deal of his collection has been dug on land at old home sites, Civil War battle areas, camp sites, and wartime hospital areas, a good portion of Beau's collection has come from fresh water hunting. He has been at it since 1983, when he was fresh out of the Army and was attending college in the lower Shenandoah Valley.

In his 2011 water hunting efforts alone, he netted four Civil War plates, hundreds of minié balls, a rare Pennsylvania lance, mili-

*(Left)* Beau Ouimette seen in his element— working a river in search of Civil War relics.

These relics displayed on Beau's pool table represent his summer 2011 best finds with a waterproof Garrett *AT Pro* detector. In the foreground are two musket barrels, a Spencer carbine and a rare 6th Pennsylvania Cavalry lance tip.

tary buttons, artillery shells, cannon shot, a rifle, a pistol, and even a whopping silver cache of 176 coins. These coins range in date from the 1780s to 1837 and may have been a family's fortune that was lost during a wagon crossing of a river in the 1830s.

"I was working an area of the river about knee deep with my *AT Pro*," said Beau. "I got a good signal, fanned back the silt and small rocks, and there I could plainly see

several big silver coins. I scooped them up and ran my coil over the area.

"To my excitement, the signals seemed to be everywhere in this little area. Each time I fanned away the silt, I could see still seven or eight more pieces of silver." This stunning river find—his best single day coin haul yet—includes not only early U.S. coins but others minted in Spain, France, Peru, Chile, Mexico and Brazil.

(*Above*) This chair rail surrounding the basement in Beau's home is lined two deep with recovered minié balls.

(*Left*) Beau is all grins as he poses with his amazing silver coin cache.

(*Below*) Closer view of some of these early coins he recovered from the river.

Beau attributes his success in water hunting to his diligent research in the colder weather of the off season. Once the fall rains set in, causing the rivers and creeks to rise, he returns to land hunting. When winter weather finally chases him indoors, Beau has another hobby that keeps him quite busy… cataloging all of his season's finds!

Beau's basement relic museum includes a trough of thousands of Civil War bullets *(upper left)* and buckets of round balls *(center)* that he has found.

*(Below)* Dan Frezza and Steve Moore examine Beau's recent relic finds, including his river haul of 176 silver coins. Note the various swords and guns of Beau's collection displayed on the wall in the background.

*(Above)* Beau found all of the Civil War plates in this case while hunting shallow water areas. Note the lack of patina on two of the shinier plates.

*(Above)* This group of Beau's recovered Civil War artillery ordnance is primarily Bormann fused cannon balls, fired from a 12-pound smoothbore cannon.

*(Right)* Inert Parrott, Read, Mullane, and Dyer artillery shells that Beau recovered from both land and water hunting.

## SEA HUNTER:
## SPANISH TREASURE OFF THE FLORIDA COAST

Scott Thomson will be the first to tell you that treasure diving on a Spanish shipwreck is not all gold and glory. For the past six years, he has put in countless hours per month toward treasure recovery and many more hours handling legal issues associated with his portion of a treasure claim.

The Spanish galleon *San Miguel de Arcangel* broke apart around 1660 off the coast of Florida. Just *how* close was unknown until Peter Leo, a local lifeguard, happened upon a cannon and an anchor with some coins attached to them while diving in 1987.

The lifeguard to began recovery work on the wreck and then formed a Florida corporation called JWI (Jupiter Wreck, Inc.), to work the Admiralty claim. Once a 78-pound silver ingot was found, things heated up on the wreck. The state of Florida assumed jurisdiction over the wreck. Legislation signed that year by President Ronald Reagan included the Abandoned Shipwrecks Act of 1987, which transferred the rights of shipwrecks close to the coast to the states whose waters they lie in. Fortunately, a compromise was reached with the *San Miguel de Arcangel* wreck allowing the local salvors the rights to the wreck and all its cargo with all one of a kind items going to the state.

Archaeological work on the wreck conducted between 1987 and 1995 recovered some 10,000 artifacts from the wreck site, as well as eight-real coins from the mint in Cartagena, Spain and two escudo coins from another mint in Bogota.

From the archaeological evidence, the salvors became convinced of their treasure ship's identity. The *San Miguel de Arcangel* reached Havana in December 1659. She later sailed for the Florida Straits loaded with treasure and 120 passengers, but never made it. The ship was grounded on a sandbar off Florida's eastern coast during a winter storm and the ship broke apart.

Scott Thomson bought out Peter Leo's interest in JWI six years ago and is thus legally permitted to treasure dive the site. One might think the job is quite simple being that the wreck is only a hundred or so yards off the Jupiter Inlet jetty in water that is calm and crystal clear most of the year.

Scott will tell you, however, that it is truly work that just happens to have exciting payoffs. His 34-foot, twin-turbo Caterpillar diesel engine *Seahunter* contains two blowers which are pointed down toward a particular gridded spot. The blowers blast out 12 to 15 feet of sand in order to clear a search area approximately ten feet square. The *Seahunter* is then positioned right

*(Above)* Scott's boat Seahunter in position above the wreck site. *(Right)* One of Scott's divers using a Garrett *Sea Hunter* detector to search for Spanish coins.

above the search spot. "It's very tough just to maintain the position," says Scott. "Once the sand is cleared, our GPS is 30 feet above the actual treasure. The wind is constantly blowing the boat around."

Scott and his team have used various detectors on this wreck over the years, but they have settled on Garrett *Sea Hunters* in recent years. Their finds through the early 2011 season include more than 160 silver coins, three gold coins, and three rare Lima Star coins, in addition to other artifacts that have been recovered. Another valuable coin type that JWI has recovered from the site is a coin known as a 1652 transitional 8 type III.

There are generally two to four divers in the water at any given time working the blown out holes. Scott's crews have found that one metal detector in the hole at a

time provides the best results while another diver swims the outer perimeter of the hole, checking other targets. Another diver helps by moving rocks aside on the bottom. The coordinated efforts have paid off in more frequent coin finds around the rocks and in the sand.

"We find treasure six out of seven days that we dive, more than any other shipwreck to date," said Dustin Juhasz, one of the JWI team members and divers. "Our *Sea Hunter* detectors spend 40 to 60 hours per week underwater and have been put through the worst conditions possible. We have beat the searchcoils through sand, shell and rock and have even had boulders roll over on them underwater."

The wreck is so close to shore that divers need not worry about missing the boat. "I have half a dozen qualified divers who

*(Left)* Silver Spanish reales after cleaning. *(Right)* Scott examines an iron vase recovered from the shipwreck with Florida archaeologist James Leavy.

*(Left)* Two gold escudos recovered in the summer of 2011. *(Right)* A gold two escudo, a 1659 Lima Star, a 1652 Transitional 8 type III Potosi coin, and a corroded silver real.

are always welcome to join our team on any given day," says Scott. "Sometimes, one of them will literally swim out to the site from the beach."

Scott is careful on who he selects to work with his team. "For some people, finding treasure comes naturally," he said. "Other people can work for a year and not find a thing."

Their finds are impressive, but as Scott points out, they are only a taste of what is to come once they hit the mother load. Until that time comes, the *Seahunter* dive teams continue to work the wreck on an almost daily basis during the better periods of the year. Coins and artifacts are brought to the surface to be tagged and packaged for fu-

ture archaeological examination. The finds are cleaned and turned over to the state of Florida at the end of each season.

Generally, they are returned within a number of months. Treasure work is not all fun and games. "Treasure brings out the best and the worst in people," Scott says. The site is therefore monitored 24/7 by web cameras that are pointed to the area.

"Treasure is a pain after you recover it," he admits. "You have to clean it, preserve it, make sure that nobody steals it, and finally deal with the federal authority." Is it all worth it? Absolutely, in Scott's opinion.

"It's the finding and it's the adventure that makes all the rest of it so worthwhile." Numerous articles and television spotlights

One of the Jupiter wreck divers holds out a day's haul of Spanish coins.

*(Left)* The *Seahunter*'s blowers are readied for excavation over the site. *(Above)* Recovered coins bagged and ready to be turned in to archeaologists.

have been produced in recent years as the Jupiter wreck divers continue to haul in the booty from this 1660 treasure ship.

Scott, Justin, and the rest of their team are confident that their years of efforts will eventually pay off big time when they finally swing their searchcoils across the big pile of treasure cargo still believed to be hidden in the sand and rocks. Finding a fortune in treasure may not come easily, but these divers will tell you that there is plenty of fun and adventure along the way.

*(Above)* Diver Jason Nowell holds a Spanish coin he has just discovered. *(Below)* A good day of working the site produced these finds.

## A CIVIL WAR RIVER SITE THAT JUST KEEPS PRODUCING

When Charlie Harris began Civil War relic hunting with a metal detector in 1968, he figured that most of the good stuff had already been found. He knows better now. Since that time, he has found thousands of relics which include Rebel and Yankee buckles, five revolvers, seven rifles and more than 100 artillery shells.

His home is literally a museum of relics found during his past four decades of metal detecting. His wife Teresa, a collector of baby bottles from the 1700s through the 1960s, has other display cases dedicated to her glass collection. Charlie's finds have come primarily from Tennessee, Georgia, Mississippi and Alabama, and a good many of them were found underwater.

"My very first Civil War find, as a matter of fact, was made underwater," Charlie related. In 1968, he began hunting a site on the Sequatchie River in Tennessee that turned out to be very productive. Confederate Major General Joseph Wheeler led a cavalry raid in October 1863 against a Union supply train on Anderson Pike that was attempting to relieve besieged Federal troops at Chattanooga. Wheeler burned an estimated 800 or more wagons and captured livestock.

"Recovering relics there is tough on tools and on searchcoils," says Charlie. "I've worn out many coils because the bottom is red clay with chert rock that can be

This case in Charlie's home contains some of his Civil War relics recovered underwater from the Tennessee river he still hunts.

razor sharp. We use Kevlar gloves to dig out our targets."

Believe it or not, Charlie's Sequatchie River site still produces Civil War artifacts even after he and his friends have hunted it for 42 years. "One of the burned Union wagons ended up in the river and we will never recover all of the items."

Although a certified scuba diver, Charlie does not bother with scuba gear for this site. He wades or stands on his tiptoes and "duck dives" to retrieve the relics he detects. "The hardest relic I retrieved from there was a huge cast iron pot," he said. "I spent at least 45 minutes duck diving to dig it free, coming up for breaths of air and going back under."

He wrote an article about this Civil War river site in 1970 and has since authored

*(Above)* A 3-inch, 12-pound Hotchkiss shell shows the effects of the 1863 Sequatchie Valley wagon train fire in the melting of the lead sabot.

Charlie and Teresa Harris' home is filled with more relics than dozens of museums. Seen at left are items recovered from underwater, including shoes from Mobile Bay and shells from the Sequatchie River wagon train fire from the Civil War.

more than 100 Civil War articles. He is currently a featured author for *American Digger* and has published two relic books including *Civil War Relics of the Western Campaigns*.

The area of the Sequatchie River that Charlie and his friends have worked is about 50 feet wide by 400 yards long. "We will never completely work it out," he states. "There was a log jam on the river about six years ago where the force of the water washed the dirt away all the way to the bedrock. That really opened things up for us again."

Charlie says their haul of Civil War artifacts from this river to date includes 125 ar-

*(Left, top)* Charlie and Teresa Harris.

*(Left, lower)* 1855 Springfield musket recovered from swamps around Richmond, VA. The x-ray shows that it is still loaded with a .69-caliber buck and ball load.

*(Below)* Charlie's collection of canister, grape and artillery shells from various Civil War locations. These range in size from 3" long to 4.56" 12-pounder canister rounds.

tillery shells, three Burnside rounds, 40 to 50 Burnside hulls, 100 complete Spencer rounds, 3,000 blown up Spencer hulls, two Union buckles, two bayonets, and about 200 pounds of shrapnel. He has also recovered, piece by piece, nearly an entire Colt Navy revolver. Charlie estimates that there are just as many relics that have settled down to the bedrock level which remain to be found over time.

*(Above)* This Colt Navy revolver, serial # 4399, was recovered piece by piece from the Sequatchie River over a period of two summers. It was rebuilt by Charlie Harris, with the only non-recovered pieces being the cylinder, the cylinder pin, the loading lever and minor interior parts. He also made a new grip for this Colt.

*(Left)* A 3", 10-pound Hotchkiss canister round from Virginia with iron balls inside the tin can. The lower one had lead balls and was recovered from the wagon train fire in the Sequatchie Valley. The lead balls have melted. Also shown is a base recovered from the Sequatchie Valley with a casting of the patent date information (erroneously stamped as 1852 instead of 1862).

*(Right)* This is one of Charlie's many cases of various minié balls and Civil war artifacts he has recovered. Note that he marks each bullet with info on its find location.

*All images are courtesy of Charlie Harris.*

# MOM, DAUGHTER MAKE SPANISH TREASURE FLEET FIND

Bonnie Schubert has spent the better part of her life on board boats or in the ocean diving for treasure. Partnered with her mother in the treasure hunting business, this mother and daughter team made one of the most significant finds ever off the Florida coast in 2010.

Bonnie and her mother Jo are co-owners of a 30-foot boat named *Gold Hawg*. Jo and her husband Walter Schubert ran a charter business in the Bahamas from a live-aboard schooner until their daughter Bonnie was born. The family business kept them living in the Bahamas during the 1960s and 1970s.

It was only natural that Bonnie would grow up with a deep love for the ocean and for scuba diving. By 1991, she had become a salvager working with veteran treasure hunter Harold Holden. Together, they worked Spanish shipwrecks off the Florida coast where she was quick to hold her own in a profession that is traditionally male-oriented.

Year later, Bonnie and her mother Jo bought their own dive boat when Harold

*(Above)* Bonnie Schubert happily displays the Spanish gold statue she has just recovered from the site of a 1715 treasure fleet lost off the coast of Florida.

retired from the salvage business. *Gold Hawg*, their second boat as a mother-daughter team, has lived up to its name and then some.

Bonnie has recovered silver reales and cobs and interesting maritime artifacts—ranging from ship's riggings and fittings to World War II Navy rings and ID tags. On August 15, 2010, however, she made the find of a lifetime. "Mom and I have been working the area of the 1715 treasure fleet for some time," she explained. "It is a very hit-and-miss area to explore. These ships left a very scattered trail. You can literally go days without finding anything."

This particular Spanish fleet is very well known to Florida treasure hunters. On July 31, 1715, a powerful hurricane struck the twelve-ship armada, sinking eleven of them between St. Lucie Inlet and St. Augustine. Modern-day salvors have only found six of these ships but the treasure finds thus far have been extraordinary. According to Bob Marx, the flagship of this fleet—the galleon *Nuestra Señora de la Regla*—carried over 3 million pesos in registered treasure, dozens of chests of jewelry made for the queen of Spain, and unknown amounts of contraband treasure.

Bonnie had gone down to work a new area on this fateful day, just hundreds of yards off Frederick Douglass Beach south of Fort Pierce. Jo remained on board the *Gold Hawg*, tending to her air lines and the boat. Their boat's prop wash deflectors had already been used to blow out a large hole in the ocean sand. Bonnie was diving in about 16 feet of water but the blowers had removed another six feet of sand to get her detector closer to the potential Spanish treasures.

"I prefer to dig all targets in such an area," she related. "A loud hit on my metal detector can often be a beer can, but you never know. This target produced a loud hit but with a more condensed sound. My first impulse was that it might be a chunk of aluminum."

Using her hand fan to swish the remaining sand away, Bonnie was stunned to see a brilliant gold figurine looking like an eagle.

This 5½-inch solid gold statue was later appraised at $885,000!

The statue is thought to be a Catholic church religious statue representing a "Pelican in her Piety." This allegorical depiction of Jesus Christ has been used in art since the Medieval Period in cathedrals, figurines and stained glass. In such art, a mother pelican is shown spilling her own blood to revive her young. Another possibility offered by Bob Marx of Bonnie's Spanish find is that it could have been a ciborium, a chalice-like vessel used by Catholics to contain the Blessed Sacrament.

By salvage law, the state of Florida will take 20% of the find's final value. Bonnie and the contractor through whom she has a salvage lease for this site will split the remaining 80% value. The rights to work this 1715 Spanish fleet were long held by the Mel Fisher family and Bonnie considers herself fortunate to have obtained a lease to work this area. The state-approved contractor is responsible for the legal work, data collection and proper conservation of all dives and recoveries made in state controlled waters.

Bonnie and Jo may not be able to top this 1715 Spanish find in the near future, but they plan to have fun trying!

Front and reverse views of the 5.5" gold Spanish religious item recovered by Bonnie.

# CHAPTER 16

# METAL DETECTORS AND ARCHAEOLOGY

Even though metal detectorists turn up history, they are not always looked upon favorably by professional archaeologists. Still, progressive countries have taken steps to help open communication between amateur "relic hunters" and professional archaeologists. Britain is among these nations that have encouraged treasure seekers to turn in their finds to proper authorities. Since the 1996 Treasure Act, detectorists have been offered market value for their discoveries. The British Museum has the first option to buy the treasure or can opt to return it to the finder.

The willingness of detectorists to report finds and claim their rewards has shown promising growth. In 1999, there were only about 25 "treasure" recoveries reported to British officials. By 2008, however, the number of finds reported had grown to 802. Roger Bland of the British Museum in London admitted in 2009, "The collections in our museums would be thinner without the detectorists' finds." British archaeologists and county recording officers now offer talks to some of the regional detecting clubs aimed at improving the detectorists' understanding of their work.

Because of the numbers of people involved in detecting and who participate in organized rallies, it is only natural that chance discoveries happen fairly often in Europe. In just the past few years, a number of significant hoards of gold artifacts, jewelry and other valuable artifacts have been discovered by detectorists who just happened to be sweeping the right area with their searchcoil.

Such was the case while I was attending the September 2009 West Hanney rally near Oxford in England. Chris Bayston from Yorkshire pursued a deep signal and dug what proved to be a grave containing ornate brooch, one that was apparently buried with an early member of a Saxon royal family.

"Archaeologists say that the person in the grave at the West Hanney rally would certainly have been one of high status and probably of royal lineage," related Weekend Wanderers rally organizer Pete Welch. "The most notable Saxon King in the area was King Alfred, who was born at Wantage just 4 miles away. It is a possibility that the person buried at West Hanney is a direct descendant but at this moment there is no way of proving that."

According to Welch, the 4-inch wide brooch is "one of only 20 known brooches of this type found in England. The garnets, which are quite comparatively large, date the brooch to the early 7th century. Garnets in later brooches were smaller as the stones became more expensive. The garnets are underlaid with gold to enhance luster. The white material in each boss is shell that probably came from the Red Sea and is set in an intricate gold wire support which is then surrounded by red garnets. Between the turrets are gold plaques inlaid with scroll work designs. Soil removed from the grave will be washed and hopefully loose stones and gold from the brooch will be recovered and the brooch can be restored to its full glory."

Archaeologists carefully inspected the soil around the skeleton for other artifacts. They lifted to body to scan below it and then reinterred the remains. Ground penetrating radar will be used in the area to assess if there are other Saxon graves. The excavation and assessment work of such an important find is tedious, but the results will certainly add to the historical knowledge of early southeastern England history.

While the items unearthed by detectorists in North America may not be stunning as Saxon gold broaches or Celtic hoards, they are archaeological treasures nonetheless. The professionals in many cases turn to experienced metal detectorists when funding

*(Above)* Archaeologists work to uncover the remains of a Saxon grave site near West Hanney, England, in September 2009. The skeletal remains are believed to be those of someone of high status, possibly royalty. To one side of this seventh century skeleton are two earthenware pots which were placed atop two iron knives *(see below left)*.

The West Hanney remains were buried with a rare brooch. " A spindle whorl and two pieces of blue/green glass were placed between the legs," noted Pete Welch, organizer of the rally in which the discovery was made. "Unusually, there was not a second brooch; they are often found in pairs. Early inspection of this skeleton while in situ shows that the bones were fused, proving that the person was at least a young adult and likely female."

*Photos courtesy of Pete Welch of Weekend Wanderers Detecting Club of England.*

becomes available for recovery work on areas of national importance in the United States—such as battlefields and historic home sites—where detecting is otherwise strictly prohibited.

---

### How Can You Get Involved with History?

• *Volunteer your time as a steward or detectorist with an archaeological project.* In most cases, there is no pay involved and plenty of hard work in the field. The reward is in preserving history and witnessing the items from early civilization that are unearthed.

My first chance to do so came in May 2008 when I worked in the field with archaeologists who were recovering artifacts south of Houston. The site was near the San Jacinto battlegrounds, where the Republic of Texas had earned its independence from Mexico in combat against General Santa Anna's numerically superior Mexican Army in 1836. The site is now preserved by the Texas Parks and Wildlife Commission and detecting is forbidden.

At the time I joined Dr. Gregg Dimmick and his team in the field, they were working on private property near the state-owned park. They believed they had found an area where the Mexican soldiers had fled in the waning minutes of the San Jacinto battle. In this area, a mass surrender took place once the Texan volunteers could be convinced to stop massacring the soldiers they felt were responsible for recent Texas Revolution atrocities at the Alamo and at Goliad.

This "Mexican retreat" area was located on the property of NRG Energy and was heavily forested. In preparation for detecting efforts, the archaeological team had contracted special land-clearing by machinery that literally mulched down the trees and undergrowth to create "zipper lanes" which zigged and zagged along the suspected line of retreat. During the course of many months of surveying this area (under exclusive permission by NRG), the archeologists found numerous items of historical significance, including clusters of bayonets where Mexican soldiers probably under Colonel Juan Almonte apparently laid down their arms and surrendered en masse. As Gregg and I detected along the zipper lanes that day, we found surprisingly few junk metal targets—only a single crushed soda can and a shotgun shell. We found a piece of chain that would have held a Mexican officer's sword to his uniform; a harness ring; a buckle from a shot pouch; and 44 Mexican Brown Bess musket balls.

All of the items recovered this day were taken back to the labs for the participating archaeological company, Moore Archaeological Consulting, to conserve for future display.

• *Join a metal detector club that is involved with historic projects where you can lend your services.* Archaeologists often train interested people in the proper techniques of preserving artifacts recovered in the field.

The Federation of Metal Detector and Archaeological Clubs (FMDAC) was organized in 1984 as a nonprofit legislative and educational organization to protect the recreational use of metal detectors in the United States. Current FMDAC membership is about 150 local metal detecting clubs and more than 5,500 members.

Steve Moore *(above and inset)* holds a Mexican musket ball he has recovered in the forest just off one of the lanes.

*(Above)* Gregg Dimmick (far left) and the archaeology team looks over a map of the area where previous artifacts have been found along this zipper lane through the forest.

• *Conduct your own research to pinpoint areas of special historic interest, making certain that you are not interfering or trespassing on areas that have been previously classified as archaeological sites.* Any area where people once worked or lived can yield coins and other interesting finds. Your discoveries could prove to be of great interest to archaeologists or county historians.

--------

### The Archaeology Process

How metal detectors are incorporated into archaeological excavations varies according to how finite the search area has been specified. For larger tracts of land where historians hope to pinpoint a specific settlement, battle engagement or other significant happenings, they must first narrow down the area.

Volunteer or government-authorized detectorists generally begin by conducting a reconnaissance-level survey of the project area. Such "recons" are not expected to provide 100% coverage of large areas; rather, they hope to use a number of detectorists to range over areas of interest until hot spots are encountered. In areas where artifact concentrations are discovered during these initial surveys, more refined block or radial survey zones are then established to work over areas of concentration more thoroughly.

Metal detector operators are expected to be proficient with their equipment, particularly able to properly ground balance their machines. Such calibrations might range from normal soil to areas of wet sand, high salt soil or highly mineralized ground. Some archeological guidelines further specify that searchcoils should be at least 23 cm (9-inches) in diameter and that headphones are required for each user. The detector's sensitivity should be raised to the highest settings allowable based on soil conditions, and the detector's volume should also be set to the highest comfortable range possible. In areas of artifact concentration, it is especially important that detectorists overlap searchcoil sweeps by 50 percent to avoid skipping any good targets.

Bullet found by author at San Jacinto believed to be a post-Civil War .36- to .44-caliber revolver bullet.

Volunteer Michelle Sunde and archaeologist Douglas Mangum lay down the search lanes for a search projected conducted on the San Jacinto battlegrounds in July 2010.

In preparation for reconnaissance-level surveys or intensive grid zone searches, the project site should be cleared of tall weeds and shrubs. It is important that searchcoils are able to sweep as close to the earth as possible in order to achieve satisfactory ground penetration. Search grids are often marked with strings tied off to corner stakes, or the ground is painted with a suitable florescent-colored paint. The detectorists are generally urged to maintain at least a three-meter distance from each other to avoid interference between machines.

All metal discoveries, or "hits," are dug for identification. The recovery team usually consists of a volunteer digger, or person who handles the excavation, and an archaeological steward, the person who records data associated with each find and tags the item. The artifacts are dug carefully to avoid damage from the shovel or hand tools. The digger will start an excavation several centimeters behind and around the target area that the detectorist has pinpointed. The excavated soil and any vegetation is carefully replaced after the item or items have been removed.

A field form is completed as artifacts are removed. Each item is given a unique location number to help map its coordinate point in relation to the block or zone it was recovered in. The steward also carefully records the depth of the item, the name of the person who pinpointed it, the date and other relevant details. The item is placed in a labeled bag, and the excavation location is mapped by GPS, conventional survey or some other approved method.

The recovered artifacts are delivered to the lab that is handling the conservation for that particular project. The items will often first receive a simple rinsing under fresh water and possibly a light scrubbing with a soft brush to remove as much of the soil as possible. The items are then dried and re-bagged for more extensive cleaning as required.

The final conservation of the specimens is handled under the supervision of a specialist in artifact conservation. The best way to experience the process of a true archaeological project is to volunteer your services to regional experts. The labor of your searches might just prove to be something from which your grandchildren will benefit.

---

### Detecting on the San Jacinto Battlegrounds

Having worked with Gregg Dimmick's team in the field near the San Jacinto site, I let him know that I would gladly help round up another group of detectorists if he needed more help. The following year, a situation presented itself where more metal detector work was required on the actual battlegrounds maintained by the state. The founders and co-owners of Garrett Metal Detectors were pleased to help efforts to recover and preserve important historic artifacts from this Texas Revolution site. Eleanor and Charles Garrett provided financial assistance, ground search detectors and *Pro-Pointers* to the Friends of San Jacinto Battleground to support their ongoing archeological work.

I rounded up a group of detectorists, including Mr. Garrett, who were willing to volunteer their time on the project. They were: Robert Jordan, Rusty Curry, Joe Hennig, Rick Anderson, Glenn Collins, Dave Totzke, Mike Skinner, Herman Denzler, Bob

A team of Garrett detectorists poses with Texas Parks and Wildlife officials, archaeologists and volunteer stewards before commencing artifact recovery work on the San Jacinto battlegrounds in June 2009. The 570-foot San Jacinto Monument is in the background.

Podhrasky and Brian Head. Gregg Dimmick coordinated the efforts of the detectorists. We were joined in the field by Michael Strutt, Director of Cultural Resources for TPWD, Roger Moore and Douglas Mangum of Moore Archaeological Consulting Inc., and Jan Devault of the Friends of the San Jacinto Battleground. The archeologists were assisted by volunteer archeological stewards trained in battlefield survey and excavation techniques. Michael Strutt and Texas State Parks Director Walter Dabney allowed Vaughan Garrett and Brian McKenzie to utilize their video and photography equipment to document the day's recoveries.

June 2009 was admittedly not the most appealing time of 2009 to conduct such labor-intensive field work. The areas we were to search, however, were in the vicinity of General Santa Anna's 1836 Mexican campground. They were also soon scheduled to be replanted in native coastal grasses present on the day of the battle. This effort will help restore San Jacinto's prairies to the conditions that existed in 1836 when Texans were able to take advantage of the cover and advance right on top of Santa Anna's camp before being discovered.

In preparation for our field work, the Texas Department of Transportation mowed several grids of the battlefield which enabled the detectors to work close to the ground surface. All the work at San Jacinto was conducted under a Texas Antiquities Permit for archaeological excavation.

The work was challenging, searching under the junk metal that had accumulated over years of park visitors picnicking and walking through the area: pop tops, shredded aluminum cans, modern coins, and various "trash" targets. Each searcher worked in groups that included one detectorist, one volunteer steward and an archaeologist to collect the artifacts. When a good historic item was unearthed, the steward carefully noted the depth and conditions where the item was found. The archeologists use a laser-guided total station to record the horizontal and vertical coordinates of each artifact recovered. The precise plotting creates a highly accurate database from which maps can be made of the site showing the distribution of all artifacts across the battle site.

Charles Garrett helped recover several Mexican musket balls and a buckle from a shot pouch using his *GTI 2500*. Several others, including myself and Rusty Curry, helped pinpoint musket balls. Gregg Dimmick switched between different brands of detectors during the day in order to field test the abilities of various machines. He had me come in behind him on several lanes where he had planted flags for the diggers to indicate a good "hit." If my Garrett did not pick up his target, I moved on. If I did find it, or if I found a target he had missed, I added a different color flag. A challenge this day for some detectorists was a layer of mineralization that lay about eight inches beneath the surface. This battleground sits on the edge of the Houston Ship Channel and is barely above sea level. The ground below was thus wet with moisture from recent heavy rains and the high water table, causing some conditions similar to wetted salt that might be encountered at the coast.

Robert Jordan and several of the detectorists working near the Mexican breastworks recovered a number of iron items. When some of them were bothered by the number of large square nails and other metal items being dug, Douglas Mangum quickly explained that these pieces were historically significant. They were the remnants of the breastworks that had long since disintegrated over time. By the time we took a lunch break, Douglas and Roger had already registered 62 items that had been sited in. The breastworks had been stacked high to form a defensive shield to the Texan rifles on April 21. Private James Hill of the Texas Army had noted in 1836 that the Mexican breastworks—stacked with "brush, blankets, sacks of corn, flour, camp equipage, aparajos [packsaddles]" and other goods—seemed initially to be "bulletproof."

Another significant item excavated was a canister plate believed to have been used by the Texas artillerymen. This plate was thick, about the size of the top half of a softball, and had four holes drilled through it. Such canisters or stands of grape, used by both the Texan and Mexican cannon, created a shotgun effect when fired from a field piece. Only two other such canister plates have been recovered from the battleground, making this an important discovery. Mapping where the plate was found, and working backwards from there, can help the archeologists locate where the Texas cannon stood when it fired the shot.

We also recovered a folding pocket knife believed to have been carried into combat by a Texan. This aged utensil was badly corroded and in pieces, although the ground had actually preserved some of the original wood of the knife.

Following our Saturday recovery work, six detectorists—Glenn, Rusty, Robert, Joe, Rick and Mike—returned on Sunday to help survey an area where the Texan cavalry under Colonel Sidney Sherman had skirmished with an advance force of Mexican cavalry, artillery and infantrymen. Their finds were not as numerous, as this area had been previously surveyed.

All told, the survey work through 2009 on San Jacinto's battlefields recovered thousands of artifacts, including more than 600 pieces of shot, ranging from Texan and Mexican musket balls to grape shot and the three canister plates. The recovered artifacts will be cleaned and conserved by expert teams at Moore Archeo-

*(Left)* Texan reenactors on the San Jacinto battleground charge through the tall prairie grass.

*(Below, left)* Mexican soldiers prepare to fire a replica of the Golden Standard cannon that was captured during the battle.

*(Below, right)* Michael Strutt of the Texas Parks and Wildlife Department thanks Charles Garrett for his team's assistance.

*(Bottom)* Texan reenactors storm General Santa Anna's breastworks where the Garrett team searched in 2009.

logical Consulting. Certain items in need of specific conservation will be passed on to Texas A&M University for special attention.

The location of artifacts or artifact clusters becomes extremely meaningful when archaeologists compile their data. "The coordinates of the artifacts are downloaded from the Total Station data collector into a Geographic Information System (GIS) program back at our office," Roger Moore explained. "This program, managed by Douglas Mangum, does more than simply make a map of our finds. Each artifact coordinate is a precise 'real-world' location that can be displayed accurately over many different maps—as long as the maps or aerial photos have been 'geo-referenced'— that is, overlaid so that their feature locations correspond with the same points on a very accurate base map layer."

Simply put, this means that Roger's team can see the artifacts with considerable accuracy against the background of a 1920 U.S. Geological Survey Quadrangle map as well as plotting these items on the current version of the same map. "We can also look at the artifacts in relation to a 1930 aerial photo as well as against a picture taken in 2009," Moore detailed. "We can easily add Garrett's 2009 artifact locations to those of the materials previously found in the breastworks area over five years ago."

The detailed GIS program allows the experts to determine where key events of the battle occurred. The location of the canister plates has helped to determine the firing locations of the cannons. "Also, the analysis of musket balls by Doug Scott Ph.D (an expert on Little Bighorn's battlefield artifacts) combined with GIS have allowed us to potentially determine small unit locations, via the similar ball molds," said Mangum.

The archaeological work will no doubt continue for some time at San Jacinto. When the results of all the surveys are compiled and published, they will certainly add valuable new knowledge to our understanding of the Texas Revolution's most significant battle. I was able to assist with the detecting work again in the summer of 2010, although the arrival of Hurricane Alex on the Texas coast caused a halt earlier than planned one day as lightning and driving bands of rains set in. This proved to be the first time I have ever been forced from the fields by an approaching hurricane.

Some of the San Jacinto artifacts previously conserved are on display in the Sam Houston Museum in Huntsville. Many other Texas Revolution artifacts unearthed by Dr. Gregg Dimmick's teams during their tracking of the Mexican Army's retreat after San Jacinto can be seen at the Alamo in San Antonio, at the Bob Bullock Texas State History Museum in Austin or in the Fort Bend Historical Museum in Richmond.

Responsible relic recovery means occasionally donating your time and your finds to a greater cause, that of conserving history for our future generations.

# DETECTING WITH ARCHAEOLOGISTS: THE PROCESS

*(Above)* A team of Garrett metal detectorists participated with professional archaeologists on a Texas Revolution battleground that is now a State Historic Site. Archaeologist Roger Moore shoots in an artifact from the total station (base).

*(Below)* The field team lines up the artifact by placing their site pole in the recovery hole as detectorist Herman Denzler takes a break from the midday heat.

Note: Garrett metal detectors were used at San Jacinto Battleground State Historic Site in Texas during controlled archaeological investigations and under the supervision of professional archaeologists. Recreational use of metal detectors is prohibited by law at all Texas State Parks and Wildlife Management Areas.

Steve Moore enjoys the recovery of a musket ball *(right and below)* on the 1836 battleground where two of his ancestors helped Texas win its independence.

The artifact recovery process. *(Left)* Detectorists Rusty Curry and Brian Head watch as the stewards dig and pinpoint artifacts.

The volunteer steward *(below, left)* records the data on a form for each artifact and then seals it in a bag *(below)* that is also marked with the data.

*(Right)* Charles Garrett shows his enthusiasm as his team recovers another artifact. *(Below)* This simplified image from the archaeologist's software shows how they learn from the plotted concentrations of artifacts recovered at San Jacinto.

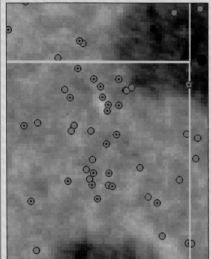

By participating in professional archaeological projects, the detectorists have the satisfaction of helping to recover significant history that can soon be enjoyed by others in museums.

Among the many items Garrett detectorists helped unearth on San Jacinto projects were *(clockwise from above left)*: a chain from an officer's uniform, a cluster of dropped musket balls found by the author, a shot pouch buckle, and this canister base from an artillery shell.

*(Above, left and center)* Front and back of a flat button found near the breastworks. *(Left and above right)* Many early square nails and other iron artifacts that were recovered are likely the remnants of the Mexican Army's deteriorated breastworks.

*(Below)* This decomposed early folding knife was found by the author at about eight inches 100 yards away from the breastworks area.

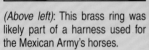

*(Above left)*: This brass ring was likely part of a harness used for the Mexican Army's horses.

*(Right)* The author and other search teams scour lanes near the monument.

# CHAPTER 17

# CAMPSITE AND GHOST TOWN RELICS

Stephen Jordan learned the value of detecting long-forgotten military campsites decades ago. His relic hunting began during the 1970s in Alabama, when he was interested in hunting arrowheads and digging Civil War pits. By the 1980s, he had become a serious metal detectorist who put in the necessary research to local Civil War campsites now overrun by modern farms and forest.

In recent years, Stephen has become close friends with several others who live near him in central Mississippi. One of them is Rob Stephens, whose father Glen bought him his first metal detector in 1980. "He got me an old White's detector that just beeped on any metal target it encountered," Rob recalled. "But the first silver coin I saw was a 1953 silver half dollar my dad found in our own front yard. That was enough to get me excited about metal detecting and to move up to improved detector models over the years."

Glenn Stephens was close friends with Autry Reynolds, who had been detecting for many years. Glenn and Autry's primary interest was in coin hunting, a sport that Glenn's son Rob came to enjoy as well. Years later, Autry and Glenn happened upon Stephen Jordan while all were detecting a rural site in Mississippi. Glenn took an interest in the Civil War relics that Stephen had been digging that day and casually showed him a button he had dug.

"What do you make of this?" Glenn asked Stephen.

Stephen quickly noted the distinctive Lone Star State emblem and "CS" letters on the nice brass button. "That's a local manufac-

*(Above)* Stephen Jordan *(left)* helped introduce Rob Stephens *(center)*, his father Glenn *(right)* and their friend Autry Reynolds to the experience of hunting Civil War campsites in central Mississippi. Their finds have produced cases of artifacts such as this one.

*(Left)* Four Civil War camp Confederate plates found by the Mississippi foursome. Rob found one of the CS two-part belt plates while Glenn recovered the large rope border plate and the other two-part plate. The half plate in the lower right was found by Autry.

*(Left)* This find by Stephen is believed to be half of a Texas officer's sash buckle. It appears to have been made by a jeweler and was found on the edge of a Texas camp in Mississippi.

*(Right)* One of Rob and Glenn's cases from their past Mississippi campsite hunts is filled with hundreds of one-piece flat buttons such as these. Such early buttons are a common find for these dedicated relic hunters.

ture Texas unit Civil War button known as a T. Miller!" he said, perhaps too excitedly. "Where did you find that?"

Glenn casually sent Stephen off searching in the wrong direction while pocketing his valuable button find. By 2005, Glenn, Autry, Stephen and Rob had all become close relic hunting companions and Glenn's little "white lie" of misdirecting Stephen was admitted one night after a few beers. Glenn and Autry were hooked on recovering Civil War artifacts after Stephen explained to them the value of Glenn's Texas star button. In their years of coin hunting, Autry and Glenn had tossed aside many such old buttons that they had assumed to be more modern and worthless.

Glenn Stephens and his son Rob each recovered half of a Confederate rope border oval plate in a Confederate camp several years ago, their first CS buckle. "He found the half with the 'C' on it and a little while later I found the half with the 'S' on it," said Rob. "My friend Leonard Short put it back together for us."

Today, this Mississippi quartet is an efficient relic hunting team that enjoys scouting for rural Civil War campsites. Their success is closely tied to the amount of research they put into finding prospective hot spots. "We hunt a lot of old house sites to find the evidence of where Civil War campsites might have been," Stephen explained. "Many of the early homes were located near spring heads in this area of Mississippi. Many early settlers made their homes near rivers or creeks, but in other areas the homes were near the head of a natural spring.

"Where we find the source of a natural spring in rural areas, we then begin scouting for signs of homesteads. Once we find the iron and household items that lead us to the home sites, then we began moving out around the home in search of campsites. Where we find evidence that troops have visited a home during the Civil War, we know that a campsite will be in the vicinity. So, we look for buttons or minié balls or things of military use that were lost near the home site and then begin our search for the camp.

"We generally find that Civil War infantry camps are not more than a quarter mile away from the home site. Cavalry camps can

*(Above)* Two T-Miller "CS" Texas buttons, one found by Rob and one found by Stephen within 20 minutes at a Civil War campsite.

*(Above)* Louisiana pelican state seal buttons. Rob found the local version (left) and his father Glen found the import (right).

*(Above)* Rob's recovered Confederate buttons include three local block "C" cavalrys, one block "R" rifleman button, a local block "A" artillery, and three cast "I" infantry buttons.

*(Above)* Gold-plated Leech and Rigdon sword hanger found in Mississippi.

*(Below)* The author's Mississippi camp finds included this bullet button, two buck and ball pieces and an early flat button.

*(Above)* Autry's central Mississippi finds include this 1850s MS or TX buckle, a cavalry and artillery button, an 1854 Seated Liberty dime and an 1853 half dime.

*(Right)* Found coins are an ideal way to help date a site. Glen and Autry have dug more than 1,000 silver coins from old school, church and home sites.

(Above) 1852 gold coin dug by Autry Reynolds. (Below) Autry dug this .37-caliber Colt round on our September hunt.

(Above and right) Stephen's 13-year-old son Dalton has found one cast "I" button and two tin-back "I" buttons in camps since starting to hunt at age 10.

(Above) Rob and Glenn's camp finds include this spur, buckles and various Civil War bullets.

(Above) Alabama local state seal "map" button found by Rob. One collector estimated its value at more than $1,200.

(Above) Three CSA eagle "D" buttons dug by Stephen.

(Right) Rob's favorite find: a 10 kt. gold Union Army badge.

(Above) Rob dug this partially carved Enfield minié ball during September 2010 campsite hunt.

be found much further away from the home. Just like the settlers, the troops and their horses needed water, so they would not be too far away from such a source in most cases."

This Mississippi hunting team has compiled an enviable collection of Civil War and early 1800s relics in the past five years by working such old campsites. Some of Stephen and Rob's finds have even been published in relic hunting magazines such as *American Digger*—with a few even making the cover because of their rarity or excellent conditions.

The lost military accoutrements they have found include minié balls, scabbard tips, belt plates, state-specific Confederate buttons, early silver coins, hat insignia, spurs, canteens, heel plates, silverware, and assorted personal items lost by the troops. Many of their better finds are displayed in impressive relic cases that Stephen, Rob and Glenn have built. Rob often sends his better belt plates and buttons to a jeweler, Leonard Short, now a Civil War relic restoration expert, to repair minor damages and to professionally clean the artifacts.

Rob's favorite finds include a gold-plated sword hangar made by the Memphis manufacturer Leech & Rigdon and a 10-kt. gold Union Army First Division of the 4th Corps badge. This jeweler-crafted piece still has a T-bar fastener on the back side and a red enamel Star of David. Apparently worn by a Jewish soldier, this rare find was estimated at about $2,000 by one Civil War expert.

Rob enjoys researching such finds almost as much as finding them. "In some cases, we can figure out what unit might have lost one of the relics," he said. In one case, he located an Alabama state seal button in a campsite and was able to track down the fact that an Alabama unit had indeed camped in that area through diary entries a soldier made during the Civil War.

Stephen, Glenn, Rob and Autry have access to literally thousands of acres of private land in central Mississippi. They are careful to fill their holes, respect the wishes of the property owners and conduct themselves in such a way that often gains them access to new areas later. Brian Pennington and I had the good fortune to join this

*(Above)* Brass camp buttons found by Stephen Jordan. At left is a prewar Confederate staff local button. The three Bingham Military School (Mebane, NC) were all found near an old house site. At far right is an office of engineer's staff button from the Union Army of Virginia. Stephen found this tin-type construction Texas hat star in a Confederate camp.

*(Left)* Four of Rob's Enfield minie balls. *Left to right:* dot-base .69-caliber ($100 value find); .54-caliber; carved-down .58-caliber; and carved .54-caliber. *(Right)* More of Rob and Glenn's bullets. *Left to right:* fused buck and ball load; sinker carved from a .58-caliber; Enfield-carved nipple protector; Burnside-carved chess piece; and Enfield-carved chess piece.

*(Above)* Campsite buttons found by Stephen, from left: Mississippi "I" cuff button he "bird-dogged" on the ground; early Virginia one-piece from early 1800s; MVC button; and Mississippi local "I" star button.

(Right) Stephen found this eagle insignia hat pin in central Mississippi. It was once part of a large sako military hat used post-Civil War.

*(Left)* The author joined this group for a campsite hunt in Mississippi during September 2010. Left to right: Autry Reynolds, Glenn Stephens, Brian Pennington and Rob Stephens.

*(Left)* Rob dug this Louisiana state seal bridle rosette in a camp in Louisiana during the summer of 2010. The soldier who once owned this gold-plated piece apparently put two holes in it to wear as a hat plate.

team for some hunting on their Civil War campsites in September 2010. The late summer heat and humidity meant that ticks, snakes, spiders and other critters were still in abundance. Since one nasty tick bite recently sent Rob to a local medical facility for treatment and antibiotics, proper treatment of our hunting clothing was a necessity. Brian prefers to completely coat his shirt, pants and hunting boots the night before to allow the tick repellent to become fully soaked in.

Once on the site, we found the need for advanced iron resolution to be a must, particularly around the sites of two old houses located in the deep forest. Near the homesteads, advanced audio features were beneficial to pick out the worthwhile target sounds from the cacophony of pops, snaps and grunts of old iron household items. As we moved out farther from the homes, we were able to locate minié balls and other Civil War period relics. Even as we hunted one piece of property, the Mississippi group was talking about where they would next like to put their research to the test with their machines.

They say the apple doesn't fall far from the tree and in the case of this hunting team, younger members of their family have already been bitten by the relic hunting bug. Stephen Jordan's 13-year-old son Dalton has already dug three cast "I" Civil War buttons since he started joining his father in the field three years ago. Although Rob's two sons are younger, he is certain they will soon follow in the footsteps of their father and grandfather.

Rob is seen digging relics while testing a Garrett *AT Pro* detector on an old campsite. *(Right)* A fired Civil War pistol ball Rob dug on the edge of a field.

---

## Ghost Towning

We all have our own mental picture of what is or what is not a "ghost town." Any deserted township or community that is being reclaimed by the land is essentially a ghost town. These are where people's desires and abilities to live have expired. Modern progress such as faster highways created many little ghost towns throughout multiple states along the famed Route 66 that twists across America.

Countless other ghost towns are created throughout the world as the industries that once supported them play out. Mining, lumber and construction industries create temporary camps and entire towns based upon the volume of work created by a project. Fishing settlements once sprung up in productive areas and communities were even formed as dams or railroad projects created work. As these industries closed, the reason to live in some of these rural areas ceased to be. Similarly, governments close military posts and advanced staging areas.

Bradley Dixon of North Carolina knows that good relics can be found close to home by researching local historic sites. He is a younger relic hunter who has been borrowing his grandfather's 1990s Garrett *Grand Master Hunter CXIII* metal detector to hunt around his hometown of Mebane. A short distance from his home is the site of the long-abandoned Civil War era military academy called the Bingham School.

"As a kid, my grandfather had taken me hunting and showed me how to use the detector," Bradley related. "I found a Wheat penny but it was years before a buddy of mine got me into detecting again. I found two silver rings on a North Carolina beach and I got hooked."

Bradley recently began hunting the Bingham School site, which is now privately owned. "The area where the school stood is now urbanized but there are still remnants of some of the old buildings out in the woods nearby," he said. "The site was used until the

(Left) Bradley Dixon's finds from an abandoned Civil War military academy, The Bingham School, include this U.S. bayonette sheath clip, an early large cent, a Bingham School uniform button, a rectangular school belt plate and a Springfield hammer lock plate.
(Below) Two of his Bingham School military button finds.

1940s, when it burned down. The buildings were made of wood, built up on two rows of bricks. There are places in the woods that wherever you dig with your shovel, you roll out a brick. There are also some old chimneys that are collapsed and laying in the woods." Although this area has undoubtedly been hit by many relic hunters in the past, Bradley's diligence has paid off for him.

He has pulled many early coins from the school site, including various Wheaties, a 1903 Barber dime and an Standing Liberty quarters. "I try to hunt where others have not taken the time to hunt, such as removing surface junk metal so that I can get a better read on what's lying beneath it," Bradley stated. "I also bend small saplings over so that I can swing my coil above them. I have dug several nice items that were lying beneath small trees."

Thus far, he has found one Civil War bullet on the site, Bingham School military buttons, an early large cent, several shell casings, a Bingham School belt plate, a U.S. bayonet sheath clip with a small piece of leather still attached to it and a Springfield hammer lock plate for a Civil War musket.

"The sheath clip and the Bingham School buttons registered as pull tab on my old Master Hunter," he said. His hammer lock find was reason enough for him to dig even some of the iron signals he picks up on this old ghost town schoolyard. Bradley's Civil War era finds have motivated him to keep working the area and to save for a new detector with more advanced discrimination for working such sites.

Regardless of where you live in America, there are probably ghost towns in short driving range. Treasure atlas books have been written for most states, identifying areas across the country where an old settlement, ferry landing, commerce area or some other point of interest once existed. One of the best ways to identify ghost towns is to use county-level research in the local libraries. Many of the spots will only be known from family stories and are often found out about by talking to the locals.

For example, there is an old Confederate hat factory that was once operated near the present small community of Italy, Texas. In history books and on the Internet, only brief mentions of its existence can be found. Detectorists Larry Simpson was determined to find its location and finally managed to do so by mingling with the local community. In the local coffee shop, he worked the locals

Ghost towns provide an excellent opportunity to find old silver money. These are just a fraction of the silver coins found by Tim Saylor and George Wyant while detecting on long-forgotten old home sites in Montana-area ghost towns.

*(Above)* There is often little visual evidence of a ghost town, such as where the author and Robert Jordan are searching in Italy, Texas. Use your detector to sniff out the patches of iron, which hopefully will also contain worthwhile relics and coins. *(Below)* In addition to horseshoes, harness rings, and other farm items, Steve and Robert were able to find several old buttons and coins. Two of Steve's recovered buttons and an 1850s French coin are seen in this photo.

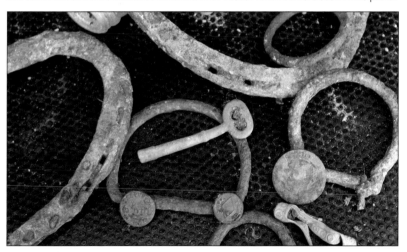

for knowledge of the old factory site and he happened upon a lady who was able to direct him to the current landowner of the property he desired to search.

Your own grass roots scouting efforts can be successful in finding such early sites. Several of the Internet research engines mentioned in Chapter 5 can be used to find old ghost town areas.

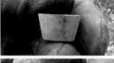

*(Left)* Only a stone chimney remains as evidence of an old home site in the Idaho ghost town that Tim Saylor is searching. One of Tim's more interesting ghost town finds *(below)* was this brass 1/2 oz. prospector's cup for measuring gold.

*(Below)* Old Chinese coins found by Gerry McMullen in old Idaho prospecting ghost towns using an *AT Gold*.

## Military Campsites

Relic hunters have long understood the value of locating a previously undiscovered camp site or mustering station. The array of goods which can be found where troops once gathered is often astounding. Soldiers pitched tents, established huts, dug trenches, cooked food, molded bullets, shoed horses, mended uniforms, discarded broken weapons, and even stashed personal goods they hoped to retrieve after a battle.

Lost coins, pocket knives, rings, good luck charms and many other personal items may be found in such areas. Serious relic hunters began scouting and hunting Civil War campsites during the 1960s and 1970s. New roads, subdivisions, and shopping centers have been built during the past 50 years where skirmish sites or campgrounds once stood in remote areas. Savvy searchers are quick to seek permission to hunt such areas during construction before new blacktop or concrete forever covers over the historic artifacts. The necessary clearing and bulldozing of timber to make way for such modern progress can expose deeper relics that may have been previously unreachable.

In the Dumfries area of northern Virginia, relic hunters Harry Visger, Paul Ervin and Brian McDonald were likely the first to discover a previously unknown camp called Camp Law. During the course of their detecting, they unearthed Mississippi sharpshooter bullets, numerous .58-caliber minié balls, .25-caliber pistol balls, an MVC button, a Virginia button, several Maine buttons, more than two dozen AVC (Alabama Volunteer Corps) buttons, two ACC (Alabama Cadet Corps) buttons, many flat and "flower" buttons, numerous round balls, tent parts, pole rings, grommets and countless other odds and ends. The Camp Law searchers also worked Confederate trash pits with entrenching tools, digging down several feet to find more artifacts, including a rare AVC buckle with a chunk of leather belt still attached.

As Union and Confederate camps were discovered by good research, hard scouting, pure chance and combinations of all three, word spread of the prized relics that were being recovered. During the summer of 1969, a rare 6th Infantry of North Carolina waist belt plate—from one of the few Confederate regiments to wear its own distinctive plates—was dug from the regiment's newly-found Dumfries, Virginia, camp site. At that time, a good Mississippi button alone could fetch between $50 and $75 for collectors. Such a rare Confederate plate obviously held considerable more value to collectors and numerous detectorists swarmed in to work the area.

Finding such productive sites is much more difficult for today's hunters but certainly not out of the question. When such "new" virgin camps are found, the excitement is the same as it was decades before. Take for instance the recent work in a virgin Union camp located in the Shenandoah Valley of Virginia. Keith Sylvester and his fiance Lana Spence from Maryland began relic hunting in 2004 and soon became fascinated with searching for Civil War history. Keith became focused on finding the camp of the Federal Army's right flank from a skirmish that was shown in his Atlas that accompanies the Official Records.

In October 2008 he secured permission to search the private property of a couple who lived in the area of his interest. Keith and Lana began searching the property that winter and soon found an area with a number of dropped three-ring minié balls. Keith dug one half of a mangled U.S. belt plate and a nicely gilted Maryland cuff button. In the weeks that followed, the couple continued to collect minié balls, camp lead, carved bullets, early Spanish reales and more Civil War buttons.

Keith and Lana gained access to the adjoining neighbor's land in early 2009 and their finds continued to multiply: three-ringers, camp lead, knapsack parts, canteen spouts, sword hangars, and Spencer and Burnside rounds. The campsite was large enough that it spilled over into a third piece of private property. Keith was again persistent in tracking down this landowner, who agreed to let the couple work his property in exchange for some of their finds. The new terrain again produced significant finds and the couple dutifully dropped a portion of their finds on the landowner's front door in a sandwich bag after each hunt.

In one hot spot, Lana literally filled her pockets with bullets from an area about 20 feet in diameter. Incredibly, Keith was able to eventually rework the spot where he had found his half U.S. plate and dig up the other half almost a year to the day later. The couple added two eagle breast plates, a beautiful U.S. bit boss, brass saddle buckles, a small powder flask, a U.S. spur. By the winter of 2009, Keith and Lana were continuing to work over these pieces of property and the virgin Union camp has not ceased to provide them with many satisfactory finds. One small rise was so loaded with old coins and more than 60 flat buttons that they

Finds from the virgin Union camp worked by Keith Sylvester and Lana Spence. *(Above)* Minié balls carved by bored Civil War soldiers. *(Left)* Episcopal High School button considered by button experts to be of a Confederate use camp from the Union camp.

*(Bottom)* These finds include buttons, two eagle breast plates, a spur, a U.S. bit boss, belt keepers, knapsack parts, and the two halves to the U.S. plate that Keith found 12 months apart.

All photos are © Keith Sylvester.

387

dubbed it "Button Hill." The couple have amassed more than 450 bullets from these sites, which they hope to visit for many more months.

The specific items found at such camp sites help to establish which forces camped on a particular site and sometimes even specific regiments or companies. The rare Waco Guards company buttons from a specific Texas Civil War company have been found as far away as a Washington, D.C.-area camp near the Potomac River which was occupied in January 1862.

----

### Discovering Rural Civil War Campsites

Careful research and determination are the keys to locating the lesser-known waysides and camping areas of Confederate or U.S. Civil War soldiers. Supply wagons, artillery companies and infantry units used existing roads and trails to move from place to place. Good campsites were often used time and again because of the shelter, water supply and favorable topography that made them a choice location in the first place.

Successfully locating such camps requires an understanding of what roads were used by the military during that time. Natural water sources such as streams, rivers and lakes along such routes should naturally be considered. Study regimental histories (either printed sources or via the Internet) to determine the movements of companies in the region you are researching. *The Official Atlas of the Civil War* provides good information on many roads used by troops during this period.

Local research can turn up more specific information on where troops crossed certain springs or made their camps near certain communities. Personal contacts and all other local-level research techniques discussed in Chapter 5 come into play in finding rural campsites. Topography maps and U.S. Geological aerial photos can be utilized to understand how older roads in use during the Civil War period tended to follow the local topography. These older dirt roadways were more curved than modern roadways because they often followed the tops of ridges for proper drainage necessary to keep artillery and wagons from bogging down. A recommended book for more coverage on this subject is *Finding Civil War Campsites in Rural Areas* (published by Blue and Grey Book Shoppe), which offers great detail on interpreting maps and aerial sources. Close scrutiny of such topographical maps can show roads that seem to end abruptly but which could logically have once connected to another road in the area that similarly seems to play out on the map.

There are a number of published and non-published diaries kept by Civil War soldiers you might want to study. The daily entry for an infantry soldier often stated how far his company marched each day before making camp. He might also point out various things of local interest which would never make it into a unit commander's report. The details of such a diary can be studied against the period maps to see what trails and roads the company would have traveled. If the diary states that the unit marched 16 miles from a known point before making camp, measure this off on your topography map.

Civil War camps established near small towns were often made less than three miles from the town—just enough distance to separate the soldiers from the locals but not too far for the purpose of supplies. The soldier's diary may or may not list a specific creek or water source that camp was made near but it is safe to assume that the stated "16 miles" or marching ended near some source of water for both the men and their animals. The average march per day for infantry was between 15 to 20 miles.

Modern highways have displaced a great number of old trails and wagon lanes that were used in the 1800s. Early churches along these forgotten roadways may have once served as an overnight camp area, as a makeshift hospital or as a gathering place. Church records can indicate if the church building was standing during the Civil War period.

Your research will lead you to a piece of property where cer-

This photo shows a Union campground in Virginia during the Civil War. Note that companies pitched their tents in tight groupings while officers' quarters and the various other sections (hospital, commissary, livery, etc.) of camp were also well defined.

tain troops camped. Now what? Unless there is an historic marker nearby pinpointing a campsite, you will have to find it. Many historic markers are placed near major roadways saying that some particular army camped in this area on this date. This more correctly means that the spot was within a few hundred yards or perhaps even a mile or more distant.

For every major battlefield that is preserved as a national park, there are hundreds of campgrounds and similar sites that are not protected. Troops obviously rendezvoused and encamped within a short distance of a major battleground. This is where you turn to letters, regimental histories and archival documents to find references to whose contemporary (and now modern) farms they camped on.

You'll have the same challenge in finding the exact area of a campsite. Decide upon a pattern for crossing the land you believe the camp to be in. If you can hunt in All-Metal mode, do so until you begin finding targets that are from the era you desire. When you find an area of concentration of targets (good or bad), slow down and work it more thoroughly.

Relic hunter Brian Pennington depends on the All Metal Mode to help snoop out camp sites. "I'm not a silent search hunter," he admits. "I want to listen to every little crackle and pop made by the metallic items in the ground. You need to find iron to locate camp sites. Iron is your best friend for finding these old places, although it can become your worst enemy once you get there!"

If the ground is littered with too many square nails, farm iron, or other trash, then use only as much discrimination as you must to eliminate the worst items. Square nails from a certain period are actually desired relics for some. As you search, use the common sense tips previously discussed in Chapter 7 (i.e. scout for elevated areas, natural water sources and the non-natural indicators that can steer you toward productive areas). **Many Civil War campsites were established on the south side of a hill** to offer almost continual exposure to the sun (particularly in winter) and to allow for better camp drainage.

If you are hunting with a group of friends, continue scouting the area until you are certain you have found the heavy areas of artifact concentration. Once relics begin coming up that indicate a good site, slow down your search and use more systematic sweep techniques (such as one of the zone patterns discussed in Chapter 7). Once you locate the old campsite, work it thoroughly with as little discrimination as you can stand. Try to find where the fire pit was located as this is an area where trash would have been tossed to burn up. The items that were not burned up in the fire were often carried a short distance away to a trash site. This could include broken buckles, shredded uniforms, malformed bullets, or any of a number of items that were scrapped. The fire pit and trash area of yesterday's camps can be today's gold mines for relic hunters.

Larger camps of both the North and the South employed common layouts. Companies camped together in neat rows while field and staff officers occupied separate areas of camp. Camps of longer duration had small wooden cabins for officers. Privies were generally dug about 150 paces from the main campground. The most common tents used during the Civil War by both sides were Wall tents and wedge tents. The Wall tent was reserved for officers and measured about 10 feet x 12 feet x 7 feet tall. Soldiers were issued one half of a wedge tent (or pup tent), which was joined with that of another soldier to make a full tent. Such wedge tents were about 5.5 feet square, made of cotton duck and contained seven metallic end buttons and nine metallic top buttons (zinc, tinned or galvanized metal).

Eyelets from Wall tents and buttons from wedge tents are common camp finds. Aside from the camping area, a Civil War camp included cooking areas, mess areas, privies (either outhouses or latrines), sutler and commissary/livery areas. Sutlers provided non-military supplies for the troops such as beverages, canned fruits, vegetables and even beer. The exchange of money for such goods means that lost coins from that period may be found in this area.

The commissary area provided food and equipment for the military while the livery maintained the animals used by the military. Relic hunters who work the camp trash pits or mess areas can find a wide variety of Civil War relics: discarded buttons, broken weapons, whiskey bottles, wine bottles, fruit cans, sardine cans, forks, spoons, canteens, iron cooking pots, and various cooking utensils.

Some Civil War campsites may have been used for mere hours as staging sites while others were occupied for weeks or even months. The types of relics found can help distinguish the officers' area of camp from that of the enlisted men and from the peripheral areas (commissary, livery, hospital, etc.). Various tools for loading artillery and for correcting the aim of a cannon can be found near battle areas. Medical and surgical tools may be found near old hospital sites. Civil War soldiers often worked on their rifles or revolvers around the camp. A bullet worm was used to extract projectiles which failed to fire from gun barrels.

The larger the campsite and the longer it was in use, the more

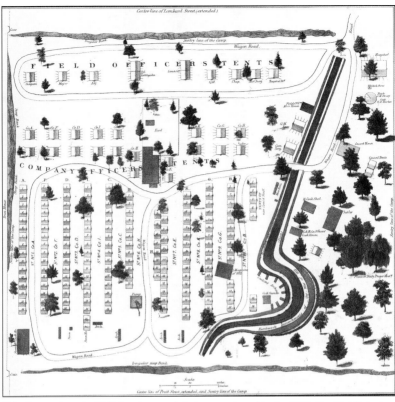

This diagram from the Civil War shows an infantry camp layout for the 110th New York Volunteer Regiment, whose Camp Patterson was located near Baltimore, Maryland. Note that the companies (A, B, C, D, E, F, G, H, I and K) were set up in proper rows with "streets" dividing each unit. The military did not keep "J" companies, perhaps to avoid the confusion of handwritten "I" and "J" companies in records. Company officers and staff officers' living areas comprised roughly half the camp space, while other areas were designated for special spaces such as a hospital. Such large camp layouts were typical of both Federal and Confederate campgrounds.

diverse and greater the number of relics will be found. Officers' areas may show window pane fragments, stone or brick fragments from chimneys and square nails from constructed cabins. Undisturbed camp areas may still even show evidence of depressions in the ground where huts were once dug out.

Large camp sites from regular army use will produce such indicative items as kepi buckles, tent grommets, knapsack parts, musket caps and cans, padlocks, shoe caps and other U.S.-issued items that would not have been carried by southern soldiers or local militiamen. Bullet finds can also help to establish which side occupied a certain camp.

The length of time a camp was occupied can sometimes be determined by the personal items that are found. Harmonicas, harmonica reeds or jew's harps indicate that there was enough idle time in camp for soldiers to turn to music for entertainment. Some soldiers passed their idle time by carving designs into their lead bullets. These minié balls, when found, are a snapshot of history—reflecting the artistic natures of some young man who perhaps did not survive his next engagement.

Carving lead was something soldiers did out of boredom around a campfire or while on picket duty. Such "boredom" carving might include Indian moccasins, a rattlesnake, dice, a chess piece or even poker chips. Other carved bullets were actually carved to serve a purpose. Some of this lead was used to make sinkers, weights, lead tampions, musket nipple protectors, bottle stoppers, and even lead pencils.

Personal items of all sorts might be found around a campsite such as pocket watches, mess kits, canteens, thimbles, candlestick holders, razors, coins, lockets with photos, rings and various other non-military items. Dating campsites can be accomplished by the buttons and bullet types that are found. The buttons may still have backmarks to indicate the manufacturer and date of manufacture. The dates on dropped coins can also help to date the camp, particularly those with the oldest (earliest) dates.

Howard Crouch spent much of the 1970s searching for and hunting Civil War campsites. He and his hunting buddies became proficient at examining the unearthed relics to determine which army's cavalry units had frequented the area. In his book *Relic Hunter*, Crouch points out some of the ways he was able to determine the original ownership of the items.

Buttons, bullets and buckles were seemingly obvious signs of who once camped at a site. He is quick to point out, however, that large quantities of U.S. manufactured items found on a site do not necessarily indicate that it was a Union camp. Confederate soldiers who had captured Federal supplies often used the same bullets for their guns. Ammunition boxes and shot pouches containing the U.S. stamped plates were quickly stripped of their accoutrements and the Federal emblems were simply destroyed, buried or tossed.

Cavalry equipment used by the South was often less ornamental and more functional. Spurs, bits and saddles were often the same gear that had outfitted farmers' horses months before. Confederate manufacturers did turn out some proper cavalry equipment and specific patterns can be identified to help determine the loyalty of the former owner. Iron spurs vary in size but often hold up well to soil exposure.

Cavalrymen left a number of other unique relics related to their trade. Rosettes and martingales were ornamental pieces found on the leather gear around the head and neck of the horse. Other horse paraphernalia include bits, curry combs used to groom the horses, iron picket pins used to stake horses to a location, horse tack, horse shoes and brass saddle shields (small tags stamped with the saddle size). Many other metal rings, hooks and links are often found that once held the leather together on a horse. Dropped buttons and other found insignia may be U.S. for Federal Army issue or "D" or "C" for dragoons or cavalry of either side.

In addition to Civil War relics, you will likely find more modern artifacts that have been lost in the past century by farmers, hunters, hikers or land owners. Some rusty iron tools or cooking utensils may or may not be "period" artifacts. It is thus important to hang onto items about which you are uncertain concerning their date. The most obvious artifacts are state specific belt plates or buttons. Unit specific relics are even more telling. The most revealing find on such a campsite is a Civil War soldier's identification disc, which contained personal information like a modern dog tag.

Maintain a finds folder either on paper or electronically as you work such a historic site. Take careful notes on everything you find, as well as the finds made by your fellow hunters. Many found relics can be indicative of either an officers' section or enlisted men's area of camp. Found camp items that most often point toward an enlisted men's area are cartridge box plates, bayonets, boot heel plates, "bat wing" carbine slings, kepi buckles, canteens, canteen necks or stoppers, harmonicas, jew's harps, knapsack hooks, bowie knives, tent grommets, rifle nipple protectors and powder flasks.

Items most likely found in the officers' area of a Civil War camp include staff buttons, swords, sword guards, sword belt hooks, officers' bar insignia, whiskey bottles and cuff link jewelry.

The types of relics found in Civil War camps range from the standard military issue items to those more personal in nature. The galleries at the end of this chapter show a representation of some of the items that can be recovered from such camps. There are so many other unique items that can be found that you may find yourself turning to forum users to help identify some of them.

------------

### World War I Camp in Big City Park Still Produces

Just about every relic hunter has a favorite hunting spot that he or she will periodically return to just to see what else can be found there. Bill Kasellman enjoys working the sand and surf of the Gulf of Mexico with his *Sea Hunter* detector. When he can get away from his business, he also enjoys organized relic hunts in Civil War territory such as the annual GNRS.

Hot spots come and go, but Bill has a favorite hunting ground that he can fall back on during the cooler winter months. Rather than being located on private property where it is protected from others who might work it out, Bill's favorite site is located in a public park in the middle of one of America's largest cities.

During World War I, Camp Logan was partially located on land that is now part of Memorial Park in Houston, Texas. This park was named in tribute to the soldiers who fought in Europe. Shortly after America's entry into World War I in 1917, the U.S. Army established 34 training camps to prepare its troops for war. Camp Logan was established on July 18, 1917, and encompassed

These images are from a World War I campsite hunted by Bill Kassellman and his friends.

*(Left)* Chunks of trees with .45-caliber bullets still embedded.
*(Below, center)* World War I soldier ID tags.
*(Bottom)* Various camp finds, including horseshoes, tent stretchers in two sizes, V nickels dated 1905 and 1911, a soldier's condom case, buckles, bullets, and the top of a hand grenade.

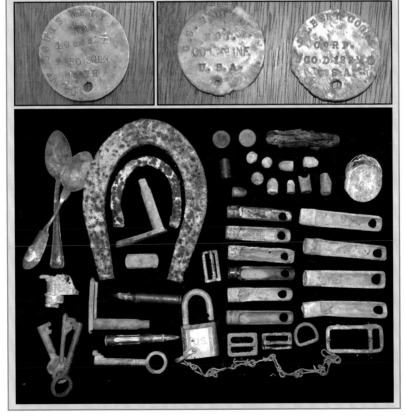

some 7,600 acres of land. It consisted of a main camp, an auxiliary remount depot, an artillery range, a rifle range and drill grounds.

During the construction of Camp Logan, members of the 3rd Battalion, 24th Infantry, were assigned to the camp as guards and were stationed about a mile to the east. This company was composed of black soldiers who were commanded by white officers. Among the troops who received training at Camp Logan included the 33rd Division—composed of the Illinois National Guard—part of the 93rd Division and other regular Army units that went on to serve in battle in France in 1918.

Houston's Memorial Park today is heavily visited by tourists, picnickers and even other metal detectorists. Bill has known for decades that Camp Logan once stood in this public park and he has hunted it periodically since 1969. "For me, this is a great winter search site," he says. "My friends and I like to search one heavily wooded area that I won't bother with in warmer weather due to the weeds, underbrush, snakes, mosquitoes and other critters.

"You can still see some of remains of the old cement bunkers," Bill relates. "Some areas appear to have been practice areas for the soldiers firing their old Thompson .45-caliber machine guns, due to the number of shells we have found." Bill and three of his detecting companions—Ron Tadlock, Ken Scanlon and Charlie Horn—work the rough areas in the forest off the beaten path.

"We have found a number of bullets by scanning the oldest trees and even the rotting, fallen logs back in the forest," Bill continued. "To me, this area will always be a fun place to detect because it is productive, if you are willing to put in the effort." The group has found hundreds of bullets and buttons, most dating to the World War I era although a few older musket balls have been found in the park woods as well. They frequently find partially loaded or fully loaded stripper clips used by the Army to hold its primary bullet, the .30-06 Springfield. Such five-shot stripper clips used little tabs that broke off and let the rounds fall off as the rifle was loaded with each .30-06 round.

Bill and his buddies have also found quite a few U.S. Army soldier ID badges or "dog tags." Army regulations of 1913 made such identification tags mandatory, and by 1917 all U.S. combat soldiers wore circular aluminum discs around their necks. Some recovered dog tags contain the letters "CL," which Bill has learned might be an abbreviation for "colored," indicating one of the black soldiers who served at Camp Logan.

---

### Hunting a Buffalo Hunters' Camp

Jerry Eckhart and his hunting buddy Vance Gwinn invited me to join them for a hunt on a buffalo hunters' camp in central Texas. In the old days, the buffalo were so numerous on the central American plains that they could literally bring a passenger train to a halt until they could be cleared from the tracks. Buffalo hunting became big business in the years after the Civil War as their hides were collected and sold for profit.

The location that Jerry had found was the first evidence that buffalo hunting was conducted near his home in Cisco (just east of Abilene). Jerry learned about this history through a friend, who then introduced him to a land owner whose property is about 15 miles from Cisco in southern Stephens County.

"When I met with the rancher, he told me he had collected a coffee can full of eagle military buttons," Jerry related. Naturally excited about the presence of military relics, he asked the man to point out the area. He found that the spot was on a hill that overlooked a large creek that runs through his property which turned out to be a major buffalo crossing area. The buffalo followed trails in their migration south, one of which crosses through the farmer's creek. The area formed a natural "draw" with a path that led down toward and across the water. Once this natural crossing area became a pattern of their migration, the buffalo continued to follow their own course for so many years that they created a roadway. Buffalo hunters of the late 19th century looked for such crossings as ambush sites to pick off many beasts in such a confined area.

*(Above)* A display case of buffalo hunters' camp artifacts found by Jerry Eckhart and his detecting club in central Texas. On the left side is a portion of a tin plate. Along the bottom of the case are *(l-r)*: metal ruler portion, knife handle, and Henry, Spencer and Winchester cartridges. On the right side are percussion cap boxes and a flattened tin cup. In the center is a bayonet and along the top row are *(l-r)*: saddle ring, melted lead and square nails.

*(Above)* Another artifact case from this central Texas buffalo hunters' camp. Center: key wind pocket watch back, decorative filigree surrounded by miscellaneous cartridge cases and a boot heel plate. *Right side:* equipment buckle and a pot handle. *Left side:* equipment buckle, matching pot handle and tube ferrule. *Bottom:* knife parts, square nails and three unidentified small parts which may be a pistol cylinder advance lever, a brass stamped gauge and a powder hole cover for a flintlock rifle.

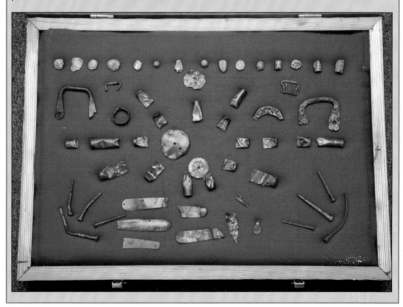

Jerry and his son-in-law worked the site initially, and he soon followed up with an organized club hunt for his local chapter. "This site is not recorded in history books, therefore making it doubly important," he explained. Jerry believes that he will continue to work the area to recover all important artifacts of this buffalo hunters' camp. Many of these are and will be on display in the local treasure hunting museum in Cisco.

Brian McKenzie and I joined Jerry and Vance in May 2010 to field test some new Garrett metal detectors on this historic site. Personally, I would have preferred cooler weather for relic hunting in central Texas but hunting privileges must always be granted when the landowner chooses. In this case, turkey season for this area ran through the end of April, so the first week of May it was.

The relics recovered from the site show that the hunters used a wide variety of firearms. These ranged from flintlock rifles, muzzle loading Sharps, cartridge-firing Sharps, Henry rifles, Spencers and Winchesters, as evidenced by the wide ranging and vast quantities of spent cartridges, musket balls and mushroomed lead found along the buffalo crossing areas of the creek. The Sharps Company manufactured the top hunting rifles of the 1870s with bore sizes of .40, .44, .45 and .50-caliber, with a variety of cartridge lengths for each. "The presence of center fire Winchesters indicates that this site was occupied between 1873 and 1878," Jerry believes.

Buffalo hunting was a way of life for hundreds of men in the depressed period following the Civil War. Some of the more famous men to engage in this trade were William F. "Buffalo Bill" Cody, Bat Masterson, Wild Bill Hickok, Pat Garrett and Wyatt Earp. Armed with powerful rifles, these men could earn a nice living by bringing down as many as 250 buffalo a day. More than 5,000 skinners and hunters earned their keep in this trade by the 1880s, when tanneries paid up to $3.00 per hide and a quarter for each tongue (a restaurant delicacy). Leavenworth, Kansas soon became a major trading center for the buffalo hides.

The Great Plains were filled with an estimated 50 to 60 million buffalo before Anglo settlers began pushing into the area. Native

Americans had long hunted bison for food, clothing and other necessities without significantly disrupting their numbers. As buffalo hunting grew in popularity among Anglos after the Civil War, the Indians became angry with the slaughter of their sustenance. Railroads even offered hunting by train, where passengers could shoot the buffalo with their long rifles for fun from the train cars. The result was more Indian attacks on the buffalo hunters and an increased U.S. Army presence to put down the violence. The government eventually forced the Indians onto reservations during the height of the Indian Wars while the Army pursued a buffalo eradication policy to extinguish their sustenance.

By 1884, the great buffalo herds had been reduced to less than 2,000 of the creatures left in the United States. Federal preserves—such as Yellowstone Park, established in 1872—helped save the animal from extinction. Today, there are an estimated 150,000 bison on such public preserves and in private hands. The history of this period has made the old buffalo hunters' camps an interesting search site for modern relic hunters.

Buffalo hunting became something of a circus in the late 1870s. As evidenced by this early illustration, advertisements were placed for hunters who wished to shoot bison for sport from the trains.

The presence of so many eagle buttons indicates that U.S. Army troops also camped on these Stephens County grounds 130 years ago to hunt buffalo. It is also possible that the buffalo hunters had been wearing old U.S. Army coats.

Texas Rangers also made camp in this part of the county at a place on Sandy Creek known to the locals today as Ranger Hole. Captain John R. Waller's 55-man Company A of Rangers camped at this site during the summer of 1874, a time in which the company was busy rounding up cattle thieves and desperados who included members of John Wesley Hardin's gang. Jerry drove us to this location on the creek during our tour of the area and pointed out where he had once dug a 1927 hunting dog tag and a 1912 Barber dime at the old Ranger camp.

Upon arriving at the property where the old buffalo hunters' camp once stood, we entered the main gate and twisted along a number of dusty roads back through the woods past deer stands and corn feeders. The soil was very rocky and tough to break through with even the sturdiest shovel but the artifacts present made it worth the sweat produced.

Vance dug a nice harness buckle a short distance from the vehicle. In several places near the creek we could still see old buffalo wallows, deep impressions in the earth where countless buffalo had rolled in the soil. Mass numbers of these heavy beasts wallowing in a certain spot over many years created deep indentions in the soil. These buffalo wallows were often used during battles as crude bunkers in which to take shelter from an opponent's gunfire. Many a good artifact has been found in old buffalo wallows by relic hunters savvy enough to spot these hollowed pits.

Near one such wallow, I followed the old buffalo trail through the draw down toward the creek and was rewarded by finding a large iron ring that once likely held a firearm or sword to a soldier's saddle. Jerry and I dug several cartridges as the temperature quickly crept into the low 90s and made the tough digging all the more wearisome. Vance soon hit upon a hot spot where he dug a number of Henry and Spencer cartridges in one tight area.

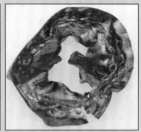

*(Top left)* These two Spencer cartridges were pushed together by the shooter, an old trick to prevent Indians from reusing the cartridges.

*(Top center)* Vance Gwinn found this nice buckle shortly after our arrival on site.

*(Top right)* This deteriorated ornamental piece was found by the author. Jerry Eckhart speculates that it might have been a decorative piece from a sword scabbard.

*(Left)* Buffalo hunters' cartridges, lead and modern bullets found by Vance during our morning hunt.

*(Below)* Jerry and the author pinpoint targets as Vance digs another buffalo hunter's cartridge.

Jerry and I naturally migrated toward this productive area and quickly had plenty of signals. In addition to the ever-present iron square nails, we found plenty of goodies, including Colt .45 short pistol cartridges (which Jerry explained could also be fired from Winchester rifles), button clasps, flattened musket balls, excess lead, a harmonica reed, half of a powder can lid, a gilded ornamental piece and an iron gun tool.

We departed the buffalo hunters' camp pleased with our day's finds and fully aware that plenty more artifacts remain for future hunts as Jerry continues to explore and preserve the history of this late 19th century site. (Flip back to page 312 for follow-up hunting we did on this interesting piece of property.)

————

### Searching Old Mining Ghost Towns

The gold rush booms of the mid to late 1800s created towns that were once thriving as the precious metal was prospected and collected. Today, there are many ghost towns in North America and in other parts of the world that can be quite productive for relic and coin hunting.

You should, as always, be aware of the laws that protect such properties. Federal public land is off limits to metal detectors without a proper permit, so your best bet is to seek areas that are owned by individuals who might grant you permission to hunt.

Gold prospectors may very well encounter old miners' camps or ghost towns while working some of their claims. It is common to find coins and relics of Chinese origin in such camps. In North America, there was a great influx of Chinese laborers who immigrated to work the gold fields during the mid-1800s. In 1848, there were only hundreds of Chinese immigrants in America; by 1880, there were more than 300,000. The majority of them came over to work the Sierra Nevadas during the California Gold Rush. They took up mining in other states and served as laborers and merchants in other areas of the country as the century progressed.

*(Top)* Vintage photo of an early Australian gold mining town in Northern Queensland.

*(Upper right)* Vintage photo of a Chinese immigrant worker smoking an opium pipe. There were more than 17,000 Chinese working the North Queensland goldfields in Australia by the late 1880s.

*(Right)* Chinese artifacts found in Australian goldfield camps by Warren McGrath. Shown are cast brass Chinese "cash" coins, brass tubes, and an ornate brass opium pipe with engraved flower motif.

*(Below)* Warren is seen hunting a northern Australia miners' camp on the banks of a gold-producing river with his *AT Pro International*.

Chinese coins minted between the 1600s and 1800s can be found in western states like Montana, Oregon, Utah, Idaho, Washington, and California. The coins obviously had no monetary worth in the American market but were still used among the immigrants for barter and as good luck pieces, gambling tokens, and markers. These circular cash coins contain square holes in the center due to their minting process. To eliminate casting irregularities, these Chinese coins were placed on a square rod or bar and then turned against a chisel or file to smooth the edges.

 Most of these square-holed round coins were made of brass or bronze. Early Chinese coins contain upper and lower characters on the obverse side to identify the issuing emperor's reign-title. By the 1600s, many such coins even included mint marks on their reverse side. Although most "Chinese coins" are assumed to be just that, there are a good number of coins actually minted in countries like Korea, Japan and Vietnam that have been found in North America—as many other Asian nationalities immigrated to work in the mines and on the railroads.

Other relics that are commonly found in old mining camps are iron tools, pieces of ceramic pottery, buttons, various brass items, antique match or tobacco tins, tokens, musket balls, opium tins, and Chinese opium pipes. Opium use was common among the immigrant miners, as they often smoked it in pipes not only as a social drug but for pain relief and appetite suppression.

I have had the chance to hunt a few mining ghost towns and camps in Idaho and even one in the northern state of Queensland in Australia. Charlie Weaver once took Brian and I hiking out to an old Chinese miners' cabin in the forest of Idaho. There was an abundance of their old trash and bottles in the area. It is therefore important to have good Target ID and iron identification in such areas. The old camps area often overgrown by weeds, brush or forest. You find them by hearing the iron in the ground with your metal detector.

Then, I like to cull through the iron rubbish with my searchcoil and listen for the higher-pitched squeaks of the better targets. In such areas, I prefer a small DD configuration coil to separate the good from the bad. Coins, buttons and large bullets will usually register with a consistent Target ID. I also like to use Iron Audio to check out the composition of the targets in such iron-infested areas. Tools and other larger ferrous items can read above the ID range of small iron, but Iron Audio can sniff out the fact that the item contains at least some iron.

There are a number of iron items worth digging at such old sites, including the picks and tools used by these tradesmen. That's the real beauty of relic hunting: you don't have to live in colonial America or "Civil War country" to find relics. No matter what part of the country you live in, there are relics waiting to be found. And some of them are unique only to your area.

Examples of commemorative medals, ornate costume jewelry, and silver coins dating to the 1870s/1880s that Warren has dug in goldfield camps.

Some of the author's Australian goldfield camp relics—musketballs, a Chinese opium pipe base, a Navy button, and a matchbox tin's lid.

*(Right)* The author searches near the ruins of a cabin once inhabited by Chinese miners in rural Idaho.

## Identification Gallery: Civil War Campsite Finds

*(Right)* A single cavity round ball bullet mold and the cherry for cutting the cavity. These tools were often used for Kentucky or Pennsylvania long rifles.

*(Left)* Copper 1-gallon moonshine still from Yankee camp in Wauhatchie, TN.

*Relics on this page are all part of the Charles Harris Civil War Museum; photos by Charlie Harris.*

*(Left)* Rifle butt plates, trigger guards and barrel bands.

*(Left)* Flint lock plate at left, plus hammers, nose caps and small pistols.

*(Right)* Recovered side knives. Left to right are: a side knife made from a file; a fraternal short sword; an ivory-handled short side knife; side knife made from a broken sword; side knife made from a broken brass handled NCO sword; side knife made from a triangular bayonet; broken CS sword; Sheffield side knife; and a homemade stilleto type side knife.

*(Left)* These brass hooks were used by Union soldiers to hang a sword off their belt. Terry Smith found them with his *Infinium* in a campsite located between two ridges.

*(Left)* These brass Union knapsack buckles include male, female and receiver pieces.

*(Left)* Civil War canteens had iron stoppers with pewter necks. To take a drink, the soldier pushed the top into the canteen. When finished, he pulled the plug back up into the neck to seal it again.

*(Below, right)* Iron candlestick holders found near Hansbrough's Ridge in Virginia. These were used in tents or huts at night to hold candles.

Iron gun tool *(above)* and iron hut hinges *(right)* found by Terry Smith near the Union camp.

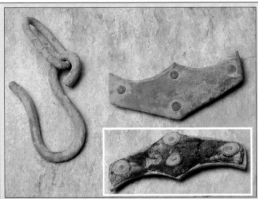

*(Left)* A brass sword hanger chain and the bat-wing tip end of a sword belt found by Terry Smith. The back of Terry's bat-wing belt piece still has leather remnants *(see inset).*

*(Above)* Pocket knives, including one non-dug and one larger, fancy type, shaving knife and cut-down table knife. *Courtesy of Charlie Harris.*

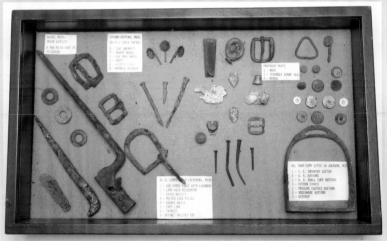

This case of Civil War relics, found in a Federal campsite in Vicksburg, Mississippi, is on display with other artifacts from Charles Garrett's collection at the Garrett Museum.

411

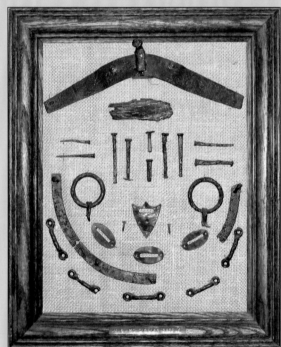

(Left) McClellan saddle parts found in a Varnell, Georgia, cavalry camp. Most all of the iron and brass parts are present.

(Below)
Intact U.S. McClellan artillery saddle. Note the small brass saddle horn behind the seat. This was either late Civil War era or early Indian War era due to its dark brown color.

*Images courtesy of Charlie Harris.*

(Above) Tool for cutting cloth or cardboard patches for use in a shotgun load. Patches were inserted into the barrel after the powder, followed by bird or buck shot loads, and then one or two more patches to hold everything secure in the barrel.

(Upper right) Colt type .44-caliber bullet mold that cast both round balls and an elongated bullet. The top plate allowed the lead to be poured into the mold and was then rotated to shear off the sprue.

(Left) Starr carbine or revolver bullet mold. The body is brass with an iron sprue cutter. A wooden handle was forced over the spike.

Relics on this page are all part of the Charles Harris Civil War Museum; photos by Charlie Harris.

(Right) A ferrier's hoof shaving tool.

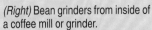

(Above) Iron gun tools. At left is an Enfield combination tool. Next is a Springfield nipple removal wrench and two screwdriver blades. Third is a pin punch. At far right is a Springfield main spring clamp for compressing and removing the rifle's main spring.

(Right) Bean grinders from inside of a coffee mill or grinder.

*(Above)* Display case of carved lead items, evidence of how some Civil War soldiers passed their idle time in camp with their pocket knives.

*(Center)* Items from the above case. Top left is a carved rattlesnake from a camp infested with rattlesnakes in Ringgold, Georgia. Horseshoe and stirrup carvings from Murfreesboro vicinity. Axe from northern Kentucky and from Wilder's Hatchet Brigade prior to capture. Also seen are a spoon, carved horseshoe nail and the start of a tongue and wreath buckle.

*(Lower)* Two carved lead writing pencils made from bullets; found in Corinth, Mississippi. Lead knife, 5.75" long from Corinth. Flute carved from lead.

*Photos courtesy of Charlie Harris from his museum.*

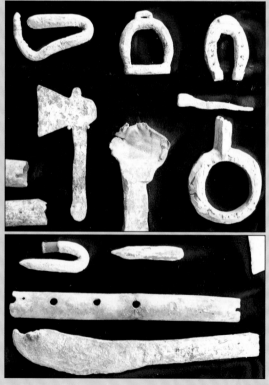

*(Right)* Lead toy "whizzer" from Lookout Mountain, TN. Lead flint pad folded from Shiloh, TN. Carved lead smoking pipe made from a French .69-caliber bullet. A fired U.S. 3-ringer that looks like an Indian moccasin.

*Photos courtesy of Charlie Harris.*

*(Right)* Miscellaneous carved items, including rifle nipple protectors, a pair of dice, rivets, a pine cone and chess pieces.

*(Below)* Top left is a flattened bullet used to make a poker chip. Top center is an ID badge from Wauhatchie, Tennessee, from an Alabama company. Top right, ID badge marked EC. Lower left is a carved ID piece marked with 72 and NYV. Bottom center is a counterfeit coin mold for a Seated Liberty half dime. Bottom right is a counterfeit mold for the back of a dime. Both molds are from a Confederate camp in Corinth, Mississippi.

*(Right)* A carved Iowa ID badge that was recovered from the Shiloh, Tennessee, vicinity.

*(Top)* Charlie Harris' spur collection. Those to far left are of Mexican design; to right are Confederates.
*(Below)* More spurs, these being mainly U.S. varieties.

*(Above)* These uniform buttons have been flattened for use as poker chips.

*(Below)* Civil War canteens. At left is an early "pick-up" from Battle of Chickamauga. Center is wooden canteen from bottom of James River. Top canteen with pick axe hole found near Chickamauga battlefield. Bottom canteen is a non-dug Yankee variety.

*(Right)* Upper wooden canteen is an early pick-up style from Chickamauga area. The bottom version is a Confederate drum canteen found in a stump hole on Lookout Mountain, Tennessee.

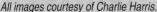

*(Left)* CS dutch oven found near Manassas with original food still inside.

*All images courtesy of Charlie Harris.*

416

# CHAPTER 18

# BULLETS, SHELLS AND FIREARMS

"Have you ever had a 'feeling' about a place?" asked Kevin of Knoxville, Tennessee. Between two east Tennessee towns he and his hunting buddy Danny had been researching Civil War battles and skirmishes back and forth. They had passed by one particular field for two years. Kevin had felt for some time that a good Civil War relic was just waiting to be found there.

The land contained acres of soybeans cut to the ground for winter. The field was near a large hill and a close water source. "We stopped in at the owners' house and luckily found them home," he wrote. "They told us of other hunters and about the minié balls they had found in the flat field by the road. For ease of first check on the site, I didn't grab my *Master Hunter 7* with a 12-inch coil (my favorite for hunting Civil War) but opted to try the field first using a Garrett *Freedom Two Plus* to see how clean the field was."

After 20 minutes of hunting, Kevin had found railroad spikes and horseshoes before getting a "great signal over the top of the hill." He began digging a foot deep to reach what at first looked to be the top on an old mason jar. After some careful digging, he probed the sides of this object. "The sound was sweet," he recalled. "Not glass."

Hollering for his friend Danny to join him, Kevin continued to gingerly excavate around the shell until he could pry it loose and realize what it was.

"The look on our faces had to be precious! *Yeehaas!* filled the

*(Above)* Kevin from Knoxville, Tennessee, proudly holds an 8-pound Confederate Burton shell he found by "following a feeling."

valley and men doing a jig in a soybean field on top of that hill had to make passersby on the road wonder what kind of crazies were loose in the fields in the winter around here! Oh, well...it's not the first time and I'm sure it won't be the last.

"My cell phone photos prove that when you have that 'feeling' you need to follow it! This eight-pound Confederate Burton shell is proof."

---

### Early North American Bullets

Crime scene investigators may have deep interest in finding recent cartridges and projectiles but for most of us, such 21st century targets are just another dug piece to go in the "junk metal" pouch. While there may be some interest in searching for projectiles from an early 20th century gangster shoot-out, the bullets that garner the most attention date back to the 1860s or earlier.

It only stands to reason that the most documented war on American soil is the one from which bullets and artillery rounds are the most highly sought. The Civil War was a period where more different styles of bullets were used than in any previous conflict on this continent. It is therefore relevant to examine some of these many types of bullets in this next section. Before we get there, however, let's look back at North American bullets you can find with your detector that predate the Civil War.

Relic hunters turn up projectiles while searching farms, old homesteads, battle sites, abandoned military posts, campgrounds, training grounds and many other places. The type of bullet you find can be an indicator dating other artifacts that you might expect to dig in an area. The earliest English settlers to arrive in Jamestown, Virginia, during the early 1600s carried swords by necessity and were proficient with bows and arrows. The colonists used muskets to protect their families from Native American attacks and to fend off encroaching Europeans. The Jamestown colony sported more than 1,000 firearms by 1625.

The earliest muskets used by the growing numbers of American colonists had primitive methods of igniting the gunpowder. With *matchlock muskets*, the powder was ignited by a match while *wheel lock muskets* ignited their powder via a small wheel that produced sparks by revolving against a piece of flint. The firearm of choice by the late 17th century was the *flintlock musket*, in which a piece of flint embedded in the hammer produced a spark that ignited the gunpowder. The early colonists of the New World also used pistols, with wheel lock or flint lock ignition variety, for very short range shooting.

German-American gunsmiths in the colonies began producing rifles with longer barrels that produced greater accuracy and were more devastating at greater distances. The colonists also learned to speed their reloading time with the introduction of paper cartridges containing powder, wad and ball in a single package. The Colonial rifles of the American Revolution had tremendous affect on British troops whose basic muskets had little accuracy beyond a 50-yard distance.

Musket balls and rifle balls from 17th to early 19th century Americana artifact sites vary widely. Pistol balls generally range from .40 to .60 caliber while muskets and rifles can vary from .62 to .87 caliber. These early weapons used lead balls that were molded to closely fit the bore size of the gun. Buck and ball loads were in

*(Above)* This 1856 model Civil War .577-caliber Enfield rifle, the standard weapon of the British Army, was imported by both the Confederates and Federals. Closeup to right show a dug .58-caliber Enfield bullet that would have been fired from this gun.

*(Above)* A Colt .44-caliber Army revolver found at Point Royal, Virginia, with four rounds in the cylinder and two rounds in the blown up barrel. Also shown is a Remington .36-caliber revolver recovered from the "Battle Above the Clouds" on Lookout Mountain, Tennessee.
*(Below)* A Savage .36-caliber Figure 8 revolver recovered from Gettysburg, Pennsylvania. *Photos courtesy of Charlie Harris.*

use by the early 1600s as evidenced by Colonial records and by detectorist and archaeological excavations in Colonial areas.

By the 1840s, conical-shaped lead bullets were in use in Europe and eventually in America for firing from percussion-cap weapons. Guns with rifled barrels have fired pointed lead bullets since about 1780 and the sophistication of bullets has progressed since that time. By the 1870s, center fire cartridges which housed the bullet, gunpowder and the percussion cap were in wide use.

---

### American Civil War Weapons

The most widely used infantry weapon of the Civil War was the *Springfield Model 1861 rifled musket*. Prior to the high production rates of this model, Union soldiers had only two modern rifled weapons, the .58-caliber Model 1855 Harpers Ferry Armory model and the .58-caliber (originally .54-caliber) Model 1841 Mississippi rifles. The two main Federal armories at the start of the war were located in Harpers Ferry, Virginia, and in Springfield, Massachusetts. The Union's standard issue Springfield Model 1861 rifle musket was produced at a rate of a quarter million arms in more than two years of production but even this rate fell short of demand.

Other manufacturers such as the Colt Patent Firearms Manufacturing Company in Hartford joined the effort to produce special versions of the Model 1861 rifle. Earlier flintlock smoothbore muskets were converted to being percussion and rifled by private arms makers such as E. Remington & Son. Some Remingtons became known as Maynard alterations because of Maynard primer locks that were installed in older flintlock muskets.

In the early days of the war, the Union imported heavily from overseas, and muskets of Austrian, French, Prussian, Belgian and German design went into battles during the Civil War. British-made Enfield rifles were the most popular import by both Union and Confederate agents during the war, with the Union securing approximately 500,000 of these arms.

*(Right)* Charlie Harris' Civil War collection includes this Star carbine (seen to left) and five out of nine Lookout Mountain guns that were recovered from a cave. Charlie is completing a book on the history of these guns.

(Below) A Spencer rifle found on Chickamauga National Military Park about 1910. Its serial number ties it to the 93rd Illinois, Company A, of Col. John Wilder's famous Lightning Brigade.
*Courtesy of Charlie Harris.*

The *Enfield 1853 rifle-musket* imported by both sides was second only in issuance to the Springfield Model 1861. When the British government refused to sell them arms after it became obvious to them that the Union would win the war, the Confederates continued buying Enfields from private contractors and gun runners. It has been estimated that more than 900,000 P53 Enfields were imported to America and saw service in every major engagement from the April 1862 Battle of Shiloh and the May 1863 Siege of Vicksburg to the final battles of 1865.

Confederate soldiers started the Civil War with many outdated flintlock rifles which had been converted to percussion cap models. At least 18 different Southern firms engaged in rifle production during the war while another seven manufactured revolvers. Traditional hunting arms such as the Kentucky rifle were transformed into shorter barrel, rebored weapons fitted with bayonets. Other rifles manufactured by companies such as Sharps and Springfield were issued in the South from existing arsenals such the Baton Rouge Arsenal during the early months of the conflict. The Confederacy's chief import was the British Enfield .577-caliber rifle musket, which fired either American or British-made .58 caliber minié balls. It had a 39″ barrel and an adjustable rear sight for ranges of 100, 200, 300 and 400 yards.

Cavalrymen of the Union carried lightweight, easily handled carbines—short-barreled cousins of the rifle and musket. No fewer than 17 different makes and models would be fielded by Federal cavalrymen, with some 80,000 being the .52-caliber Sharps carbine New Model 1859 version. This lever-cocked rifle fired a .56-56 Spencer rimfire cartridge whose actual bullet measured .52 inches in diameter. The Spencer rifle was reliable in combat and could fire up to 20 rounds per minute as compared to only about three rounds per minute from a standard muzzle-loader.

More than 115,000 Remington Army .44-caliber, six-shooter revolvers were manufactured during the Civil War for the Union troops. Remington and Colt both manufactured a .36-caliber, six-shooter Navy revolver which also found its way onto many battlefields. Other Federal units carried revolvers manufactured by Starr, Savage, Whitney and other armories, while many soldiers purchased their own private sidearms from other companies such as Colt or Smith & Wesson. Common revolver models used by the Union fired .32, .36, .41 or .44-caliber balls. The Confederacy captured thousands of Union pistols for its use, imported others, and manufactured some of its own. The primary Southern handgun factories were Spiller & Burr, Griswold & Gunnison and Leech & Rigdon of Georgia.

Hundreds of different types of weapons were used during the Civil War. Rifles and muskets are less common finds unless you have come upon a virgin hunting ground. Pistols and revolvers, smaller in size and more apt to have been missed by casual searchers over the years, are sometimes found.

Knives, bayonets, swords and scabbards from both the Blue and the Gray are possible weaponry finds as well. Officers' swords were usually more decorative than useful while the more serviceable sabers were generally carried by the cavalry and light artillery officers. Bayonets and bayonet tip covers are found more often than swords. Many of the dug bayonets do not hold great value because of the amount of decay that has usually been inflicted upon these relics by time in the earth.

---

### Minié Balls

The most common and distinctive to its period Civil War finds are the bullets, or minié balls, of both the Federals and the Confederates. In contrast to its name, the minié ball is a reference widely used for both round balls and the spherical-shaped lead bullets that were cast from a different type mold. Prior to 1855, rifled longarms were considered less practical for infantry use because loading a solid lead ball down the grooves of a rifled barrel was slower than loading a smoothbore.

A French Army captain named Claude Minié devised a simple solution in the form of an elongated soft lead projectile with a hol-

## Examples of Commonly Found Civil War Bullets and Shot

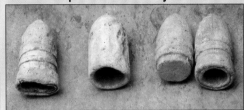

*(Above)* Confederate Enfield and Gardner bullets found by Terry Smith.

*(Below)* Terry found this group of .58-caliber Union minié balls while hunting a camp near Hansbrough Ridge in Culpeper County, VA.

*(Above)* Solid Spencer .52-caliber bullet and .56-caliber Spencer cartridge found by Terry at the Union campsite.

*(Left)* Terry dug this cluster of Confederate iron grape shot at four- to six-inch depths near the Virginia camp.

*(Below)* One of Charlie Harris' type trays of mainly Confederate minié balls. Top right corner is a buck and ball load and a shotgun load of buck shot. *Courtesy of Charlie Harris.*

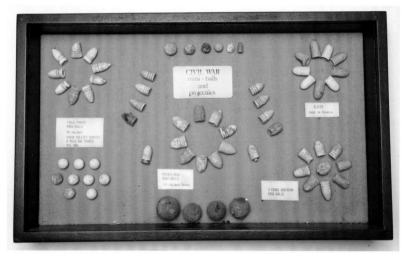

This case of Civil War minié balls, grape shot and rifle balls is on display with other artifacts from Charles Garrett's collection at the Garrett Museum.

low, cone-shaped base. James H. Burton, master armorer at Harpers Ferry, perfected Minié's design so that a lead bullet slightly smaller than the diameter of the rifled bore easily slid past the rifling during loading. The soft lead of the bullet's hollow base expanded into the grooves of the rifling when the gunpowder exploded. This put a spin on the bullet that stabilized its flight, thereby increasing range and accuracy. Burton's improved minié ball design is commonly referred to as the "minié ball."

Such dug bullets have a distinctive, white, powdery appearance when they are retrieved due the metal's oxidation from so many decades in the soil. Such bullets that were never fired are referred to as "drops" or "dropped shot." These may have been lost in combat, dropped on the march or simply stashed away for later use and never recovered. Drops hold more value because of their condition. Minié balls retrieved from a battle or skirmish area will often be flattened or partially crushed from impact with a person, a horse, a tree, a rock or some other obstacle. It has been estimated that as many as 600 different varieties of bullets were used during the Civil War. As many as a *billion* bullets may have been spent during the four-year conflict.

*(Above)* Roger W. of Indiana located this 12-pound cannonball with his *ACE 250*.

*(Left)* Civil War grape shot, also called canister fill, that was recovered by Jimmi K. of Marietta, Georgia. Using his *GTI 2500*, he was able to pinpoint a large quantity of this artillery shot near Cartersville over a multi-week period.

*(Left)* A variety of cast iron shot collected near Perryville, Kentucky Civil War battlegrounds. Sizes range from a 12-lb. cannon ball, an 8-lb. ball, 2-inch cannister shot, smaller grape shot and standard musket ball.

The average recovered minié ball does not command a high street price because of widespread availability on the trading market. It is possible to acquire many of the common Civil War bullets for a few dollars apiece from the Internet or antiquities dealers. Calibers range from .36 to .69 caliber on most Civil War bullets.

There are some fairly rare Civil War bullets which do fetch high prices among collectors. There are many Internet sites on which you can search to find the type of minié ball you have recovered. One suggested printed source is W. Reid McKee and M. E. Mason Jr.'s *Civil War Projectiles II: Small Arms & Field Artillery with supplement.*

---

### Artillery Shells and Grape

Many relic hunters consider the recovery of a complete artillery shell to be a coveted prize. Some Civil War shells can weigh as much as 90 pounds or more, although the discovery of an intact, live round is a rare treat. More often than not, you may encounter fragments from detonated shells of varying size and weight. Large projectiles were named after such designers as Parrot, Schenkl and Hotchkiss. It is estimated that some 1.5 million artillery shells and cannonballs were fired between Union and Confederate troops during the war and that one in five were duds.

Please note that any shell that might still be live should be treated with extreme caution. When in doubt, call in the experts to help handle an artillery shell that you believe to be a live round.

Point in case to this caution is the story of one veteran relic hunter from Virginia who was killed in February 2008. Sam White was a 53-year-old veteran Civil War hunter who had dug plenty of bullets, buttons and artillery shells. During his life, he had worked on restoring about 1,600 shells for collectors and museums. At the time of his death, White was reportedly trying to disarm a 9-inch, 75-pound naval cannonball. He was using either a drill or a grinder to remove grit from the cannonball, causing a shower of sparks.

The ensuing blast killed him as he worked in his driveway and sent a chunk of shrapnel through the front porch of a house a quarter-mile from White's suburban Richmond home.

Cannon balls and grape shot can also be recovered in areas where a significant battle took place. The smaller sized "grape shot" was a load of iron balls ranging from large marble-size to billiard ball-size which were packed into a canister before being fired from the cannon. Once a load of grape shot was fired, the smaller balls spread over a wider area to knock down men and horses. Today grape shot can fetch $10 to $20 per piece.

Cannons were generally classified by the weight of the projectile fired and were known by "pounder" (i.e. 10-pounder, 30-pounder, etc.). Other such weapons were classified by the diameter of the bore of the tube or barrel, such as a 3-inch rifle. At the beginning of the Civil War, Union Army weapons were generally formed in batteries, or groups of six weapons—such as four guns and two howitzers. A *gun* was a long-barreled, heavy weapon which fired solid shot from long range while a *howitzer* had a shorter barrel that could throw shot or shells at a shorter range but at higher elevations. One of the most famous guns of the war was the "Whistling Dick," a rifled 18-pounder Confederate siege and garrison weapon. The shells fired from the gun made a peculiar whistling sound because of some erratic rifling, thus the nickname.

*Mortars* were stubby weapons which used small powder charges to fire heavy projectiles in a high arc. Mortar shells exploded and spread large fragments across approaching enemy troops. Another cannon type was the *Columbiad*, a heavy artillery piece first used in the War of 1812 which could fire shot and shell at a high angle of elevation using a heavy powder charge. Columbiads were most often mounted in fortifications along rivers and seacoast waterways. More innovations with heavy guns took place during the Civil War than during all previous wars combined.

Robert Parker Parrott, a West Point graduate, resigned from the U.S. Army and went to work for the West Point Foundry in New York. By 1860 Parrott had designed a new method of attaching the reinforcing band on the breech of a gun tube and Parrott cannons of 10-, 20- and 30-pound variety were in production during 1861. His name is thus associated with the ammunition fired by Parrott cannon.

The Model 1861 3-inch wrought iron rifle or ordnance rifle adopted by the Federal Ordnance Department early that year soon became popular with the Confederate Army as well. Ordnance rifles could accurately fire Schenkl and Hotchkiss brand shells about 2,000 yards at a five-degree elevation, using a one pound charge of gunpowder. The popular Hotchkiss shell had three pieces: a nose which contained the powder chamber; a sabot (a soft lead band fitting into an intention in the middle of the shell); and an iron forcing cup at the base which forced the lead sabot to expand upon firing. Schenkl shells were cone-shaped projectiles with ribs along a tapered base and papier-mâché sabot, which was driven up the taper by the force of the gas produced upon firing.

There were many more types of cannon produced during the Civil War. Some of the common names referenced by relic hunters apply to either the cannon, its preferred shell brand or to both. They include the Whitworth cannon, the Blakely gun, the Confederate Brooke gun, Dahlgren guns (used on small boats patrolling waterways). Artillery fire produced mass casualties but also served to unnerve advancing soldiers in a battle. Whitworth projectiles by design made an eerie whining sound during flight. Many Civil War soldiers would recount the screams of Hotchkiss, James or Parrott shells that were produced by damaged or hanging sabots.

Because of the weaponry innovations of the Civil War, this conflict has been deemed by some to have been the end of the ancient wars and the start of the modern wars. It is little wonder that Civil War collectors and relic hunters have special admiration for the weapons and ammunition that are still recovered in the field today from this broad conflict.

8 inches tall

8 pouces de haut

3 1/4" large

*(Above)* This empty nine-pound British 1863 Armstrong muzzle loading rifled cannon shell and 24-pound cannon ball were found by Canadian detectorist Jocelyn Savoie. He has found two of the Armstrong shells and other fragments of explosive-filled cannon balls on the shores of Orlean Island on the St. Lawrence River between Quebec and Lévis.

*(Left)* Jocelyn and his son Anthonin pose with one of the shells they found near the river.

He recommends joining a forum to learn as much as you can about the type of relics you wish to find. "Then, go to your library and do a little research on old maps that relate to that area you want to metal detect," Jocelyn adds. In his case, his artillery-finds area is on public land but he advises that you should make sure you seek proper permission before hunting anywhere that is not public or that may contain historic items.

*(Left)* Jocelyn also uses his *GTI 2500* to find artillery percussion fuses. These inert fuses range from a Mark I dated 1872 to an 18-second time delay Mark IV dated 1896. He searches in All Metal mode but often switches to Relics mode. "I dig most of my targets, knowing that I'll find brass, copper, lead and iron relics. If possible, hunt after a good rain," he adds.

# CIVIL WAR ARTILLERY SHELL GALLERY

A 3.87", 20-pound James shell recovered from the vicinity of the Shiloh battefield. It was designed to be fired out of a 6-pound smooth bore and the slanted grooves helped create the spin of rifling.

This 3" CS Archer bolt was recovered near the Sulphur Creek Bridge bordering Alabama and Tennessee.

This 3", 10-pound Reed shell was also recovered near the Sulphur Creek Bridge bordering Alabama and Tennessee.

This 3", 10-pound CS Mullane (Tennessee Sabot) shell was recovered from Murfreesboro, Tennessee.

3.67" Shenkl shell from Moccasin Bend, Tennessee, near the foot of Lookout Mountain. Charlie Harris recovered this shell in eleven different pieces and reconstructed it. The Shenkl used a paper machet sabot so as not to injure forward friendly troops.

*All images courtesy of Charlie Harris.*

## CIVIL WAR BULLET IDENTIFICATION GALLERY

There are more calibers and types of Civil War minié balls, pistol balls and cartridges to find than there is space to show them in this text. This section is included for general reference on some of the various sizes and styles which you might recover.

**All bullets and cartridges below from the Tom Henrique collection.**

### Rifle Musket Percussion Cap Ignition Bullets

Tennessee Rifle minié ball, .45-cal., two groove

Wilkinson North Carolina rifle bullet, .50-cal., two-ring

Enfield .54-cal. with cone cavity (CSA)

Northern manufacture, .54-cal., three groove

Northern manufacture, .577-cal., three groove

Enfield .577-cal. with cone cavity (CSA)

Gardner one-groove .58-cal.

Williams regulation bullet, .58-cal., three-ring

Enfield over-sized .61-cal. with cone cavity (CSA)

British Pattern 1851 .69-cal. bullet

Gardner Patent .69-cal., two-ring

Nessler muzzle loader bullet, .69-cal., one-ring (CSA)

(Left) 3-ring Minie ball, .577-cal., Southern manufacture

(Above, right) Cylinder cavity of same CSA .577-cal.

Carcano .58-cal., 3-rings raised (CSA)

Williams Type I bullet, .57-cal.

New Austrian .577-cal., 2-ring (CSA)

 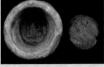 

(Left) French Model 1859 .69-cal., 1-ring

(Above) Two views of Enfield .577-cal., plug cavity w/plug

Shaler 3-piece bullet, .58-cal., percussion cap ignition (Union)

## Carbine Rifle Bullets and Cartridges

Sharps .52-cal., percussion cap ignition, 4-ring

Ballard .44-cal., rim fire ignition

Maynard .50-cal., percussion cap ignition

Spencer .52-cal, rim fire (Union)

Gallager .50-cal., drawn brass, percussion cap

Burnside .54-cal., percussion cap

Maynard .37-cal., 1-ring, percussion cap ignition

Henry Rifle, .44-cal., rim fire ignition (Union)

Sharps .46-cal., multi-ring (Union)

Burnside .54-cal., 2-ring, breech load

Merrill .54-cal., 3-ring, percussion cap ignition

Starr .54-cal., percussion cap ignition (Union)

## Revolver and Pistol Bullets and Balls

Smith & Wesson .31-cal. revolver, 2-ring, rim fire

Whitney revolver .36-cal., 1-ring, percussion cap

Colt Pattern for .36-cal. Navy revolver

Colt revolver, .44-cal., 1-ring, percussion cap

Volcanic self contained .42-cal., pin fire

Complete CSA four-piece buck and ball load with .69-cal. ball

Round buckshot, .32-cal. (.313"-diameter) for buck and ball load

Pistol ball, .44-cal. (.40"-diameter)

Musket ball, .69-cal. (.65"-diameter)

**All bullets and cartridges above from the Tom Henrique collection.**

*(Above)* A display of revolver bullets and cartridges from the collection of Charlie Harris. Left to right are: .44-caliber Colt Long (smooth and serrated bases), .41-caliber Derringer, French .41-caliber, .50-caliber pin fire, .42-caliber pin fire, .32-caliber pin fire, .44-caliber Sharps multi-ring, and a .44-caliber Colt revolver bullet. *Courtesy of Charlie Harris.*

This 121-pound, 11-inch Dalhgren shell was found at Fort Sulakowski at Velasco. It was fired at the Confederate fort by a Federal gunboat during the winter of 1863–1864. *Image courtesy of Bobby McKinney.*

This group of minié balls was dug from Camp Irene near Sandy Point, Texas, Brazoria County. It includes Gardners, Enfields, 3-ringers and a Tom Greene bullet. *Image courtesy of Bobby McKinney.*

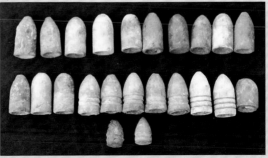

## Miscellaneous Minié Balls, Bullets and Cartridges

Colt revolving rifle, .56-cal., 2-ring, percussion cap

Eley .44-cal. cartridge for Tranter cylinder revolver

Williams square shank .58-cal. bullet for Union repeating gun

5mm revolver cartridge, pinfire ignition

Sharps sporting rifle bullet, .38-cal., 2-rings raised, percussion cap

Double ended revolver bullet, .31-cal., percussion cap (CSA)

Dimick rifle bullet, .50-cal, percussion cap (Union)

Hanoverian rifle bullet, .69-cal., 2-groove (CSA)

Believed to be a Vandenburg double end volley gun bullet, .45-cal. (Union)

Whitworth cylindrical rifle bullet, .45-cal. (CSA)

*All bullets and cartridges above from the Tom Henrique collection.*

*(Above)* A display of carbine cartridges from the collection of Charlie Harris. Top row, left to right are: .44 Henry, .54 Burnside, .54 Maynard blunt nose, .36 Maynard Sporting Cartridge, .54 Maynard pointed nose, .54 Gallagher, and a .56-56 Spencer rim fire. To the left and right of the paper tag are a teat fire and a cup fire cartridge, which were attempts to get around the Rollin-White bored-cylinder design patent owned by Smith & Wesson. *Courtesy of Charlie Harris.*

# CHAPTER 19

# BUCKLES, BUTTONS AND BADGES

Gene Bakner and his brother-in-law Mike are two more examples of the fact that impressive relics remain to be found by those who conduct proper research. Their book work has led the pair to the forests of Pennsylvania, where both men made exciting recoveries in June 2009.

"We were metal detecting an area that we had researched for months on the Confederate retreat from the battle of Gettysburg," Gene related. "Our research lead us to a wooded area miles from the battle. We split apart and proceeded to search. My first recovery was a fired Gardner bullet, and soon after a Sharps ring-tail bullet. As I was digging another signal, my brother-in-law yelled for me. I looked over to him about 30 yards away, where he was kneeling to the ground.

"Mike had this big grin on his face and he was holding his hand up. I could just make out a loop, so I rushed over to see him in total astonishment. He opened his hand and staring us in the eyes were the letters CS; he had just recovered a CS belt tongue! The high fives and the laughter could be heard for miles."

Gene quickly grabbed his *GTI 2500* to search the immediate area before his brother-in-law could retrieve his own *GTAx 550*. "On the first sweep I got that strong high bell-tone," he said. "Could it be! The other half? The wreath to make it complete? Exactly two inches below the CS tongue, I recovered another CS belt tongue! The hairs on our arms were rising, as we stared in amazement at each other. One wreath was rare, but to find two together...it was like hitting the lottery."

Mike and Gene spent several more days searching the area in hopes of finding the wreaths that once were part of these Confederate belt tongues but it was to no avail. They did, however, find plenty more Gardner and Sharps bullets, along with canteen parts, a pewter spoon and a friction primer. "This is a piece of local history that will be with us forever," Gene professed.

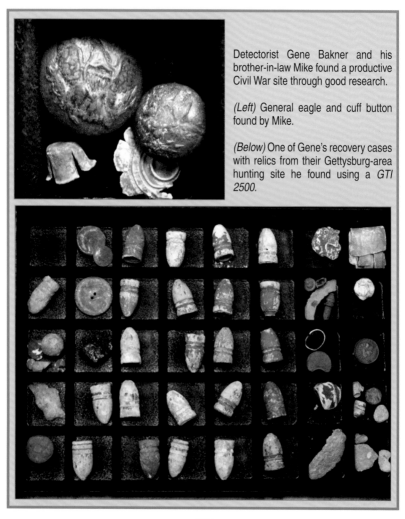

Detectorist Gene Bakner and his brother-in-law Mike found a productive Civil War site through good research.

*(Left)* General eagle and cuff button found by Mike.

*(Below)* One of Gene's recovery cases with relics from their Gettysburg-area hunting site he found using a *GTI 2500*.

Detectorists in North American and European fields have long appreciated their finds of buttons, buckles, bronze brooches and other military fasteners. These accoutrements, made of various metals and in various sizes, are key indicators as to the age of other relics found on a site. The majority of metallic buttons recovered by detectorists are of more recent origin—generally dating from the 18th to 20th centuries.

*(Left)* Confederate belt tongues, iron buckle and friction primer found by Mike with his *GTAx 550* at the Pennsylvania site.

*(Below)* This case contains more than 100 pieces of Mike's recovered shot, including dozens of smooth Enfields, three-ring Sharps ringtails, and two-ring Gardner bullets.

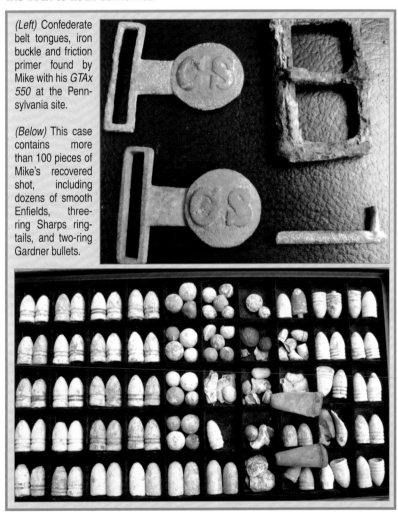

Wounded Union soldiers lie beneath large oaks after the battle of Chancellorsville in Virginia. On such old camp and field hospital sites, relic hunters commonly find discarded buttons, uniform paraphanelia and even belt plates.

Soil acids and time cause most excavated buttons to lose their surfacing through deterioration, thus making the recovery of a decorative button in perfect condition a rare occurrence. Buttons recovered which are made of precious metal are more scarce, and may command a nice price from a collector.

Why were so many plates, buttons and insignia lost or discarded during the Civil War? There are many answers but the best clues lie in where you recover them. Local made pieces may have had poorly soldered clasps that caused them to be lost in action. One side may have captured goods from another and stripped off the offending enemy insignia. Broken or discarded pieces were tossed into camp dumps. Federal troops reportedly realized that their shiny eagle breast plates made ideal aiming points for Confederate sharpshooters. Some soldiers thus opted to dispose of their sun-catching "bullet catchers." Regardless of how such insignia pieces were lost, they are prized finds for today's relic hunters.

## Rare Confederate Officer's Breast Plate

*(Left)* Al Winters poses with his *GTA 350* metal detector and the rare Confederate breast plate *(above)* he recovered in Tennessee. The eleven stars represent the eleven Confederate States.

Al Winters' best Civil War relic came from his own front yard. "We live in an area in Tennessee where a battle was fought in the Civil War and produced over 8,000 casualties," he explained. "I decided to try out my *GTA 350* metal detector in my yard. After digging up some small coins and Hot Wheels, I had a real strong signal. I dug up a Civil War breast plate that was buried about 3–4 inches deep. I also dug up several square nails and a tool of some sort."

He found that the oval plate was made of brass and measured roughly 1.25" x 3" in size. "Research revealed it had been sand cast in a foundry in Memphis, TN between 1861 and 1864," Al detailed. "I was informed that only about ten or 12 breast plates like this one have ever been recovered. I was told that the theory behind the breast plates was that this was typical of General Nathan Bedford Forrest. He may have had the breast plates commissioned for his staff officers.

"General Forrest was a Tennessee native who fought several battles in this area and later served as Mayor of Memphis, Tennessee. I was also advised the square nails would have come from the wood supply boxes that the soldiers would have emptied and then used the boxes as fire wood for their camp fires. The tool was partially rusted away and it may have been used to hold the cooking pot when they prepared a meal.

"I eventually sold the breast plate for $15,600 to a doctor who indicated that he had a collection of breast plates but needed this particular one to complete his collection."

### Plates and Buckles

The ultimate goal of many Civil War hunters is to find a belt plate, breast plate or buckle engraved with unit or army loyalties. Since there is a market for forged plates, digging your own is the safest way to authenticate it. Be careful of using the term "belt buckle" when referring to a Civil War "buckle." These are often referred to as plates versus buckles.

*Belt plates* were used by both Union and Confederate troops. There were decorative *sword belt plates* as well as the traditional *waist belt plates* which are similar to what would be called a "belt buckle." Federal belt plates come in a variety of styles and sizes but generally feature the Federal eagle or large "US" letters. Because such pieces are less rare, prices for a US plate in good condition (either dug or non-dug) can range from about $150 to $400 or more. The Model 1851 sword belt plate in very good condition can fetch more than $1,000 from a serious collector.

Confederate belt plates were often die-struck and made of either brass or pewter. Prices for these may run from $2,000 to more than $5,000, depending upon their condition and scarcity. These may be stamped "CS" or "CSA" (Confederate States of America). Various die-struck, sheet-brass patterns were used by the Confederates on their interlocking sword belt plates.

Belt plates with the highest value are those excavated that are specific to one of the states. Federal troops were more often properly supplied with uniforms, weapons and ammunition that was manufactured for regular army use. Still, local militia companies and city-specific units were organized which had their own special uniforms. Some of these included buttons and buckles of local creation with special logos, mottoes and abbreviations to designate their loyalties. For example, an oval "SNY" belt plate was used by Union soldiers from the State of New York.

Collectors may pay many hundreds or even thousands of dollars depending upon the scarcity of a particular state or unit's

*(Above)* George Wyant will tell you that Civil War relics can turn up almost anywhere in North America. He found this Union buckle in 2009 in southwestern Montana while searching with his *GTI 2500* near a crumbling foundation that once supported a pioneer's cabin. "I had seen these Civil War-era buckles in books but I had never found one before," George admitted. "It was pretty awesome." He and his buddy Tim Saylor also recovered a military button *(right)* and 1897 Liberty Head nickel from the same site.

plate emblem. Confederate belt plates specific to their state of issuance are very valuable, with prices that can easily exceed $10,000. Southern companies were often dressed out in locally manufactured uniforms with belt plates that indicated their local state. Many soldiers marched to war in civilian dress or farm clothes, particularly from states that had limited pre-war militia systems. Buttons are thus far more rare from states such as Tennessee and Arkansas, where their accoutrements were locally made and in limited distribution.

As of the early 1990s, only nine Arkansas state seal belt plates were known to have been found. Union belt plates can fetch more than $100 but Confederate buckles are again higher in value. One Garrett searcher recently sold a 13-star officer's CSA buckle for more than $15,000 to a collector. Others have been seen on the trading shows with starting bids above $10,000. Due to their size and thickness, such plates can be detected well beyond a foot in depth by quality metal detectors.

*Breast plates* from Union soldiers are more commonly found and can fetch hundreds of dollars. Many of these feature the Federal eagle design. Ammunition was often carried by infantrymen in leather pouches which were often adorned with an accoutrement plate affixed to its outside. While time in the ground will have destroyed the leather pouch, the plates and the minié balls once held inside are a prized find.

Breast plates were worn by both the Federals and Confederates as part of their uniforms. These were often worn suspended in the center of the soldiers' chests. A common story is that Confederate soldiers quickly learned that the USA breast plates worn by their opponents made an excellent target for a good marksman. Even if the shooter missed his mark by inches, he was likely to drop his opponent. Union soldiers, realizing that the plate glittered in the sun and drew enemy fire, often disposed of their breast plates in the heat of battle.

There were also plenty of buckles that can be found on Civil War or Revolutionary War sites. Leather waist belts often had non-ornamental brass frame buckles. Knapsacks, blankets, mail pouches, holsters, cartridge boxes, canteens, sword belts, cap pouches and other accouterments were often attached with snaps, buckles or plates of varying styles and composition. Soldiers carried their rations in haversacks, their ammunition in cartridge boxes and their clothing and personal items in knapsacks. Buckles from any of these items may be found on Civil War sites long after the leather has disintegrated into the soil.

---

### Badges, Shoulder Scales and Other Insignia

Relic hunters can also find various metallic insignia from the caps, knapsacks and uniforms of the soldiers who fought in the Civil War. A soldier's uniform often included thin, brass plates known as shoulder scales, which were attached to the shoulders of the uniform.

Other uniform keepsakes include badges, hat pins and company identification pieces. Both the Blue and the Gray often sported their company's letter or some other symbol which identified their unit as infantry, artillery or cavalry. Such pieces are often very decayed and oxidized when recovered and can be quite fragile to handling. Artillerymen's insignias were often crossed cannons while cavalrymen's metal logos might include crossed swords.

Some Southern soldiers and civilians displayed their support for the Confederacy by pinning state secession cockades to their jackets and hats. These badges were generally made of ribbon and often included a brass or pewter button with varying insignia. Although Maryland did not secede from the Union, many Confederate soldiers from that state wore a variety of metal pins whose design was adapted from the Calvert heraldic cross. Some Texan soldiers sported "lone star" shaped emblems engraved with the word Texas around the five star points.

More rare to recover are the identification tags worn by some U.S. Army soldiers around their necks like a modern dog tag.

These were often about the size of a quarter and made of brass. They contained personal information about the soldier identifying the command and unit he belonged to, which was particularly helpful as war casualties mounted.

Unit specific badges for Union soldiers were originally cut from colored cloth but as the war progressed many Federal soldiers sported more elaborate badges craft from coin metal, bone or even solid gold.

---

### Military Buttons

Officers of both the U.S. and Confederate armies wore specially prescribed buttons with a letter designation for their branch: "A" for artillery, "C" for cavalry, "I" for infantry, "D" for dragoons and "R" for rifles. Staff officers and generals wore buttons with an eagle surrounded by stars. Confederate brigadier generals wore coats with double-breasted rows of two buttons while major generals used rows of three buttons to denote their rank. Other Confederate junior officers and enlisted men generally wore gray-colored jackets with a single row of buttons as their standard issue. More prized buttons that relic hunters find even indicate national, state or local unit loyalties. Other specialized buttons were created for surgeons and engineers.

Union buttons issued by the Federal government also bore branch-of-service initials for infantry, rifles, cavalry and artillery or were simply general service eagle buttons. Only the states of New York and Massachusetts issued large number of uniform buttons with state specific designs to their men during the war.

French designers influenced the dress garb of some Union companies. The broad category of Zouave garb originated in the French colonies of North Africa and this style became popular with some regiments, including the 5th New York Regiment, which was also known as Duryée's Zouaves. Soldiers of this regiment wore a French style uniform of a dark blue jacket trimmed in red, baggy red trousers, and a red fez with tassel. Zouave jackets contained either a single or double row of buttons which are found in either a standard ball design or more ornately stamped convex shapes.

As with plates and buckles, Confederate buttons are less common and thus more highly prized. Most Southern buttons were made in the North prior to the Civil War. After fighting commenced, the Rebels were forced to turn to European-made buttons for their uniforms until blockades eventually choked off these supplies. This left only smaller southern state companies to produce crude button versions which are known as *locals*.

Many of these local buttons are quite collectible. The Waco Guards of Texas and the 2nd Arkansas Regiment are examples of locally-fitted companies whose buttons are rare and thus valuable to today's hunters and collectors.

There are *three general types or groups of early uniform buttons* that may be found from the time of the American Revolution through the Civil War. *One-piece buttons* were generally cast, molded or die-struck on the face with a shank backing to adhere it to clothing or uniforms. These were most often cast from white lead or pewter or yellow brass. The shank on a one-piece button was formed as an integral part of the button in the same casting. Some later struck buttons included a separate, looped-wire shank that was brazed to the back of the face. One-piece buttons were popular on both civilian and military uniforms during the nineteenth century.

Detectorists often refer to these buttons as "flat buttons." Other solid one-piece buttons are called *bullet buttons*, a style that originated in Europe and was in use in North America by the late 1700s. As the name implies, bullet buttons are similar in shape to the molded round balls of that period.

In 1813, a *two-piece button* design was invented by Benjamin Sanders in England and it became popular on American uniforms. In such designs, the button's convex front "shell" holds the design struck from the die while the back "plate" contains the shank. After being struck, the front shell was attached by rolling it over the edge of the back plate. Some locally made Confederate two-piece buttons had the shank fastened with a soft solder mixture of tin and lead.

A third button style that may be found by Civil War searchers is the *staff button* style that became popular in the U.S. during the 1830s and continued in use for the military into the 20th century. This type of button was first produced for army staff officers in the 1830s by the Scovill Company. The convex staff button contains both a separate front shell and back plate which are held together by a separate, narrow, flat rim piece which is crimped around.

Another button type that may be recovered by relic hunters is commonly referred to as a *tombac button* (tomback or Hessian buttons). Tombac buttons are flat-faced with a very pronounced boss on the backs, into which an iron-wire eye was anchored. The name is derived from the fact that these buttons originally were made of tombac (copper/zinc alloy), or thin brass, depending on the color of the regiments' metal. This style of button was worn by British Army troops during the Revolutionary War period.

Flat tombac buttons were cast by colonial workers throughout most of the eighteenth century and became larger in size by the early 1800s. Most of these buttons have copper or brass wire loop shanks and are virtually indistinguishable from civilian buttons of the same period.

Many buttons can be further identified by the presence of a *backmark*, a stamped manufacturer name and/or date and place of manufacture. Civil War and Revolutionary War button prices can run into the hundreds of dollars, especially for state specific versions in quality condition or of small manufacture. Most non-commissioned officers' buttons were made with gilt (gold) finish while most enlisted mens' buttons were not.

Button identification can become a hobby in itself as you strive to determine just what exactly you have recovered. Many relic hunters post their finds on forums enabling more experienced hunters to help with identification. There are also a number of good reference books on early American uniform buttons. Among those which have become popular with collectors are:

Albert, Alphaeus S. *Record of American Uniform and Historical Buttons.* Boyer Publishing Company, 1976.

McGuinn, William F. and Bruce S. Bazelon. *American Military Button Makers and Dealers: Their Backmarks & Dates.*

Tice, Warren K. *Uniforms of the United States, 1776–1865.* Thomas Publications, 1997.

Tice, Warren K. *Dating Buttons: A Chronology of Button Types, Makers, Retailers & Their Backmarks.* Essex Junction, VT: W. K. Tice, 2002.

There are also a number of published sources for identifying Civil War and other military belt plates. Among these are:

Kerkis, Sydney C. *Plates and Buckles of the American Military, 1795–1874.* Stone Mountain, GA: Stone Mountain Press, 3rd Edition, 1987.

Mullinax, Steve E. *Confederate Belt Buckles & Plates. Expanded Edition.* Alexandria, VA: O'Donnell Publications, 1999.

O'Donnell, Michael J. and Duncan Campbell. *American Military Belt Plates.* O'Donnell Publications, 1996.

These and other publications should be studied to properly identify your finds. The galleries presented on the following pages are only a small sampling of the buttons, belt plates and other insignia that relic hunters have found.

## CIVIL WAR PLATES AND BUCKLES GALLERY

*(Left)* Greg T. of Anderson, SC found this Civil War buckle using his *Infinium LS* metal detector while hunting an old Union camp with highly mineralized ground in Culpeper County, Virginia.

### Federal (U.S.) Buckles and Plates
*circa 1861–1865*

*(Above and below)* Front and back of a US buckle dug by Butch Holcombe in Marietta, GA. *Photos by Butch Holcombe, courtesy of American Digger Magazine.*

*(Above and below)* Front and back sides of US belt plate found at Pickett's Mill, GA. *Photos by Jerry Solomon, courtesy of American Digger Magazine.*

Front and back of U.S. Eagle breastplate found at Pickett's Mill, Georgia. *Photos by Jerry Solomon, courtesy of American Digger Magazine.*

Bullet-struck plates from the Eddie Shuman Collection. *Courtesy of American Digger Magazine.*

## Federal Buckles and Plates *(Continued)*

Five Union plates, including one from New York, found in one hole by a lucky digger in Waugh Point, VA. *Photo by Butch Holcombe, courtesy of American Digger Magazine.*

*(Above)* This well-worn stock militia "panel" plate was made of rectangle rolled brass. Available to northern and southern militiamen before the Civil War. *Photo by Butch Holcombe, courtesy American Digger Magazine.*

*(Left)* Brass stock militia square belt plate, eagle with 13 stars design. Available from 1810s to 1830s, such early plates were worn by both Union and Confederate soldiers. *Butch Holcombe photo, courtesy American Digger Magazine.*

*(Below)* Federal eagle militia plate. Such rectangle "panel" plates were available for purchase by militia units in the 1840s and 1850s and may have been worn by either side in the 1860s. *Photo by Jerry Solomon, courtesy of American Digger Magazine.*

U.S. two-piece artillery sword plate, currently on display at the Old Court House Civil War Museum in Winchester, Virginia. *Courtesy of Harry Ridgeway and www.relicman.com.*

*(Right)* Federal eagle sword waist belt plate recovered in the water (note the lack of patina). *Photo by Butch Holcombe, courtesy of American Digger Magazine.*

## State-Specific Buckles and Plates: United States

California two-part belt buckle, made of gilt cast brass, used by the local militia to defend the gold region. *Courtesy of Harry Ridgeway and www.relicman.com.*

Volunteer Militia of Maine (VMM) stamped brass oval belt plate, recovered in south Louisiana. *Courtesy of Charlie Harris.*

Massachusetts state seal officer's sword belt plate. *Courtesy of Harry Ridgeway and www.relicman.com.*

New Hampshire State Militia (organized in 1862), stamped brass belt plate. *Courtesy of Harry Ridgeway and www. relicman.com.*

*(Above)* State of New York oval belt plate and *(below)* New York militia "panel" plate, recovered in Orange County, Virginia. *Images courtesy of Harry Ridgeway and www.relicman.com.*

*(Above)* A broken New York sword plate and buttons found by Terry Smith in a Virginia campground.

## State-Specific Buckles and Plates: United States *(Continued)*

Ohio Volunteer Militia stamped brass, solder filled oval belt plate, recovered in Savannah, Georgia. *Courtesy of Charlie Harris.*

Pennsylvania Militia, Philadelphia Reserve Brigade (RB) brass oval belt plate. *Courtesy of Harry Ridgeway and www.relicman.com.*

Ohio Militia shoulder belt plate, recovered in Farmville, Virginia. *Courtesy of Harry Ridgeway and www.relicman.com.*

Volunteer Militia of Maine oval cartridge box plate dug by Scott Aylor. *Photo by Anita Holcombe, courtesy of American Digger Magazine.*

Half of a snake buckle that was likely part of a sword belt. *Courtesy of Spencer Barker.*

This disk badge found by Spencer Barker has not been positively identified but it was found on a site that produced other Civil War relics. Spencer believes that it might be a script "I" hat or belt insignia worn by a Civil War infantryman.

## Confederate Buckles and Plates

Confederate two-piece belt plate with oak leaf wreath, recovered by Larry Connors of Virginia. *Courtesy of Harry Ridgeway and www.relicman.com.*

Confederate belt plate, sand cast with rounded corners. *Photo by Butch Holcombe, courtesy of American Digger Magazine.*

"Standard" CS frame buckle with integral raised hooks, found in Jonesboro, GA. *Butch Holcombe photo, courtesy American Digger Magazine.*

Regulation die-stamped, oval CS rope border brass belt plate, from Shiloh, Tennessee. *Courtesy of Charlie Harris.*

Two-part imported English snake buckle dug by Bill Hunt in South Carolina Lowcountry. *Photo by Butch Holcombe, courtesy American Digger Magazine.*

CS frame buckle with small "forked tongue" style. *Courtesy of Harry Ridgeway and www. relicman.com.*

*(Above)* Such egg shaped oval plates were hand cut or irregularly formed. *(Below)* Rare, oval belt plate symbolizing original 11 states of the Confederacy. *Images courtesy of Harry Ridgeway and www.relicman.com.*

*(Above)* Sand cast CSA rectangle belt plate and Georgia state seal oval waist belt buckle, found by Butch Holcombe. Photo by Barry Banks. Image *courtesy of American Digger Magazine.*

## State-Specific Buckles and Plates: Confederate States

Alabama Volunteer Corps stamped brass oval belt plate.*

Alabama state seal "map on tree" solid cast brass sword belt plate.*

Georgia Militia stamped brass oval cartridge box-plate, found in Savannah by R. S. Durham.*

Georgia state seal, cast two-part belt plate with oak leaf wreath.*

Kentucky Military Institute brass stamped buckle, found by Kenny Copelin.*

Louisiana two-part state seal belt plate, sand cast local manufacture.*

Louisiana pelican belt plate, stamped brass, solder filled, from west Tennessee. *Courtesy of Charlie Harris.*

Maryland stamped brass state seal, oval cartridge box, found in Fredericksburg.*

Maryland state seal sword belt plate, used by Maryland militia units.*

Mississippi oval belt plate, stamped brass. Recovered from Mill Creek Gap near Dalton, Georgia. *Courtesy of Charles Harris.*

Mississippi sword belt plate, solid die cast brass. Recovered in Richmond, Virginia. A minor bend has been straightened.*

*\* Indicates an image courtesy of Harry Ridgeway and www.relicman.com.*

## State-Specific Buckles and Plates: Confederate States *(Continued)*

North Carolina 6th Infantry solid brass belt plate. This was the only southern regiment formed during wartime to have a custom buckle. Found near Richmond.*

North Carolina oval belt plate, stamped brass. Recovered in 1973 in Fredericksburg area.*

South Carolina militia panel plate, solid brass. Recovered from Charleston, SC.*

South Carolina stamped brass oval belt plate. *Photo by Butch Holcombe, courtesy of American Digger Magazine.*

South Carolina two-part belt plate, state seal, die stamped brass with laurel leaf wreath. Recovered in Savannah, Georgia.*

Rare Texas cast brass sword belt plate, found on plantation in Fort Bend Co., Texas, by Bobby McKinney.

Texas belt plate, stamped brass, from battle of Chancellorsville, VA. Three punched holes indicates field repair made for broken keeper.*

*\* Indicates image that is courtesy of Harry Ridgeway and www. relicman.com.*

Virginia stamped brass waist belt plate, recovered by Harry Ridgeway in 1864 camp.*

Virginia two-part belt plate, recovered by Jerry Levin in Spotsylvania trench lines.*

## BUTTON IDENTIFICATION GALLERY

There are many identification books on specific historic periods which can be consulted to help identify your finds. This section is included for general reference on some of the many styles of buttons that North American relic hunters can recover.

### Revolutionary War
*circa 1770s–1780s*

*(Above, left)* Civilian one-piece brass buttons recovered by Sergei of New York from a British camp site in Saratoga County, NY. *(Above, center)* One-piece, plain brass buttons. *(Above, right)* One-piece pewter buttons. *(Right)* Continental Army, general service USA button, circa 1777. Images courtesy of Sergei and his website *www.metaldetectingworld.com*.

### War of 1812
*buttons circa 1808–1830*

Images courtesy of Sergei and his website *www.metaldetectingworld.com*.

| Army, general service small button, circa 1808–1830. | Light Artillery, 1st Regiment button, circa 1808–1821. | 2nd Regiment of Artillerists button, circa 1811–1813. | 3rd Regiment of Artillerists button, circa 1811–1813. | War of 1812 artillery button, circa 1808–1821. |

### Other Button Types
*buttons circa 1780s–1830s*

One-piece early bullet button (right) seen beside a .69-caliber rifle ball. Both artifacts recovered from 1839 Cherokee War battleground.

Revolutionary War era mother-of-pearl buttons and drilled shell made from mussel shells from Tennessee River. Recovered from Rev. War fire pit with iron items. *Courtesy of Charlie Harris.*

This flat button was found on an 1836 Texas Revolution site.

## Miscellaneous Button and Badge Types
*buttons circa 1780–1860s*

Republic of Texas Navy 1-piece brass button (circa 1836–1845) dug by Earl Boyd on an Alabama plantation. *Courtesy of Brian Pennington.*

An 1812-1820 era Rifleman's coat button, coin type with shank back. *Courtesy of Charlie Harris.*

Various size "flower buttons" recovered from Antebellum home sites. *Courtesy of Brian Pennington.*

*(Right)* Mid-1800s cuff size "flower" buttons dug in South Carolina Low-country with gilt finish. *Courtesy of Butch Holcombe.*

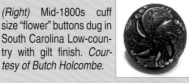

*(Below)* Late 1700s buttons dug by Kenneth Blevins. *Photo courtesy of Butch Holcombe and American Digger Magazine.*

*(Above)* Riveted and soldered Navy button found in Camp Waters, Fort Bend Co. *Courtesy of Bobby McKinney.*

*(Above)* Eric Schoppmann of Florida and his three sons—Caleb, Cian and Alexander—have become hooked on treasure hunting. Their favorite find to date is this 1903–1905 Coastal Artillery officer's pin, found in one of their local parks using an *ACE 250*.

*(Above, left and center)* Dug coat-size tombac button from 1700s era. Front is silver color with copper shank. *(Above, right)* Dug 16 mm coat-size solid Zouave ball button (circa 1700s–early 1800s). *Images courtesy of Butch Holcombe.*

*(Right)* Colonial brass buttons found by Tom Ference in Pennsylvania. The dates of these relics range from the mid-1700s to around 1800. The thimble (shown for button size reference) was found on a late 1700s tavern site.

*(Below)* Tom also dug this rare hot air balloon cufflink, circa 1780–1790. In January 1793, Jean Pierre Blanchard was the first to fly a hot air balloon across America. George Washington was present to see the balloon launch.

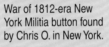

War of 1812-era New York Militia button found by Chris O. in New York.

War of 1812 officer's button. Depicts eagle with shield.

*(Below, left)* Brian Hanisco of Philadelphia, a veteran coin shooter, had just decided to try his hand at relic hunting when he dug this beauty using his *ACE 350*. It is a 1-piece cast pewter Pennsylvania State Regiment militia button from the American Revolution.

*(Below, right)* Late 18th century (post Revolutionary War) Rattlesnake and Stars patriotic 1-piece button found by Steve Evans. The 13 stars represent the 13 colonies, protected by the rattlesnake which forms the outer border.

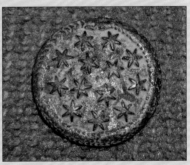

## American Civil War
*buttons circa 1861–1865*

*All images on this page courtesy of Larry Cissna and The Treasure Depot (unless otherwise noted).*

Confederate
Staff
(local)

Confederate
Staff
(local)

Confederate
Staff found by
Gary Koger

Confederate
General Service

CSA coat-size
button (non-dug).
*Courtesy of Charlie
Harris.*

Confederate
Artillery

Confederate
Cavalry
(Texas)

Confederate
Cavalry

Confederate
Engineer's button
(non-dug)
*Courtesy of Charlie
Harris.*

Confederate
Script "I" button,
English made.
*Courtesy of
Charlie Harris.*

(Left) Confederate block Infantry button
and (center) cast brass CS block "I" button, both from Lookout Mountain.
*Courtesy of Charlie Harris.*

Confederate
Engineer, script
"E" found in Caney
Creek support camp
*Courtesy of Bobby
McKinney*

Confederate
Infantry
(London
manufacture)

Confederate
Rifleman
(local
manufacture)

Confederate
Rifleman, script "R"
found in Fort Bend
County
*Courtesy of Bobby
McKinney*

## Civil War Buttons: Federal Service

U.S.
Staff

U.S.
Staff

U.S.
Artillery

U.S. Artillery,
found by
Robert Vaughn

U.S.
Cavalry
(2-piece)

U.S.
Dragoon (circa
1840s-1850s)

U.S.
Dragoon
(1-piece)

U.S.
Rifleman
(2-piece)

U.S. Ordnance
(2-piece)

U.S.
Infantry

U.S. Infantry
(2-piece)

U.S.
General Service

U.S. Topographical
Engineer's button,
coin type, from
Virginia. *Courtesy
of Charlie Harris.*

*All images on this page
courtesy of Larry Cissna
and The Treasure Depot
(unless otherwise noted).*

U.S.
Navy

U.S. Navy
(2-piece, brass)

U.S. Dept. of
Treasury (1-piece)

*(Left)* Front and back sides
of a Marine button dug by
Ken Weitlauf. *Photos by
Butch Holcombe, American
Digger Magazine.*

## State-Specific Civil War: Confederate Buttons

Alabama*
Volunteer Corps,
Officers (2-piece)

Mid-1800s era Alabama Corps of Cadets buttons,
University of Alabama. *Courtesy Brian Pennington.*

Alabama "map on tree"
coat button from Look-
out Mountain. *Courtesy
of Charlie Harris.*

Arkansas*
state seal,
Staff button

Florida state seal
with six-pointed star
button, produced by
Scovill around 1860.**

*(Above, left)* Georgia state seal 2-pc. button dug in
Savannah. *(Above, right)* Irish Jasper Greens button
found by Butch Holcombe in Savannah. This Georgia
Civil War Militia group had only about 200 members,
making these buttons very rare.

Georgia Military
Institute, found by
Danny Snider (photo
by Butch Holcombe)

Louisiana state seal
button recovered by
Earl Boyd

Mississippi Infantry
button, courtesy of
"Dad in AL"

Mississippi Militia
button, courtesy of
Brett McWilliams.

North Carolina state
seal 2-pc. button dug
in Savannah. *Courtesy
of Butch Holcombe.*

North Carolina state
seal button from
Shiloh, TN. *Courtesy
of Charlie Harris.*

Rare North Carolina
Hornet's Nest button;
photo by Butch
Holcombe

North Carolina
"sunburst" button dug
by Michael DeAngury

*(Left and right)* The remaining gold gilt finish on this
North Carolina button, dug by Bradley Dixon, is highly
sought by button collectors.

\* Image courtesy of Larry Cissna, The Treasure Depot.
\*\* Image courtesy of Harry Ridgeway and www.relicman.com.

## State-Specific Civil War: Confederate Buttons

North Carolina, Charlotte Military Institute cadet *

South Carolina state seal palmetto tree button recovered by Brian Pennington.

Another South Carolina state seal button dug in Petersburg, Virginia, by Bert Alderson.

A rare Tennessee state seal button found by James Shaner.

University of the South button found by James Disney. CSA General Polk taught at this 1850s TN school.*

Texas Staff Officer button, a rare find made by Paul Shipe*

Virginia state seal, 2-piece button

Virginia coat button from near Richmond, Virginia. *Courtesy Charlie Harris.*

* Indicates image courtesy of Larry Cissna, The Treasure Depot.

*(Above and below)* Two of Beau Ouimette's Virginia state seal button finds. The silver coating still present on the lower button gives it a high collector's value.

### Split Loyalty States

*(Left)* Kentucky state seal button. *(Center and right)* Both sides of a 2-pc. Kentucky Military Institute (KMI) Cadet button. Brian Pennington searched and found the front half after his buddy dug the back piece. Kentucky citizens served both for the Union and Confederacy but this pin is considered a "Yankee pin."

Maryland state seal, © Keith Sylvester

Maryland state seal, dug by Beau Ouimette

Missouri state seal button

## Texas Relics of the Confederacy

Rare Texas sword plate dug by Bobby McKinney at Camp Walters in Fort Bend Co., Texas. Only two examples are known to exist.

Texas star belt plate dug in Virginia in a Hood's Brigade retreat route camp.

1851 sword belt plate dug at Camp Walters in Fort Bend Co., Texas.

Star sash buckle dug in old town Brazoria, Texas.

Two-piece Confederate belt plate dug in Jackson County, Texas.

CSA belt plate dug in Jackson County, Texas.

CS solid cast plate dug at site of Confederate shipyard near Lynchburg, Texas.

CS rope border plate dug at Confederate supply depot near Millican, Texas.

Plain face sword belt plate dug at CS campsite near Crosby, Texas.

Texas hat star dug in Camp Waters, Fort Bend County, Texas.

Another Texas hat star that was dug in Camp Waters, Fort Bend County, Texas.

Texas hat star dug in camp of 8th Texas Cavalry near Murfreesboro, Tennessee.

*All images courtesy of Bobby McKinney.*

## Confederate Buttons Dug in Texas

Cresent Infantry Regiment from Louisiana button dug in Camp Buchel in Brazoria County.

Texas button found on a plantation site in the ghost town of Pittsville, in Fort Bend County.

Texas buttons with T. Miller backmark, known as "TX 25." The star has "CS" in the center with TEXAS spelled around the it. *(Left)* Dug at Sabine Pass. *(Right)* Dug in Brazoria County camp site.

Local-made Texas star cuff button, dug in CS campsite near Columbia in Brazoria County.

Texas Military Institute (TMI) button dug in CS campsite in Matagorda County.

Texas button made by Hyde & Goodrich in New Orleans. Dug at Camp McNeel on Gulf Prairie.

This Texas CS star T. Miller button, known as "TX 26," does not include the state's letters.

Louisiana button dug in Camp Waters, Fort Bend County, Texas.

Voltigiers button dug in Brazoria County CS campsite.

Confederate "muffin" Houston Depot buttons dug in Brazoria County camp sites.

*(Left)* Script "I" and Texas button dug in Brazoria County CS camp site.

*(Right)* T. Miller back-marked "C" buttons dug in Brazoria County CS camp site.

*All images courtesy of Bobby McKinney.*

## State-Specific Civil War: U.S. Buttons

California
state seal button

Connecticut state
seal button (non-
dug Scovill)*

Indiana state seal
(staff button)

Maine one-piece
state seal button

Maine button found
by John Chaplin in
South Carolina**

Massachusetts
state seal
(1-piece)

Michigan
state seal
(staff)

Minnesota
state seal

New Hampshire
Volunteer Militia
(2-piece)

New Jersey state
seal (staff)

New York Ulster
Guard button
found by Roger
Morgan in VA**

New York Militia
button dug by
Butch Holcombe in
Marietta, GA.**

New York National
Guard button dug
near Harper's
Ferry**

New York school buttons: *(Above, left)*
Poughkeepsie Military Institute (PMI);
*(Above, right)* Hudson River Institute (HRI)
*Courtesy of Larry Cissna & The Treasure Depot*

New York Militia cuff
button dug by Steve
Moore in West
Virginia

* Indicates image courtesy of John and Nikki Walsh and Fort Donelson Relics.
** Indicates image courtesy of Butch Holcombe, *American Digger Magazine.*

## State-Specific Civil War: U.S. Buttons

Pennsylvania
National Guard
button dug in VA*

Pennsylvania
state seal
(staff)

Ohio State (postwar)
of superior quality
*Courtesy of Fort
Donelson Relics*

Rhode Island
state seal (staff)
with 24 stars
around border **

Rhode Island state
seal 2-pc. button
recovered by Butch
Holcombe*

Rhode Island,
Providence Marine
Corps of Artillery,
2-pc. button
dug by Beau Ouimette

Vermont Militia
1-pc. button
*Courtesy of Harry
Ridgeway and
www.relicman.com*

Vermont Militia
Artillery 1-pc. button
*Courtesy of Harry
Ridgeway and
www.relicman.com*

Vermont state seal
(non-dug) 2-pc.
*Courtesy of Fort
Donelson Relics*

Wisconsin
state seal button
(staff)

*(Above)* These Civil War buttons (including a state-specific from Rhode Island) were found by Butch Holcolmbe in a three-day span in Fredericksburg, Virginia.*

*(Left)* A Confederate Infantry button found with uniform remains in a Dalton, Georgia, winter camp where old uniforms were discarded.*

* Indicates image courtesy of Butch Holcombe, *American Digger Magazine.*
** Indicates image courtesy of Larry Cissna and The Treasure Depot.

*(Left and above)* Civil War artillery and infantry buttons, dug by Albert Jewel in South Carolina.

*(Above right)* "RB" Militia Button dug by Butch Holcombe in Savannah. These are attributed to both the Republican Blues and Pennsylvania Reserve Brigade. *Photos by Butch Holcombe, courtesy of American Digger Magazine.*

*(Left)* Confederate Bingham School buttons—one coat and two cuffs—found by Michael DeAngury of Charlotte in York County, SC. *Photo courtesy of "Panther Mike."*

*(Left)* Horse or Sportsman's button, overcoat size. Many different animals are found on such Sportsmen's buttons, often found in Confederate camps. *(Right)* The Putnam is a cloth die button of the Civil War era, this recovered from Lookout Mountain. *Courtesy of Charlie Harris.*

*(Above)* William Harrison presidential campaign button, found in middle Tennessee. Harrison campaigned as being from a log home (as in design), although he came from a mansion. *Courtesy of Charlie Harris.*

*(Right)* These Civil War buttons—including artillery, cavalry, infantry and several state specifics—were dug by Gregory Heath along General Lee's retreat route in Virginia. *Photo by Butch Holcombe, courtesy of American Digger Magazine.*

## Other Civil War Insignia

Case of hat plates, snake buckles and other insignia from Charlie Harris' collection. In up-per left are two varieties of cast brass snake buckles. Top row, second from left: crude U.S. tongue and wreath buckle made from pewter. Top, third from left: officer's artillery crossed cannon hat plate from FL. Top, far right: belt adjuster.

*Second row, starting second from left are:* 1840s era Shako hat plate from Mobile Bay area; Confederate Cavalry coat button from VA; Cavalry crossed sabers hat plate from Shiloh; snake buckle with iron belt loops; and an enlisted man's artillery crossed cannon hat plate from Wauhatchie, TN.

*Third row, from left are:* crossed cannon artillery hat plate; U.S. eagle button; infantry officer's french horn hat plate from Sequatchie Valley, TN; and cape pin.

*Bottom row, from left are:* unknown belt plate; thin, stamped brass Naval sash buckle from Vicksburg, MS; smaller officer's infantry french horn hat plate from Sequatchie Valley, TN; small cast brass belt buckle from middle TN; and tongue and wreath U.S. sash buckle of thin stamped brass, from Knoxville, TN. *Courtesy of Charlie Harris.*

*(Right)* Buttons that have been hammered out to make poker chips or that were put on railroad tracks. Top left to lower right are: Louisiana, North Carolina, U.S. Cavalry and Wisconsin Civil War buttons. *Courtesy of Charlie Harris.*

469

**Case of cavalry plates from Charlie Harris' collection.** Details for those with numerals:

① Group of four rosettes. Top left was sweated onto the side of an officer's stirrup. Top right is a Confederate officer's bridal rosette. Lower left is a cast pewter bridal rosette with silver foil cover. Lower right is a bulls-eye rosette.

② Pewter "CS" saddle shield, stamped brass "US" saddle shield, stamped brass "CS" saddle shield and "US" stamped brass shield with the seat size on it.

③ Large stamped brass solder-filled bridal rosettes (US, intertwined USA and a bulls-eye type design).

④ Moving left to right: "US" martingale plate from Murfreesboro, TN; eagle martingale plate from Mobile, AL; and enlisted man's martingale plate from northern GA.

⑤ Moving left to right: Brass eagle cut out of a breast plate; officer's style eagle martingale plate from Knoxville, TN; and cut-out sheet brass martingale from Little Rock, AR.

⑥ Two small U.S. bridal rosettes from Sweden's Cove, TN, and a small martingale heart or possibly a mule's leather nose decoration from near Fort Payne, AL.

*Courtesy of Charlie Harris.*

Front and back side of a martingale dug at Harper's Ferry.
*Photos by Butch Holcombe, courtesy of American Digger Magazine.*

## World War I
*buttons circa 1914–1918*

*(Above)* American World War I uniform buttons recovered by European metal detectorists. On the top row, the central button secured the pocket of a jacket. The four infantry buttons on the top row, 17 mm in diameter, were used for closing cartridge pouches. The second row of buttons (23 mm size) were used to close an American jacket and the bottom three buttons (30 mm in size) secured an American coat. Trademarks on the backs of these buttons indicate that they were manufactured in 1910 in Newark, New Jersey, and in Philadlephia, Pennsylvania, in the United States. *Courtesy of Gilles Cavaillé, Loisirs Detection.*

David H. of Natchez, MS recovered these two World War I brass relics using an *ACE 250*.
*(Left)* A Mississippi National Guard collar button.
*(Right)* A World War I General Service button.

(Right) These buttons are from the drill plate of a tunic, part of the uniform of a Bavarian light horseman. The top three buttons on the left, 23 mm in size, fastened the right sleeve of the soldier's tunic. Note that the lion faces in, with his tail on the left. The top three buttons on the right face the opposite direction. The two bottom buttons, 18 mm in size, also face opposite directions. The small photo below shows how these rows of lion buttons secured the Bavarian light horseman's drill plate.
*All photos courtesy of Gilles Cavaillé, Loisirs Detection.*

(Left) These Bavarian buttons are made of tombac, an alloy of copper and yellow zinc. The larger buttons on the top row indicated rank of warrant officers. The second and third row buttons were used to secure the soldier's uniform. The button on the bottom with the numeral "1" indicates the company number.

Various uniform buttons, U.S. Army and National Guard insignia from Camp Logan, a World War I campsite in Houston where Bill Kassellman, Ron Tadlock, Ken Scanlon and Charlie Horn have recovered many buttons.

## Button Bonanza From Massachusetts Shoddy Mill

David Thatcher, a member of the Silver City Treasure Seekers Club of Massachusetts, has hunted the site of a 19th century shoddy mill for the past several years with some of his companions. Such mills created inexpensive woolen cloth by grinding woolen rags from old clothing, including a fair amount of discarded military uniforms. David and his fellow detectorists have made button finds which number into the many hundreds from the ruins of this old Massachusetts factory. Brass and copper buttons, buckles and other adornments are regularly unearthed from this site.

"Rob Fahey, a fellow bottle digger/metal detectorist discovered this old mill site about four years ago while searching for old bottles along a river bank," Dave explained. "While at a club meeting, he told me about this site he came upon where buttons of every size, shape and color imaginable were literally popping out of the ground. The site on the other hand gave up few bottles and Rob lost interest."

Dave and other club hunters returned to the old shoddy mill site to hunt for buttons, which they quickly found in abundance. "Many are metal but there are also plenty of non-metallic buttons we find as we dig," he related. "I use my *GTI 2500* to locate targets and then my Garrett *Pro-Pointer* to separate the metallic buttons from the plastic and bakelite. We have found a wide variety from military to postal service, police, railroad, and even fire buttons. Most of our finds date from around World War I, but I did find several buttons from the Civil War period. Bill Ladd, an acquaintance of Rob and myself and an accomplished metal detectorist, has also visited this site and made many successful recoveries."

Various buttons David has collected from the Massachusetts shoddy mill include: *(left)* unknown BRT button, *(center)* World War I era U.S. Army Artillery Corps button, and *(right)* World War I U.S. Army collar disk button.

*(Above)* David Thatcher and his buddies have detected the site of a 19th century button factory in Massachusetts for some time. David *(left)* uses his *GTI 2500* with a *Super Sniper* coil to find the metallic targets and then sifts through the plastic buttons for metallic ones with his Garrett *Pro-Pointer*.

More of David's shoddy mill button finds. Left: A World War I era postal service button. Second from left: World War I U.S. Navy button. Third from left: Central Hanover Bank & Trust Co. button. Far right: one of twelve found uniform buttons.

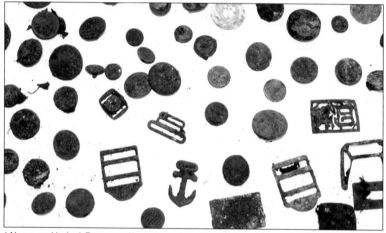

(*Above and below*) Recovered buttons and buckles from the Massachusetts shoddy mill.

## Gallery of Military Buttons and Buckles

*(Left)* Union buttons found by Terry Smith hunting in Virginia. Both have an eagle insignia but the one on the left has an "A" for artillery and the one on the right has an "I" for infantry.

*(Below)* Iron knapsack buckles Terry found near a Union camp.

*(Above* These two-piece U.S. cuff buttons include fronts, backs and intact sets. Terry uses minimal cleaning for such relics and dips them in olive oil to stop oxidation.

*(Above)* This flat brass button would have been either gold or silver gilded. Often, only the brass remains after 145 years in the ground. Note the open loop fastener on the back side of this button *(see inset)*.

*(Above)* Various relics Brian found at a Confederate mustering area in Newbern, Alabama. Includes a piece of a powder flask, a .44-caliber Colt bullet, and an Infantry eagle button.

*(Below)* Front and back of a Scoville flower button, after cleaning, found by Brian at an 1800s Alabama ghost town site.

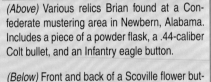

*(Left)* An early U.S. Navy button—found by Brian in Greensboro, Alabama—shown atop his button identification book pages.

Many relic hunters carry a digital camera to capture a prized relic as it appeared when first dug. *(Above left)* A Civil War bridal rosette dug in Alabama by Brian Pennington. *(Above, right)* An eagle breast plate in the soil where Melvin Lane has just recovered it.

*(Right)* Melvin Lane of SC holds a local palmetto plate at the dig site. *(Below)* The Civil War era South Carolina palmetto plate Melvin is holding is shown in more detail below. He found these relics, including 29 palmetto buttons, in a one-month span while hunting a productive South Carolina plantation in 2011.

The lure of relic hunting is spreading to the next generation of diggers. Seventeen-year-old Michael Bennett of North Carolina is just one example. He videotapes many of his hunts and posts them to YouTube (under the handle "NuggetNoggin"), where he is viewed by thousands of followers per week. Some of Michael's favorite relic finds *(above, left)* include buttons from the Carolinas, War of 1812 buttons, and a Confederate tongue. In the upper corner, moving down are: the front and back view of a War of 1812 era 1st Regiment of Artillery button found by Michael, and one of his North Carolina state seal button finds.

Megahn White *(above)* joined her boyfriend to hunt a house site in Mebane, North Carolina. Before the day had ended, this first-time searcher had found a U.S. belt plate *(above, right)*.

*(Right)* This bronze World War I Victory lapel pin, given to servicemen after returning home, was found by George Zuk of Britsol, CT, with his *AT Pro.*

## Montana's Team Anaconda Racks up Buttons, Tokens, Relics

For the past eight years, buddies Tim Saylor *(seen at left)* and George Wyant *(right)* of Montana have been relentlessly hunting coins, relics, and rare tokens. They have amassed an enviable collection of treasure in that time, and have gained some media attention—including an appearance on ABC's *Good Morning America* in 2011. Calling themselves Team ATC (for Anaconda Treasure.com), George and Tim have produced a number of light-hearted treasure hunting DVDs and even a book on their various adventures and advice.

Based in Anaconda and Butte, Montana, this metal detecting duo ranges far and wide throughout the year in search of old coins and relics. When the snow becomes too deep in the winter, their off time is spent researching potential new sites to scour when the warmer season returns. Tim and George have given back to their communities in the form of relic cases they have donated to local museums for their hometowns to enjoy.

Two of Tim's state-specific buttons. *(Left)* Montana state seal button, circa 1890s, found with his *AT Pro. (Right)* Kentucky state seal button with gold gilt, circa 1870s–1880s, with Waterbury back mark.

*(Above)* Some of Tim and George's favorite button finds, all made using Garrett detectors.

478

*(Above, left)* These rare Montana historical pins found by Tim include several campaign medallions proclaiming Anaconda to be the capital of Montana. In 1894, voters chose Helena over Anaconda as the new state capital.

*(Above, right)* This tag, found by George with his *AT Pro*, announced the 1864 death date of a man hanged in what is now the ghost town of Virginia City, Montana.

*(Right)* Several of George and Tim's military relic finds: a U.S. box plate, a carbine sling buckle, an 1851 sword belt plate, and an 1851 Colt brass trigger guard.

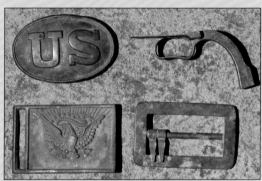

*(Left)* This group of historic tokens found by Tim dates from about 1910 into the 1930s. Some of the rare trade value tokens are highly valuable to modern collectors.

## A Button Hunter Who's Not Afraid to Get Dirty

Bobby DePalo *(left)* of Rhode Island is not your average relic hunter. Although he is a newcomer to the hobby, he has an inner drive for success that will not let any potential roadblock stand in his way.

"Being a paraplegic sometimes presents obstacles," he admitted. An avid historian and big game hunter, Bobby was not about to let his own wheelchair distract him from his new desire to take up metal detecting.

"My dream was to find a military button," he said. So, he began researching an old dump site that dates back to the 1870s with connections to the military. He made arrangements to go out with relic hunter David Thatcher, who lives in his area.

After arriving at the site, David pushed Bobby in his wheelchair along a grassy pathway "bordered by trees on one side and a thicket of bramble, brush and briars on the other." David cleared off a hunting area and began detecting while Bobby leaned over from his chair to alternately detect with his Garrett *Pro-Pointer* and dig with his trowel. Less than five minutes later, Bobby was calling out to David, "Look what I found!"

Bobby had dug a brass World War II Medical Corps button (left and below) from the dump site. His dream of finding a military button was fulfilled on his first hunt but he feels that his relic hunting is only just beginning. "That independent feeling that I get is something that I just can't describe," Bobby said. "My head becomes clear, the workout feels great and I don't think about my disability."

# CHAPTER 20

# ORGANIZED HUNTS

One of the things I enjoy about relic hunting is organizing group hunts. Sometimes it is an effort to pinpoint a battleground. One trip involved volunteers willing to work with us and the Texas Parks & Wildlife folks on a Texas Revolution site for archaeological purposes. Other times, it's simply a farm or homestead where the owner has granted us the permission to conduct a search and shoot a video.

Such hunts make for a great day of simply seeing what will be found. The more people on these outings, the better the odds that someone will find something of value or interest. During one Saturday ranch property hunt, we even threw in a few dollars apiece to make a pot for the best find and for the oldest find, to be split by two winners. No serious money changed hands but it gave everyone the opportunity to return home with a few bucks more in their pocket that they had started the day with.

The key to being invited back to private property lies in how the group conducts its business. Once our search group has gathered at a site, one of us (or the landowner) gives a brief talk to lay out the ground rules: where to go, where not to go, what to avoid, and any potential hazards that may exist.

By following the basic rules, we have always left the properties on good terms. This simply involves removing trash items that are discovered, filling in the holes and leaving the property in as good or better shape than we found it. On farmland, you should always make sure to close gates properly behind you to keep livestock from escaping. The landowners are naturally curious to see what, if anything, of value or historical interest comes out of their soil.

We therefore make it a common practice to compare finds at the end of the afternoon and show the owners what was unearthed. They are usually pleased if a few of the found items are offered to them. Regardless of whether I have a good day or a bad day in terms of finds, I always come away from the field with additional knowledge of scouting relic sites.

---

### Historic Texas Ranch Hunt

In November 2009, we organized a hunt with 20 detectorists from the Dallas area Lone Star and East Fork treasure hunting clubs to search on an historic Texas ranch. The landowners had purchased this property from another family in the late 1800s. Over the decades, the family has picked up Indian arrowheads and other artifacts from some of their pastures.

During this pre-hunt briefing, the landowner is able to express any concerns he has to our search group. Complete cooperation with such requests is the key to being invited back.

Gary, one of the landowners, described various Indian tribes that centuries before had roamed, camped and farmed along the creek which twists across the back of his land. The research of Larry Simpson—who had worked with Gary to gain permission for us to detect this site—indicated a strong Indian presence in this area. According to Gary, the Indians reportedly had some type of skirmish with Texas frontiersmen in the early 19th century along the creek which bordered his property.

Many of our searchers were eager to hunt around the old farm-house and barn structures for early coins and homestead relics. Few of us had much good fortune around these buildings, aside from a piece of silverware and a 1907 Liberty Head nickel dug at eight inches by James Ford. Many of the others headed for the back of the property to begin working along the creek. I chose to work my way from the homestead area slowly across the pastures toward the creek, hoping to run across an area of interest en route.

By the time I reached the "back 40," Robert Jordan and a couple of other fellows had each discovered a musket ball. The most exciting recovery of the day came while Robert was using his *Pro-Pointer* to retrieve a musket ball. As he reached in to retrieve the lead shot, he found to his great joy an Indian arrowhead in great condition. By the appearance of these items at this same depth, it certainly added to the possibility that frontiersmen and the Native Americans had clashed in this area.

Before I could reach the area where Robert was whooping about his arrowhead, I stopped to retrieve a nice .69-caliber musket ball. More and more of our detectorists moved back to help sweep this skirmish area as the word got around of good finds. During the next few hours, dozens of pieces of shot were detected and recovered. I ended the day with 14 balls ranging from .69-caliber down to what may have been pistol balls of about .40-caliber.

Like many old sites, recovering relics is only half the fun. The other part is going back and trying to figure out what certain items really are or how they came to be there in the first place or in the condition in which they were found.

## HISTORIC TEXAS RANCH HUNT

*(Above and below)* Robert Jordan retrieves an Indian arrowhead in the same dug clod with a pistol ball.

James Ford *(above)* digs near old fencing. *(Inset)* A 1907 Liberty Head "V" nickel he found.

*(Left)* Steve pinpoints a musket ball.

*(Above)* Some of our group works a productive area near the old Indian village site. *(Inset)* Robert Jordan shows his finds of the day.

484

These various size pieces of lead shot were recovered by Robert Jordan and the author during their second visit to the old Indian village site.

Robert Jordan and I returned to this farm in the fall of 2010—along with Vaughan Garrett and Brian McKenzie to document our finds—to continue exploring the site with our latest detectors. Although the hot spots were somewhat overgrown with goat weed, the area continued to produce musket balls of varying sizes and ages. As has been par for the course in past hunts, Robert was the first to dig a round ball this time and he had the better luck during the early going.

By afternoon, I had caught up and we ended up nearly dead even in total recovered relics. My first find was a fired buck and ball-size piece of buckshot, followed by more than a dozen other pieces of lead. They varied in size from pistol balls to standard .69-caliber musket balls to a three-ringed solid bullet similar to a Civil War minié ball.

The landowner discussed with us the variety of Indian relics that his family had found while cultivating their fields in past years. In addition to arrowheads, they recovered primitive hand tools, hide scrapers and other items.

---

### Battle Creek, Pleasant Hill and Other Hunts

Some relic quests take longer than others; some people will search their lifetime for buried caches of Jessie James, Sam Bass or some other renegade. Regardless of whether your quest is an historic site or a rumored outlaw hoard, research and contemporary maps can help steer you to a site. Your time, patience and detector skills then become the required ingredient for success...and even then, success is never guaranteed.

Some time after locating the July 16, 1839, Cherokee War's main battlefield, I decided that it would be worthwhile to one day pinpoint the area of the first day's battle of July 15. It occurred in present Henderson County along a particular body of water that is appropriately named Battle Creek.

Julie Reiter, who had hunted with us on the July 16 battle-grounds, did some scouting in this area. In the end, Julie's best lead was Kenneth Cade, who, ironically, I had visited in 1996 while writing a biography of an early Texas Ranger. Kenneth said that he had walked the July 15 battlefield many years ago. He said that the older gentleman who had walked him along Battle Creek pointed out a particularly unusual iron marker that had been driven into the ground to mark where two Texans had been buried close to the battlefield. This was exciting to me, as an early source on this battle mentions these iron markers. I reviewed plat maps of the county to determine the current owner of land parcels. The first property of interest to us was that of Helen Cade, one of Kenneth's relatives who owned property along Battle Creek.

Although several promising signs existed, we found that the area was too large and too overgrown to be tackled in a single day. For our first trip to Helen's land, Brian and I were joined by detec-

Relic hunters without four wheel drives should beware of marshy conditions. *(Left)* Dave Totzke surveys how deep our Suburban has sunk into a saturated roadway. *(Right)* Paul Wilson puts his relic shovel to work digging out one of the rear wheels.

torists Andy Mearos, Robert Jordan, Dave Totzke, Mike Skinner, Paul Wilson, Julie Reiter, Ron Rutledge and Ronnie Morris.

The grounds in this area were saturated. The Dallas area had received a foot of snow—a record amount—during the previous three weeks and this had been followed by heavy amounts of rainfall. The result made driving into the actual site impossible. In fact, we buried the Garrett Suburban long before we even reached the entrance gate to the Cade property. The extra detectorists and their shovels came in handy to help dig out the deeply bogged vehicle.

Our detecting team hiked into the land and split up to scour the area. The metallic targets were few and far between and all proved to be contemporary bullets. I did, however, come upon a significant rock formation that appeared to be of Indian creation. The early Native Americans were known to leave trail signs and other markers to steer others toward a treasure or a meeting place. These stones clearly were stood up and leaned against each other in a way that simply would not have happened naturally in this terrain. There are very few stones in the area, and it would have taken many men to move these.

Natural formation or early signs? *(Left)* These large rocks were leaned together long ago, perhaps as an early guidepost or marker for Native Americans. Note that small trees have grown between the boulders over time. *(Above)* Robert Jordan searches the crevice between these large rocks.

At the end of the day, we had explored large areas of the Cade land, but had nothing of significance to show. Not one to give up, I returned with Brian and Robert a few weeks later to search further up and down Battle Creek.

We had talked about whether snakes would be out on this spring day since the temperatures were finally warming up. That thought had long since left my mind as I finished digging a target and holstered my *Pro-Pointer*. As I prepared to stand, I caught a long, black shape out of the corner of my eye. Not four feet away was a four-foot black and grey snake slithering past me!

I used my *Infinium* coil to get him out of my way. He coiled up to strike for a moment but quickly slithered away and dropped into Battle Creek once I took a couple of steps back. Needless to say, I was on extra alert the rest of the day in this thick stuff along the creek banks.

Our searches went without luck, so after lunch we joined Helen and went to visit neighbors of hers who own about 500 acres just north of her land. I suspected that we really needed to be searching south of Helen's land, but it seemed worth the effort to continue scouting along the creek as far as we could. We searched the area and Robert did find one musket ball on a high ridge line above Battle Creek.

This interested us enough to return with a large group to the Griffin property. With more detectorists, we were able to cover

The author's organized hunts along Battle Creek have succeeded only in narrowing down the land to the most likely area. Until permission can be obtained from that landowner, this solitary musket ball dug by Robert Jordan is the only "period" relic we have unearthed from this 1839 frontier fight.

*(Above)* Some of the searchers who helped contribute to the Battle Creek search efforts were *(left to right)*: James Massey, Retchey Davis, Stan May, Ed Verboort, Robert Jordan, Bob Bruce, Ron Rutledge, Lewis Murray, author, Danny Norris, James Ford, William Godfrey and Steve Doering.

The author searches for artifacts in a turn of Battle Creek in April 2010.

significant portions of the farm, searching the ridge lines and low country near the creek in earnest. Our best efforts, however, failed to produce any more evidence of the battle between the Cherokees and the Texas frontiersmen. Members of our group did turn up several interesting relics near the old home site above the creek.

We returned with a smaller group in the fall of 2010 and made a recon of another large section of land just south of where we suspect the key action to have taken place. By that point, we had scouted the Battle Creek area sufficiently enough to convince me about whose land we need to search. That individual has not been interested in allowing even a single person to search his land, so this particular relic quest will remain a future endeavor.

Fortunately, there are always plenty of other relic hunting spots to pursue. The size of the group we organize is contingent upon the amount of acres we plan to cover. We often end up with a group of four to six searchers, and that's a comfortable size group to work a large piece of land.

One of these smaller group hunts that I particularly enjoyed was a visit to Louisiana in early 2013. Brian and I drove with Rusty Curry to Pleasant Hill, the site of a significant Civil War battle. I was excited because several of my ancestors had fought there and one of my great-great uncles was killed at this location. We met up with our friends Jason Ebeyer and Spencer Alan Reiter, who had secured permission with some of the locals for us to hunt.

The challenge in this case was seeing how well we could do in an area that we knew very well had been pounded by treasure hunters for more than forty years. We were joined by two relic hunters from the Pleasant Hill area who knew the area well and helped with gaining access to other properties.

The land we hunted ranged from heavily forested to pasture land to another patch that had been clear cut. As expected, our finds volume was not tremendous but I was still very pleased. My goal was to pick up a few relics from a battle site that had meaning to me and to that end I was not disappointed. Everyone had some fun and came away with at least a handful of items. Rusty found

## GROUP DIG IN LOUISIANA CIVIL WAR COUNTRY

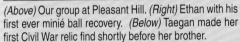

*(Above)* Our group at Pleasant Hill. *(Right)* Ethan with his first ever minié ball recovery. *(Below)* Taegan made her first Civil War relic find shortly before her brother.

*(Right)* Rusty's finds included a group of five dropped Confederate round balls.

*(Lower left)* Spencer's finds included a flattened scabbard tip.

*(Lower right)* Steve's digs included a more modern 1909 Barber dime.

five Confederate round balls in one hole, proving that you should always double-check your dig spot before closing it up.

The most enjoyable part of our couple of days of digging at Pleasant Hill was in seeing Spencer's kids dig their first Civil War relics. His daughter Taegan was first to dig a minié ball, and she was soon followed by Ethan making his first 1860s find. The grins on their faces said it all: they are hooked now!

Our Garrett team will continue to go out on small group hunts in various states and countries. I learn something every time and I value the new friendships that are made.

———

### DIV, GNRS, North/South and Club Hunts

Organized regional relic hunts have become quite popular in the past two decades. The size, scope and nature of these depends on the amount of available land and whether it is a "seeded" hunt or one in which non-planted relics are to be discovered.

An example of a popular seeded hunt that has been held in past years is the Fort Donelson Relic Hunt. John and Nikki Walsh have held five relic hunts in near Fort Donelson, Tennessee, and they may host another one in the future. For them, it is a labor of love, as they personally acquire and plant many thousands of Civil War-era artifacts in the ground. Relic hunters then pay entry fees for the right to hunt for their share of period relics and tokens that can be redeemed for prizes such as metal detectors.

The East Texas Treasure Hunters Association has held very similar style seeded Civil War hunts near the Louisiana and Texas borders. The planted targets included thousands of minié balls, hundreds of eagle buttons, and various other relics. Some of the relics were painted with special numbers. These lucky pieces could later be traded in for big prizes, such as metal detectors and Civil War relics such as belt plates.

Detecting clubs across the country periodically hold other group hunts, both on historic properties and on land where the

The items in this case helped Brian Pennington win the 2006 North/South Hunt. The 2006 hunt was held near the Union post of Fort Powhatan in Colonial Heights, Virginia. Brian found all of these items in a very small space that he believes was an old hut site. These are .54-caliber Starr carbine bullets, a kepi buckle (hat buckle) and a Federal soldier's ID tag.

These close-ups show the front and back side of the Union identification disc seen in Brian's case. The soldier's name was George Washburn, from Company I of the 20th New York Cavalry under Major General George B. McClellan. Brian's research shows that this soldier entered and departed the Civil War as a private. Such identification tags are a prized find and can be quite valuable.

finds have been seeded. Some of the larger relic hunts are invitation-only hunts in which forum members submit applications in hopes of being selected. Two of the most well-known relic hunts are commonly referred to as the GNRS and DIV events.

The annual relic hunting competition known as the Grand National Relic Shootout (GNRS) was founded by Larry Cissna in 1998 for teams of 16 hunters to compete metal detector brand against metal detector brand. Most recently, the hunt has consisted of detectorists representing seven manufacturer's teams: Bounty Hunter, Fisher, Garrett, Minelab, Nautilus, Tesoro and Whites. In 2013, the latest GNRS also featured an XP team. It should be noted that these team members operate detectors that are production models available to the general public.

The hunt field's boundaries are explained and each team has alternate hunters in case one or more members needs a break. Warnings and penalties are assessed for teams and individuals who do not keep their team areas clean or for those who are caught not filling in their holes properly.

During the 2010 GNRS in the South Carolina Lowcountry, Mike Wheless dug a cache of 25 silver coins. Several pre-war home sites were found in addition to the numerous colonial and Civil War relics that were dug. Wheless' find won him find-of-the-hunt honors and a free trip back the following year.

Many of the prior hunts were held in Virginia or Connecticut, before organizer Larry Cissna moved the GNRS to South Carolina in 2009. Teams are given maps of the area and then hunt until a designated daily turn-in time to present their finds. One point is issued for every relic determined by a panel of judges to date back to the Civil War or earlier. The highest points earner for each team wins a free trip to the following year's hunt and an overall team is declared champions based on total points. The teams range over a wide space of land. In 2009, the GNRS hunters had 2,000 acres at their disposal.

Finds include Civil War buttons, breast plates, colonial flat buttons, coins, cannon balls, scabbard tips and the like. The top find

The GNRS is an annual competition hunt. *(Above, left)* Artillery pieces and relic cases on display at the end of a day's hunt at GNRS. *(Above, right)* A cache of 35 silver coins dug by Mike Wheless at the 2010 GNRS on the first day. *(Below)* GNRS hunters gather around for the official morning start at a recent hunt. *Photos courtesy of Larry Cissna and www.treasure depot.com.*

in 2009 was also a coin cache, one dug by Jack Akins that included more than 100 coins, two of which were gold.

In addition to the GNRS, Cissna has organized dozens of other special hunts on Civil War sites. The North/South Hunts, the Git-R-Dun Hunts and Mardi Gras Hunts have been held since 2002 in various states. Each hunt includes groups of relic hunters based upon the available acreage open for the hunt. In these individual events, judges award prizes for the best finds versus tallying the points for team competition. The top winners have generally been awarded a special ring created specifically for the hunt.

Another very popular organized relic hunt conducted on the East Coast is the DIV (Diggin' In Virginia). DIV is a fully licensed and insured Limited Liability Corporation in the state of Virginia operated by event organizers John and Rose Kendrick. Their invitational hunts are conducted in the early spring (usually around mid-March) and again in late October or early November in the fall. Announcements for upcoming hunts are made on the *mytreasurespot.com* website approximately three to six months in advance of the hunt week. Participants are invited to register online. Since these are strictly invitational hunts, the number of hunters selected is based upon the size of the property to be hunted and the organizers' "best guess as to the amount of relics still left." An alternate list is created for those who might be asked to fill a slot left open by someone who could not make the trip.

The current cost to enter a DIV hunt is $250, which includes three full days of relic hunting, a meal each day and water and sodas. Security and transportation for the hunt sites are handled by DIV committee members and a pre-hunt meeting is held on the night before the first day of hunting.

For DIV XV, held in late October 2010, a total of 350 hunters were invited to search on private property in Virginia. In addition to the organizers, committee members and helpers, more than 100 other searchers remained on a waiting list, eager to fill the spots of any last-minute dropouts.

Joining this hunt for me was as exciting as some of the large European rallies I've been on. The hunters know that they will be working known productive areas and other historic sites that may not have been previously worked. The DIV hunts are held near Culpeper, Virginia, on land where the Civil War was fought. The area is rich in American history. The town was originally founded in 1748 as Fairfax, although its name was changed in 1869 to Culpeper. A pro-Independence militia company known as the Culpeper Minutemen had formed in the town during the Ameri-

DIV hunters take to the field at daybreak for DIV XXII in November 2012. Several of the finds from that hunt are seen below. *Clockwise from left are:* A gilt finished soldier's ID tag found by Don Lenhart; a breastplate and two box plates dug by father and son team Ed Wiggart Sr. and Jr.; and a Civil War sword dug by Don Dodson of Georgia.

can Revolution and the area continued to be an historic hot spot during the Civil War. Culpeper was a crossroads for both the Union and Confederate armies, as evidenced by three major battles which were fought in this area: the Battle of Brandy's Station, the Battle of Kelly's Ford and the Battle of Cedar Mountain.

Eager detectorists descend upon Culpeper and fill the local hotels. Anticipation is in the air as old friends reunite and swap stories of their recent relic hunting successes. During the pre-hunt meeting the night before the first day of hunting, Rose and John Kendrick run through the rules of the field, pass out maps of the hunt area and offer advice for the safety and conduct of their searchers.

There was a 100-acre new parcel of land opened to the DIV XV hunters, including section of a key ridge known as Cole's Hill. This hill and the adjacent Hansborough's Ridge contained trenches and camp sites dating from the 1863 actions around Culpeper. These hillsides are obviously popular areas for the deep diggers. They have produced many bottles, buttons, belt plates, bullets and other relics in past DIV hunts.

The Kendricks take their organized hunts seriously and expect their participants to make a good impression on the landowners and the local townspeople during their visits. They also go to great lengths to document all relics that are recovered. Artifacts are photographed and all diggers are required to submit complete lists of everything that is recovered, all in the desire to document the history of the battles waged around Culpeper nearly 150 years ago.

For those who are able to travel to such organized relic hunts, I strongly encourage them to put in their application for at least one of these events. The areas that are secured to hunt offer each person the potential to make significant finds. At the very least, I believe you will come away from such an event with many new acquaintances in the relic hunting world and perhaps some new skills learned from the seasoned veterans.

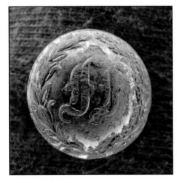

*(Left)* Military buttons are prized finds at such organized relic hunts. Ian Conway found this cuff-sized "FF" Fitchburg Fusileer button on Cole's Hill during DIV XV. He has traced it back to the 15th Mass. Co. B. According to the Tice button identifcation book, it is a pre-Civil War button that was manufactured up to 1855.

## DIV XV (2010): Culpeper, Virginia

(Above, left) Searchers gather at the command post tent for the first day's start.
(Above, right) DIV hunters gather for the pre-hunt meeting held by Rose and John Kendrick.

*(Above)* This rare Confederate brass rosette was dug by Joe Dinisio of Maryland during the first day of the hunt.

*(Above)* This industrious dig team is working a trash pit.
*(Below)* Reggie inspects a freshly dug eagle button he has just rinsed.

Ready to go at daybreak are (left to right): Reggie Simmons, Brad Saunders, Doug King and Tom McDowell.

Diggin' deep has it rewards, as evidenced by this nice whiskey bottle that was recovered.

Beneath this mineralized red iron Virginia soil lay many fine relics waiting to be unearthed.

*(Left)* More finds by Reggie Simmons, including a button back, two general service Eagle buttons and an Infantry cuff button.

*(Left)* Northern Virginia was the scene of many Civil War battles. There are a number of battlefield parks open to tourists within a short distance of the DIV dig sites.

*(Left)* An eagle breastplate dug from a firepit on the second day.

*(Below)* Cartridges, lead bullets and buttons found by Reggie Simmons on his third day of hunting.

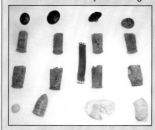

*(Left)* A U.S. box plate and knapsack hook dug by *Infinium* user Terry Smith on the first day.

*(Below)* Minié balls, camp lead, a Spencer cartridge and buckshot found by author on Day 2.

*(Below)* There is frost in the field at daybreak as the hunters start off on a cold morning.

*(Above)* Hut diggers began pulling more Civil War buttons, bottles, and plates on day two.
*(Right)* These serious searchers even used a power auger to dig test holes.
*(Below)* DIV finds made by Ted Smith of Virginia.

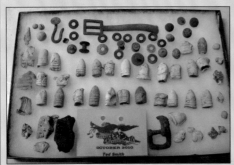

*(Below)* DIV XV finds of Steve Evans of Pennsylvania include colonial era buttons, coins and buckles.

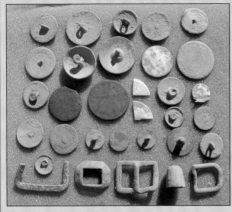

*(Clockwise from above)* Minié balls, 1738 King George III coin and bits of cut Spanish silver dug by Steve Evans.

## 2011 North/South Hunt: Yemassee, South Carolina

*(Left)* The searchers gather at the central meeting site to hear hunt organizer Larry Cissna give his pre-hunt briefing.

*(Below)* Near the SC plantation hunt site, we visited old Sheldon Church, which dates to the 1750s and was twice burned.

A few of the North/South button finds include: a Jefferson College button found by Wilson Smith *(left)*; a New York button *(center)* dug by Rick Hutson; and a Phoenix button *(upper right)* dug by Mitch King.

*(Right)* Two buttons, a minié ball and a shoe buckle found by a hunter named Dan at an old house site on the second day of the hunt.

*(Left)* Some of the scenery on this Yemassee plantation almost still feels like the 1860s.

*(Above)* Jason Reep from Tennessee dug this fired 12-pound cannonball in the forest during his first day at the 2011 North/South Hunt. He made the find at a 16" depth while hunting with his *AT Pro* detector.

*(Above)* Mitch King works an area of the plantation where skirmishing took place during the Battle of Pocotaligo. Mitch's first day finds included this Confederate .69-caliber "shotgun slug" projectile *(right)* and these cannister fragments and large piece of round shot *(left)*.

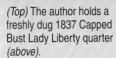

*(Top)* The author holds a freshly dug 1837 Capped Bust Lady Liberty quarter *(above)*.

*(Upper right)* Bill Kasselman from Houston works the forest during a light rain on the second day.

*(Right)* Bill's relic box after the third day includes three pieces to a silver chain, round balls and minie balls, and an 1867 kerosene lamp burner.

*(Left)* At the close of the hunt, Steve and Bill joined a local, Melvin Lane (far right), to take him up on an invitation to hunt private property that was rich in Civil War history.

*(Below)* This piece of pine recovered by Steve contains a minie ball that has been completely sealed over by growth. Steve dug another minie right beside the chunk of tree.

*(Below)* The author's four-day collection of better digs from the 2011 hunt include numerous round balls, buck and ball shot, a broken miniature cannon, a .69-caliber Gardner bullet, various early buttons, a percussion cap, and an 1891 V-nickel.

### European and UK Organized Hunts and Rallies

American organized hunts can often number several hundred detectorists. In England, some of the larger rallies I've attended have included 1,000 or more hunters. Most of the excitement overseas has to do with the chance of finding breathtaking Roman, Celtic or Anglo-Saxon artifacts that have been hidden for literally thousands of years (see Chapter 9).

Rallies and club hunts of various sizes are actually held in quite a few countries. The ones that I've attended outside the UK have varied in size from a few dozen participants to a couple hundred, depending upon the region and how well it was advertised. Such hunts are often held on large farms or orchards that provide ample space for large numbers of diggers.

These hunts are a good way to make new friends from other countries. This might lead to future travel to dig with your new friends in new areas. It is not uncommon to see searchers from half a dozen countries show up at an open rally. Some plan their vaca-

John Howland checks out a button that Nigel Ingram has just dug near Corfe Castle in England. Jim Leonard was among several Americans who attended a rally there in 2010.

tion time around a major organized hunt. They enjoy the food, the fellowship, and the competition, and then enjoy sightseeing in a new country.

It is well to exercise caution when deciding upon a reputable hunt. I asked Jim Leonard from Georgia—publisher of online magazine *Relic Hunter*—for his tips on attending such events. He has gone on a number of UK hunts in the past 15 years, and he returns any chance he can.

Jim books his airfare early to get the best deal and prefers direct flights to avoid the loss of baggage during connecting flights overseas (a fact I can relate to!). "Bring a GPS and have it pre-programmed to your destination," he adds. "Most inns and B&Bs have websites where you can book early for your room or you can just camp out, if you're inclined to do so." Many local inns near a major rally will give special lodging rates.

"Many Americans come to England to metal detect because of the age and possible values of items they may find. There are several commercial ventures making lots of money off of interested, 'addicted' relic hunters," Jim warns. "Check them out before you sign up and pay their fees. Keep in mind, it's easy to purchase old Roman coins on Ebay and other sites and plant them in a 'reserved' field to be discovered by hunters. This insures that the detectorist always comes home with a 'prize' discovery after they've paid thousands of dollars for the thrill of the hunt.

*(Left)* Jim's Roman coin finds from a UK organized hunt in 2010. These were found near the Corfe Castle, an area rich with Roman, Celtic and English artifacts in the southwestern part of England.

"Moreover, if they've found a gold coin, that coin may have been purchased for $300 to $400 dollars, yet the hunter has paid approximately $2,000 for the outing—hope you see the profit margin and the possible deception. I'm not saying that all of these ventures are rip-offs; just be careful in choosing the right adventure. If the 'red flags' are present in what they've found, you'd do better to buy a bag of coins off of Ebay!

"Check out your hunting tour. Do your research first. Ask for references. Talk to those who have gone before, see if they'd go again, and ask what they found. The best way to have a fun trip is to make a good friend across the pond and go hunting with them."

*(Above)* These diggers are waiting for the starter's gun at an organized hunt in Belgium.

*(Right)* This group is enjoying the food and drink during lunch break. They were taking part in an international rally held in an olive tree grove in Toledo, Spain.

These are European relics and coins found by the author during a visit in 2012.

# CHAPTER 21

# CLEANING YOUR FINDS

Once you have recovered significant relics, you will be faced with the decision of *how* or even *if* you want to clean away any corrosion or oxidation. *Corrosion* is the primary means by which metals deteriorate as they react to their environment.

Different metals react differently to the effects of the soil or water in which they have been lying until you recover them. Gold is one of the precious metals that generally holds up well to the effects of oxidation. Pure gold coins may be retrieved with only minor discolouration or a thin film visible to the naked eye. Because pure gold is soft, coins were generally created with an alloy of other metals such as silver or copper, which results in further deterioration in the ground.

Pure silver does not oxidize because silver does not combine naturally with oxygen. Silver alloys, however, will corrode and oxidize. Pure copper was often used in coins of the ancient days, but it became a more common alloy in coins of recent eras. Brass is a mixture of copper with 10 to 50 percent zinc mixed into its formula. Three of the most common forms of degradation of copper and its alloys that occur are *tarnish* (usually dull, gray or black in color), *copper carbonate* (bluish-green weathering of metal) and *verdigris* (a green patina that forms on copper, brass or bronze long exposed to air or salt water).

Copper and copper alloys such as bronze and brass often emerge from the ground with various colored *patina*, the result of

511

years or centuries of external chemical influences on the surface of the coin or artifact. The thickness of this patina and its color vary based upon the chemical influences. Dirt, moisture, carbon dioxide, salt content and organic acids all influence the appearance of an old coin. Some coins emerge from the ground with a green patina while others can take on a red or brown layer of corrosion.

Patina is a characteristic of relics and old coins that is desired by most collectors. If the item has been in the ground long enough for *pitting*—the formation of small divits in the patina—to occur, this can reduce the value of the item.

The natural tendency is to begin rubbing the dirt from an old coin immediately to learn its mint date. Be advised, however, that the most valuable coins or buttons can be damaged by even the simple process of rubbing off the soil with your fingers. The value of your coins can best be preserved by leaving the dirt on the coin until you are able to work with them later. It is better to place the dirty coin into a protective pouch or cotton-filled container in your treasure pouch while you are still hunting. Some relic hunters are happy to maintain some of their less valuable finds just the way they appeared when first unearthed.

Many relics will take some effort to identify. There are many reference books that can be used to identify artifacts. Internet forums are another good way to post a picture of your find that others may be very familiar with. Once you know what you are working with you can make better decisions on how or if you should clean it.

———

### How Should I Clean My Relics and Coins?

Most of your finds will be covered to some degree with a layer of dirt which can be rinsed off with water. If you decide to clean your coin or relic more thoroughly, **you must first decide what type of metal it is.** The safest process, of course, is to trust your potentially valuable finds to an expert on cleaning such items.

# Cleaning Your Finds

If you choose to clean your own finds, be aware that it is easy to ruin them. Yet, you will hear and read about numerous home solutions that people use to clean recovered items. Among the many solutions are: malt vinegar applied with a soft brush; white vinegar or lemon juice; soaking coins in Coca-Cola; and even using red-hot sauce to remove dirt from exterior surfaces. Some may prove successful; others could completely ruin your precious find. *If you have recovered coins that may be of great value, visit a reputable coin dealer or other expert before attempting to clean them yourself.*

Another product used by relic hunters is Top Job, a liquid detergent originally made by Proctor & Gamble that works quickly on buttons, buckles and other items. Try soaking such items in a Top Job solution for a few minutes and then rinsing thoroughly. (Note: This cleaning agent is not distributed in mass any longer but can be found through some independent distributors.)

Never attempt to remove dirt from a coin's surface with any sharp object that can permanently scratch its surface, such as a knife or a needle. One of the first steps to safely cleaning your recovered coins and artifacts is to soak them in a solution of warm water to help loosen the surface grime. Coins should never lie on top of each other while soaking.

The basic rule of thumb for bronze items with a green patina is to simply not try to clean them. Oxidized silver items can be cleaned with a baking soda or citrus acid solution or through electrolysis. Modern scouring machines should not be used as they will remove patina from objects. The fine detail of older items can quickly be destroyed forever by these more automated processes.

Some coin hunters use a very soft-bristled brush with a toothpaste substance to gently brush away some of the tarnish on old silver coins. Be advised that as you uncover more of the coin's nice surface features, you are also scrubbing away the natural patina that helps give the coin its value!

In extreme cases, scientists or restoration experts employ aggressive cleaning methods to remove corrosion and oxidation. *The use of drain cleaner is not recommended* because of the poison-

513

ous nature of the fumes and the fact that this treatment may ruin already damaged coins. Scientists sometimes use this method, however, to strip brass and copper-nickel artifacts with undamaged surfaces.

Others clean coins and silver jewelry recovered from the ocean in an **electric tumbler** used to polish rocks. This method is not suitable for antique items and must be experimented with before you take a chance on damaging an old coin. Another method used by some hobbyists and scientists is **electrolysis**, which uses a vinegar/water solution and electricity to strip items via a chemical reaction.

Experts trained in archaeological restoration have access to more elaborate mechanical and chemical methods and even use x-ray machines. Some restorers use a scalpel under a microscope to peel away loose outer layers of patina to improve the appearance of a badly corroded coin or other artifact. **Be advised that in general you should not attempt to remove a relic's patina.**

———

### Metal Identification and Cleaning

To properly clean and preserve your finds, you must correctly identify the type of metal. Your field experience will increase with your finds and you will be able to better judge an item's composition by the types of patina or rust covering that has formed on it. By carrying a small pocket magnet in your treasure pouch, you can quickly verify if an item contains iron, nickel or steel (an iron alloy). Other pure metal objects (gold, silver, tin, lead, copper, bronze, brass, etc.) are non-magnetic.

You can begin cleaning your artifacts before you even leave the field. Some hunters bring sealed plasticware containers partially filled with water and a mild soapy solution. The relics are added to the containers to soak during the return trip to begin loosening the soil and grime while driving home. A soft brush can then be used on buckles, buttons, minié balls, etc. to gently loosen the remaining soil which has not soaked off. The following list is intended to serve for general reference as you learn to identify treasure items for cleaning. In addition, notes on how to clean or whether to clean an item at all are given. Some of the cleaning methods listed under these metals will be more fully described.

• **Bronze**—This metal alloy of copper and up to 10% tin is a hard and heavy substance. Some Bronze Age variations even contained small percentages of lead. Bronze items, which can date back to 2,000 BC, are not pliable and can break under pressure.

Corrosion on bronze artifacts and coins can be in a green, brown or bluish patina. A soft patina layer is a form of corrosion that should not be disturbed. Experts advise not to clean the patina from antique bronze because it may ruin its value.

• **Silver**—Pure silver coins tarnish easily to a yellowish-brown, gray or black color. Old silver pieces may include a maker's mark, town mark or a number for its percentage of silver (such as 800 for 800 parts silver to a thousand). Many silver items were alloyed and can thus tarnish differently. Some colonial silver coins with a high copper alloy will turn greenish or brown like bronze. High quality silver remains smooth even if it turns black.

You may also find fairly clean high quality silver in the field because ammonia in a farmer's fertilizer has acted as a cleaning agent on the silver item. The best methods for cleaning silver will depend upon the amount of oxidation present and the quality of the silver alloy. When in doubt, start with the least invasive method *(see next section)* and determine results from there.

• **Gold**—This precious metal had been used for jewelry since the Bronze Age and relics made with it remain virtually unchanged in the ground. Gold is not affected by acidity, is heavy and is relatively soft. Gold is therefore generally mixed with other metals to give it strength. Items made of gold alloy may show spots of green (copper mix) or purple (silver mix). Jewelry from the past several hundred years may contain a hallmark to indicate the object's gold percentage. For example, 8-carat gold is shown with the numerals 333, 14-carat as 585 and 18-carat as 750.

- **Brass**—Brass, an alloy of copper and zinc, became more prevalent than bronze during the Middle Ages because brass was easier to work with. Copper is a red-brown metal but brass and bronze are yellow metals that can appear to be gold when dug from the ground. Brass turns dark brown after being in the ground for a long period of time, and it can also take on a green color when its surface is corroded. Brass items clean up easier than silver. Start with soap and a soft brush to scrape away the corrosion layer and use lemon juice to rub away any marks. Then, rinse the object and lightly polish it with a soft cloth.

- **Copper**—In its pure form, copper has a red shine. This metal can easily be confused with brass, but copper is softer and thus polishes well. Copper coins often remain in better condition in the soil than coins made of brass or bronze. The ground will eventually turn copper coins dark brown, and corrosion can turn them black or green in color. Axes, spears and other tools made using copper have been found that date back thousands of years.

Cleaning copper is similar to cleaning brass. Start with a simple soapy water and soft brush combination.

- **Nickel**—Many modern coins are made of a nickel-copper alloy that can cause them to oxidize to a brownish color. Any pure nickel artifact, however, will not rust or take on a patina. Nickel is more brittle than silver and is magnetic if it has not been alloyed. This metal has been used since the 18th century for buttons and buckles, which generally hold up well. Very acidic soil can cause corrosion, however, particularly when the item is a nickel alloy.

Wash nickel items with soap and a stiff brush or use the ammonia cleaning method covered in the next section.

- **Lead**—Lead has been used for many centuries to create bullets, musket balls and weights because of its low melting point. After it has been in the ground for many years, lead begins to turn black and corrode with a white or brown patina as it reacts with the ground acids. You should not try to remove this coating of patina when cleaning lead artifacts. Simply wash such items with soap and water and use a soft bristle brush to remove soil.

• **Tin**—This soft metal has been used since 2000 BC as an alloy when making bronze. It was used by the Romans and Greeks for spoons and other utensils. By the 14th century, tin was heavily alloyed with lead, which produces a harder, darker-colored artifact. Tin pest or tin disease corrosion creates rough, black porous marks on the surface of items high in tin content.

Medieval tin is very soft and should be cleaned only by using warm water, soap and a soft brush to avoid scratching it. Experts can remove some of the tin pest with the electrolysis method.

• **Aluminum**—This lightweight metal was used by countries such as France, Germany and Greece prior to World War II for some of their lesser denomination coins. Aluminum coins and artifacts will be fairly recent in age (compared with other finds). Corrosion causes aluminum to take on a yellow or whitish color as it loses its sheen. Cleaning should be attempted only with soap, water and a soft brush that will not mar the metal. You can preserve the item with a coating of Vaseline.

• **Wrought iron**—Such items are generally preserved well only if they have been dug from mud or dry clay, because soil acids, moisture and oxygen cause such items to quickly rust. Magnetic wrought iron, used since around 700 BC, will form a thick reddish or brownish crust after being in the soil for a few years.

You can remove some of the exterior crust from a wrought iron artifact by tapping it with something hard. Some detectorists use Coca-Cola (which includes phosphoric acid) as a soaking solution to remove rust. Others use a 5:1 water and citric acid bath and soak artifacts up to 20 days. Once the worst of the rust has been removed, carefully remove and dry the artifact while avoiding contact with your bare hands, which would cause the item to rust further. You can conserve the item by treating it with gun oil.

• **Cast iron**—This tough yet brittle metal was molded into shapes beginning in the 19th century. It corrodes with light to dark brown layers of rust which are uneven. Some loose outer layers can be removed by tapping the item with something hard. Some of this rust can also be removed with a strong steel brush. Citric acid or phosphoric acid can also be used to remove it. Add a layer of Vaseline to cast iron coins after cleaning them. Wire brushes such as paint scrapers which are used on any artifact other than iron can permanently mar the item's surface. Brass bristled brushes are available which are used to scrub coins and relics more gently.

Iron artifacts can be successfully cleaned through one of two *common electrolysis methods*. The first is an electrical method whereby a weak current is run through the item being cleaned. This negatively charges the surface and sends a stream of electrons to the other (positive) terminal. Dirt and rust are removed from the artifact during this process. To conduct such an electrolysis cleaning, you will need a plastic (non-conductive) container, a water based solution and a controlled power source, such as a battery charger.

Working with electricity of any sort requires a high degree of caution but those who have interest in this method can find plenty of "how-to" articles on the subject. One that I would recommend is "Saving the Iron Age: Preserving Iron Through Simple Electrolysis" by G. M. "Doc" Watson. This was published in the January-February 2009 issue of *American Digger* magazine.

In this article, Doc Watson also details the other common electrolysis method for cleaning iron artifacts which involves a chemical reaction in place of an electrical power source. In this method, a caustic chemical such as lye is used in conjunction with a piece of zinc to cause a chemical reaction between the solution and the two disparate metals which remove rust and dissolves the zinc.

***Disclaimer:*** This process is being described as a point of reference to how electrolysis is used by some to clean relics. The author and the publisher of this book do not advocate attempting such a process and will not be held liable for those who attempt such a procedure. Consult a professional in such restoration and cleaning if you wish to attempt such a procedure. Extreme caution is necessary for such a process as electrolysis creates gases that can be harmful if inhaled. Water and electricity poses obvious dangers and such procedures should only be conducted outdoors in well ventilated areas. The gases produced by such electrolysis can be flammable so those attempting such a procedure should never have a lit cigarette or any flame near the process.

A good power source for an electrolysis setup is a motorcycle battery charger with a 6 volt/12 volt selector switch to vary the amount of power being sent against the item based on its encrustation. Fill a plastic (non-conductive) tub half full with a water solution that includes salt and lemon juice. Connect the iron object to the negative lead from the power source and drop it into the water solution. Connect a stainless steel item such as a spoon to the positive lead and drop it into the water. Make certain that the positive and negative leads never come in contact with each other.

Flip on the power to the battery charger and then observe the bubbling effect that takes place as the solution and electricity work on the corroded item. Start by trying this for about 5 minutes and see what results you see. Turn off the power, remove the item being cleaned, rinse it off and inspect. If necessary, repeat the process until positive effects are observed. Be aware that some iron relics can be so badly corroded that your cleaning process may simply destroy what is left if the corrosion goes throughout the item.

I have experimented with several electrolysis methods to see how well they would clean up some of my artifacts. I purchased an inexpensive Schumacher brand motorcycle battery charge from Wal-Mart (about $20) that works for 6v/12v charging. I used an inexpensive 5-gallon plastic tub and filled it half full (2.5 gallons) with tap water. I stirred in 1/4 cup of Cascade dish washing detergent, making sure to thoroughly stir it into the water.

I then connected the negative lead's clamp directly to the iron artifact to be cleaned. I then connected the positive lead to the side of the plastic tub with a plastic clip and inserted a stainless steel bolt into the teeth of the positive lead. I positioned the positive lead so that the attached bolt was inserted about two inches into the solution. Only after all was set did I plug in the charger to let the power begin.

The electric current created a slow, bubbling effect that looks similar to an Alka-Seltzer dissolving in water. The more bubbling

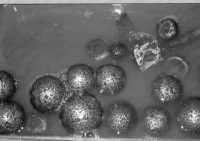

*(Above)* Jimmi K. of Marietta, Georgia, shares some before and after pictures on how he cleans artillery relics. Jimmi found this grape shot with his *GTI 2500* during several weeks of working a site in Georgia.

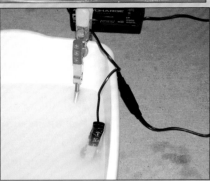

*(Above left and right)* The author experiments with cleaning several iron Civil War relics with a Schumacher brand motorcycle battery charger in a plastic tub. The electric current creates a bubbling reaction as the corrosion is removed.

you see, the more that the electrolysis is working on the artifact's corrosion. After about 15 minutes, the bottom of the pan began showing small flakes of rust coming off the artifact. I have also experimented with changing the solution from the Cascade detergent to 1/3 cup of baking soda, which produced more bubbling reaction.

After you have completely cleaned your item, dry it thoroughly by placing it near a heat source that will help draw any moisture from the item, such as placing it in an oven on a very low heat setting. Many relic hunters recommend a spray-on lacquer to keep moisture from re-entering the artifact and further destroying it. Others recommend a simple application of a Vaseline coating to give the item a fresh look and to protect it.

Bill Kassellman of Houston recommends Evaporust to take the rust off recovered iron or steel relics such as guns that have become corroded from immersion in saltwater. This non-caustic cleaner can be obtained from retailers such as Harbor Freight or automotive parts stores. Electrolysis can help restore an artifact to its original form even though the rust still remains. Pour the Evaporust into a plastic tub and place the iron or steel artifacts in the solution for an overnight soaking.

"Once I am happy with the results, I simply remove the items from the tub," said Bill. "The Evaporust only works on the rust and will not continue to deteriorate the rest of the artifact. I return the Evaporust to the bottle and continue to reuse it until it simply loses its effect." The more discolored the water in the tub appears the next morning, the more it has improved the appearance of the corroded relic.

---

### Common Cleaning Methods

The method you use to clean finds varies by metal type. Several methods will be explained that have been used by detectorists to clean up their finds. Refer to the preceding section to learn if any of these methods are suitable for the metal composition of your treasure item. *After completing any of these methods,* your final step should be to neutralize most items by washing them under running water and drying them well.

• **Pure water or soap and water solution**—Metals can be soaked in pure water overnight or for a full 24-hour period to begin loosening deposits. The water is doing its job if it is dirty after several hours of soaking. Use a soft brush to gently loosen other deposits. For the most delicate artifacts, a cotton swab can be rolled carefully over the item to absorb water and dirt.

Add pure soap flakes or soft soap (with no additives) to a tub of warm water. Soak any non-ferrous metal find in this for up to 24 hours and gently brush off excess sediment with a soft brush or cotton swab. Be sure to rinse off all traces of the soapy solution before final drying.

• **Citric Acid Mixture**—Mix citric acid crystals and distilled water in a 1:4 ratio in a container. Pure lemon juice is used by some hobbyists but beware of other additives in the lemon juice that could be harmful. This method is best for silver coins and artifacts with only light tarnishing. Soak items in this solution for several hours or overnight and then use a soft brush or cloth to gently remove the loosened crust. Because citric acid can strip objects down to their bare metal over time, monitor this process closely. Dilute the solution with more water if cleaning seems to be happening too quickly. A citric solution can be used with most metals to help loosen corrosion. For early buttons, try a mild solution of diluted lemon juice with a Q-tip to gently clean the button.

• **Household Ammonia Mixture**—Use a small container to mix a solution of 1:3 ammonia to water for silver coins. Cover the solution and do not inhale the fumes as you let coins soak for about 20 minutes. Use a soft brush to gently remove tarnish and dirt. Repeat this process if necessary. A solution of 50% ammonia and 50% warm water can be used to give Civil War minié balls a nice white appearance. Gently removed caked-on dirt from the bullets with a soft toothbrush and warm water.

Then, allow the minié balls to soak for about ten minutes in the warm water/ammonia solution. Gently brush away any remaining grime, dry thoroughly and then place them in a display box.

• **Sulfuric Acid Mixture**—Pour water into a container first and then add sulfuric acid at a ratio of 1:20. Be sure to observe the warnings pointed out by labels on the sulfuric acid; avoid breathing it or getting it on your skin or clothing. If you choose this

## Discovering What Was Hidden Inside a Coral Rock

Restoration of recovered relics is a labor of love, as evidenced by these photos shared by Florida relic hunter Bob Spratley. While searching a Florida beach in November 2010 with his *Infinium LS* metal detector, Bob "got a solid strike. I knew it was silver immediately."

"The item came from about 12 inches deep and was covered with coquina and coral," he said. He took the "mystery rock" home and gave it *(right, top)* "a swift hit with a hammer to expose a Spanish 8-reale cob.

"I immediately put it in one of my electrolysis tanks *(right, center)* with a solution of baking soda in water with an increased voltages of 5 volts to hurry the cleaning process."

Shown below are before and after pictures of this Spanish 1689 Potosi mint cob.

aggressive method, you should soak coins in this solution for no more than ten minutes.

Make sure the coins you soak in this mix do not contain any significant percentage of copper, because the acid will damage copper. This treatment is mainly for removing heavy oxidation on silver artifacts and coins.

- **Silver cleaners**—Various commercial silver cleaning compounds are sold by coin dealers and other retailers. Coins that have become badly discolored can be cleaned with one of these solutions and cotton balls. Use this solution conservatively, swabbing or soaking the item. Some hobbyists swab down gold items with such a solution as well, but be warned that the chemical can strip some items (particularly copper alloys) down to bare metal if they are not used with care.

-------

### Final "Polishing Up" Methods

Techniques for cleaning coins and relics vary widely, and great caution should be taken concerning the method you choose to employ. Some detectorists use common office supplies such as masking tape to remove tarnish from old coins. A high-tach masking tape can be used to remove some of the dirt and tiny debris from coin surfaces by carefully adhering and slowly peeling off clean pieces of tape from the coin. While this process will remove much of the dirt, be advised that it can also remove unstable patina.

Underwater treasure recovery expert Bob Marx offered another trick he uses to clean old Spanish reales. In his final cleaning, he sometimes uses a simple rubber eraser to "erase away" the tarnish on big silver coins. Be aware, however, that the use of an eraser on newer coins can cause shadowing or scratches on the coin's face.

Iron relics become flaky and powdery to the touch as the moisture in the iron begins to evaporate. To preserve the item after it has been cleaned, many collectors add a polyethylene sealant which improves the artifact's coloration and offers a slightly shiny

## An Amazing "Before and After" Restoration Project

Bob Spratley recovered this bronze rail cannon *(left)* several years ago. It had been buried for several hundred years on a Florida beach. Two years of restoration work gave the cannon this amazing finish *(right)*.

So, just how did Bob manage to achieve these results? He related, "I cleaned down to the bronze by gently chipping away at the encrustation on the inside of the barrel. I used a vibrating engraving tool that made simple work on the shells, etc. This was to get a good connection for the electrolysis without causing any further damage to the exterior of the cannon.

"Since I did not have it x-rayed I did not know what surface fractures it may have had so I took the safest place to start…inside the barrel. I then hooked up the electrodes and put it in one of my larger tanks. It took quite a while to get it done but was well worth it. It came out looking like a new cannon but that is not the way I desired it to be. I used a patina agent (#C1 - Triple Brown) for bronze that I obtained from Triple-S Chemical to get the cannon back to the original look of aged bronze patina. Now it looks like a museum piece.

"Finding a relic is just part of the job. Correctly preserving it is most important so we have something to pass down to others."

appearance. The polyethylene can be applied with a small paint brush to prevent the rusty flaking of your relic in future years. Varnish is not recommended for relics because it will crack, peel or begin yellowing over time.

---

### Photographing and Displaying your Finds

In some countries, the government may keep your rare finds and offer monetary compensation. Photographing your discoveries before reporting them is one way you can preserve the memory of a special item.

Digital single lens reflex (SLR) cameras with high resolution have become more affordable in the past few years. With a little experience behind the lens, such cameras enable you to take high quality photos with crisp detail. Basic non-SLR digital cameras can be more challenging for the operator to achieve good focus on a small object such as a coin.

When using a digital SLR or a point-and-shoot digital camera, always review the detail of your photo on the camera's LCD screen. If possible, zoom in on the photo to look closely at the image's sharpness. If the coin details appear shaky or fuzzy, delete the image and try again. Many digital cameras have a "macro" setting (often the symbol of a flower) that will help you capture the fine detail on such coins. Consult your camera's owner's manual about shooting extreme close-up photos. More serious photographers mount their camera on a tripod to keep it steady. Even the slightest shake as you push the button will throw the picture out of focus. Digital cameras can also capture the date when your photos are taken. This can be beneficial later if you maintain a journal or logbook of your finds.

Excessive handling of ancient coins can damage the surface appearance due to moisture and acids in your fingertips. Some detectorists protect valuable silver coins after cleaning by applying a thin coating of plastic lacquer for protection from handling. Coins can be stored in albums with plastic sheets. Be careful, however, that sheets of heavy coins do not damage the patina on small coins on adjacent pages.

Iron relics are also easily damaged by handling. The natural moisture in a recovered iron artifact begins to evaporate once it is exposed to air and the rusty areas of the relic crumble to the touch as this drying process continues. Many collectors thus use a polyethylene sealant such as those used to protect finished wood surfaces. This can be applied with a small paint brush and may require more than one coat as the artifact soaks up the sealant. Please note that varnish is not a recommended alternative to polyethylene because varnish can crack, peel or yellow over time.

If you create your own display case, make certain to use acid-free materials and avoid allowing bare metal objects to come into contact with each other which can cause corrosion to spread.

## PHOTO QUALITY VARIANCE

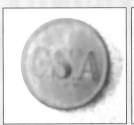  

Each of these three photos was taken of the same button. *(Left)* This photo taken with a point-and-shoot digital camera shows lack of focus. *(Center)* This image was taken with the same point-and-shoot camera under the same lighting using the camera's macro setting. *(Right)* This image was taken with a higher quality digital SLR camera using a macro lens.

Items that are corroded should always be isolated from others. Another option is to use high quality plastic artifact and coin tray display cases. These are available from many metal detector dealers, coin dealers and even from some arts and crafts retailers. Most of these come with protective cotton lining to help separate and offer contrast to the generally darker-colored relics you have collected. Add period illustrations or photos in with the relics as you desire to dress up your case. Many collectors add small notes into their case which detail the types of artifacts, the date and place found and other interesting facts. As you fill and collect more display trays you can further protect these trays from moisture by storing them in special cabinets built to house multiple trays or in airtight plastic storage tubs.

Riker cases can be purchased to present your items. Add notes to the back of the case or prepare info cards that can go inside the case. This makes your case more interesting, helps you remember about the item and can make an artifact more valuable if you do indeed sell it later. Collectors who know which battle area a rifle ball was retrieved from will pay more than if it is unknown.

There are books available with complete details on restoration and preservation of coins and artifacts. One that I recommend was given to me by longtime RAM Books distributor Joe Bogosian from St. Louis. Written by German numismatist Gerhard Welter, it is titled *Cleaning and Preservation of Coins and Medals*. This book goes far beyond the commonly recommended cleaning methods used by veteran relic hunters, offering precise scientific details on oxidation, corrosion, melting temperatures of metals and numerous cleaning methods that are used by professionals. As an added bonus, the tenth edition printing of this book includes the article "Paper Money Restoration and Preservation" by James J. Curto.

Your best discoveries are the result of countless hours in the field. The extra effort you put into properly preserving them will enable you and your friends to enjoy these items for a lifetime.

# CHAPTER 22

# RELIC HUNTING
# ETHICS AND THE LAW

The Federation of Metal Detector and Archaeological Clubs (FMDAC) was organized in 1984 to preserve, promote and protect the recreational use of metal detectors. FMDAC established a Code of Ethics for the proper use of detectors that is supported by most metal detector manufacturers. Many relic hunters print this code on small cards to hand to property owners as a showing of the respect they will show on someone else's property.

---

### U. S. Metal Detecting Laws

American relic hunters enjoy more freedom than those living in many international countries but that freedom is being challenged more and more. Any new legislation that is introduced quickly makes the rounds in the metal detecting community.

In 2010, the South Carolina Legislature addressed a new bill to further protect private property and state-owned land. Its goal was to penalize those who "wilfully, knowingly, or maliciously enter upon the posted lands of another or the state and investigate, disturb or excavate a prehistoric or historic site for the purpose of discovering, uncovering, moving, removing or attempting to remove an archaeological resource." In this case, "archaeological resource" is defined as "all artifacts, relics, burial objects, or material remains of past human life or activities that are at least 100 years old and possess either archaeological or commercial value, including pieces of pottery, basketry, bottles, weapons, weapon projectiles, tools, structures or portions of structures, rock paintings, rock carvings, intaglios, graves, or human skeletal remains."

Trespassing onto private property or state property is an offense punishable by fines and/or imprisonment. Second offenses in the case of the above South Carolina act can include prison time of up to three years and fines "in the discretion of the court." Third and subsequent offenses become a felony. Consult your local state laws on trespassing to understand what the penalties are.

*The best course of action is to never enter into state, federal or private property to metal detect without permission.* The earliest U.S. laws protecting archaeological items have been in place more than a century. The *Antiquities Act of 1906* was the first federal law passed in the U.S. to address the collection of artifacts on federal land. President Theodore Roosevelt was behind this law, which passed half a century before metal detector usage had even become a consideration to legislators. This act became law on June 8, 1906 (34 Stat. 225, 16 U.S.C. 431-433) and has been amended once.

The Antiquities Act states in part: "Any person who shall appropriate, excavate, injure, or destroy any historic or prehistoric ruin or monument, or any object of antiquity, situated on lands owned or controlled by the Government of the United States, without the permission of the Secretary of the Department of the Government having jurisdiction over the lands on which said antiquities are situated, shall, upon conviction, be fined in a sum of not more than $500 or be imprisoned for a period of not more than 90 days, or shall suffer both fine and imprisonment, in the discretion of the court."

The President of the United States was empowered to declare certain areas of land to be national monuments and to protect items of interest located on such lands. Permits for excavations and gathering of items from these lands may be issued with a view of "increasing the knowledge of such objects, and that the gatherings shall be made for permanent preservation in public museums."

Additional legislation in 1916 created within the Department of the Interior "the National Park Service, which shall be under the charge of a director who shall be appointed by the President, by and with the advice and consent of the Senate." The National Park Service was charged with maintaining national monuments, reservations and parks "to conserve the scenery and the natural and historic objects and the wild life therein and to provide for the enjoyment of the same in such manner and by such means as will leave them unimpaired for the enjoyment of future generations."

The National Park Service was given further powers to protect, preserve and research national monuments in the *Historic Sites Act of 1935*. Further laws include the *Archeological and Historic Preservation Act of 1960* (Public Law 86-523, 16 U.S.C. 469-469c-2), which has been amended six times. This act was originally known as the "Reservoir Salvage Act" but by amendments has also become known as the  Act became known as the "Moss-Bennett Act" or the "Archeological Recovery Act." It provides for the preservation of historic sites which might be lost or damaged due to the creation of roads, highways, dams and other improvements. Funds can be made available to collect important archaeological artifacts that might be otherwise lost in the course of progress.

More specific laws have been passed in the United States since the early 1970s. Among them are the *Archaeological Resources Protection Act (ARPA) of 1979*, which had been amended four times. ARPA provides for the protection of archaeological resources on public lands and Indian lands which are "an accessible and irreplaceable part of the Nation's heritage." Some of the relics to be protected by this Federal Historic Preservation Law include "pottery, basketry, bottles, weapons, weapon projectiles, tools, structures or portions of structures, pit houses, rock paintings, rock carvings, intaglios, graves, human skeletal materials, or any portion or piece of any of the foregoing items" which are more than 100 years of age.

The laws enacted by ARPA cover all 50 states, the District of Columbia, Puerto Rico, Guam, and the Virgin Islands. They pro-

vide for the proper use of permits to conduct work on such protected areas and set penalties for those who excavate, remove,
damage, sell, purchase, exchange, transport or receive any archaeological resource from public lands or Indian lands. Convictions
can result in fines up to $10,000 or imprisonment up to one year, or
both. If the value of such items exceed $20,000, the fines can reach
as much as $20,000 and imprisonment up to two years, or both, can
be levied against the violator. In the case of second or subsequent
violations upon conviction a person "shall be fined not more than
$100,000, or imprisoned not more than five years, or both."

The American Battlefield Protection Act was passed in 1996 "to
assist citizens, public and private institutions, and governments
at all levels in planning, interpreting, and protecting sites where
historic battles were fought on American soil during the armed
conflicts that shaped the growth and development of the United
States, in order that present and future generations may learn and
gain inspiration from the ground where Americans made their ultimate sacrifice." This act generally provides for partnership work
to identify, research, evaluate, interpret and protect historic battlefields and associated sites on a National, state and local level.

Laws regarding archaeological protection and the use of
metal detectors have been passed on the state level as well. The
FMDAC offers the following basic guidelines concerning state
parks: "FMDAC recommends that you check with the specific park
service you are going to visit in order to be certain of their park
regulations. Every state has limitations within parks and some
state parks are off limits. Some of the information encountered
and the replies from various states were a bit vague and open to
interpretation so to be safe check with a state park representative
before your visit."

FMDAC further states this basic rule: "If it is a historical park
in any sense of the word, then consider it off limits." This organization's web site offers information on a state level for those
who wish to seek permission to metal detect with a permit. Some
states do allow detecting with a proper permit from park authori-

ties or in some cases only along beach areas within a park. The states listed on FMDAC's site that *do not allow* any metal detecting within state parks are Georgia, Kentucky, Louisiana, Minnesota, Mississippi, New Mexico, North Carolina, North Dakota, Texas, Tennessee, Utah and Wisconsin. Idaho and Montana state that detecting is permissible, but that nothing can be removed from their parks. This information should always be verified with park authorities before you turn on a metal detector in a state-controlled area. The potential consequences are obviously not worth the risk.

---

### European Metal Detecting Laws

Treasure hunting in Europe and other countries is controlled tighter than it is in America. In many of these nations, metal detecting is strictly forbidden without proper permits to conduct specific archaeological recovery work. General metal detecting for non-archaeological items is permissible in some of these countries, but local regulations should always be checked before you travel to a country in hopes of relic hunting.

Cultural antiquities are tightly governed in many nations. In Portugal, for example, metal detecting is not allowed inland because of the significant number of archaeological sites. The country's beaches are generally the best place to search because they offer the least restrictions. Metal detecting is against the law in Romania without a special permit. Detecting is outlawed in Sweden with the exception of individuals who have been given special permission to do so for a specified time.

Other European governments have adapted a more progressive system regarding treasure hunting. In the United Kingdom, for example, the British Treasure Act of 1996 was passed to replace the medieval law of Treasure Trove which had existed in England and Wales. A visionary reporting plan known as the Portable Antiquities Scheme was created to record archaeological objects found by members of the public.

More than 13,500 historical objects were reported during the first year of the pilot scheme, and this led to extensions of the program to provide a comprehensive national plan for all of England and Wales. At present, there are 36 Finds Liaison Officers (FLOs) who cover each county of Wales and England, plus additional advisers to work with the detectorists. Any detectorist who finds a treasure item that falls within stated parameters must report their discovery to a district coroner within 14 days of making the discovery. The first offense penalty for failing to report a treasure find carries a sentence of up to three months in jail or a fine not to exceed £5,000 or both.

More specific information—where known—on metal detecting laws in Europe is presented in Chapter 15 of the RAM Books title *European Metal Detecting Guide*. Because such regulations are often amended, always check with the proper authorities in each particular country for any revisions.

In short, learn your local, state and federal laws concerning the use of metal detectors on both private and public lands before you hit the field. Failing to do so might result in the loss of your metal detecting equipment, stiff monetary penalties or even jail time. Relic hunting is a hobby we can all enjoy if a little common sense and legal knowledge is followed to maintain responsible recovery of artifacts.

---

### Codes of Ethics

Today's dedicated metal detector hobbyist must do more than simply fill in excavation holes and protect landscaping. Antiquities laws are tough in many countries and will become tougher if individuals and organizations do not follow a strict code of ethics. Several codes of conduct have been written by metal detector groups in Europe and in the United States over the years. More recently a voluntary "Code of Practice for Responsible Metal Detecting in England and Wales" has been adopted by a number of organizations. They include: the British Museum; the Council for British Archaeology; Country Landowners and Business Association; English Heritage; Federation of Independent Detectorists; Museums, Libraries and Archives Council, National Council for Metal Detecting; National Farmers Union; National Museum Wales; Royal Commission on the Historic and Ancient Monuments of Wales; Portable Antiquities Scheme; and the Society of Museum Archaeologists.

In a greatly condensed format, the Code of Practice for Responsible Metal Detecting in England and Wales basically reads:

1. Do not trespass; before you start detecting, obtain permission to search from the landowner/occupier, regardless of the status, or perceived status, of the land. Remember that all land has an owner. To avoid subsequent disputes it is always advisable to first get permission and agreement in writing regarding the ownership of any finds subsequently discovered.

2. Adhere to the laws concerning protected sites. Take extra care when detecting near protected sites: for example, their boundaries are not always clear.

3. Join a metal detecting club or association that encourages cooperation and responsive exchanges with other responsible heritage groups.

4. Familiarize yourself with and follow current conservation advice on the handling, care and storage of archaeological objects.

5. If detecting takes place on undisturbed pasture, be careful to ensure that no damage is done to the archaeological value of the land, including earthworks.

6. Minimize ground disturbance through the use of suitable tools and by reinstating excavated material as neatly as possible.

7. Record findspots as accurately as possible for all finds (i.e. using an Ordnance Survey map or hand-held GPS device) while in the field. Bag finds individually and record the National Grid Reference (NGR) on the bag. Findspot information should not be passed on to other parties without the agreement of the landowner/occupier.

8. Respect the Country Code (leave gates and property as you find them and do not damage crops, frighten animals or disturb ground nesting birds, and dispose properly of litter).

9. Report any finds to the relevant landowner/occupier; and (with the agreement of the landowner/occupier) to the Portable Antiquities Scheme, so the information can pass into the local Historic Environment Record.

10. Abide by the provisions of the Treasure Act and Treasure Act Code of Practice (www.finds.org.uk), wreck law (www.mcga.gov.uk) and export licensing (www.mla.gov.uk). If you need advice, your local Finds Liaison Officer will be able to help.

11. Seek expert help if you discover something large below the plowed soil, or a concentration of finds or unusual material, or wreck remains, and ensure that the landowner/occupier's permission is obtained to do so. Local Finds Liaison Officers may be able to help. Reporting the find does not change your rights of discovery, but may result in far more archaeological evidence being discovered.

12. Call the police, and notify the landowner/occupier, if you find any traces of human remains.

13. Call the police or HM Coastguard, and notify the landowner/occupier, if you find anything that may be a live explosive: do not use a metal-detector or mobile phone nearby as this might trigger an explosion. Do not attempt to move or interfere with any such explosives.

Metal detector organizations and local clubs across the world have adopted similar policies for proper conduct. Charles Garrett has for many years published a basic code of ethics in his treasure hunting books:

• I will respect private and public property, all historical and archaeological sites and will do no metal detecting on these lands without proper permission.

• I will keep informed on and obey all laws, regulations and rules governing federal, state and local public lands.

• I will aid law enforcement officials whenever possible.

- I will cause no willful damage to property of any kind, including fences, signs and buildings, and will always fill holes I dig.
- I will not destroy property, buildings or the remains of ghost towns and other deserted structures.
- I will not leave litter or uncovered items lying around. I will carry all trash and dug targets with me when I leave each search area.
- I will observe the Golden Rule, using good outdoor manners and conducting myself at all times in a manner that will add to the stature and public image of all people engaged in the field of metal detection."

Policing these codes is an important job of local metal detector and treasure hunting clubs organized throughout the world.

*RELIC QUEST*

# SELECTED BIBLIOGRAPHY

## ARTICLES, JOURNALS AND PAMPHLETS

Barker, Spencer. "Follow Those Dozers." *Western and Eastern Treasures*, February 1998 (Vol. 32, No. 2), 64–66.

Barker, Spencer. "Native Tongue." *Western and Eastern Treasures*, April 1996 (Vol. 30, No. 4), 23–24.

"Brits Really Dig Generous Finder's Fee." *The Dallas Morning News*, May 15, 2009, 16A.

Carr, Matt. "Colonial Cache." *The Treasure Depot Magazine*. November/December 2009 (Vol. 2, No. 6), 46–47.

Chemerka, William R. "Uncovered Artillery Piece at the Alamo." *The Alamo Journal*, December 2010.

Delgado, James P. "The Trouble with Treasure." *Naval History Magazine*, August 2010 (Vol. 24, No. 4), 18–25.

Eckhart, Jerry. "Texas' Treasure Hunting Museum." *Western & Eastern Treasures*, November 2009 (Vol. 43, No. 11), 50–53.

Eckhart, Jerry. "Tips For Hunting Freshwater Beaches." *Western & Eastern Treasures*, July 2010 (Vol. 44, No. 7), 42–44.

Fried, Stephen. "Who Were the First Americans?" *Parade*, June 13, 2010, 6–8.

Jack, Malcolm. "Top 10 Metal Detector Discoveries." *Heritage Key*, September 24, 2009.

Leonard, Jim. "Relic Hunter Returns to England." *Relic Hunter*, November–December 2010 (Vol. 1, No. 4), 28–36.

Rippey, Kelly. "How I Made The Find of a Lifetime Where 'Nothing Was Left.'" *American Digger Magazine*, November-December 2009 (Vol. 5, No. 6), 38–39.

Spencer, Keith. "Camp Union Plate and Bullet Hill.'" *Treasure Depot Magazine*, March-April 2010 (Vol. 3, No. 2), 11–17.

Spratley, Bob. "Medieval Armor in the Sunshine State." *American Digger Magazine*, July-August 2010 (Vol. 6, No. 4), 18–23.

——. "In Search of French Treasure in the New World." *American Digger Magazine*, March–April 2009 (Vol. 5, No. 2), 48–52.

"The Vale of York Hoard." *The Searcher*, November 2009, 9.

Velke, John. "A Mile in His Shoes. We Spend an Afternoon with William G. Gavin: The First Man to Recover Civil War Relics Using a Metal Detector." *American Digger Magazine*, May/June 2010 (Vol. 6, No. 3), 26–31.

Watson, G. M. "Doc." "Saving the Iron Age: Preserving Iron Through Simple Electrolysis." *American Digger Magazine*, January-February 2009 (Vol. 5, No. 1), 52–55.

Workman, Alan. "Google Your Way to Better Relics." *American Digger Magazine*, July-August 2007 (Vol. 3, No. 4), 31–34.

## BOOKS

Albert, Alphaeus S. *Record of American Uniform and Historical Buttons: Bicentennial Edition.* Oakpark, Va.: SCS Publications, 1976.

Appels, Andrew and Stuart Laycock. *Roman Buckles & Military Findings.* Witham, Essex: Greenlight Publishing, 2007.

*Arms and Equipment of The Confederacy.* Alexandria, Va.: Time-Life Books, 1998.

*Arms and Equipment of The Union.* Alexandria, Va.: Time-Life Books, 1998.

Awbrey, Betty Dooley and Claude Dooley. *Why Stop? A Guide to Texas Historical Roadside Markers.* Fourth Edition. Houston: Lone Star Books, 1999.

Bailey, Gordon. *Buttons & Fasteners: 500 BC—AD 1840.* Witham, Essex: Greenlight Publishing, 2004.

Blair, Clay, Jr. *Diving For Pleasure and Treasure*. Cleveland: The World Publishing Company, 1960.

Campbell, J. Duncan and Michael J. O'Donnell. *American Military Headgear*. Alexandria, VA: O'Donnell Publications, 2004.

Coggins, Jack. *Arms and Equipment of the Civil War*. Wilmington, NC: Broadfoot Publishing Company, 1990.

Crouch, Howard R. *Historic American Spurs. An Identification and Price Guide*. Oakpark, VA: SCS Publications, 1998.

——. *Civil War Artifacts: A Guide for the Historian*. Fairfax, VA: SCS Publications, 1995.

——. *Horse Equipment of the Civil War Era*. Oakpark, VA: SCS Publications, 2003.

——. *Relic Hunter: The Field Account of Civil War Sites, Artifacts and Hunting*. Oakpark, Va.: SCS Publications, 1978 (5th Printing with Supplement).

Dammann, Dr. Gordon. *Pictorial Encyclopedia of Civil War Medical Instruments and Equipment. Volume I*. Missoula, Mont.: Pictorial Histories Publishing Co.

Dickey, Thomas S. and Peter C. George. *Field Artillery Projectiles*. Atlanta: Arsenal Publishing Co., 1980.

Eckhart, Jerry M. *Relic Hunting Tips & Techniques*. Cisco, Tex.: Jerry Eckhart Enterprises, 1996.

Fletcher, Edward. *Reading Land*. Witham, Essex: Greenlight Publishing, 2009.

Gaede, Frederick C. *The Federal Civil War Shelter Tent*. Alexandria, VA: O'Donnell Publications, 2001.

Garrett, Charles. *The New Successful Coin Hunting*. Garland, Tex.: RAM Books, 2005 (Thirteenth Revised Edition).

——. *Treasure Hunting for Fun and Profit*. Garland, Tex.: RAM Books, 2005 (Eighth Printing).

——. *Understanding Treasure Signs and Symbols*. Garland, Tex.: RAM Books, 2009.

Gott, Kendall D. *Where the South Lost the War: An Analysis of the Fort Henry–Fort Donelson Campaign, February 1862*. Mechanicsburg, PA: Stackpole Books, 2003.

Harris, Charles S. *Civil War Relics of the Western Campaigns, 1861–1865*. Mechanicsville, VA: Rapidan Press, 1987.

Hathcock, Steve. *Behind the Third Dune: Beachcombing, Treasure Hunting and History of South Padre Island, Texas*. South Padre Island: Padre Island Trading Company, 2002.

———. *Old Indio: Last of the the Karankawa Indians on Padre Island and Other Short Stories*. South Padre Island: Padre Island Trading Company, 2010.

*Illustrated Atlas of The Civil War*. Alexandria, Va.: Time-Life Books, 1998.

Jones, Charles H. *Artillery Fuses of the Civil War*. Alexandria, VA: O'Donnell Publications, 2001.

Kerkis, Sydney C. *Plates and Buckles of the American Military, 1795–1874*. Stone Mountain, GA: Stone Mountain Press, 3rd Edition, 1987.

Lewis, Russell E. *Warman's Civil War Collectibles. Identification and Price Guide, 3rd Edition*. Iola, WI: Krause Publications, Inc., 2009.

Marx, Robert F. and Jenifer. *The World's Richest Wrecks: A Wreck Diver's Guide to Gold and Silver Treasures of the Sea*. Garland, Tex: RAM Books, 2009.

McGuinn, William F. and Bruce S. Bazelon. *American Military Button Makers and Dealers: Their Backmarks & Dates*. Manassas, Va.: Bookcrafters, Inc., 2001.

McKee, W. Reid & M.E. Mason, Jr. *Civil War Projectiles II: Small Arms & Field Artillery with supplement*. Orange, VA: Publisher's Press, Inc., 1995.

Melton, Jack W. Jr. and Lawrence E. Paul. *Introduction to Field Artillery Ordnance, 1861–1865*. Kennesaw, GA: Kennesaw Mountain Press, 1994.

Moore, Stephen L. *European Metal Detecting Guide: Techniques, Tips and Treasures*. Garland, Tex: RAM Books, 2009.

———. *Last Stand of the Texas Cherokees: Chief Bowles and the 1839 Cherokee War in Texas*. Garland, Tex: RAM Books, 2009.

Mullinax, Steve E. *Confederate Belt Buckles & Plates. Expanded Edition*. Alexandria, VA: O'Donnell Publications, 1999.

Noe, Kenneth W. *Perryville: This Grand Havoc of Battle.* Lexington: The University Press of Kentucky, 2001.

O'Donnell, Michael J. and Duncan Campbell. *American Military Belt Plates.* O'Donnell Publications, 1996.

O'Donnell, Mike with Charles "Hap" Hazard and Sue Boardman. *Gettysburg Battlefield Relics & Souvenirs.* Alexandria, VA: O'Donnell Publications, 2009.

O'Donnell, Mike. *U.S. Army & Militia Canteens, 1775–1910.* Alexandria, VA: O'Donnell Publications, 2008.

Pierce, Gerald S. *Texas Under Arms: The Camps, Posts, Forts & Military Towns of the Republic of Texas, 1836–1846.* Austin: The Encino Press, 1969.

Phillips, Stanley S. *Excavated Artifacts from Battlefields and Campsites of the Civil War, 1861–1865.* Lanham, MD, 1974.

Phillips, Stanley S. *Excavated Artifacts from Battlefields and Campsites of the Civil War, 1861–1865. Supplement 1.* Lanham, MD, 1980.

Poche Associates. *Finding Civil War Campsites in Rural Areas.* Independence, MO: Blue and Grey Book Shoppe.

Poche Associates. *Interpreting History from Relics Found in Rural Civil War Campsites..* Independence, MO: Blue and Grey Book Shoppe, 2002.

Robinson, Charles M. III. *The Men Who Wear the Star: The Story of the Texas Rangers.* New York: Random House, 2000.

Saylor, Tim with George Wyant. *Treasure Hunting with Team ATC.* Anaconda, Montana: Anaconda Treasure.com, 2008.

Sylvia, Stephen W. and Michael J. O'Donnell. *Illustrated History of American Civil War Relics.* Orange, VA: North South Trader's Civil War, 1978.

Tice, Warren K. *Dating Buttons: A Chronology of Button Types, Makers, Retailers & Their Backmarks.* Essex Junction, VT: W. K. Tice, 2002.

——. *Uniforms of the United States, 1776–1865.* Thomas Publications, 1997.

Trevillian, Bob. *In Search of...The Civil War: Volume One.* Linthicum, MD: Expedition Press, 1992.

Villanueva, David. *Cleaning Coins & Artefacts.* Witham, Essex: Greenlight Publishing, 2008.

von Mueller, Karl. *Treasure Hunter's Manual # 7.* Dallas: RAM Publishing Co., 1972.

Webb, Walter Prescott. *The Texas Rangers: A Century of Frontier Defense.* Austin: University of Texas Press, 1991, reprint.

Welter, Gerhard. *Cleaning and Preservation of Coins and Medals.* Rockville Centre, NY: Sanford J. Durst, 2001 (Tenth printing).

Wolf, Norfolk. *Advanced Detecting.* Witham, Essex: Greenlight Publishing, 2005.

Wooster, Ralph A. *Texas and Texans in the Civil War.* Austin, Tex.: Eakin Press, 1995.

## INTERNET SOURCES

Civil War Artillery.com—Accessed http://www.civilwarartillery.com/ on July 22, 2010.

www.civilwarhome.com

FMDAC State Park Regulations Compendium. Accessed http://www.fmdac.org/parks/parks.htm on May 24, 2010.

Geographic Names Information System (GNIS). Accessed http://geonames.usgs.gov/ on April 21, 2010.

Library of Congress Maps Collection. Accessed http://memory.loc.gov/ammem/gmdhtml/ on June 18, 2010.

National Park Service's Federal Historic Preservation Laws. Accessed http://www.nps.gov/history/history/hisnps/fhpl.htm on May 23, 2010.

North South Trader's Civil War. Accessed http://www.NSTCivilWar.com/ on June 19, 2010.

Official Records. Accessed http://digital.library.cornell.edu/m/moawar/waro.html on May 25, 2010. See also ttp://ehistory.osu.edu/osu/sources/records/ for the OR's.

University of Alabama Historical Maps Archives. Accessed http://alabamamaps.ua.edu/historicalmaps/ on June 17, 2010.

# ABOUT THE AUTHOR

Stephen L. Moore, a sixth generation Texan, is the author of thirteen other books on World War II, Texas history and metal detecting. His Texas history titles include *Savage Frontier*, a four-volume series on the early Texas Rangers, and *Eighteen Minutes: The Battle of San Jacinto and the Texas Independence Campaign*. Moore, a frequent speaker at book conferences and metal detecting club events, writes for local historical journals, including *The Texas Ranger Dispatch*.

In recent years, he has combined his passion for history with the use of metal detectors to promote responsible relic recovery. His other metal detecting titles from RAM Books are *European Metal Detecting Guide* and *Last Stand of the Texas Cherokees*. His relic hunting trips include visits to locations in Alabama, Arkansas, Colorado, Connecticut, Florida, Georgia, Idaho, Kentucky, Louisiana, Maryland, Massachusetts, Mississippi,

 Missouri, Nevada, New Mexico, Oklahoma, Rhode Island, South Carolina, Texas, Tennessee, Virginia, West Virginia, Mexico, Australia, Canada, England, France, Spain, Italy, Belgium and the Netherlands so far. Steve currently serves as the marketing and advertising manager for Garrett Metal Detectors. He, his wife Cindy and their three children live north of Dallas in Lantana, Texas.

# THE GARRETT LIBRARY

Standard-size 5.5" x 8.5" format books offer treasure hunting techniques, hints and history from Charles Garrett and other RAM Books authors. Each book is soft cover format unless otherwise noted.

*Visit garrett.com to watch for new titles!*

Sample RAM Books are shown.

## SECRETS REVEALED!

Treasure hunting advice is at your fingertips with Charles Garrett's 3.5" x 5" shirt pocket-size field guide series.

## TO ORDER RAM BOOKS

RAM Books, the publishing division of Garrett Metal Detectors, continues to release new titles related to treasure hunting, gold prospecting, coin hunting and relic recovery.

**To see a current list of titles available from RAM Books, please consult a Garrett Metal Detectors hobby catalog or visit:**

## www.garrett.com

After reaching Garrett's website, visit the Hobby Divison section and select "RAM Books" to see all of our current titles. An order form is available on our site which can printed and mailed with your requested titles and payment.